A
GLOBAL
AGENDA

Issues Before
the 50th
General Assembly
of the
United Nations

A GLOBAL AGENDA

Issues Before the 50th General Assembly of the United Nations

An annual publication of the United Nations Association of the United States of America

John Tessitore and Susan Woolfson, Editors

University Press of America
Lanham • New York • London

Published by
University Press of America,® Inc.
4720 Boston Way
Lanham, Maryland 20706

3 Henrietta Street
London WC2E 8LU England

ISSN: 1057-1213
ISBN 1-880632-33-0 (cloth : alk. paper)
ISBN 1-800632-34-9 (paper : alk. paper)

Cover by Scott Rattray

 The paper used in this publication meets the minimum requirements of American National Standard for Information Sciences—Permanence of Paper for
Printed Library Materials, ANSI Z39.48-1984.

Contents

Foreword

The United Nations has turned 50. In San Francisco, the site of the U.N. Charter Conference in 1945, thousands of people from throughout the country (and the world) gathered in June 1995 to commemorate and celebrate a major milestone in the history of relations among nations. A few months later, the heads of state of more than 150 nations as well as the Pope would be arriving at U.N. Headquarters in New York to commemorate the 50th anniversary of the ratification of that Charter—U.N. Day, October 24. But when all the speeches and all the dinners and all the media attention have faded, it is hoped that we will not lose sight of what the anniversary was really about—something far more important and more complex than can be reduced to a simple sound bite.

World War II is a distant memory for most of those who are old enough to have lived through it, and today there is a whole generation (maybe two) who have no real understanding of what it means to experience—in the words of the U.N. Charter—"the scourge of war." And though we know perfectly (and painfully) well that millions have continued to experience the horror of warfare all over the world, we have not, at least, experienced that most dreaded of all confrontations—World War III. For this we owe no little thanks to the United Nations.

At a time when some Americans—notably members of the new Congress—are expressing doubt as to the efficacy of the U.S.–U.N. relationship, particularly the return on our peacekeeping dollars, it is vital that we reexamine the role of the U.N. system throughout the world and its relevance to the welfare and security of our own nation. The editors of this volume might be forgiven if they suggest that *A Global Agenda* does much to point out that relevance. Taking as its subject the full scope of the Organization's agenda—as opposed to merely the highly publicized activities of peacekeeping and peace enforcement—*A Global Agenda* offers a comprehensive overview of the U.N.'s enormous social and humanitarian programs, accounting for fully 70 percent of the U.N. budget. Does the movement of millions of refugees and displaced people have an effect on the social and economic stability of other nations in the region? Does major human rights abuse by one government have an impact on other, neighboring governments? Can a health epidemic in Africa spill over to countries on yet other continents? The answer to each of these questions is, of course, a resounding "yes."

The boat people of Cuba, Haiti, and even Vietnam and Cambodia have—literally and figuratively—landed on U.S. shores. The abused and oppressed of El Salvador, Guatemala, South Africa, and China have sought sanctuary in our communities. And the AIDS pandemic, as with all deadly viruses, is as mobile as an airline flight to any U.S. city. Polls show conclusively that the vast majority of Americans have accepted the ineluctable truth that we live in an interrelated world, where cooperation and "multilateralism" are essential and inescapable. Yet there are still those—including some in high places—who would like to ignore this reality and pull us into an anachronistic and dangerous neoisolationism. May this volume give them cause for reevaluation.

* * *

If, as we believe, *A Global Agenda* contributes to the discussion and understanding of the work of the United Nations, then the credit must be given to those who have made this work possible. First we must acknowledge our contributing authors, whose expertise and commitment are the warp and woof of this volume. These dedicated men and women are identified in the following pages, and to each of them we offer our deep gratitude.

Also participating in the publishing process have been UNA-USA's Manager for Media Affairs, Nick Birnback, and University Press of America's Maureen Muncaster and Lynn Gemmell. They have been there to assist with what is a long and at times painful delivery.

Finally, there is—as there has been each year—a small cadre of interns to be acknowledged, young people who have freely given large amounts of their time and energy over the spring and summer months. These are Daretia Austin, Kestrina Budina, Thomas Carson, Felicia Gross, Eric Hesse, Sara Ann Mahmoud, Erin Meyer, Katherine Mossman, Adam Williams, and Anne Witt-Greenberg.

John Tessitore
Susan Woolfson

New York, July 1995

Contributors

Ricardo Alday (Haiti) is U.N. correspondent of the Mexican News Agency.

José E. Alvarez (Legal Issues) is a professor of law at Michigan Law School in Ann Arbor, where he teaches international law and international organizations.

Daretia J. Austin (Other Social Issues: Human Settlements; Disabled Persons), a UNA-USA Communications Intern, has recently completed a master's degree in international political economy and development at Fordham University.

Frederick Z. Brown (Cambodia) directs Southeast Asian studies at the Paul H. Nitze School of Advanced International Studies of Johns Hopkins University and has followed the Cambodian peace process under a grant from the U.S. Institute for Peace.

Kestrina Budina (Other Social Issues: Aging), a UNA-USA Communications Intern, is completing a master's degree at Columbia University's School of International and Public Affairs, with a concentration in security policy and East European studies.

Toula Coklas (Finance and Administration) was an administrative officer in the Budget Division of the U.N. Department of Administration and Management, primarily responsible for the drafting of the Rapporteur's reports for the Fifth Committee. She has also contributed to the *United Nations Yearbook* on issues related to administration and finance.

Felice D. Gaer (Human Rights) is director of the Jacob Blaustein Institute for the Advancement of Human Rights of the American Jewish Committee. She was appointed a public member of the U.S. delegation to the World Conference on Human Rights in 1993 and to the U.N. Commission of Human Rights in 1994 and 1995. Previously, she served as executive director of the International League for Human Rights, as executive director for European Programs at UNA-USA, and as a program officer at the Ford Foundation.

Jules Kagian (The Middle East and the Persian Gulf) covered the United Nations and the American scene for a number of Middle Eastern newspapers and radio and TV stations during more than two decades. He is currently U.N. correspondent for *Middle East International* (London).

Gail V. Karlsson (Environment and Sustainable Development; The World Summit for Social Development) is a New York-based attorney specializing in international environmental law. She attended the World Summit for Social Development as UNA-USA's press representative.

Lee A. Kimball (Law of the Sea, Ocean Affairs, and Antarctica) is a specialist in treaty development and international institutions on environmental and development issues. She works as a consultant in Washington, D.C.

Craig Lasher (Population) is a senior policy analyst and legislative assistant at Population Action International, a private nonprofit organization that works to expand the availability of voluntary family planning services worldwide.

Martin M. McLaughlin (Food and Agriculture) is a consultant on food and development policy.

Erin Meyer (The Status of Women), a UNA-USA Communications Intern, is a 1995 honors graduate from the University of Texas at Austin. Specializing in World War II studies, she will begin classes at the Université Libre de Bruxelles in the fall of 1995 as a Rotary International Ambassadorial Scholar.

George H. Mitchell Jr. (Economics and Development) is an assistant professor of international politics at Tufts University, where he is a member of the Department of Political Science and of the Fletcher School of Law and Diplomacy.

Howard A. Moyes (Arms Control and Disarmament) is a research assistant with the Project on Rethinking Arms Control, based at the Center for International and Security Issues at Maryland, and a graduate student in public policy at the School of Public Affairs, University of Maryland.

Edmund T. Piasecki (Africa) is a graduate fellow at the School of Public Affairs, University of Maryland.

Constantine V. Pleshakov (The Former Soviet Union) heads the Geopolitical Studies Center of the Institute for U.S. and Canada Studies of the Russian Academy of Sciences. At the time of writing he was a visiting professor at Amherst College.

Christina M. Schultz (Refugees and Internally Displaced Persons, with Heidi R. Worley) is a research assistant at the Washington-based Refugee Policy Group, where she specializes in U.S. refugee policy, complex emergencies, and special populations.

John Tessitore (Co-Editor) is Executive Director of Communications at UNA-USA.

Adam M. Williams (Drug Abuse, Production, and Trafficking; Other Social Issues: Crime), a UNA-USA Communications Intern, is majoring in English at Yale.

Ian Williams (Beyond Peacekeeping; The Former Yugoslavia) is president of the U.N. Correspondents Association and writes for, among others, *The Nation.*

Anne Witt-Greenberg (Other Social Issues: Children and Youth), a UNA-USA Communications Intern, is completing a law degree at the City University of New York and a master's degree in international affairs at C. W. Post College of Long Island University.

Susan Woolfson (Co-Editor) is Managing Editor of Communications at UNA-USA.

Heidi R. Worley (Refugees and Internally Displaced Persons, with Christina M. Schultz) is a research assistant at the Washington-based Refugee Policy Group, where she specializes in internally displaced persons, special populations, and the environment.

I
Making and Keeping the Peace

1. Beyond Peacekeeping
By Ian Williams

This past year has been a momentous 12 months for U.N. peacekeeping, involving more operations, more people, and more money than any other year in the world body's 50-year history. It was also a year in which the failures received far more publicity than the successes, such that the United Nations now finds itself an organization sorely pressed from all sides.

The **major issue** facing the U.N. member nations in this 50th anniversary year is the **absence of a coherent policy on peacekeeping.** Unclear mandates, insufficient resources, and blurred lines of command have all put the Organization's credibility on the line at a time when its services are more necessary than ever. Rather than an "end to history" after the Cold War, the world has seen a rapid acceleration of history, at least in the sense of wars and conflicts. U.N. Secretary-General Boutros Boutros-Ghali enumerated 89 armed conflicts between 1989 and 1992, of which only three were between states [Speech in Sydney, Australia, 4/27/95]. It has been fashionable to blame these conflicts on ancient ethnic hatreds, but other contributing factors include economic and social upheaval, ambitious politicians, and the ready availability of sophisticated weaponry.

A Very Bloody Year

The past year has witnessed **a record 18 peacekeeping missions,** involving some 78,000 peacekeepers in both intra- and interstate conflicts, as well as mixtures of the two. In some cases, missions have suffered from the lack of a firm commitment from the major powers, making an already complex job even more difficult. In recognition of the changing requirements of increasingly complex peacekeeping operations, the Secretariat undertook some strategic thinking on peacekeeping operations as reported in the Secretary-General's now famous 1992 report, *An Agenda* *for Peace*. Commissioned by a Security Council Heads of State Summit, the report sets out the necessary preconditions to make the United Nations an effective and efficient tool in promoting world peace and security. The Secretary-General proposed, among other things, the "preventive deployment" of troops in trouble spots, "the earmarking of military units for U.N. use," and heavy "peace-enforcement operations" when necessary. However, some key member states viewed such proposals with suspicion and skepticism. The big powers, in particular, balked at the notion of creating a significant U.N. "standby" force. And while they were unsympathetic to the Secretary-General's innovative attempts to provide secure funding for the operations, it must be noted that they offered no constructive counterproposals.

In the face of such lukewarm support from the major powers, the Secretary-General issued an addendum to *An Agenda for Peace* in January 1995. It suggested that the only alternative for very large operations was U.N. authorization for member states themselves to take the initiative, as effectively happened in Desert Storm and, later, in Haiti. The Secretary-General's difficulties on the issue were dramatically illustrated when **U.S. Ambassador Madeleine Albright denounced the document** to the press even before the document was officially released, and without first advising the Secretary-General of U.S. views. The incident demonstrated—in a somewhat brutal fashion—the addendum's conclusion that there did not exist sufficient international support to permit large-scale peace-enforcement operations.

Curiously, the permanent Security Council members' lack of interest in renovating the mechanisms of peacekeeping has not stopped them from mandating new operations. Few states ever vote against a peacekeeping operation when requested, although they do—for various reasons, budgetary and political—occasionally procrastinate. The reluctance of the Perm Five to commit adequate and timely resources to operations that they have initiated has helped to contribute to the overall perception that peacekeeping operations are doomed to failure from the very outset. As such, the United Nations is caught in a bind when member states routinely authorize the deployment of peacekeeping operations with unclear mandates, insufficient resources, and inadequate infrastructural support. The **tragic U.S. Rangers operation in Mogadishu** in October 1993 is an unfortunate but crystalline example of the willingness of member states to leave the United Nations to twist in the wind should an operation become too controversial.

One partial solution the Secretary-General has suggested is employing **regional organizations** which, he says, "should take on more responsibility for peacekeeping in future as called for by the U.N. Charter" [Special Committee On Peacekeeping Operations, 4/95]. However, current examples of regional security arrangements being employed to keep the peace have not been unqualified successes. The African initiatives in Somalia and Liberia showed a serious lack of resources; and even NATO, the best-funded regional organization with over 40 years of preparation for military operations, has not been especially eager to work on its own doorstep in the former Yugoslavia. Further, developing countries again see such efforts as another attempt by the industrialized countries to stick them with the financial and military burdens of peacekeeping.

The Potential of Peacekeeping

Despite the problems, there is no denying that U.N. peacekeeping represents an extraordinary multinational enterprise. No fewer than 82 nations contribute peacekeeping troops, ranging from France's 5,149 to Albania's one [U.N. spokesman's office, 3/31/95]. Even nonmember Switzerland contributes 26 troops and police. Operations of this scope are not without cost: 135 peacekeepers died in 1994 while serving under the U.N. flag.

Perhaps the most successful, cheapest, and least publicized operation was the **U.N. Observer Group in the Aouzou Strip (UNASOG)**, which epitomized all that the Charter had intended for the conduct of world affairs. Both parties, Chad and Libya, had agreed to refer the dispute to the International Court of Justice in The Hague, and both accepted the decision, which was effectively in favor of Chad. The tiny U.N. force, drawn from six countries, monitored the agreed withdrawal of forces, thus fulfilling one of the primary stipulations for traditional peacekeeping operations (PKOs)—that all parties concerned must want the peacekeeping force. Consequently, the United Nations was able to act as a neutral buffer between the two parties, and in less than two months the agreement was implemented and the mission over. UNASOG also highlighted the important and underused capability of the International Court of Justice (ICJ) to resolve problems between states.

Of course the ICJ has no jurisdiction in internal conflicts and, strictly speaking, neither does the United Nations. Nonetheless, the Secretariat—and specifically the Secretary-General—has chalked up some impressive successes when its good offices have been welcomed by all the parties concerned. For example, the successful termination on May 1, 1994, of ONUSAL, the U.N. operation in El Salvador, showed that the presence of an outside, impartial, third party could bring to an end a vicious internecine conflict. In this case it provided sufficient guarantees of security for the opposing sides to stand down their forces and effect a reconciliation. "No Salvadoran . . . would deny that the United Nations has left a strong base on which to build," commented Larry Rohter of the *New York Times* [4/29/95]. The success of UNASOG and ONUSAL clearly demonstrates the important positive role that peacekeepers can play when the missions are provided with clear mandates, achievable objectives, and the consent of all parties concerned.

However, the measure of success is not always this clear. The operation in Cyprus (UNICYP) has averted war between Turkey and Greece for some 30 years. But in doing so, it has fossilized the armistice line and ethnic division that, in principle at least, every party considers unacceptable. While it is true as the Secretary-General states that an outbreak of hostilities would be even more unacceptable, the government of Croatia, for one, cited its fear of "Cypriotization" as a reason for its insistence on changing the mandate of the U.N. Protection Force (UNPROFOR) within its borders. Zagreb's impatience with what it perceived as a static situation also led to the overrunning of Western Slavonia by the Croatian Army in May 1995, rendering moot the presence of U.N. forces in the region.

The successful U.N.-sanctioned intervention in Haiti by U.S. troops—begun in September 1994 and concluded on March 1995—provides a clear example of the Secretary-General's observation that the only alternative to well-funded and clearly mandated U.N. operations is U.N. authorization for unilateral action by member states. The Haiti operation followed an emerging pattern of "franchise" operations first illustrated by Desert Storm.

In the case of Rwanda, as news came of the massacres in April 1994, the small and badly equipped U.N. force in Kigali was left to its own devices. Washington, beset by a Congress reluctant to commit more money, stalled on finance. Other countries stalled on troop contributions. The eventual unilateral response by the French, dubbed Operation Turquoise, was widely viewed as a move to prop up France's Rwandan client government, and was accepted only as a *faut de mieux* in June 1994 by other Council members. The Russians followed the trend toward franchising by getting a U.N. badge for their operation in Georgia. Although the "farming out" of missions can certainly be effective in peace-enforcement operations, the method relies on the great powers to decide that an operation is directly in their own national interest. Thus, Haiti was above all a U.S. operation and, as New Zealand Ambassador Colin Keating said archly, he hoped that the Council would show similar alacrity when other democracies "farther away" were threatened.

And the Pitfalls

A similar clear-cut franchise operation in Somalia (UNOSOM II) might have avoided the ignominious exit of U.N. forces from that war-torn nation. UNOSOM II raised many questions about the wisdom of the U.N. undertaking peace-enforcement operations at all, and in particular missions undertaken with unclear mandates and an uncertain chain of command. (The U.N. forces in Somalia somehow became identified as colonists and invaders.) The Secretariat pointed in vain to its success in delivering humanitarian aid, but the image of a defeated and demoralized operation staging a heavily armed retreat in the face of hostile forces was fixed firmly in the public consciousness, eroding support for future similarly ambitious operations.

These problems were amplified by the situation in the Balkans, where UNPROFOR has been depicted almost as an accomplice of the Serbs by the Bosnian government and significant sections of the media. Public opinion is understandably perplexed when victims and transgressors are treated as moral equals in accordance with traditional peacekeeping doctrine. As the Secretary-General explained: "We are not allowed to intervene in favor of the victims. . . . We are supposed to be neutral and objective, so we are limited by our mandate" [Press conference, National Press Club, Australia, 4/28/95].

Perhaps the fundamental problem with the UNPROFOR operation has been that the essential premise of peacekeeping—that the parties involved should want peace—is clearly inapplicable in Bosnia and Croatia. The Serbs have wanted to hold on to what they seized in defiance of U.N. resolutions, and the Bosnians and the Croatians want it back. In fact, the Secretariat was originally correct in its contention that Bosnia, in particular, is not a suitable subject for peacekeeping. The clear implication of the imposition of sanctions against Belgrade as the aggressor was that this should have been an undisguised Chapter VII peace-enforcement operation similar to that which it had undertaken in the Persian Gulf. However, the Security Council members—seeking a way of balancing domestic pressure for something to be done against their unwillingness to commit the forces necessary to be effective—chose instead to attempt a traditional peacekeeping operation under untraditional conditions.

The problems of implementation are increasingly worsened by political differences among members of the Council. A continuously shifting U.S. position was countered by an increasingly firm Russian tilt toward the Serbian side, making it impossible to fine-tune the resolutions in the face of changes in the region. The differences of opinion and focus were reflected in a confusion of diplomatic moves, which frequently acted at cross-purposes. Although the Secretary-General welcomed these various initiatives, they actually reflect the weakness of the United Nations itself, which in turn represents the inability of the major powers to achieve a firm consensus.

However, the situation in the Balkans does provide a living example of the efficacy of the type of preemptive peacemaking ("preventive deployment") called for in *An Agenda for Peace*. In contrast to the initial failure to station troops on the Bosnian border, the speedy deployment of forces—including a major U.S. component—on the Macedonia-Serb border has proven visibly successful in securing the region. Now called UNPREDEP (since UNPROFOR divided into three separate operations on March 31, 1995), the U.S. troop contingent has been reinforced to 800.

Financial Problems

Since peacekeeping is not explicitly provided for in the Charter, it must be financed by a special assessment. Once the proposal has made its way through the international committees, authorization to pay for it must then survive national decision-making processes. In the case of the United States, that means that the funding voted for in the Security Council may not be approved by the Congress, if the legislature judges the operation to be too expensive or not in America's own best interests. With the United States as the largest contributor by far, **Capitol Hill's current hostility** toward the world organization has made it even more difficult for the Organization to plan or operate effectively.

However, polls indicate that congressional attitudes toward the United Nations do not necessarily reflect the views of the American people. Even after a year of bad press over Somalia and Bosnia, 67 percent of those polled still strongly supported U.N. peacekeeping operations. Remarkably, support remains at this level despite a widespread overestimation of the cost to the United States. Many polled thought that the U.S. commitment of troops should be halved from 40 percent of peacekeeping forces to 20 percent, when in fact only 4 percent of U.N. troops are from the United States. Similarly, the majority of those polled believed that 22 percent of the federal budget went for U.N. operations, when in fact less than 1 percent of the U.S. defense budget goes to such operations [*New York Times,* 4/30/95].

The lack of funds and the member states' unwillingness to take up the Secretary-General's suggestions for funding reform and pretraining units for U.N. operations has led to unusual problems, such as those caused by the Croatian government's demands that troops stationed there should be from, first, NATO, then Western Europe, then the Contact Group (i.e., the United States, Russia, the European Union, and the United Nations) [*Christian Science Monitor,* 3/13/94]. Since the primary common feature of these groups is the skin color of most of their inhabitants, this was seen as a form of racism, but the official explanation did raise a serious question. Peacekeeping operations used to involve contingents of well-equipped, well-trained troops from a fairly selective group of, usually, neutral countries. Most U.N. observers agree that the vast expansion of U.N. operations has diluted the overall quality somewhat, and it seems undeniable that at least a few contributing nations see their contingents more as a source of hard currency than as a contribution to peace.

Faced with a rapidly expanding demand and a shrinking supply,

U.N. Headquarters cannot always be too demanding about the contingents it recruits. Increasingly there have been complaints of black-marketeering, partiality, and lawlessness on the part of some contingents. This was highlighted early in 1995 when Russian General Alexander Perelyakin in Croatia was recalled for offenses ranging from black-marketeering to facilitating the resupply of Croatian Serbs by Belgrade while commanding Sector East [*Financial Times*, 4/12/95].

Sanctions as an Alternative

In general, the purpose of sanctions under the U.N. Charter (Chapter VII, Article 41) is to be persuasive rather than punitive, which means that there should be a clear equivalence between "sin" and sanctions. Compliance is rewarded by easing, and defiance by tightening, of those sanctions. In conjunction with or instead of peacekeeping operations, sanctions can be a useful tool. However, they tend to be a very blunt instrument, hitting both transgressors and their victims.

Currently Libya, Iraq, and Serbia are at the blunt end of this weapon, and in each case Council members have widely diverging views on what should happen. The United States and the United Kingdom are unable to secure a tightening of sanctions on Libya, while Russia is unable to lift the sanctions on Serbia, as it increasingly shows signs of desiring. Some ambassadors have toyed privately with the idea of a "sunset clause" in future sanction resolutions so that they cannot be maintained in the face of majority opposition. Member states are also increasingly reluctant to support sanctions. One reason is that, despite promises, the Council has not taken any concrete steps to implement Article 50, which states that members whose economies suffer as a result of sanctions or another nation can "consult" with the Council. The implication that they would get help has not been followed through. "Assistance" has therefore taken the form of ignoring widespread violations of the sanctions by neighboring countries (such as Macedonia) whose economies would crash unless their trade was replaced by international aid.

Despite these notes of caution, sanctions have in certain cases been quite effective. They played a major role in ending the racist regimes in Rhodesia and South Africa, and currently they have extracted a considerable degree of cooperation from Iraq with regard to inspection of its nuclear and chemical weapons facilities. In the Balkans, Belgrade's compliance with some resolutions has been the direct result of the economic problems it has suffered as a result of U.N. sanctions.

Tribunals

In a highly interconnected world, the failures of peacekeeping operations reverberate across the globe. The debacle in Mogadishu and the U.N.'s seeming tentativeness in dealing with Serb aggression in Bosnia strengthened the resolve of gangs in Port-au-Prince to brush off the U.N.'s first attempt to land police and monitors in Haiti. The bureaucratic delays in setting up the International Criminal Tribunal on the Former Yugoslavia (ICTFY) made it too late to save the victims of the early days. However, the appointment of Judge Richard Goldstone as a prosecutor in 1994 has invigorated the tribunal system. Indictments have been issued, the first prisoner has been extradited, and the court's notice of pending indictments against major political and military figures has sent a message across the region.

Indeed, the extension of the tribunal's work to Rwanda may already have had some effect in neighboring Burundi, where a Rwanda-like situation simmered for much of 1994 without boiling over. Unfortunately, there is still wrangling between the General Assembly and the Security Council about which budget should cover the cost of the tribunal, regular or peacekeeping. Some legal critics have pointed out that if the appropriation comes under the regular budget, it will weaken the Council's control over the tribunal—making it potentially possible to indict permanent members, such as Russia over its handling of the revolt in Chechnya. The tribunal does send a signal that the world community will take some action against war criminals, and it is hoped that this will lead to some degree of prevention.

Conclusion

Despite all the problems, it seems unlikely that there will be any going back on multilateralism. In a sense, the concept has already succeeded in the "market" of world diplomacy. Although involvement in internal conflicts is not as new as the Secretariat has taken to claiming (e.g., Cyprus and the Congo), the degree of such involvement is certainly increasing, and there is no mechanism other than the United Nations to deal with these conflicts legitimately. A peaceful globe is in every government's national interest, as is a strong United Nations with an enhanced peacekeeping capability.

Efficient and effective peacekeeping demands a serious enhancement of the U.N.'s institutional capacity. A promising innovation this year was the setting up of a special "Learning From Experience" unit after the Mozambique operation. It needs extension, and perhaps generalizing. Similarly, there have been efforts in the procurement section to preposition equipment from one operation in readiness for the next, and the United Nations has acquired a military base in Brindisi, Italy, to store the equipment. These are small but significant steps on the road toward the serious intellectual and material preparation for future operations that will undoubtedly be necessary in the ongoing quest for global peace and stability.

2. The Former Yugoslavia
By Ian Williams

After three years of warfare in the former Yugoslavia, the U.N.'s involvement in that part of the world has so diverged from its original mission of providing humanitarian relief to a civilian population that in May 1995 the Secretary-General ordered a complete reassessment of the operation. Indeed, many had come to believe that the U.N. Protection Force in the Former Yugoslavia (UNPROFOR) had become more of a problem than a solution. And with mounting pressure on U.N. budgets, the operation's annual cost of $1.6 billion for peacekeeping and over $600 million for humanitarian aid made such a reassessment almost inevitable [UNDPI, *U.N. Peacekeeping*, 2/95].

Boutros Boutros-Ghali's 1992 comment that the conflict in Europe was "a rich man's war"—however tactless—was not without some foundation. Far more people died in the conflicts in Somalia and Rwanda than in the former Yugoslavia. However, there are strong reasons for U.N. involvement in the former Yugoslavia, even beyond a desperate desire by Western governments to avoid greater intervention. There was clearly a danger to international peace and security, and as the Security Council admitted in its resolutions, there had indeed been an act of aggression by the Federal Republic of Yugoslavia, which is why sanctions were imposed and Chapter VII of the U.N. Charter was invoked.

Another branch of the United Nations, the International Court of Justice (ICJ), determined that there was a prima facie case of genocide taking place in Bosnia and Herzegovina, adding that "great suffering and loss of life has been sustained by the population of Bosnia and Herzegovina in circumstances which shock the conscience of mankind and flagrantly conflict with moral law." The Court ordered Yugoslavia to "take all measures within its power to prevent genocide" [ICJ, 9/13/93].

Inescapable Involvement, Escapable Conclusions

The Security Council was unanimous in accepting U.N. membership applications from Slovenia, Croatia, and Bosnia and Herzegovina on May 22, 1992. Although it did so on the same "as is" basis as it had previously accepted the former Soviet republics, without questioning the boundaries or establishing the rights of minorities, their membership set the stamp of approval on them as independent sovereign states. Thus, they were entitled to the full protection of the U.N. Charter.

Once it became clear that the former Yugoslav People's Army (JNA) was directly engaged in fighting in Croatia and Bosnia, the United Nations was faced with an immediate problem. Though the Security Council was founded to stop aggression by one state against another, there was no enthusiasm within the Council for a Desert Storm-style peace-enforcement operation to stop the invasion. The risk of casualties was certainly not acceptable to the West Europeans, and even less so to the United States. Recoiling from the implications of their recognition of the new states, the Western nations tended to present the conflict in terms of a civil war, referring to "warring factions" and "ancient hatreds." The Bosnian government in particular was subject to a form of creeping delegitimization in this way, being referred to as the "Muslim" government by the press.

Almost as a reflex action, before the conflict spread or the republics were recognized, the Security Council had imposed an arms embargo on all parts of the former Yugoslavia. Not surprisingly, it was urged to do so with the support of the Belgrade government [SC/713, 9/5/91]. Although leaky, the embargo has meant that the massive weapons stocks that the former Yugoslav People's Army had built up to resist a Soviet invasion were and are mostly available to the Serb forces, while the Croats to some extent, and the Bosnians to a very large extent, were and still are relatively underequipped.

Ensuring the disarmament of the victims implies a heavy responsibility on the international community to protect them. In the confusing welter of mandates, however, this responsibility has been shirked. As the Secretary-General has himself outlined, successful peacekeeping requires certain preconditions. The "basic conditions for success remain unchanged: a clear and practicable mandate; the cooperation of the parties in implementing that mandate; the continuing support of the Security Council; the readiness of the Member States to contribute the military, police and civilian personnel . . . required; effective United Nations command at Headquarters and in the field; and adequate financial and logistical support" [*An Agenda for Peace*, p. 29].

By those standards, it is hardly surprising that UNPROFOR has been bogged down, despite its 38,848 personnel [Spokesman's office, 3/31/95]. Its multiple mandates are muddled and impracticable, its lines of command tortuous, its troop contributions conditional and sparse, and the warring parties—the Serbs most of all—uncooperative. In addition, the traditional peacekeeping posture of neutrality led the United Nations to defend a status quo that its own resolutions make morally indefensible.

It is not surprising that the U.N.'s involvement in the region has led to an extraordinary devaluation of Security Council resolutions and presidential statements. The more of each there are, the less notice the warring parties take. Ominously for the future credibility of the Organization, the major powers have convinced the world that this is the U.N.'s war, even though they call the shots both at U.N. Headquarters and in the region.

Despite the frequent talk of withdrawal by the European governments with troops on the ground—notably France and Britain—such a withdrawal seems unlikely. When in April 1995 President Franjo Tudjman of Croatia called for the removal of U.N. troops from his country, the United Nations realized that if the Western component of UNPROFOR were withdrawn, the Secretariat would have little option but to accept the ready offers from Muslim nations to supply troops, or to pull out completely. If the latter happened, it would cease to be the U.N.'s war and would become Western Europe's war. And as it escalated, there is little doubt that a much larger force would be needed. Thus, while the European forces may regroup, there seems little chance of outright withdrawal.

Peacekeeping in the Former Yugoslavia

UNPROFOR was originally set up as the **U.N. Protection Force**, that is, a force intended to look after the U.N. Protected Areas in Croatia (see "Croatia," below). The name was later the cause of considerable confusion, when no one was sure who it was supposed to be protecting. In fact, it has not always proved effective at protecting itself. For example, during a government offensive in November 1994, the Serbs took some 400 U.N. troops hostage—a threat that has been implicit throughout the conflict and one that has been invoked by UNPROFOR commanders as the reason they are unable to fulfill their mandates. The Serbs repeated this threat when NATO airstrikes hit a Serb ammunition depot outside Sarajevo on May 25, 1995 [*New York Times*, 5/26/95]. In addition, casualties among peacekeepers have been high. On May 15, 1995, a 23-year-old French peacekeeper died from sniper fire in Sarajevo—the 37th French peacekeeper to be killed in Bosnia and Croatia since 1992 [Associated Press, 5/16/95]. Total UNPROFOR fatalities to date number well over one hundred.

The innumerable, contradictory, and sometimes frankly rhetorical resolutions on the region began on September 25, 1991, when Security Council Resolution 713 enforced an embargo on all arms supplies to the region. The resolution followed the path of its many predecessors, with good intentions not always achieving good results. Belgrade's urging of the resolution should have given someone food for thought.

In addition to freezing in place a disparity of weapons between the warring sides, Resolution 713 has threatened a major rift between the United States and its NATO allies, and it has provoked a major challenge to the U.N.'s authority by the U.S. legislature. Attempts by the United States and others to lift the resolution have failed in the face of opposition by Britain, France, and Russia. However, as soon as Congress convened in 1995, Senate Majority Leader Bob Dole introduced a bill to lift the arms embargo on Bosnia unilaterally. For his part, President Bill Clinton has already announced that U.S. forces would not take part in enforcing the embargo [David Rieff, *Slaughterhouse: Bosnia and the Failure of the West* (New York: Simon and Schuster), 1995].

Croatia

Resolution 721 (11/27/91) considered a peacekeeping force for Croatia, which was later confirmed in Resolution 724 (12/15/91). A preparatory team was sent, and following a meeting between the Croatian and Yugoslav armies in January 1992, the United Nations sent an initial mission of 50 liaison officers. With Resolution 743 (2/21/92), UNPROFOR was formally established.

The accretion of mandates began almost immediately. UNPROFOR was originally deployed in the U.N. Protected Areas (UNPAs), defined as "areas in which the Serbs constitute the majority or a substantial minority of the population and where intercommunal tensions have led to armed conflict" [UNDPI, *U.N. Peacekeeping*, 2/95]. In return for providing this protection, UNPROFOR was supposed to disarm Croatian Serb forces, ensure the departure of the Yugoslav Army, and monitor the police.

To these areas were added the Serb-controlled "pink zones," which were to be returned to the control of the Croat authorities. Resolution 769 (8/7/92) gave authority to UNPROFOR to control immigration and customs on the international boundary between the Protected Areas and other countries, such as Bosnia and Serbia. It was the failure of UNPROFOR to provide such control that led the Croatian government in 1995 to threaten to withdraw its permission to allow UNPROFOR to remain within its borders.

Bosnia and Herzegovina

During this early period, UNPROFOR was headquartered in the relatively tranquil city of Sarajevo. The Bosnian government had tried hard to keep the Yugoslav Federation alive, but the secession of Croatia and Slovenia would have left them in the hands of Serbian President Slobodan Milošević, whose treatment of the Muslim Albanians in Kosovo did not augur well for Bosnians under Belgrade's hegemony. A referendum on March 1, 1992, gave a clear majority for secession. In May 1992 the United Nations withdrew two-thirds of its staff when the situation in the Bosnian capital became too much for them. The Council passed a series of resolutions in effect telling the Yugoslav and Croatian armies to get out of Bosnia.

Resolution 757 (5/30/92) invoked Chapter VII to impose sanctions on Belgrade. It also demanded unimpeded access for humanitarian supplies to Sarajevo and, theoretically, established a security zone for the now besieged city and its airport. By the end of the year UNPROFOR had established the strictest definition of "supervision" with the Serbs. Its monitors watched and counted at the artillery emplacements as the Serbs broke the Geneva Conventions by pouring (monitored) shells into the city below, using guns that had earlier been withdrawn with U.N. permission from JNA bases in Croatia.

UNPROFOR was given a new mandate by Resolution 776 (9/14/92) to help the U.N. High Commissioner for Refugees (UNHCR) deliver humanitarian supplies. In the face of the concern of governments not wanting to be drawn into the conflict, 776 deliberately did *not* invoke Chapter VII. Consequently, the convoys have moved only at the will of the Serb forces, who take up to a third of their contents for "humanitarian" purposes in their own zone and demand fuel for "roadworks" [*Christian Science Monitor*, 10/11/94]. Later Security Council mandates authorizing the use of force if deemed necessary have not been used by local U.N. commanders.

On March 24, 1994, the U.S.-brokered "Washington Agreement" provided for a federation between Muslims and Croats in Bosnia, thus ending the fighting between the two groups. In the summer of 1994, secure from Croat attack, Bosnian government forces moved against the rebel Muslim leader Fikret Abdić, who had arranged a mutually profitable modus vivendi with surrounding Bosnian and Croatian Serbs [*Financial Times*, 8/22/94]. The initially successful attack was followed later that year by highly successful assaults against Bosnian Serb-held territories. However, Croatian Serbs then joined in the fray, with the result that Bihać and other towns in the enclave have been under heavy attack ever since. Despite this being a designated Safe Area, the NATO and U.N. response was to play down the significance of the attacks. Following an air attack from the Croat-Serb–controlled Udbina Airport on November 18, and with the will of the Security Council as expressed in Resolution 958 (11/19/94), NATO did respond with an air attack. Even then, however, NATO was careful to target the runway only, avoiding any damage to the attacking planes [*Balkan War Report*, 12/94, p. 9]. Continued U.N. inaction led Haris Silajdžić, the Bosnian Prime Minister, to accuse UNPROFOR leaders of actually "helping the Serbs use the crisis in a bid to force the Government to accept a complete end to the fighting in Bosnia" [*New York Times*, 11/27/94]. The NATO option was not used again until May 25, 1995.

The long period of inaction affected not just Bosnian civilians under artillery attack. A Bangladeshi detachment in Bihać—ill-clothed, ill-fed, and ill-armed—appeared to be abandoned by UNPROFOR for a long period, during which time they were the frequent targets of Serb attacks.

To many observers, it appeared that they were being sacrificed to UN-PROFOR's policy not to defend the safe area and, as Silajdžić suggested, to teach the government a lesson.

By the end of 1994, military commentators were talking of the complete defeat of the Bosnian government's Fifth Brigade, but then the front line stabilized, with fighting continuing throughout the alleged cease-fire. Indeed, in April 1995 the government made new advances in several areas.

Mission Fission

Perhaps the dubious honor of being the most flouted resolution belongs to 781 (10/9/92), which mandated a no-fly zone over Bosnia for all military flights except those of U.N. agencies. After a bombing raid by aircraft from Serbian territory against Srebrenica, Resolution 816 (3/31/93) extended the ban to include helicopters, and made it a Chapter VII operation, which eventually recruited NATO.

The cumbersome chain of command has inhibited response most of the time, but on February 28, 1994, NATO fighters shot down four out of six Serb planes on a mission over Bosnia. However, this was the exception rather than the rule. By the end of April 1995 there had been 4,462 "apparent violations" of Resolution 781 [S/1995/5/Add.26]. Included in those violations was what appeared to be a heavy resupply effort from Serbia proper to the Bosnian Serbs in February and April 1995. Bombing raids in May went unanswered, despite threats by UNPROFOR civil and military chiefs.

On March 31, 1995, the Security Council split UNPROFOR into three separate organizations at the insistence of Croatian President Franjo Tudjman. He had pointed out that large portions of the agreement under which the Blue Helmets had entered the country had not been implemented, such as the disarmament of Croatian Serb troops and the return of refugees. As noted above, Tudjman gave the United Nations notice to quit Croatia unless its mandate was separated from that of UNPROFOR in Bosnia and redrawn to include something like the original, unimplemented peace plan.

Since UNPROFOR's mission in Croatia was to protect the Croatian Serbs in the U.N. Protected Areas, and UNPROFOR in Bosnia admitted that those Serbs were attacking the U.N. Safe Area across the border in Bihać, there was indeed room for tidying up the mandates. In reality, Tudjman no more wanted the United Nations to quit than the Europeans did. Even the Serbs wanted it to stay. Bosnian Serb General Ratko Mladić insisted that the United Nations had to stay in Croatia, or he would insist on it pulling out of Bosnia as well [*Financial Times*, 3/8/95]. After much mutual brinkmanship, a fudged agreement was produced. Resolutions 981 and 983 on March 31 reorganized the peacekeepers. In Bosnia, UNPROFOR retained its name, while in Croatia it became the U.N. Confidence Restoration Operation (UNCRO). In Macedonia, UNPROFOR transmuted into the U.N. Preventive Deployment Mission (UNPREDEP). The main effect has been to hive off UNPROFOR's only unqualified success story, Macedonia's intact borders.

Within a month the newly renamed UNCRO proved utterly ineffective when the Croatian Army swept aside both U.N. and Serb forces to gain control of the Western Slavonian enclave. Initial reports of serious human rights violations by the Croat Army in May seemed to lack substantiating evidence, and the conflict appeared to be contained. Indeed, cynics suspected a deal between Croatian President Tudjman and Serb President Milošević, who has his own quarrels with the leadership of the Serb enclaves in Croatia and Bosnia.

After the Croat attack, there was a gruesome irony in Serb demands for strong action by the United Nations and NATO against the Croats. As the four-month cease-fire agreed to in late 1994 came to an end in April 1995, the Bosnian Serbs closed down Sarajevo airport to U.N. diplomats and to relief flights. Their allies in Croatia bombed Bihać, all without the slightest military response from the United Nations or NATO. In fact, few of the developments that had been greeted with guarded enthusiasm last year came to fruition [see *A Global Agenda: Issues/49*]. The "permanent ceasefire" between Zagreb and Knin can be presumed to have gone up in smoke with the attack on Western Slavonia. As of late May 1995 the Serbs continued to block the reopening of Tuzla airport to humanitarian shipments, and the heavy weapons ban in the zone around Sarajevo, established under threat of NATO airstrikes following the "market massacre" of February 5, 1994, was being flouted with impunity. That came to a halt on May 25, when the patience of even the United Nations ran out.

On May 16, 1995, Secretary-General Boutros-Ghali returned from Europe after consultations with UNPROFOR commanders, armed with suggestions for redrawing the mandates for the Organization. It was clear to even the most optimistic U.N. official that the mission was drifting rudderless. Among the options canvassed were a more "robust" enforcement of the mandate, a pullout from the safe zones, and the total disarmament of government troops in them. At a press conference following a meeting of the Security Council (5/16/95), the Secretary-General echoed earlier French military complaints about the lack of definition for a safe area, and seemed to be favoring the evacuation of the safe zones.

UNPROFOR already seemed to have anticipated a policy retreat by taking no action whatsoever at violations of the exclusion zone. However, the Bosnian Serbs decided the situation themselves, if in a negative way. The following week, a Serb sniper killed a French peacekeeper, the Serbs refused to allow a medevac flight, Serb forces seized heavy weapons from U.N.-monitored depots, and they resumed heavy shelling of Sarajevo.

Collectively, these acts provided the impetus necessary for the United Nations to adopt the U.S.-favored policy of NATO airstrikes.

On May 25, NATO struck ammunition dumps in Pale, destroying them. The Serb response was savage, as usual aimed at noncombatants, and almost certainly politically stupid. One shell alone reportedly killed over 70 civilians in Tuzla. UNPROFOR and NATO showed that a new policy was in operation by striking at more ammunition dumps in Pale on May 26. The Serbs then took hostage peacekeepers, chaining some of them to ammunition dumps. Apart from the civilian deaths, they did not advance their cause by including a Russian officer among the human shields [Reuters, 5/26/95].

NATO warned the Serbs that they had anticipated this, and that further strikes would follow if the heavy weapons were not returned to U.N. control and the hostages released. Having tried peaceful persuasion, sanctions, and downright appeasement, it almost looked as if UNPROFOR had finally been pushed into the more robust action that it had long eschewed—and which was far from the policy that the Secretariat had favored only a week before.

Diplomacy

Soft-spoken diplomacy by a variety of intermediaries has proven totally ineffectual, given that the parties concerned are convinced, on very good empirical evidence, that their refusal to cooperate will result in no ill-consequences. From October 8, 1991, when then Secretary-General Javier Pérez de Cuéllar appointed former Secretary of State Cyrus Vance as his Personal Envoy to the former Yugoslavia, the United Nations has been involved in continuous "stickless" diplomatic efforts. Usually it has been in partnership with a European nominee as co-chair of the International Conference on the Former Yugoslavia, although the personnel have changed.

First among these was Lord Carrington, who was replaced by Lord Owen. Then, in 1993, Cyrus Vance was replaced by Thorvald Stoltenberg [U.N. press release, 4/2/93]. In retrospect, this partnership may have been a mistake. The European Union was usually unsure of what it wanted, and its principles of consensus made it even more indecisive than the Security Council. At an early stage European diplomats were saying that some form of cantonization was inevitable. So it was no great surprise when, on October 28, 1992, the "Vance-Owen plan" called for Bosnia to be divided into ten cantons. The plan was rejected by all parties but the Croats, who got everything they wanted out of it. France, Germany, Russia, the United Kingdom, and the United States formed what has been known as the Contact Group, which briefly showed a united face to the world and the parties, but which fell apart at its first serious test.

Since December 1, 1993, Under-Secretary-General Yasushi Akashi has been the Secretary-General's Special Representative and head of UN-PROFOR. Both he and his military commanders are involved in continuous local negotiations. In addition, the Zagreb Group (also known as Z-4), composed of the European Union, Russia, the United States, and the United Kingdom, have been equally unsuccessful in achieving lasting agreements in Croatia, although some progress has been made there on economic links.

Given all these efforts, not to mention the freelance activities of various international figures (such as the Carter initiative, described below) and the various meetings between Tudjman and Milošević and between Tudjman and Bosnian President Alija Izetbegović, it is safe to say that international diplomatic efforts have been as thoroughly Balkanized as their subject matter.

This was exemplified on September 21, 1994, when the Contact Group came up with a plan that gave the Serbs 49 percent of Bosnian territory. Sarajevo was pressured to accept with the promise that serious leverage would be exerted on Bosnian Serb leader Radovan Karadžić, if he did not agree. The United States, for example, spoke of lifting the arms embargo on Bosnia and Herzegovina. Still, the Bosnian Serbs said no, despite the urging of Milošević to accept. Eventually, it turned out that the Russians on the Contact Group either had changed their minds about the consensus, or had never joined it, with the result that the carrots offered the Bosnian government were not delivered.

Milošević then publicly parted company with his former proteges in Bosnia and Croatia, Radovan Karadžić in Pale and Milan Martić in Knin, and imposed his own sanctions on his former allies. In return for closing the border with the Bosnian Serbs, to be monitored by a force from the International Conference on the Former Yugoslavia, the Security Council lifted some of the sanctions on Belgrade (notably restriction on air travel) on condition that they be reviewed every 100 days. If the border regime was not maintained, sanctions were to be reimposed in full, immediately.

The Contact Group plan was still officially on the table when in December 1994 former President Jimmy Carter joined in with his own initiative. The result was an "Agreement on the Complete Cessation of Hostilities" (12/31/94) in Bosnia. This was slightly longer lasting than most previous declarations, but as usual it was honored more in the breach than the observance. It was midwinter and most of the parties made little secret that they were preparing for the next military round. At the end of April 1995 the Agreement's passing was hardly noticed, since fighting had already been taking place across the country.

The hopes and prayers of diplomats seemed to be concentrated on Milošević as someone who could deliver peace. However, while the Russians were prepared to go all the way with Milošević and advocated the immediate lifting of all sanctions on Belgrade, Western diplomats were much warier. They wanted to monitor progress and, after concern over reported breaches of the border regime with Bosnia, to reduce the review period to 75 days.

The Croat-Muslim Federation

Forced on the Bosnian and Croatian governments by the Washington Agreement of March 24, 1994, the Croat Bosnian Federation is best regarded as an armistice between the two governments. Croatia was on the verge of facing sanctions as a result of its troops' presence in Bosnia. Fighting the Bosnians, and thus acting as de facto allies of the Serbs, did not play well at home for Tudjman, and the behavior of Croat forces surrounding the eastern half of Mostar was regarded around the world as on a par with events in Sarajevo. After a year of intensive effort by the European Union, the minuteness of the progress toward connecting the two communities, let alone uniting them, set the Agreement in perspective. The Special Rapporteur on Human Rights, for example, referred to "local Bosnian Croat authorities in the western part of the city who refuse to countenance cooperation with the authorities in the Eastern part of the city" [E/CN.4/1995/57, p. 9].

The Federation's cumbersome arrangements dealt several ideological blows to the multinationalists in Sarajevo, since it was to be between two ethnic communities—Muslims and Croats. The thousands of Serbs loyal to the Bosnian government, in particular the Serb Civic Union in Sarajevo, were not institutionally represented, although they have since been given some representation. However, the Agreement detracted from the legitimacy of the Sarajevo government by presenting it as an ethnic community, thereby detracting from any argument against a Serb community confederating with Knin—or Belgrade [New York Times, 5/7/95]. It also raised questions about the U.N. seat. As Russian diplomats asked, who wields the vote—the Federation or the Bosnian presidency?

The Federation's fragility was demonstrated in March 1995 when the Croat side almost pulled out after General Vlado Santić of the Bosnian-Croat militia was kidnapped by Bosian government troops [Financial Times, 4/17/95]. On the other hand, it was threatened even more seriously the following month when an alleged Croat war criminal was to arrive in Sarajevo to represent the Croat side of the Federation. The Croats also levied duties on goods carried across their line of control into Bosnian government territory [ibid.].

A Small—But Significant—Success

In contrast to the many failures, Resolution 795 (12/11/92) could perhaps be considered the only timely and unqualified success of the conflict. It set up UNPROFOR (later UNPREDEP) with a force of 700 troops on the Macedonian/Serbian border. This was the first preventive deployment of its kind, and, enhanced by U.S. troops the following year, the border has remained quiet and intact. Ironically, the Bosnian authorities had requested a similar force at an early stage of the conflict there, but were refused. The two contrasting experiences make a strong argument in favor of timely preventive deployment with a clear mission.

However, in larger terms, the UNPROFOR/UNPREDEP successful containment of the borders is a strictly limited success. The nonrecognition and blockade of Macedonia by Greece have severe consequences, beyond the Balkan Republic's unorthodox name at the United Nations, where it is known as The Former Yugoslav Republic of Macedonia (filed under "T" and usually referred to as FYROM). It means that the international community turns a blind eye to the militarily sound but economically porous frontier between Macedonia and Serbia. Inside those borders the large Albanian majority was growing restless, especially over the Skopje government's refusal to allow an Albanian-language university to open in Tetovo. That resulted in a death on February 17, 1995, when an Albanian attempt to open the premises was thwarted by police.

Embargo

The very first Security Council resolution on the Balkan war, Resolution 713, created an arms embargo on the entire former Yugoslavia. There is clear evidence that this is not totally effective. Belgrade owned most of the supplies and has its own manufacturing capacity, and so the Serbs have maintained a very high level of superiority in heavy artillery, tanks, and aircraft. Croatia has clearly been reinforcing itself, reportedly buying former Warsaw Pact weapons from various sources. Bosnia has to resupply itself via Croat-controlled territory, and anecdotal evidence suggests that the Croats take a percentage on the deal. However, the Croats are reluctant to allow heavy weaponry to pass on to the Bosnians in case they (the Croats) once again take up arms against the neighbors to the south.

As part of the package to persuade Bosnia to sign up for the Contact Group proposal, the United States had promised to seek the lifting of the U.N. arms embargo, if the Serbs did not accept the plan. In the face of heavy bipartisan domestic presssure, President Clinton announced that U.S. forces would not take part in enforcing the embargo, but his rather half-hearted diplomatic efforts at the United Nations came to naught.

Legislation now before Congress would explicitly defy the United Nations over the resolution—and cause a major rift with America's European allies, not to mention Russia. The Europeans have insisted that there would be even more bloodshed were the embargo lifted, and they have threatened to withdraw their forces from UNPROFOR in the event that it is.

Sanctions

Resolution 757 has had far more effect on Belgrade than almost any other Security Council decision. The Chapter VII sanctions have both political and economic effects. Politically, it has isolated the government and branded it as the aggressor. Internally, some observers suggest that it has given Milošević an excuse for economic incompetence while also rallying support from the public. The state's "firm" control over electronic news media in the former Yugoslavia has ensured that only one version of events reaches most of the public [Commission on Human Rights Report, E/CN.4/1995/54].

Ironically, attempts to follow the Commission on Human Rights (CHR) Special Rapporteur's recommendations on aid to the independent media in the former Yugoslavia were blocked in the Sanctions Committee by the Russians, who cited freedom of the press as a reason why supplies must go to the government press as well. Smuggling from neighboring countries has alleviated many of the worst effects of sanctions, but they are still clearly making Milošević more amenable to cooperating with the United Nations, as shown by the Security Council decision on September 23, 1994, to partially lift sanctions in return for his pledge to close the border with the Bosnian Serbs. Russia's desire to lift sanctions completely has so far been unsupported by other members of the Security Council, who are less convinced of Milošević's change of heart and who continue to insist on a rolling 100-day review.

In April 1995 concern about UNPROFOR reports of helicopters flying across the border into Bosnia led to that review period being reduced to 75 days. Remarkably, the border monitors, who were not from UNPROFOR but from the International Conference on the Former Yugoslavia (ICFY), failed to see anything in February—this despite sightings by Dutch UNPROFOR contingents in Srebrenica. Later in April the ICFY monitors reported that there had been some 80 radar contacts that looked like helicopters moving across the border from Serbia to Bosnia. Citing "sufficient reason to defer judgement on possible violations of the air border," the Mission coordinator agreed to wait for analysis of the radar tapes [S/1995/302]. One reason to defer judgment was, of course, that according to the Security Council, the full range of sanctions should have been reimposed on Serbia and Montenegro immediately.

Human Rights

Unhindered by the United Nations and seemingly unworried by the International Court of Justice or the U.N. tribunal established in The Hague to investigate and prosecute human rights violations in the former Yugo-slavia, ethnic cleansing continued in Bosnia throughout 1994 and 1995. In Banja Luka, a well-attested reign of terror drove out thousands of Croats and Muslims [*New York Times*, 8/29/94]. Appeals by the International Commit-tee of the Red Cross to Boutros-Ghali and to heads of governments on April 18, 1994, produced no effective results. Former Polish Prime Minis-ter Tadeusz Mazowiecki, who has served since 1992 as the U.N.'s Special Rapporteur on the Situation of Human Rights in the Territory of the Former Yugoslavia, reported in April 1995 [E/CN 4/1995/3] that in the Banja Luka region 90 percent of the Muslims and 85 percent of the Croats had been driven out since the beginning of the war. He further reported that in the first three months of 1995, some 3,000 refugees crossed from the region into Croatia alone, driven out by persistent persecution.

Mazowiecki pointed out that the local Serb authorities had never al-lowed access by human rights monitors, which was one of the conditions of the cease-fire agreement, and he called upon the international commu-nity to "exercise all possible pressure to obtain access of U.N. civil police officers and human rights monitors."

Missing Persons

In 1994 the Special Rapporteur and the U.N. Commission on Human Rights set up a "Special Process on Missing Persons in the territory of the former Yugoslavia," with a strictly humanitarian, "non-accusatory" mandate [E/CN.4/1995/37]. Admitting the difficulties of calculating exactly how many people are affected, Manfred Nowak of the Commission quoted estimates of up to 20,000 "disappeared" in Bosnia [ibid., p. 14]. The process had only 600 cases registered with it at the time of its report, but it does not seem to have secured much success other than to conclude that most of these cases were "enforced disappearances," and that apart from six people "of Serbian origin" who disappeared after being detained by Croatian military police, the others were mostly Muslims or Croats seized by various Serb authorities.

Since those "authorities" are still in power and still detaining people, it seems unlikely that they will offer the cooperation necessary for the Special Process to succeed.

The International Criminal Tribunal on the Former Yugoslavia

The International Criminal Tribunal on the Former Yugoslavia (ICTFY) has been forcefully accusatory in comparison with the determination of so many UNPROFOR officials not to place blame. The appointment of Judge Richard Goldstone of South Africa as prosecutor for the ICTFY on July 8, 1994, has breathed life into what was looking increasingly like a stillborn body. His courage in pursuing charges against the South African security's "dirty tricks" department has clearly been a good preparation.

For a long time the procrastination in providing facilities and a prosecutor for the tribunal, accompanied by a seeming desire to overlook the voluminous work of the Commission of Experts established by Resolution 780 (10/6/92) to investigate alleged war crimes, had left many human rights workers worried that the tribunal was being set up for failure. Those fears seem to have dissipated. In establishing its headquaraters at The Hague in the Netherlands, the tribunal has also "leased" prison facilities from the Dutch government. The first tranche of indictments named 22 suspects, one of whom, Dusko Tadić, has already been extradited from Germany. Perhaps the biggest test of credibility was passed when it was clear that Goldstone was not content with indicting only low-level figures. In April 1995 he gave notice that indictments were likely against such major figures as Radovan Karadžić and Ratko Mladić, the civilian and military leaders of the Pale Serbs [Christian Science Monitor, 4/26/95]. This move was politically inconvenient for the many statesmen and diplomats who were trying to cajole the Bosnian Serbs into some form of compromise.

Goldstone was even more undiplomatic when, on May 8, he gave notice that the tribunal was considering indictments against Croats suspected of mass killings of Muslims in Ahmici, Vitez, and other towns in central Bosnia. Perhaps Goldstone's confidence was boosted when the future of the tribunal seemed to be assured after the Fifth Committee approved a $7 million tranche for it. There is still a wrangle between the Security Council and developing countries in the Group of 77 as to just how this money should be paid. The latter say that the cost should be treated as peacekeeping, with the Perm Five paying more. The Council says it is a General Assembly matter that should come from the regular budget. Even so, tribunal officials are confident that financing will be forthcoming.

Humanitarian Aid

U.N. spokesmen frequently excuse their inaction in the face of attacks on civilians by saying that their mandate is restricted to ensuring the delivery of humanitarian aid. The UNHCR appeal for 1995 cited 2,244,000 people as "beneficiaries," but its footnotes point out that "in practice food distribution reaches a wider population based on assessment of food deficit by region." Of these, 450,700 are officially designated as refugees, but to describe the unusual situation in Bosnia, the 1,400,000 beneficiaries there are all listed as "assisted persons." For this relief, the international community will pay an estimated $691.9 million in 1995 [U.N. Revised Consolidated Inter-Agency Appeal for Former Yugoslavia, 11/94]. The U.N. agencies involved include

UNHCR, WFP, UNICEF, WHO, UNESCO, FAO, and of course, UNPROFOR.

The big breakthrough for the relief agencies was the cease-fire between the Croats and the Bosnian government, which freed up the routes from the coast to central Bosnia. Convoys to Sarajevo and the safe area enclaves are still held at the mercy of the Serbs. In fact, 80 percent of the food needs of Sarajevo are met by air, which ensured that the city did not suffer the full severity of the past winter. Serbian obduracy has also caused the continuance of airdrops to some of the enclaves. In particular Bihać, besieged by both Pale and Knin regimes, has suffered severe shortages and interruptions of supplies.

Lessons Learned?

Many observers have questioned whether Bosnia will prove to be for the United Nations what Abyssinia was for the League of Nations—the point of no return in the Organization's decline. The Third Annual Peacekeeping Mission of the United Nations Association of the USA, which toured UNPROFOR in November 1994, reported that it is "structural incoherence—calling upon an intentionally weak peacekeeping force to compel strong military antagonists to stop fighting—that is behind UNPROFOR's difficulties." Many commentators have added that behind that undoubted structural incoherence is a moral and political incoherence, emanating from the capitals of the major powers. And that incoherence has, of course, been reflected in the Security Council.

Even so, it would be too facile to blame the Council and its members for all the failings of the United Nations. The Secretariat has allowed control of UNPROFOR to slide into the hands of various national interests, and has allowed its military and civil leadership to follow an agenda that not even the kaleidoscopic mandates from the Council can justify. Under-Secretary-General Akashi told the UNA-USA mission, "We do not take a moral position on the conflict." Most of the world, however, thinks that the United Nations should. To be impartial between a member state and an aggressor, between the perpetrators of genocide and its victims, is to ignore the U.N. Charter, the Genocide Convention, and numerous human rights conventions that the peoples of the world almost certainly assume to be the "common law" of any U.N. operation.

3. Haiti
By Ricardo Alday

In late June 1994, in the face of the Haitian military rulers' continuing refusal to comply with Security Council demands that they step down, and with a **global embargo** already in effect for 40 days, the Security Council decided to extend for one more month the mandate of the yet-to-be deployed **U.N. Mission in Haiti (UNMIH)** [S/Res/933, 6/30/94]. The same resolution directed the Secretary-General to offer by July 15 "specific recommendations" on the strength, composition, cost, and duration of an extended UNMIH that would be deployed "after the departure of the senior Haitian military leadership."

The situation became more tense over the next few days as reports of continuous violations of human rights increased and as nongovernmental organizations (NGOs) monitoring Haiti asked both the United States and the United Nations to review their options. Among the calls for action were a number strongly advocating military intervention to oust the coup leaders. On July 5, 1994, overwhelmed by the flow of Haitians trying to reach U.S. shores by boat, the White House changed its Haitian policy for the second time in two months and decided to bar Haitians from entering U.S. territory. Two days later the United States sent over 2,000 Marines to patrol the waters off the small island nation.

As with previous U.S. and U.N. demands over the past year, Lt.-General Raoul Cédras and the coterie of officers around him ignored the Council's pressure, and on July 11 they delivered to the Executive Director of the **U.N.–OAS International Civilian Mission (MICIVIH)**, Colin Granderson, an "executive decree" by which they declared the mission "undesirable," giving the human rights monitors and other MICIVIH personnel 48 hours to leave Haitian territory. The members of the mission, along with Granderson, left Haiti on July 13.

Secretary-General Boutros Boutros-Ghali's report to the Security Council [S/1994/828, 7/15/94] proposed the creation of a multinational force under Chapter VII of the U.N. Charter, and—with the authorization of the Council—the establishment of a "safe and secure environment" in Haiti, in order to begin the implementation of the **Governor's Island Agreement** [A/47/975–A/26063], signed on July 3, 1993 [see *A Global Agenda: Issues/ 49*].

This proposal was one of three options presented to the Council, none of which included diplomatic or political negotiations among the parties—a fact that infuriated several Latin American and other Third World countries, which strongly criticized Boutros-Ghali for considering only military options and opening the door to a U.N.-blessed intervention of the impoverished Caribbean nation. **Chapter VII,** these countries insisted, should be invoked and used only when there is a threat to international peace and security. The Secretary-General did not explain or suggest that the Haiti situation posed such a threat, and the Security Council had never before authorized the use of military force in this hemisphere.

Boutros-Ghali stressed that the situation in Haiti had deteriorated to the point at which it had become "intolerable." The Council recognized "the unique character" of the present situation in Haiti "and its deteriorating, complex, and extraordinary nature, requiring an exceptional response." On July 31, the Security Council voted 12 in favor, 0 against, with 2 abstentions (Brazil and China) and 1 member absent (Rwanda), authorizing the use of "all necessary means to facilitate the departure from Haiti of the military leadership, and the prompt return of the legitimately elected President," clearing the way for a U.S.-led invasion [S/Res/ 940, 7/31/94].

Deposed President Jean-Bertrand Aristide asked many times, both before and after the adoption of **Resolution 940,** for a military intervention that "could liberate the suffering of civilians" in his country. Nevertheless, Venezuela, a member of the Secretary-General's "Group of Friends" for Haiti (together with France, the United States, Canada, and Argentina), decided not to sponsor the draft resolution, citing "the principle of non-intervention in the internal affairs of another country." Venezuela had been the first country to give asylum to Aristide in 1991 and had played an influential role among the "friends" during several talks and negotiations with the deposed President. Within hours of the adoption of the resolution, Haiti's military-backed president, Emile Jonaissant, who had been "appointed" on May 11, 1994, declared a stage of siege.

Stepped-Up Pressure

In the days following the Council's "green light" to establish a multinational force for Haiti, the U.S. government engaged in intense consultations, both domestically and abroad, carefully considering its options and the risks involved in a potential military intervention. By mid-August two attempts by Latin American nations to send high-level delegations to Haiti to try to convince Cédras to go into exile and avoid an invasion were aborted by the United States. Plans to put more pressure on the military by strengthening the enforcement of the embargo with increased monitors along Haiti's 240-mile border with the Dominican Republic also failed.

The Secretary-General dispatched a mid-level official, Rolf Knuttson, to warn Cédras and other military rulers to accept exile voluntarily or face a U.S.-led invasion. Political and logistical preparations for this option were further complicated at the end of August when the United States faced a large flotilla of Cuban refugees. Any decision on the Haiti issue was to be put off.

On August 29, 1994, the **Reverend Jean Marie-Vincent,** a Roman Catholic priest who aided Aristide, was killed in a northwestern district of the country. A day later, special U.N. envoy Knuttson left Haiti empty-handed after an attempt to meet with military leaders had failed.

It was at this point that the Secretary-General gave up all hope of resolving the Haitian crisis by diplomatic means and left the U.S. government with two choices: Use force to restore Aristide to power, or wait to see if the near-total blockade of Haiti would force out the military. "Once again the military regime had discarded a possibility of peacefully implementing the Governor's Island Agreement and the relevant Security Council resolutions," the Council said in a prepared statement on August 30 [S/PRST/1994/49].

The 13 English-speaking members of the Caribbean Community (CARICOM) announced their support of a U.S.-led invasion of their neighbor. Deputy Secretary of State Strobe Talbott declared publicly for the first time "that the multinational force is going to Haiti" [*Washington Post*, 9/2/94]; and on September 5, President Bill Clinton told a news conference that "one way or another, the de facto government is going to be leaving," although he added that there was no "specific deadline."

A week later, Secretary of State Warren Christopher said that some **17 countries had pledged to commit at least 1,500 troops to a multinational force.** Events then moved quickly. Two troop-laden aircraft carriers left the United States for Haiti on September 13, and two days later President Clinton said in a televised address that General Cédras must be held accountable for the "terrible human tragedy" in Haiti—an obvious suggestion that invasion was imminent. "Your time is up," Clinton said. "Leave now or we will force you from power."

Eleventh-Hour Negotiations

Lt.-General Raoul Cédras responded in a CBS television interview that he was not interested in U.S. offers to live in comfortable exile. On September 17, as the world awaited the arrival of the first U.S. Marines in Haiti, it witnessed instead the arrival of a political delegation headed by former U.S. President **Jimmy Carter** for last-minute talks with Cédras. Carter was accompanied by Senator Sam Nunn and the former Joint Chiefs of Staff Chairman, General Colin Powell.

On the evening of September 18, Clinton announced that the United States and Haiti's military leaders had reached **an agreement to allow the de facto government to step down** by October 15 in return for a promise of amnesty. President Jean-Bertrand Aristide would then be restored to power. The invasion had been called off.

The accord called for both Cédras and his military chief of staff, Brigadier General Philip Biamby, to step down. In addition to amnesty the offer included safe passage to exile and the preservation of the fortunes they had amassed during a rule of three years. On September 19, the day after the accord was reached, the 90 percent-U.S. multinational force began its peaceful entrance into Haiti to begin the task of establishing a "safe and secure environment," as provided by Security Council Resolution 940.

Special **U.N.-OAS envoy Dante Caputo** presented his resignation that same day, sharply criticizing the U.S. government for not consulting with him or the two multinational organizations regarding its plans to go through "unilateral channels." The Secretary-General appointed Algerian diplomat **Lakhdar Brahimi** as his new **Special Representative to Haiti.**

Angry with the White House for having negotiated an agreement with the very same military rulers that the United States had earlier called "criminals," the still-deposed Aristide asked the Clinton administration to disarm the Haitian forces and paramilitary units that were endangering civilians and U.S. troops. With the Somali quagmire fresh in the American memory, Clinton ignored the request.

In the first two weeks **following the arrival of U.S. troops,** a series of events led to a more optimistic picture of the country's future, although the situation in general was fragile, and in several regions of the country it was business as usual, with violence and demonstrations on the increase. On September 26, 1994, the U.S. government announced the suspension of all unilateral sanctions against Haiti, except those affecting the military leaders and their immediate supporters. On September 28 the **Haitian parliament,** meeting in an emergency session, approved the amnesty for the coup leaders. One day later the Security Council decided to authorize the lifting of U.N. sanctions—to take place a day after Aristide's return to power [S/Res/944, 9/29/94]—and requested the Secretary-General (in consultation with the Organization of American States) to take steps to ensure completion of deployment of the observers and other elements of the 60-person UNMIH advance team provided for in Resolution 940.

An advance team began to work out the details of the **transfer of power from the 20,000-member multinational force to UNMIH,** which was to go ahead once the Security Council determined that a "safe and secure environment" had been established in Haiti. A triumphant President Aristide addressed the U.N. General Assembly and reaffirmed that those who ousted him from power three years earlier would not be charged or prosecuted for their act. On October 13, a year after they were supposed to leave Haiti by virtue of the Governor's Island Agreement, Lt.-General Cédras and Brigadier General Biamby left for Panama. President Aristide returned to power two days later, in a ceremony attended by Bill Clinton and Boutros Boutros-Ghali.

Remaking a Nation

In accordance with **Resolution 944,** U.N. sanctions were then lifted, and the human right observers of MICIVIH were redeployed throughout the country. The Security Council then approved a resolution reaffirming "the willingness of the international community to provide assistance to the people of Haiti, with the expectation that they will do their utmost to rebuild the country" [S/Res/948, 10/15/94]. On November 29, and with no major incidents on the ground after more than two months of occupation, the Council authorized the Secretary-General to increase the original 60-member advance team to 500, and asked him to accelerate preparations for transfer of power from the multinational force to UNMIH.

According to the **U.N. High Commissioner for Refugees,** more than 16,000 of the nearly 22,000 Haitians who had fled their country after Aristide was ousted were back at home within the first three months of the President's return. During the same period, crime skyrocketed throughout the island as the government struggled to revive **an economy devastated by economic sanctions** and cope with tens of thousands of unemployed civilians.

Security was and continues to be a major concern. A U.S. soldier was killed on January 12, 1995, after a gun battle near a checkpoint on the outskirts of the town of Gonaïves. By this time, the number of U.S. soldiers was around 6,000, down from nearly 21,000 at the height of the intervention. Renewed violence brought new demands for the disarmament of **paramilitary forces and former police officers,** but both the United States and the United Nations kept their distance and stressed that disarmament was not part of the multinational force's mandate, nor would it be part of UNMIH's.

The **interim police,** consisting of about 4,000 officers under the supervision of international monitors, has struggled to earn public respect. On January 13, President Aristide announced a **purging of Army ranks,** weakening its apparatus and making it dependent on him. So far the move by the priest-turned-politician has proved to be successful, as some of the oppressors of the past are no longer able to act as an autonomous body. Also in January the new permanent police force began to undergo **informal training,** and its first team of 375 graduates was expected to be fully operational by midsummer 1995.

At the end of January 1995 the Security Council had fixed March 31 as the date for UNMIH to assume responsibility from the multinational force once the Council had determined that a "safe and secure environment" had been established [S/Res/975, 1/30/95]. The handover took place in Port-au-Prince with the same sort of ceremony that marked Aristide's return to power. This was just three days after **Mireille Durocher Bertin,** a long-time opposition figure, was shot to death in Port-au-Prince. The killing, by far the worst incident since the end of military rule, underscored the importance of the role that U.N. peacekeeping forces will play in the future of the country. Until the expiration of their mandate in February 1996, the 6,000 soldiers and 900 police officers of UNMIH will have to maintain a safe and secure environment as well as to provide assistance in the "professionalization of the Haitian armed forces and the creation of the separate police force" [S/Res/940/1994].

After two postponements, U.N. and U.S. officials pressed Haitian authorities to move quickly on preparations for **parliamentary elections,** considered a first and crucial test in the country's quest for democracy. The whole process, consisting of two rounds of elections monitored by MICIVIH staff and other international civilian organizations, has proved to be a complicated one, though attended by far less violence than many people expected. According to Horacio Boneo, director of the U.N. Electoral Assistance Unit, 3.6 million of Haiti's 7 million citizens are eligible to vote. More than 800,000 ballot cards were reported missing in the weeks prior to the first round, on June 25, but fears that this would invalidate the elections were quickly put to rest. The second, runoff round was scheduled for July 23, but was rescheduled for August when political parties protested widespread irregularities in the first round. In addition, new first-round elections were scheduled for July 28 in eight towns where arsonists burned ballots in the original June 25 vote [*New York Times*, 7/6/95].

Almost 10,000 candidates competed for 83 seats in the Chamber of Deputies, 18 seats in the Senate, membership in 133 municipal councils, and membership in 565 community boards across the country. **Presidential elections** are scheduled for December 1995.

Today, the nation's citizens and the international community face what is viewed as an even harder job—that of bringing stability and security to Haitian society and setting the country on the path to economic development.

4. Africa
By Edmund T. Piasecki

The United Nations scored several peacekeeping successes in Africa through 1995, including the first free multiparty elections in Mozambique and the conclusion of a second peace agreement for Angola. Western Sahara was still awaiting its referendum on self-determination, however, and in Rwanda and Burundi the world body had at best stopped the mass killings but was only just beginning massive rehabilitation and reconstruction efforts. The civil war in Liberia intensified, forcing a downsizing of the U.N. observer mission there, and the United Nations completed its long withdrawal from Somalia with only vague promises of continued diplomatic involvement.

In all these conflicts, the Security Council continued to show ingenuity and perseverence, managing arms embargoes, dispatching its own fact-finding missions, and digesting a flood of information in off-the-record briefings from the Secretary-General and his special representatives. The Organization of African Unity (OAU) also continued to expand its own diplomatic and peacekeeping efforts, a development welcomed by the General Assembly [A/Res/49/64]. In addition to its annual item on cooperation with the OAU, the Assembly will consider at its 50th Session reports on special economic assistance to Mozambique, Liberia, and Somalia (as well as Djibouti, Lesotho, Malawi, and the Sudan) [A/Res/49/21], the New Agenda for the Development of Africa in the 1990s [A/Res/49/142], the Program for the Second Industrial Development Decade for Africa [A/Res/49/107], and the Educational and Training Program for Southern Africa [A/Res/49/17].

Rwanda

The United Nations was still struggling to reinforce its **Assistance Mission in Rwanda (UNAMIR)** in June 1994, two months after the renewal of civil war and the outbreak of unprecedented ethnic slaughter. Although the Security Council had authorized the deployment of up to 5,500 troops to protect massive numbers of displaced persons and refugees [S/Res/918, 5/17/94], just 503 UNAMIR personnel were on the ground by June 18. The problem, the Secretary-General pointed out, was the inability of eight of the nine African states offering troops to fully equip them and the refusal of other states to supply the necessary equipment or offer troops themselves. UNAMIR could not be fully deployed, the Secretary-General estimated, before September [S/1994/728, 6/20/94].

But the dimensions of the humanitarian crisis were already staggering. From a population of 7 million, the Secretary-General had reported estimates of between 250,000 and 500,000 dead, 1.5 million displaced persons, and 400,000 refugees [S/1994/640, 5/31/94]. Most of the dead were ethnic Tutsis, hacked to death by militias of the ruling Hutu tribe; those fleeing the fighting were mainly Hutus, fearing reprisals from the forces of the Tutsi-dominated **Rwandan Patriotic Front (RPF)**, now advancing from the north.

Boutros-Ghali recommended that the Security Council accept the offer from France [S/1994/734, 6/21/94] to send an "interim force," pending the full deployment of UNAMIR, to protect displaced persons, refugees, and civilians, especially through the establishment of "safe humanitarian areas." The French got the Chapter VII mandate they were seeking—authorizing them to use "all necessary means" to achieve their objectives—in Resolution 929 [6/22/94], which also limited the mission to two months and emphasized its "impartial," "neutral," and "strictly humanitarian" nature.

Billed as a multinational force, **"Operation Turquoise"** consisted of 2,300 French and a mere 32 Senegalese troops when it entered what remained of government-controlled territory in southwest Rwanda on June 22, 1994. As the number of Hutus seeking protection surged, the French began to establish a large safe zone in the triangle of land between the towns of Cyangugu, Kibuye, and Gikongoro on July 2. It was already offering sanctuary to some 850,000 Hutus in 50 camps [S/1994/798, 7/6/94].

Despite the intervention, fighting continued. The RPF captured the capital of Kigali on July 4 and the government stronghold of Ruhengeri on July 14. "Alarmed" that the "massive exodus" of Hutu civilians and soldiers unleashed by the fall of these two cities would deepen the humanitarian crisis and threaten stability throughout the region, the Security Council demanded an immediate cease-fire, the resumption of peace talks, and respect for the neutrality of the humanitarian zone by government and rebel forces alike [S/PRST/1994/34, 7/14/94]. France, for its part, announced that it would "not tolerate any political or military activity" within the zone after discovering the presence there of the former Rwandan president and four of his cabinet ministers [S/1994/832, 7/15/94]. It also turned back "armed RPF elements" that had attempted to enter the area [S/1994/834, 7/18/94].

After chasing the bulk of the government Army northwest into neighboring Zaire—along with an estimated one million Rwandan refugees—the RPF declared a unilateral cease-fire on July 18 and the establishment of a broad-based "Government of National Unity" the next day. Despite the name, the previous ruling party and an anti-Tutsi party were excluded from the coalition. Pasteur Bizimungu of the RPF was named President for a five-year interim period, and Lieutenant General Paul Kagame, military commander of the former rebel force, became Vice President and Minister of Defense [S/1994/924, 8/3/94]. The bloodletting sparked by the death of Rwandan President Juvenal Habyarimana in a suspicious plane crash on April 6 came to a sudden end.

The Security Council was doing its best to exercise what control it had over the situation on the ground. On June 20 it had extended the mandate of the **U.N. Observer Mission for Uganda-Rwanda (ONU-MUR)** for a final period through September 21 [S/Res/928, 6/20/94]. Since the signing of the Arusha Peace Agreement between the government and the RPF in August 1993, ONUMUR's 81 observers had been patrolling Rwanda's border with Uganda, verifying that no military assistance (arms or armed personnel) reached the rebels from the north.

As the war neared its close, the Council became more farsighted, requesting the Secretary-General to establish an "impartial Commission of Experts" to investigate allegations of "grave violations of international humanitarian law," including the possible "genocide" the Secretary-General himself mentioned in his report of May 31 [S/Res/935, 7/1/94]. The Council was making good on its pledge to find those responsible for such acts and hold them individually responsible [S/PRST/1994/21, S/Res/918, 5/17/94].

Though voting for the Commission, China argued that the decision infringed on the mandates of U.N. human rights bodies and should not be considered a precedent for future action [S/PV.3400, 7/1/94]. On July 29 the Secretary-General announced the names of the Commission's members: Atsu-Koffi Amega (Togo), Habi Dieng (Guinea), and Salifou Fomba (Mali) [S/1994/906].

The situation in the safe zone began to stabilize somewhat with the full deployment of the Operation Turquoise force on July 13. The Senegalese had been joined by troops from six other African countries, bringing the number of "foreign" troops to 508 of 3,060. The French began a gradual pullout on July 31 and handed control of the zone over to UNAMIR on August 21. The operation had provided protection, food and water, and medical attention to some 1.4 million displaced persons and refugees [S/1994/1100, 9/27/94].

But the U.N.'s difficulties in deploying additional troops to UNAMIR continued. On August 3 the Secretary-General reported that just 503 troops were on the ground, 1,000 were on the way, and 2,790 were still awaiting equipment. Only a few countries had accepted the U.N.'s suggestion to bilaterally "adopt" and supply specific contingents directly, which would bypass cumbersome legal and accounting procedures and speed deployments. Without more troops, the Secretary-General warned, UNAMIR would not be able to establish the safe and secure conditions required for the repatriation of refugees, the resettlement of displaced persons, and a return to normal conditions [S/1994/923].

By August, a half-million more Rwandans had crossed into Zaire from the northwest, and displaced persons in the southwest numbered as many as two million. To meet emergency and rehabilitation needs through the end of 1994, the United Nations launched a $434.8 million Interagency Consolidated Appeal on July 22 [S/1994/924, 8/3/94]. The Security Council, for its part, denounced attempts by Hutu extremists in the refugee camps to prevent repatriations and emphasized the responsibility of the current government to make good on its commitments to encourage returns and provide security to returnees [S/PRST/1994/42, 8/10/94].

The U.N. system took steps to put the Council's words into action. The new **U.N. Special Representative to Rwanda, Shaharyar Khan,** suggested separating from the one million Rwandan civilians at risk in Zaire the relatively small number of former officials, soldiers, and militiamen who exerted de facto control over the refugee camps there. He oversaw the establishment of a joint Zairean/U.N. working group in September to propose specific action. As radio broadcasts were a major factor in inciting both the massacres and the refugee flows, UNAMIR was also establishing its own broadcasting capability to counteract continued misinformation in the camps. The new **High Commissioner for Human Rights** deployed 31 human rights officers throughout Rwanda as of September 30, with plans for 116 more. The officers were to investigate suspected rights violations, prevent future violations, and assist in the reestablishment of the criminal justice system. Further, 30 of 90 civilian police observers had been deployed as part of UNAMIR to help train members of a new national police force. UNAMIR's military contingent finally reached a respectable 4,270 by early October, and the consolidated humanitarian appeal had received 70 percent of its revised goal of $552 million [S/1994/1133, 10/6/94].

Despite these efforts, only 360,000 Rwandans had returned since the cease-fire, and the Secretary-General had revised his casualty figures upwards once again: as many as a million dead, more than two million refugees, and between 800,000 and two million internally displaced persons [ibid.]. The Security Council welcomed the progress to date but, with an eye toward the just issued interim report of the Commission of Experts, it took the opportunity to stress that individuals implicated in human rights abuses could not "achieve immunity from prosecution by fleeing the country" [S/PRST/1994/59, 10/14/94].

The Commission reported serious breaches of international humanitarian law on both sides, including murder, torture, and summary executions; crimes against humanity on both sides, including murder and extermination, persecution, and mutilation; and acts of genocide by the Hutus against the Tutsis "in a concerted, planned, systematic, and methodical way." It did not uncover evidence of any attempt by the Tutsis to destroy the Hutu group as such [S/1994/1125, 10/4/94].

With the approval of the government of Rwanda, the Security Council accepted the Commission's recommendation to establish an International Criminal Tribunal for Rwanda essentially by adapting arrangements already made for the U.N. tribunal for the former Yugoslavia. By Resolution 955, the Council established the Rwandan tribunal and directed that it should use the prosecutor, rules of evidence, and five-judge appeals chamber already in place for the other body. Six additional judges would be elected by the General Assembly upon the recommendation of the Security Council. Rwanda objected to these (and other) arrangements and voted against the resolution; China, citing Rwanda's objections, abstained [S/PV.3453, 11/8/94].

Turning again to the refugees in Zaire, the Secretary-General proposed in November 1994 that the Security Council consider three options for separating some 230 former political leaders and approximately 60,000 former government soldiers and militiamen from 1.2 million civilians. In addition to deploying a peacekeeping force to gradually close the numerous camps while protecting returnees, the Council could take peace enforcement action to relocate the extremists—a move favored by Rwanda and Zaire—or authorize a multinational force to do so [S/1994/1308, 11/18/94]. The Council condemned preparations in the camps for a suspected "armed invasion" of Rwanda but requested further information before taking action. It did support deploying "security experts" to train and monitor local authorities on an interim basis [S/PRST/1994/75, 11/30/94]. Repatriations from Burundi and Uganda, mainly Tutsis who had fled decades ago from previous massacres, reached 400,000.

Some semblance of normalcy was beginning to return to Rwanda, such as the opening of small shops and schools and the resumption of agricultural activity. The government had incorporated more than 2,000 former soldiers in its new army and reappointed two local officials from the previous regime [S/PV.3473, 11/30/94]. The Council extended the UNAMIR mandate through June 1995 [S/Res/965, 11/30/94].

By February 1995, UNAMIR was finally fully deployed and was cooperating with the RPF in **"Operation Retour,"** the resettlement of the 350,000 remaining displaced persons in the country's southwest region. The contingent of human rights monitors had nearly reached its authorized limit of 88, and was beginning to provide technical assistance in such areas as prison administration and the treatment of detainees. UNAMIR's civilian police had also taken on the additional task of training communal police as well as the national gendarmerie. To meet continued emergency needs, the United Nations was seeking $710 million for the first half of 1995. The government was looking for $764 million more in longer-term rehabilitation assistance [S/1995/107, 2/6/95]. To justify such expenditure, the Security Council wanted to see the government do more to promote national reconciliation and repatriate refugees [S/PRST/1995/7].

The Security Council also got the international tribunal on track, deciding on Arusha, Tanzania, as its seat [S/Res/977, 2/22/95], although Rwanda had sought to host the tribunal itself. After receiving the final report of the Commission of Experts [S/1994/1405], the Council also urged states to arrest and detain individuals implicated in those crimes as well as persons who may have committed attacks in the Rwandan refugee camps [S/Res/978, 2/27/95].

As he had done in Mozambique and Burundi, **Ambassador Ibrahim Gambari of Nigeria led a Security Council mission to Rwanda,** February 12–13, to make recommendations on enhancing the government's role in repatriation and national reconciliation. The mission proposed the establishment of a "framework for dialogue" among the government, refugee representatives, and the United Nations; a civic education program to promote national harmony; and guarantees of property rights to returnees. It also urged the prompt publication of a list of suspects sought by the international tribunal [S/1995/164, 2/28/95]. In a big boost to dialogue and reconciliation, Radio UNAMIR began broadcasting on February 16, but the Secretary-General reported in April that the security situation was deteriorating [S/1995/297, 4/9/95].

"Armed saboteurs" were entering the country, targeting local officials as well as UNAMIR personnel. The government was also beginning to complain about U.N. violations of Rwandan national sovereignty and talk about the need to renegotiate UNAMIR's mandate or begin phasing out the operation. Moreover, 200,000 displaced persons were still awaiting resettlement, and increasing insecurity had limited repatriation of refugees to just 60,000 by March [ibid.]. Security in the camps around Goma, Zaire, improved somewhat with the deployment of 1,500 soldiers to the Zairean Camp Security Contingent under a January 27 agreement between the government and the U.N. High Commissioner for Refugees. Up to 60 international experts were also to be deployed under the agreement as a **Civilian Security Liaison Group.** But **as of April 1995, 1.1 million Rwandans refugees remained in Zaire,** along with **600,000 in Tanzania** and **240,000 in Burundi** [S/1994/304, 4/14/95].

Perceptions that the displaced persons camps contributed to the general atmosphere of insecurity by sheltering rearmed government soldiers and militiamen spurred the government to accelerate Operation Retour. By mid-April only eight camps remained, including the largest and most troublesome at Kibeho. But the government's attempt to encircle and close the camps, beginning on April 18, resulted in massive riots and the deaths of at least 2,000 unarmed persons at Kibeho on April 23.

An Independent International Commission of Inquiry appointed by the United Nations at the request of the Rwandan government placed most of the blame on armed extremists in the camp, who had instigated the initial panic, and on the army for disproportionate use of lethal force. But the Commission also found fault with UNAMIR's failure to respond earlier to the existence of "hard-core criminal elements" among the civilian populations under its protection. The Commission also cited U.N. agencies and NGOs for their slowness in evacuating displaced persons, and called on the world body to ensure that future peacekeeping operations are "not held hostage or bogged down by one or several agencies and organizations with limited mandates and responsibilities" [S/1995/411, 5/23/95].

Burundi

Since May 30, 1994, the interim government in Burundi had been wrangling with the question of an acceptable successor to **President Cyprien Ntaryamira,** killed in a suspicious plane crash on April 6 along with the head of state of neighboring Rwanda, **Juvenal Habyarimana.** While Habyarimana's death unleashed a wave of ethnic killings in Rwanda, perpetrated by his governing Hutu majority against the long-oppressed Tutsi minority, Burundi remained relatively calm. With roughly the same ethnic makeup as Rwanda—85 percent Hutu, 15 percent Tutsi—Burundi had already experienced its own massacres the previous fall, after a failed coup by Tutsi soldiers claimed the life of Ntaryamira's predecessor, Melchior Ndadaye. Both Ndadaye and Ntaryamira had been Hutus, the first to govern their country.

Replacing Ntaryamira posed difficult legal questions, as his election by the Burundian parliament had been ruled unconstitutional: Presidents could be elected only by popular vote. On July 11, in the face of dead-locked negotiations, Burundi's Constitutional Court extended the rule of the interim government for another three months [S/1994/1039, 9/9/94].

Since denouncing the attempted coup in 1993, the Security Council had been monitoring events in Burundi with the aid of briefings from the Secretariat. The Secretary-General, too, had been active, appointing a **Special Representative, Ahmedou Ould-Abdallah,** and dispatching a **two-man fact-finding mission** to carry out a preliminary investigation of the coup and the subsequent massacres. Simeon Ake and Martin Huslid had transmitted their report to the Secretary-General in May 1994, but a year later he had yet to make the document public or share its contents with the Security Council [ibid.]. In response to rising political tension and violence, the Security Council in July 1994 again condemned "extremist elements" for their attempts to incite "ethnic hatred" and to scuttle the talks on succession. It encouraged political, military, and religious leaders to persevere in their efforts at dialogue and peaceful settlement [S/PRST/1994/38, 7/29/94].

On August 11 the Council directed the fact-finding mission it had earlier dispatched to Mozambique to travel on to Burundi for a two-day visit, beginning August 13. Under the chairmanship of Ambassador Ibrahim A. Gambari of Nigeria, the four Council delegates (including Ambassador Karl F. Inderfurth of the United States) reported that the Hutu and Tutsi political parties had reached agreement on concluding negotiations by August 26. But citing a "general breakdown of law and order," the mission stressed that "impunity from justice is one of the most serious problems" facing the country. It also stressed that some 1.3 million people in the region were in desperate need of humanitarian relief, including 550,000 displaced persons and 250,000 Rwandan refugees in Burundi and 270,000 Burundian refugees in Rwanda. The mission called on the U.N. system to "prevent a repetition of the tragic events that engulfed Rwanda."

Among its recommendations, the mission proposed the establishment of U.N. airlift capability in the capital, Bujumbura, to speed emergency aid; immediate assistance to restore the judicial system; the deployment of human rights monitors; and the bringing to justice of those responsible for the coup and the ensuing violence [S/1994/1039]. The Security Council reiterated its support for the ongoing talks, and endorsed judicial reform and the deployment of "civilian" observers [S/PRST/1994/47, 8/25/94].

An agreement on powersharing emerged from the negotiations between Hutus and Tutsis on September 10. Ten of the 13 political parties in the "Forum of the Negotiations" signed the "Convention of Government," which called for a four-year transition period, a 25-member cabinet (55 percent Hutu), a prime minister from the opposition, and an equally divided National Security Council. Finally, on September 18 the ten parties also approved an annex to the Convention covering the procedures through which the National Assembly would select a new president. The constitution was amended to incorporate the convention and its annex. **Interim President Sylvestre Ntibantunganya, a Hutu, was elected the new head of state** on September 30, ending the constitutional crisis [S/1994/1152, 10/11/94].

But the underlying tension remained, exacerbated by charges from both Hutus and Tutsis of partiality in the government-led investigation of the 1993 coup and by clandestine radio broadcasts urging violence against Tutis. The presence of Hutu refugees from Rwanda in neighboring Zaire further destabilized the situation, and the Secretary-General reiterated in his October 11 report a proposal for the preventive deployment of a "military presence" in Zaire, should violence erupt along the border. In another preventive move, the **High Commissioner for Human Rights** established an office in the capital to implement a "technical assistance program" aimed at encouraging respect for human rights and fundamental freedoms. The Secretary-General also proposed other measures to prevent another "Rwandese tragedy": the deployment of guard contingents, such as those sent to Iraq, as well as human rights observers; preparations for a regional summit; and continued visits by "eminent persons" to highlight international concern and commitment [ibid.].

The Security Council did not take up all these matters but did endorse a proposal for U.N. assistance in bringing violators of international law to court. It likewise welcomed the appointment of **Robert Dillon as the Secretary-General's Special Humanitarian Envoy for Rwanda and Burundi,** who was to study the refugee problem from a regional perspective. Similarly, the Council supported U.N. assistance for the convening of an international conference to examine the problems of the sub-region. It also agreed to the strengthening of the office of the Special Representative, who had done much to mediate the political debate and keep the Secretary-General and the Council informed of developments [S/PRST/1994/60, 10/21/94].

But continued disagreements within the new government on appointments, this time concerning allegations that the nominee for the Speaker of the National Assembly had incited violence against Tutsis, prompted new unrest and another presidential statement from the Security Council in December. In it, the Council urged "all sides to reject confrontational tactics, violence, and extremism, and to work toward compromise and conciliation in a spirit of national unity which transcends ethnic origins" [S/PRST/1994/82, 12/22/94]. The speakership was resolved on January 12, 1995, but attacks on the Tutsi prime minister from his own party, culminating in calls for the overthrow of the entire government, moved the Secretary-General to join the Security Council in underscoring the international community's support for the existing coalition and the Convention of Government [S/PRST/1995/5, 1/31/95].

In a further demonstration of support, on February 10 the Council again dispatched Ambassador Gambari to Burundi, this time with five of his colleagues. This second mission was to identify additional ways in which the United Nations could be of service to the Special Representative while expressing the Council's concern about recent developments and its continued support for the Convention of Government. In his brief report [S/1995/163], Gambari called the usurpation of the political initiative by "extremists" on both sides the "root cause" of the continued instability. The more "fundamental problem," however, remained the "culture of impunity" and the lack of prosecutions against participants in the 1993 coup and the ensuing massacres.

In addition to previous recommendations on the deployment of human rights monitors and continued international visits, the mission proposed the establishment of an "international commission of inquiry" into the coup and its aftermath and an expanded U.N. presence to reform the judiciary, train civilian police, and help establish effective governmental administration in the provinces. It also called for increasing the number of observers from the Organization of African Unity (OAU) from a mere 46 and the denial of visas or access to foreign bank accounts to members of extremist groups [ibid.].

The Security Council repeated its condemnation of those opposed to powersharing in the new government but fell short of taking further action. It said a commission of inquiry and human rights monitors "could" play important roles, and it "encourag[ed]" the Secretary-General to augment the U.N.'s presence in the country and the OAU to increase the number of its monitors there. The Council also reiterated its support for the Special Representative's efforts to facilitate the holding of a "national debate" as called for in the Convention on Government [S/PRST/1995/10, 3/9/95].

The murder of the moderate Hutu energy minister on March 11, the killing of three Belgian nationals on March 19, and retaliatory action by the army later that month that left "several hundred" Hutus dead in Bujumbura unleashed an exodus of some 25,000 Hutus from the city, and sparked press reports of a return to civil war [*Washington Post*, 3/29/95]. Despite warnings from UNHCR that the flow could reach 100,000, the Secretary-General was reportedly unable to convince the permanent members of the Security Council to plan for the deployment of "several thousand" peacekeepers, should war erupt.

The Council satisfied itself with a more strongly worded statement of its previous position. It issued an "urgent" call for a national debate in Burundi and accepted the Gambari mission's proposal to deny visas and outside financial assistance to "extremists." It also announced its intention to bring to justice any individual committing acts of genocide in Burundi and requested the Secretary-General to report on procedures for establishing the commission of inquiry called for by the mission. In addition, the Council "call[ed] on" (but did not require) states to deny arms and sanctuary to the extremists. A regional conference on peace, originally endorsed in October 1994, had now become a matter of "urgency" [S/PRST/1995/13, 3/29/95].

Reporting to the Security Council in April on the Rwandan refugee camps, the Secretary-General noted that 240,000 Rwandans remained in seven camps in the north of Burundi, some 78,000 having fled increasing insecurity into Tanzania since mid-February. They had been joined by some 8,000 Burundians, with another 24,000 having sought refuge in Zaire [S/1995/304, 4/14/95].

Angola

A resolution to the question of national reconciliation continued to elude negotiators from the government of Angola and the rebel forces of the **National Union for the Total Independence of Angola (UNITA)** in May 1994, seven months after the opening of formal peace talks to resolve one of Africa's longest civil wars. Although representatives of **President José Eduardo dos Santos** and **UNITA leader Jonas Savimbi** had already reached agreement on 5 of 7 items on the peace agenda and 12 of 18 "specific principles" relating to national reconciliation, the issues of UNITA troop withdrawal from occupied territory and powersharing in a new government and legislature stymied the U.N.-brokered talks, held in the Zambian capital of Lusaka. Fighting intensified through June, and UNITA bombardment of population centers and its refusal to authorize relief flights and humanitarian convoys of the World Food Programme (WFP) led to the complete suspension of aid deliveries on June 13. Another crisis loomed in Angola's already precarious humanitarian situation [S/1994/740/Add.1, 6/20/94].

The government had already accepted compromise proposals on powersharing put forward by the **three Observer States to the peace process** (the United States, the Russian Federation, and Portugal) on May 28, and on May 30 it announced its "last offers" of positions in the provincial and local administrations for UNITA members [S/1994/637, 5/31/94]. The parties reached agreement on all 18 specific principles relating to national reconciliation on June 27, but "implementation mechanisms"— where and at what level UNITA would actually participate in the "management of state affairs"—remained outstanding. The final agenda item—the future roles of the United Nations and the Observer States—was not expected to require prolonged or difficult negotiations once the national reconciliation issue had been resolved.

On June 30 the Security Council reaffirmed its arms embargo against the rebels [S/Res/864, 9/15/93] and threatened UNITA leaders with trade sanctions and restrictions on their international travel, should they fail to endorse the compromise package by July 31 [S/Res/932, 6/30/94]. The Council also extended the mandate of the **68-member U.N. Angola Verification Mission (UNAVEM II)** through September 30 and promised to "review" the U.N.'s role in Angola, should a full peace agreement not materialize by that date. Finally, out of concern about alleged violations of the embargo by neighboring states, the Council requested a report on compliance with that measure by July 15. The sanctions committee reported that neither the Congo nor Zaire had fully responded to requests for the relevant information, and it recommended consideration of the matter by the full Council [S/1994/825, 7/15/94].

Toward the end of July, UNITA had generally lifted its prohibitions against relief flights, but the delivery of humanitarian assistance continued to be interrupted by government and rebel forces engaged in largely "stalemated" battles throughout the northern and central provinces. The Secretary-General hoped that the **recent involvement of South African President Nelson Mandela in the peace process**—among other things, he was to host Savimbi in Pretoria for direct talks—would facilitate progress. The parties were currently considering a "compromise text" on the whole question of national reconciliation prepared by the **Secretary-General's Special Representative in Angola, Alioune Blondin Beye** [S/1994/865, 7/22/94].

Believing that a "just and comprehensive peace agreement [was] within reach," the Security Council expressed its impatience over the continuing delays and warned UNITA that it would "not tolerate further procrastination in the peace process." To allow time for unspecified diplomatic overtures by Mandela and Zambian President Frederick Chiluba, the Council declined to further sanction UNITA but promised to do so should Savimbi fail to accept the compromise on national reconciliation by August 31. The Council also declared its readiness to take "appropriate action" against those states (the Congo and Zaire) mentioned in the sanctions committee report, should they not reply "forthwith" to requests for information from the committee [S/PRST/1994/45, 8/12/94].

The breakthrough in the negotiations on national reconciliation occurred on August 30, when the UNITA delegation to the Lusaka talks "formally expressed" its acceptance of the U.N.'s compromise text. UNITA confirmed its position in a letter to Blondin Beye dated September 5 [S/1994/1069, 9/17/94]. The Security Council considered the letter "formal acceptance" by UNITA of the proposals already approved by the government on May 28. It urged quick work on the last agenda item, the future U.N. and observer roles, and the conclusion of the entire peace agreement by the expiration of UNAVEM II's current mandate on September 30 [S/PRST/1994/52, 9/9/94]. By mid-September, the WFP had gained access to major cities from which it had been largely or completely barred since mid-May, but the number of Angolans in need of such emergency relief had climbed to 3.7 million [S/1994/1069].

To allow for the conclusion of talks, the signing of the peace agreement, and preparations for an expansion of UNAVEM, the Security Council agreed to a short extension of the operation's mandate through October 31 [S/Res/945, 9/29/94]. By September 21 the parties had agreed to 60 articles on the future U.N. mandate, five articles on the role of the Observer States, and 13 more on joint monitoring and verification. Final details on the issue of national reconciliation—the apportionment of local administrative offices to UNITA members—were agreed to on October 14. The final accord "could be initialed within weeks," the Secretary-General said on October 20 [S/1994/1197].

The Security Council extended the UNAVEM II mandate once again, through December; authorized the Secretary-General to restore the operation's original strength of 350 military and 127 police observers; and stated its readiness to consider the establishment of a much larger peacekeeping force to replace the current observer mission. The Council made the actual deployment of additional personnel contingent, however, on the parties' initialing of the peace agreement and especially on the implementation of a cease-fire [S/Res/952, 10/27/94].

As expected, the government and UNITA delegations initialed what would be called the **Lusaka Protocol** on October 31 [S/1994/1241, 11/3/94]. The agreement was a follow-up to the "Accordos de Paz" or Bicesse Accords of 1991, which had paved the way for U.N.-monitored elections the following fall—and renewed civil war. The offer of a peacekeeping force was an effort to avoid a third round of killing and mass starvation. But the deployment of such a force required not only a peace agreement but the actual cessation of hostilities. Instead, fighting intensified. The government pressed its attack on the provincial capital of Huambo, a major population center and the site of UNITA's headquarters. Besides endangering thousands of civilians, the attack threatened to cut off egress from the city for a UNITA military delegation, scheduled to hold talks with its government counterpart prior to the official signing of the protocol. The Security Council called on both sides to "refrain from any action that could jeopardize the signing" set for November 15 [S/PRST/1994/63, 11/4/94].

In response, the government offered an immediate truce on November 13, provided the military delegations could agree on the date and time of the entry into force of the protocol [S/1994/1290, 11/14/94]. Military talks took place with a four-day delay on November 14, and the truce took effect two days later. On November 20, five days later than originally scheduled, Angolan Minister for External Relations Venancio de Moura and UNITA Secretary-General and chief negotiator Eugenio Manuvakola met to sign the protocol [issued as S/1994/1441, Annex] in Lusaka. Curiously, neither dos Santos, present at the ceremony, nor Savimbi, who refused to attend because of security concerns, signed the document. The Security Council marked the occasion with a brief statement [S/PRST/1994/70, 11/21/94]. A cease-fire finally entered into force on November 22, but not before the government had retaken all the provincial capitals, including Huambo on November 6 as well as the oil-producing town of Soyo. Except in the central and northern provinces of Huambo and Zaire, humanitarian relief began flowing more freely, up to 400 tons a day [S/1994/1376, 12/4/94].

The Secretary-General reported on December 7 that the cease-fire was "generally holding" and that both parties were "reasonably satisfied" with compliance by the other side. The government and UNITA also requested that the planned enlargement of UNAVEM take place "as soon as possible" to allow the deployment of observers throughout the country. UNAVEM II was to monitor and verify the implementation of the Lusaka Protocol and investigate as needed alleged violations of the agreement until a peacekeeping force could be planned, established, and deployed [S/1994/1395, 12/8/94]. Noting that the parties had fulfilled their pledges to sign the protocol and respect a cease-fire, the Security Council approved the enlargement (at a cost of $7.5 million) and extended the current mission through February 8, 1995 [S/Res/966, 12/8/94].

Relations between the government and UNITA improved during December 1994 and January 1995 as a result of ongoing military and diplomatic contacts called for in the Lusaka Protocol. To oversee the implementation of the complicated agreement—while continuing to build confidence between the parties and to discourage violations in the sensitive transition period from war to peace—the Secretary-General wasted no time in recommending an extensive peacekeeping operation for Angola on February 1 [S/1995/97 and Add.1].

UNAVEM III's military component of 6,450 troops and 350 military observers would oversee the disengagement of government and UNITA forces; monitor the cease-fire; supervise the withdrawal and demobilization of the former rebels; and verify the formation of a unified Armed Forces of Angola. In addition, the military forces would protect humanitarian convoys, set up quartering areas for troops, repair water facilities and roads, and assist in the clearance of some 10 million land mines. The 260-strong civilian police contingent would monitor the activities of the Angolan National Police and oversee the integration of 5,500 UNITA personnel into that force and the Rapid Reaction Police.

The already established Office for Coordination of Humanitarian

Assistance would continue to provide for the nearly 3.5 million Angolans currently in need, some 35 percent of the population. Politically, UNAVEM III would chair the newly established Joint Commission to verify, among other things, the "extension of state administration" throughout the country. The Secretary-General's Special Representative would have the responsibility of determining when a second round of presidential elections could be held—the first having gone to dos Santos shortly before the renewal of the civil war in November 1992. The United Nations placed the cost of the operation at $383.1 million for 12 months [press release SC/5994, 2/8/95]. The government announced its intention to make in-kind contributions of $374 million toward the $1.262 billion it estimated as the "general costs" of implementing the Lusaka Protocol and $67.4 million in cash for UNAVEM itself [S/1994/1451, 12/28/94].

After an extraordinary day-long debate in the Security Council, led by a 12-member delegation of the Council of Ministers of the Organization of African Unity (OAU), the Council approved the operation and authorized the immediate deployment of sufficient personnel to establish the quartering areas for demobilizing UNITA troops. Infantry would be sent once the parties furnished data on their own troop deployments. The Council also set a strict monthly reporting requirement on the Secretary-General and announced its intention to conclude the operation by February 1997. Over objections from the Angolan government, the Council approved additional provisions relating to the establishment of a U.N. radio station, the inclusion of human rights specialists in UNAVEM III's political component, and the parties' obligation to devote resources to "humanitarian and social needs," not arms and materiel [S/Res/976, 2/8/95].

Progress achieved by March in deploying UNAVEM III was not encouraging. In a statement on March 10, the Security Council criticized the parties for numerous infractions, including the failure to disengage their forces, to facilitate the unimpeded movement of U.N. personnel, and to refrain from attacks on civilians, relief aircraft, and aid workers [S/PRST/ 1995/11]. Both sides completed the first phase of disengagement by April, and the number of restrictions and attacks on U.N. and nongovernmental personnel lessened. The Secretary-General decided to proceed with the preparations for deploying UNAVEM III's infantry units, although neither side had even begun its own preparations: clearing mines, repairing main roads, and designating quartering areas for their troops. The Security Council reiterated its call, first made in February, for a meeting between dos Santos and Savimbi to iron out these problems and expedite the process [S/PRST/1995/18, 4/13/95].

The long-waited meeting finally took place on May 6 in Lusaka, with both men embracing warmly for the cameras but signing no agreements. Nevertheless the meeting itself had fulfilled an "unofficial condition" for the full deployment of UNAVEM III, scheduled to begin May 9 [*Washington*

Post, 5/7/95]. In fact, the first U.N. peacekeepers—approximately 300 Uruguayan infantrymen—arrived on May 31, with battalions from India, Zimbabwe, Brazil, and Romania scheduled to arrive in the following weeks [*New York Times,* 6/1/95].

Somalia

The Secretary-General put the best face possible on developments in Somalia through July 1994 but admitted that the **U.N. Operation in Somalia II** stood little chance of completing its mandate before its scheduled withdrawal date of March 1995. Progress continued to be made in agricultural production and the rebuilding of the police and judicial system after three years of famine and civil war, but the return to near normal conditions in many regions of the country was not matched by developments in the capital, Mogadishu. There inter-clan fighting and banditry were again on the rise, and neither the National Reconciliation Conference planned for May nor its Preparatory Meeting were close to convening [S/1994/839, 7/18/94].

The lack of progress on the political front and the continued deterioration of the security situation moved the Secretary-General to call for a formal review of the prospects for national reconciliation and of the need to maintain 18,790 troops and support elements in Somalia. The Security Council was "seriously concern[ed]" and "disappointed" about the political and security failures and supported the Secretary-General's comprehensive reviews [S/1994/898, 7/30/94].

Although the U.N. had had some success in sponsoring reconciliation meetings at the regional and district levels throughout 1993 and 1994, which had enhanced the prospects for national reconciliation, the **major obstacle remained the ongoing conflict in Mogadishu between Ali Mahdi and Mohammed Farah Aidid,** both members of the dominant Hawiye clan. The Secretary-General's new **Special Representative, James Victor Ghebo,** reported in August 1994 that the convening of a Hawiye peace conference by September might pave the way for a national conference—and the establishment of an interim government—by year's end. Both Ali Mahdi and Aidid were reportedly willing to attend such a peace conference.

On the question of troop withdrawals, the Secretary-General proposed an immediate reduction of 1,500 personnel and further reductions to 15,000 "as soon as possible," the lowest level at which UNOSOM II could still offer "some degree of protection to humanitarian operations." Arguing that "it is . . . too early to conclude that UNOSOM II cannot achieve [its] objectives," Boutros-Ghali requested a mandate extension through October 31 [S/1994/977, 8/17/94]. The Security Council, however, wanted some indication that a Hawiye conference would actually take place before it would agree to even a one-month extension. It supported the initial troop reductions and stressed that continued international involvement in Somalia "depend[s] very much on the resolve of the Somali parties to achieve political compromise. . . . The future of their country lies in their hands" [S/PRST/1994/46, 8/25/94].

With the assistance of a Somali religious leader, the Imam of Hirab, Ghebo initiated intensive discussions throughout August and early September to resolve differences among the various Hawiye subclans (Abgal, Habr Tgedir, Hawadle, and Murusade) in preparation for the peace conference. Agreements were reached on withdrawing the ersatz military vehicles known as "technicals" from Mogadishu and dismantling checkpoints and roadblocks in the city. The Secretary-General reported a "salutary effect" on the security situation.

Progress was also made toward the convening of the Preparatory Meeting, especially the inclusion of two remaining clans in the peace process—the Somali Salvation Democratic Front (SSDF) of the northeast and the Somali National Movement (SNM) of the northwest. In addition, a joint delegation of northern clans opened talks in Mogadishu on August 30 in an attempt to mediate a compromise between Ali Mahdi's Group of 12 and Aidid's Somali National Alliance (SNA). The joint delegation was "confident" about holding the Preparatory Meeting by the end of September [S/1994/1068, 9/17/94].

Despite these accomplishments, security in Somalia deteriorated further. Technicals continued to roam the streets of Mogadishu, and outside the capital the situation remained "very volatile and virtually uncontrollable." The Secretary-General reported 11 UNOSOM deaths since the end of July and the complete withdrawal of several nongovernmental relief organizations as the result of continued fighting and banditry as well as reductions in UNOSOM personnel. Despite the good harvest expected in the fall, Somalia was still unable to shift from emergency relief to longer-term recovery and development [ibid.].

With the expiration of the UNOSOM II mandate at hand, the Security Council was essentially forced to continue the operation through October 31, by which time the Secretary-General was to offer his final assessment of the prospects for national reconciliation. In the interim, he was to intensify contingency planning for the future U.N. role in Somalia, "including withdrawal of UNOSOM II within a specified timeframe." The Council also weighed the possibility of dispatching its own mission to the country to meet directly with political leaders [S/Res/946, 9/30/94]. The United States abstained in the vote, citing the deaths of 140 peacekeepers since the operation began, costs of $2.5 million a day, pressing needs elsewhere, and the "trail of broken promises left by the Somali factions." Washington had pushed for an immediate decision to withdraw UNOSOM II by the end of the year [S/PV.3432, 9/30/94].

The Secretary-General did not have good news to report in October on the prospects for national reconciliation. Not only did the Hawiye peace conference not take place but General Aidid had declared unilaterally that harmony was such among the subclans as to make the conference unnecessary. Moreover, Aidid insisted that he, not the U.N. Special Representative as agreed, would issue invitations to the Preparatory Meeting for the National Reconciliation Conference, a position vehemently opposed by Ali Mahdi and the Group of 12.

Progress had likewise stalled on the humanitarian front, with the Secretary-General reporting that the lack of long-term development initiatives and a functioning government made Somalia vulnerable to a "renewed massive emergency" in the face of any "natural or man-made disaster." In particular, no action had yet been taken to repatriate 500,000 Somali refugees or 400,000 displaced persons. Humanitarian agencies and nongovernmental organizations reported through the Inter-Agency Standing Committee on Somalia that even the continuation of current relief efforts would be impossible "without the support of UNOSOM troops" [S/1994/1166, 10/14/94]. By the end of October, UNOSOM had been reduced to 15,000 troops and withdrawn from all but the three locations with major airports or seaports—Mogadishu, Baidoa, and Kismayo—a 50 percent reduction in coverage since mid-1994.

Although the Security Council was in no mood to renew the UNO-SOM II mandate through March 1995 as the Secretary-General recommended, it was under increasing pressure from the Arab Group to avoid a sharp reduction in forces that could lead to a power vacuum and renewed warfare [S/1994/1204, 10/22/94]. During informal consultations on October 20, the Council accepted the Group's suggestion to dispatch its own mission to Somalia before making a final decision on troop withdrawal [S/1994/1194, 10/21/94]. In the interim, it renewed the UNOSOM II mandate through November 4 [S/Res/953, 10/31/94].

The mission, chaired by New Zealand Ambassador Colin Keating and including Ambassador Karl F. Inderfurth of the U.S. Mission, made a two-day visit to the country beginning October 26. In identical statements to Ali Mahdi and Aidid, the mission called for Somali cooperation with an "orderly and progressive phasing-out" of UNOSOM II by March 1995 and held open the door to a "facilitating or mediating political role" for the U.N. beyond that date, should the parties so wish. The statements also called for a "broad-based" national reconciliation conference, to include all 15 signatories to the Nairobi Declaration of March 1994 and the SNM (and not just invitees of Aidid). Finally, the mission promised the U.N.'s best efforts to "sustain humanitarian activities" and "provide rehabilitation and construction assistance" when requested, but emphasized that the U.N.'s ability to do so would "depend almost en-

tirely on the degree of cooperation and security offered by the Somalis"
[S/1994/1245, Annex II, 11/3/94].

Both Ali Mahdi and his factional allies as well as Aidid and his factions pledged to cooperate with the withdrawal, protect humanitarian
workers remaining behind, and seek "genuine" political reconciliation.
While concluding that the March 1995 deadline was appropriate (as neither leader nor any of the humanitarian organizations requested an extension), the mission was left with "a profound sense of unease." "The risk
of return to civil war," the report stated, "is real" [ibid.]. As if to underscore the point, Aidid unilaterally declared open a national reconciliation
conference on November 3, risking warfare with the Ali Mahdi factions
[UNOSOM II press statement by the Special Representative, 11/3/94].

On November 4, the Security Council finally agreed to extend the
UNOSOM II mandate for "a final period" until March 31, 1995 [S/Res/
954, 11/4/95]. As its primary task, the operation was to facilitate political
reconciliation, especially through the activities of the Special Representative, who was to continue his efforts beyond the formal expiration of the
mandate. In case of a withdrawal under fire, UNOSOM II was authorized
to "take those actions necessary" to protect its personnel and assets; relief
workers would receive protection only "to the extent . . . practicable."
The Secretary-General was also to continue to monitor the humanitarian
and security situation in Somalia and report on suggestions for a further
U.N. role beyond March.

In remarks after the vote, U.S. Ambassador Madeleine Albright
counted among UNOSOM II's accomplishments the prevention of hundreds of thousands of death from starvation and the provision of a "win-
dow of opportunity for the Somalis to put their country back together
again." She argued that should a transitional government not be established by March 1995, the U.N. "effort will not have been a failure," for
"the true value of peacekeeping is the chance it offers for people and
nations to help themselves." Ambassador Keating of New Zealand, for
his part, emphasized that the resolution restored consensus in the Council
and reflected the view that "UNOSOM had, in effect, achieved all it could
achieve in Somalia." The United Nations had "stayed the course" and
demonstrated that the "collective security mechanisms of our Organization [are] equally available for the benefit of the small and underprivileged
as they are for the larger and more powerful" [S/PV.3447, 11/4/94].

To help guarantee the continuation of humanitarian assistance, the
Inter-Agency Standing Committee on Somalia (IASC) announced
plans to establish a U.N. "coordination team" for program support and
possible "protected humanitarian operations bases" at essential ports and
airports. Consisting of representatives of all the U.N. agencies active in
Somalia, the coordination team was to see to emergency and rehabilitation
programs "whenever and wherever" security conditions permitted. To es-

tablish the operational bases, the IASC requested the transfer of UNO-SOM equipment and assets as well as humanitarian and security staff to the U.N. humanitarian agencies and nongovernmental relief organizations already on the ground [S/1994/1392, 12/7/94]. Without addressing the question of operational bases, the Security Council welcomed the IASC's intention to continue providing services in Somalia and reminded the Secretary-General of his pledges to play a "facilitating or mediating role" after the withdrawal and to monitor the safety of humanitarian relief personnel [S/1994/1393, 12/7/94].

Out of concern for the security of its personnel and equipment, the United Nations did not make public a detailed withdrawal plan, but the press reported that India's 4,700 troops, UNOSOM II's largest contingent, would be the first to leave. The United States promised ships and planes to the operation but had not approved a formal plan by the end of November [New York Times, 11/27/94]. By December 11, India had withdrawn the last of its troops from Kismayo after renewed clan warfare in the city [ibid., 12/12/94], and U.S. plans were taking shape for a 3,000-strong Marine force to be deployed for about a week in late January or early February [Wall Street Journal, 12/19/94]. Fierce fighting broke out in Mogadishu on December 20, and further violence in Baidoa prompted the United Nations to announce the withdrawal of all its foreign humanitarian staff in mid-January 1995 [New York Times, 12/20/94, 1/13/95]. As the date for total withdrawal neared, Somali U.N. workers in the capital harassed or seized UNOSOM II staffers in numerous protests over back pay allegedly owed them and U.N. equipment they demanded be left behind [ibid., 1/15/95].

By the time the first U.S. troops arrived in neighboring Kenya on January 28 to cover the final withdrawal, 9,000 UNOSOM troops remained [ibid., 1/29/95], and looters were helping themselves to the contents of the vacated U.N. headquarters in Mogadishu—as well as stripping the buildings themselves [ibid., 2/2/95]. After concentrating at the port and airport in Mogadishu, the last 4,800 peacekeepers were scheduled to be withdrawn by the first week of March under the protection of a U.S.-led flotilla of some 20 ships from seven nations [ibid., 2/23/95]. By February 28 all international staff had been withdrawn and only a 2,500-man rearguard remained; U.S. Marines landed to cover their departure, accomplished March 3. With the completion of "Operation United Shield," UNOSOM II offices were "temporarily relocated" to Nairobi, and the United Nations donated some $236,000 worth of equipment to Somali district councils. The Secretary-General placed the **total cost of UNOSOM I and UNOSOM II (May 1992 through February 1995) at $1.64 billion** [S/1995/231, 3/28/95].

In its own final assessment, the Security Council noted that U.N. intervention in Somalia "helped save many lives" and "contributed to the search for peace." The Council reiterated that the international community could only "facilitate, encourage, and assist" in that search and could not "impose" a solution. Noting that the factions in Mogadishu had succeeded in reaching agreement on control of the port and airport there, the Council said it would continue to support such progress and welcomed the Secretary-General's intention to continue a "small political mission" in the country. Likewise, the Council endorsed the decision of some U.N. relief agencies (some 30 staff had stayed behind) and nongovernmental organizations to remain in those areas where their security could be guaranteed [S/1995/PRST/15, 4/6/95]. The Secretary-General had noted, however, that the latest interagency appeal for Somalia, covering the January through June period, had collected less than 10 percent of the $70 million requested for long-term rehabilitation, recovery, and reconstruction [U.N. press release SC/6012, 4/6/95].

Although the United Nations had repeated its claims since November 1994 not to "abandon" Somalia, the Secretary-General nevertheless conceded the "limited possibilities" for its continuing political efforts there. Accordingly, he intended to replace his departing Special Representative with one D-2 staff member and two professional officers, who would be relocated to Mogadishu when security conditions permitted [S/1995/322, 4/21/95]. As for the lessons to be learned from the Somalia experience, the Secretary-General reiterated in his March 28 report the need for member states to realized that "responsibility for political compromise and national reconciliation must be borne by the leaders and people concerned." The United Nations, for its part, would have to draw a clearer line in the future "between peacekeeping and enforcement action," a point elaborated further in his "Supplement to an Agenda for Peace" [S/1995/1].

Liberia

An outbreak of intrafactional fighting in Liberia in early 1994 reignited all-out civil war in that small West African country and threatened to scuttle the U.N.'s first attempt at cooperative peacekeeping with a regional organization. Disagreements within the **United Liberation Movement for Democracy in Liberia (ULIMO)** on the question of representation in the new government called for in a July 1993 peace accord split the movement along ethnic lines and led to armed conflict in February 1994. By May the fighting had engulfed most of western Liberia, while in the southeast similar disagreements within the **National Patriotic Front of Liberia (NPFL)** led to the formation of the breakaway **Liberian Peace Council (LPC)** and additional combat. The renewed fighting frustrated efforts by the United Nations and the **Economic Community of West African States (ECOWAS)** to help disarm combatants and monitor elections, scheduled for September 1994 [S/1994/760, 6/24/94].

With the cease-fire in tatters, progress on implementing other aspects of the comprehensive peace plan, known as the **Cotonou Agreement,** was not much more encouraging. The five-member Council of State, the country's new executive, was operational, but only the NPFL and the Interim Government of National Unity (IGNU) had taken up their deputy ministerial posts in the cabinet, and disagreements continued between the Council and the various factions on the distribution of other senior positions in the transitional government. Moreover, neither the executive branch nor the Transitional Legislative Assembly enjoyed much real control over political decision-making or territory [ibid.].

Adding to the U.N.'s worries in sorting out this increasingnly complex and dangerous situation were charges from ULIMO and the NPFL that the military observer group dispatched by ECOWAS—known as ECOMOG—had surrendered its impartial observer role and become actively involved in the conflict. Mistrust and active combat continued to prevent the full deployment of ECOMOG throughout the country, and the **U.N. Observer Mission in Liberia (UNOMIL)** was fully deployed only in the relatively peaceful central and northern regions. These delays brought the process of disarmament, begun in April 1994, to a virtual standstill: By mid-June, only 3,192 of an estimated 60,000 combatants—including 6,000 children—had been demobilized. The renewed fighting also increased the number of internally displaced Liberians by 150,000, for a total of 800,000. The refugee count stood at 700,000 [ibid.].

Disturbed by the "limited progress" achieved in implementing the peace plan, especially with respect to disarmament, the Security Council called on the **Liberian National Transitional Government (LNTG),** ECOWAS, and the **Organization of African Unity (OAU)** to convene a meeting of the factions by July 31 and set target dates for resuming and completing the disarmament process. It also used especially harsh language in dealing with the fallout of the fighting, "condemn[ing]" the instigators, "deplor[ing]" attacks on ECOMOG, and "demand[ing]" an end to such attacks and full cooperation in the delivery of humanitarian assistance [S/PRST/1994/33, 7/13/94].

The meeting of the factions never materialized, and the security situation deteriorated further. By late August, UNOMIL withdrew its forces completely from the western region and from two of nine monitoring sites in the north, the scene of yet more fighting by another new faction, the **Lofa Defense Force.** The Secretary-General reported "serious command and control problems" among all the factions, leading to "an increase in banditry, harassment, . . . and looting." Concluding that "there is no clear prospect as to when elections will or can be held," the Secretary-General recommended reassessing UNOMIL on the basis of the outcome of the "Liberian National Conference," scheduled to conclude

September 7. He dispatched a fact-finding mission to attend and report on that meeting [S/1994/1006, 8/26/94].

While the Security Council was denouncing the kidnapping of 43 UNOMIL observers on September 13 [S/PRST/1994/53], the NPFL, ULIMO, and the **Armed Forces of Liberia (AFL)** were announcing that they had reached agreement the day before on a nationwide cease-fire and a recommitment to the main provisions of the Cotonou Agreement. Worked out with the assistance of the **U.N. Special Representative, Trevor Gordon-Somers,** and the current **ECOWAS chairman, President J. J. Rawlings of Ghana,** the Akosombo Agreement [S/1994/1174, 10/16/94] reconfirmed UNOMIL's authority to monitor the cease-fire and supervise the surrender of weaponry to ECOMOG. After an attempted coup against the Transitional Government by nonparties to the agreement, the Secretary-General proposed a two-thirds reduction in UNOMIL's strength but an extension of its mandate through January 13, 1995.

In its Resolution 950 of October 14, the Security Council agreed to the reduction in forces and the mandate renewal and endorsed the Secretary-General's intention to dispatch a high-level U.N. mission to consult with ECOWAS on the future roles of both organizations in the peace process. The Council also approved a provision, despite reservations by Nigeria and Brazil, forcing the Secretary-General to seek the Council's approval before redeploying UNOMIL at full strength. Such an outcome would depend, the Council said, on a "real improvement" in the security situation [S/PV.3422, 10/21/94].

Further pressure from ECOWAS and the United Nations produced yet another amendment to the Cotonou Agreement by year's end. The **Accra Agreement of December 21, 1994** [S/1995/7] improved upon its immediate predecessor by including all the warring factions along with a revised timetable for implementation. In addition to the NPFL, ULIMO, and the AFL, signatories included the Central Revolutionary Council (split off from the NPFL); the United Liberation Movement of Liberia for Democracy and the "General Johnson Roosevelt wing" of ULIMO (both offshoots of the main ULIMO faction); the Liberia Peace Council; and the Lofa Defense Force. The Accra Agreement called for a cease-fire from December 28; a new Council of State; elections on November 14, 1995; and the installation of a new government on January 1, 1996 [S/1995/9, 1/6/95; press release SC/5979, 1/13/95].

By mid-January 1995 the cease-fire was holding, but UNOMIL's 90 observers (down from 368) and ECOMOG troops were restricted to the 15 percent of Liberian territory under international control. The humanitarian crisis had grown also, with the United Nations seeking $65 million through June 1995 to feed and shelter the 1.8 million Liberians it estimated were in need. Welcoming the cease-fire, the Security Council extended the UNOMIL mandate through April 13 but criticized the failure of the parties to reach agreement on the composition of a new Council of State, as provided in the Accra Agreement [S/Res/972, 1/13/95]. The Council also supported the call of the high-level mission for an ECOWAS summit meeting to "harmonize" members' policies on Liberia, especially with respect to the often-flouted U.N. arms embargo called for in Resolution 788 (11/22/92).

The Secretary-General reported no significant progress on the reestablishment of a Council of State or an agreed-to "Cease-fire Verification Committee" by the end of February. Moreover, he estimated that the expansion of ECOMOG to carry out disarmament and monitoring functions under the Accra Agreement would require some 4,250 additional troops, for a total of about 12,000 troops at an annual cost of $90.7 million. Were sufficient contributions received to expand ECOMOG, the Secretary-General would propose maintaining UNOMIL at its authorized strength. Should contributions fall short, however, he might propose the establishment of a U.N. peacekeeping force to replace UNOMIL or, in the absence of political progress, that UNOMIL be reduced further or completely withdrawn [S/1995/158, 2/24/95].

By early April a gradual upswing in the level of skirmishing posed a serious threat to the general cease-fire, but the Secretary-General expressed hope that the provisional agreement on an ECOWAS summit for May might strengthen the arms embargo and jumpstart the peace process [S/1995/279, 4/10/95]. Boutros-Ghali proposed a further reduction in UNOMIL to only 20 observers, and the Security Council agreed to a mandate extension through June 30. To add teeth to the embargo, the Council also established a committee of the whole to monitor compliance and recommend "appropriate measures" against violators. A continued U.N. presence in Liberia, the Council warned, was dependent on the reestablishment of an effective cease-fire and the receipt of sufficient contributions to ECOMOG by troop contributors [S/Res/985, 4/13/95].

Western Sahara

By the summer of 1994 the United Nations had finally succeeded in registering the first voters in Western Sahara's long-delayed referendum on self-determination. This milestone of sorts came four years after **Morocco and the guerrilla-backed Frente POLISARIO** first agreed to submit their dispute over control of the former Spanish colony to a popular vote under the **U.N.-brokered Settlement Plan of 1990.** The plan also called for an end to the 15-year-old civil war in the territory and the international monitoring of a cease-fire. Approximately 240 military observers of the **U.N. Mission on the Referendum in Western Sahara (MINURSO)** have overseen compliance with the cease-fire accord since its coming into force in September 1991.

Impatient with the failure of the parties to resolve long-standing disagreements on the exact criteria to be observed in determining voter eligibility, the Security Council had directed in March 1994 [S/Res/907, 3/29/94] that actual registration proceed according to the U.N.'s compromise proposal of April 1993 [see *Issues/49*, p. 59]. Accordingly, the **Identification Commission,** appointed by the Secretary-General to verify the eligibility of individual applicants for voting cards and to register those who qualify, began accepting completed applications from potential voters in May 1994. However, by early July the Commission had processed only 20,000 of the 76,000 applications then received; and new charges from Morocco disputing the impartiality of observers from the **Organization of African Unity (OAU)** sent to monitor the work of the Commission prevented that body from interviewing individual applicants, the crucial step in determining eligibility. These developments forced the Secretary-General to delay the referendum once again, from December 1994 to February 1995 [S/1994/819, 7/12/94]. In a brief Statement of the President, the Security Council expressed its satisfaction with the initiation of the identification process, noted the revised timetable for the vote, and welcomed the Commission's intention to set August 31, 1994, as the deadline for the receipt of completed applications [S/PRST/1994/39, 7/29/94].

After the Secretary-General personally intervened to settle the question of OAU representation, the Identification Commission began interviewing applicants and registering voters on August 28, 11 weeks behind schedule. The delay pushed the deadline for applications back to October 25, and a flood of some 250,000 completed forms submitted just before that date created a four-month backlog in the registration process. By early November the Commission had been able to register only 4,000 applicants, some 2 percent of the total. The Secretary-General nevertheless called the start of voter registration "a significant step toward the fulfillment of the United Nations mandate in Western Sahara" and announced plans to visit the area in an attempt to expedite the process [S/1994/1257, 11/5/94]. Although it agreed with the Secretary-General's overall assessment, the Security Council criticized the slowness of the process and called for "no further undue delay" in holding the referendum. The Council hoped to be able to set a firm date for the voting—and to approve the required expansion of MINURSO—by the next reporting period [S/PRST/1994/67, 11/15/94].

Following his November 25–29 visit to Algeria, Western Sahara, and Morocco, the Secretary-General concluded that the Identification Commission could complete its work in a timely manner only through a "major reinforcement of personnel and other resources" [S/1994/1420, 12/14/94]. As of the end of November, the Commission was operating only two identification and registration centers and four teams of Commission personnel—three to a team—and processing just 1,000 voters weekly. Two more centers came on-line in December, and the Secretary-General requested Security Council approval for 51 additional Commission personnel to staff six more centers and five mobile teams (crucial for a nomadic population). He placed the total cost of the expansion, including civilian police, administrative staff, and OAU monitors, at $18.1 million for the eight-month period beginning January 1995 [S/1994/1420/Add.1, 12/19/94]. Were the pace of registrations to increase as expected, the Secretary-General reported, he would turn his attention to expanding MINURSO in preparation for voting in October 1995.

The Security Council approved the expansion of the Identification Commission on January 13, 1995, and extended MINURSO's mandate through May 31. But the Council also continued to push for a rapid conclusion to the overall mission, requesting the Secretary-General to report by March 31 on the resources required to enlarge MINURSO. Despite the delays, the Council warned, MINURSO "should be subject to periodic consideration" like other peacekeeping operations [S/Res/973, 1/13/95].

Although the United Nations could control the activities of its personnel in Western Sahara, it had little say over the territory's "sheikhs," or tribal leaders, who were to testify as to the identity of each potential voter. Calling the "issue" of the tribal leaders "the single greatest obstacle to identification," Boutros-Ghali complained in his March 30 report that work at individual identification centers was often completely shut down when tribal subfactions were unable or unwilling to make their leaders available. Moreover, a third of the subfactions were without a recognized leader, making identification and registration of their members impossible. Working through his **Deputy Special Representative, Erik Jensen,** the Secretary-General arrived at a formula by which the Identification Commission would appoint tribal leaders from lists obtained from both Morocco and the Frente POLISARIO. But the insistence of each side on "strict reciprocity" in the number of centers available to their tribal allies and "limits" each placed on the number of voters identified daily continued to delay the process. By mid-March, the Identification Commission had registered only 21,300 applicants at seven centers [S/1995/240].

Estimating that the full complement of 10 centers would increase registrations to 25,000 a month, the Secretary-General could not foresee a vote before January 1996. He also rescheduled from June to August 1995 the start of the "transition period," during which an expanded MINURSO was to oversee final preparations for the referendum: the reduction of Moroccan troops in the territory; the confinement of combatants from both sides to designated locations; the release of political prisoners; the exchange of prisoners of war; the return of refugees; and the finalization of a "code of conduct" for the referendum campaign. Boutros-Ghali placed the preliminary cost of bringing MINURSO to full strength (1,695 troops and observers, 300 civilian police, and 410 civilians) at $77 million for six months [S/1995/240/Add.1, 4/13/95], more than double the current three-month commitment of $17 million. Despite the increased costs, holding the referendum had "become a real possibility" [ibid.].

Expressing its "regret" that insufficient progress in identification had again delayed the scheduled vote, the Security Council called for "continuous and rapid progress" by May 1995, when it would consider the "possible extension of MINURSO's mandate" [S/PRST/1995/17, 4/12/95]. Showing signs of frustration, the Council agreed on May 27 to extend the mandate for one month—to June 30, 1995—in order to allow a delegation of Council members to travel to Morocco and the Sahara to push for the referendum [S/Res/995, 5/27/95]. Accordingly, six Security Council envoys from the United States, France, Argentina, Honduras, Oman, and Botswana were to be in the region the first week of June.

Mozambique

It was far from certain in the summer of 1994 that the government of President Joaquim Chissano and Alfonso Dhlakama's Mozambican National Resistance (RENAMO) movement would be ready to participate in Mozambique's first multiparty elections set for the fall. In the 18 months since the conclusion of the General Peace Agreement, the government and the former rebels continued to bicker over the timetable for the demobilization of their forces and even the number of troops to be disarmed. The disputes further delayed the full deployment of a unified Mozambican Defense Force (FADM), to consist of 30,000 soldiers drawn equally from both sides. Should the pace of demobilization not pick up, the Secretary-General warned in July, Mozambicans would be forced to hold their first free elections with three armies still in the field [S/1994/803, 7/7/94].

The parties took a big step toward accelerating demobilization by resolving a dispute dating from April 1994 on the size of the Mozambican Armed Forces (FAM), i.e., the number of government troops to be demobilized. After investigations by the joint Cease-fire Commission and the Supervisory and Monitoring Commission set up under the peace accord, the parties signed a June 17 statement revising FAM troop levels downward, from 76,405 to 64,466. (Estimates of RENAMO forces remained unchanged at 18,241.) Nevertheless the government was unable to meet its own July 1 deadline for assembling its troops in 29 designated areas in preparation for demobilization by August 15.

The Secretary-General reported that by July 4 the government was 4,517 soldiers short of full assembly and had demobilized only 22,832 troops. RENAMO, for its part, had assembled 17,317 but demobilized only 5,138. Although progress was sufficient to allow for the closure of three of the total 49 assembly areas, neither side was in position to meet the Security Council's July 15 deadline for completion of the process, set May 5 [S/Res/916, 5/5/94]. Moreover, the delays in assembly and demobilization limited the number of trained FADM personnel to 3,000, a tenth of the expected level. The Secretary-General termed the training of even half the force by election time "unlikely" [S/1994/803, 7/7/94].

Deployment of a U.N. police force was somewhat more successful. The Secretary-General had been able to deploy 817 **civilian police observers (CIVPOL)** by July against a total authorized strength of 1,144. Attached to the **U.N. Operation in Mozambique (ONUMOZ)**, CIVPOL continued to monitor the activities of the national police and investigate and resolve any complaints of misconduct against them. Although the government had opened its own police installations to inspections by July, residual suspicions of RENAMO further delayed the deployment of national police and CIVPOL contingents to areas formerly under rebel control. Some local RENAMO leaders also actively blocked such deployments, crucial to the reestablishment of central authority throughout the country—a main tenet of the peace agreement [ibid.].

The U.N.'s electoral and humanitarian missions were proceeding much more smoothly than its military and police functions. The 148 officers of ONUMOZ's Electoral Division were busy monitoring the electoral process, including the training of voter registration and education teams, which was completed in May with the assistance of the U.N. Development Programme (UNDP). By July, 15 political parties (excluding RENAMO) and 2.5 million voters (of an estimated 8 million eligible) had registered. The U.N. Office for Humanitarian Assistance Coordination (UNOHAC) completed its review of funding needs for the May through December period and announced the results to donor states: $117 million would be sought for emergency relief, $31 million for the repatriation of 1.4 million refugees, and $47 million for training, counseling, and job referrals for demobilized soldiers. The United States, the United Kingdom, and Norway were funding programs to clear land mines from key roads, according to a national mine survey, completed June 9 [ibid.].

The Security Council welcomed the "significant progress" made in the peace process, but reiterated previous concerns about delays in demobilizing forces and establishing a national army. Completing demobilization by the government's own August 15 deadline was "essential," the Council said, adding that there was "no margin for further delay" in dissolving the rival armies and forming the National Defense Force. Looking forward to elections—and the hoped-for end of U.N. involvement in Mozambique—the Council also announced "its intention to endorse the results," should they be judged free and fair, and called on the parties "fully to respect" them [S/PRST/1994/35, 7/19/94].

The Council also mentioned in its statement the possibility of dispatching its own mission to Mozambique—an unusual but not unprecedented action—to help ensure that the provisions of the General Peace Agreement, including the call for elections, were carried out in full and on time. Representatives of nine Council members (the United States among them) visited the country August 7–12 and reported a "positive impression of the pace of the peace process" and "cautious optimism about its prospects" [S/1994/1009, 8/29/94].

By the end of August, 52,242 government and 17,844 RENAMO troops had been demobilized; some 11,500 remained to be processed. Only 7,400 had joined the new army, however, forcing both parties to abandon hopes of fielding a force of 30,000 or even 15,000 members before the elections. Voter registration stood at 6.1 million, and both Chissano and Dhlakama gave commitments to the mission to abide by the election results. Among the mission's disappointments were a $1 million shortfall in contributions to the RENAMO Trust Fund (used to finance the movement's political participation) and the slow pace at which mines were being cleared and a domestic mine clearance capability developed [ibid.].

In his own assessment of the situation on the ground, the Secretary-General claimed that demobilization had "substantially concluded" by August 22, just a week beyond the Security Council's deadline [S/1994/1002, 8/26/94]. Seventy-five percent of the 3.7 million displaced persons had been resettled, and the United Nations estimated that it could increase the number of Mozambican deminers from 119 to 450 by November. "By all indications," the Secretary-General concluded, "the necessary conditions exist for holding the elections in Mozambique as scheduled." The Security Council pronounced itself "satisfied" with the progress to date [S/PRST/1994/51, 9/7/94].

A week before the elections the Council again met on the situation in Mozambique and declared that the "necessary conditions have now been established" for the vote. Reiterating previous pleas for calm, impartiality, and nonviolence, it also urged the parties to be "guided, after the elections, by the spirit of reconciliation as well as the principles of democracy and the need to work together in harmony to reconstruct their country" [S/PRST/1994/61, 10/21/94]. In a statement on the voting issued November 2, **U.N. Special Representative Aldo Ajello** reported a "massive voter turnout nationwide," more than 90 percent in some provinces. Because some of the 7,244 polling stations opened late or not at all on the first day, voting was extended through October 29. But a "remarkable absence of violence, intimidation, [or] coercion" prevailed, Ajello said, and RENAMO was eventually convinced to participate officially, after sitting out the first day. Ajello concluded that monitoring by U.N. and 2,300 other international observers "would not support any possible claim of fraud or intimidation" [S/1994/1282, Annex, 11/11/94]. To allow for a U.N. presence in the country up to the installation of the new government, the

Secretary-General requested the extension of the ONUMOZ mandate through December 15 [ibid.]. The Security Council complied with that request on November 15 [S/Res/957, 11/15/94].

In his "Final Report" on ONUMOZ [A/1994/1449, 12/23/94], the Secretary-General informed the Council of the official election results, announced by the National Elections Commission on November 19. Of the 12 presidential candidates, Chissano received 53.5 percent of the vote against 33.7 percent for Dhlakama. In the legislative contests, Chissano's FRELIMO party was likewise triumphant, 44.3 percent (129 of 250 seats) to 37.8 percent (109 seats) for RENAMO, with 12 other parties or coalitions competing. Turnout was 5.4 million, or 88 percent of registered voters. Ajello immediately declared the elections "free and fair," and the Security Council endorsed the results on November 21 [S/Res/960, 11/21/94].

After the installation of the Mozambican Assembly on December 8, the inauguration of Chissano on December 9, and the appointment of his cabinet on December 16, the mandate of ONUMOZ officially terminated. Its accomplishments were impressive. The operation's 4,150 troops and 322 military observers had overseen the demobilization of 78,000 combatants and the enlistment of 11,500 soldiers in the new defense force. CIVPOL's 1,086 personnel investigated 511 complaints against the national police, including 61 alleged human rights violations. With the help of some 40 nongovernmental organizations, U.N. agencies resettled 4.3 million refugees, displaced persons, and former combatants, built 700 schools and 250 health facilities, and dug 2,000 wells. International donors contributed more than 78 percent of the $650 million spent on humanitarian assistance in Mozambique [ibid.].

Serious threats to security remained, however, including numerous arms caches, undisposed weaponry, incomplete administrative control by the central government, a poorly trained police force, and an undersized army. Nevertheless the Secretary-General termed the achievements "remarkable" and declared ONUMOZ's mandate "successfully accomplished" [ibid.]. Its forces and assets would be completely withdrawn by January 31, 1995, save for equipment donated to the "accelerated demining program," scheduled to continue through November 1995. Offering its congratulations to the people of Mozambique and commendations to the Secretary-General and ONUMOZ, the Security Council encouraged future proposals for a U.N. role in the country during its "important and delicate" postelection period [S/PRST/1994/80, 12/14/94].

5. The Middle East and the Persian Gulf
By Jules Kagian

Iraq

During the first week of October 1994, President Saddam Hussein pushed Iraq toward a serious confrontation with the United Nations. **Iraqi elite**

troops took up positions near the Kuwait border, prompting President Clinton to dispatch Navy and Marine forces to the region and to warn that the United States would once more defend its allies in the Gulf [*New York Times,* 10/8/94]. Pentagon officials said that Iraq had moved 10,000 troops to the area near Basra, 30 miles from the Kuwait border, bringing the total number of Iraqi troops in the area to between 40,000 and 50,000.

At a White House press conference Clinton said he had ordered "precautionary steps" and would not allow Hussein to intimidate the United Nations into lifting sanctions. Clinton warned, "It would be a grave mistake for Saddam Hussein to believe for any reason that the U.S. would have weakened its resolve on the same issues that involved us in that conflict just a few years ago" [ibid.]. Because the deployments took place one week before the Security Council was to take up its regular review of the sanctions, many observers believed that Baghdad was looking to underscore its demands that sanctions be lifted. To win support in the Security Council for continued sanctions, the American delegate, Madeleine Albright, showed satellite photos of a T-72 tank in an area north of the Kuwait border and units from an elite guard division that had escaped the allied attack during the Gulf War.

After the Council meeting on October 9, Sir David Hannay of Britain issued a statement reaffirming the U.N. commitment "to the sovereignty and territorial integrity of Kuwait." All along, Iraqi officials maintained that their intentions were peaceful and that it was within their jurisdiction to move troops within their borders. In the meantime, the Council urged the U.N. Observer Mission in Kuwait (UNIKOM) to report any violations of the border and expressed concern over Iraq's threat to prevent U.N. monitoring of its military sites if the Security Council did not ease the economic sanctions [S/PRST/1994/58].

As the United States lobbied hard for a new Security Council resolution to deter Iraq from repeating its threatening moves, **Russia's Foreign Minister, Andrei V. Kozyrev, was conducting a diplomatic mission in Baghdad** to defuse the crisis. Together with Iraq's Deputy Prime Minister, Tariq Aziz, he announced an agreement on October 13 that would lead to Iraqi recognition of Kuwait. The joint Russian-Iraqi statement indicated that Iraq was still seeking to link Kuwait's recognition to a Russian promise to get the sanctions partly lifted in six months, when the weapons monitoring system set up by the United Nations had been fully tested. The joint communiqué, as quoted by the Itar-Tass news agency, stated that "Following Iraq's official recognition of Kuwait's sovereignty and borders, Russia will support an official commencement of long-term monitoring in accordance with U.N. Security Council Resolution 715 and a simultaneous start of a limited 'deadline' period, which in the opinion of Russia should not exceed six months, to check monitoring efficiency, after which the U.N. Security Council would decide on the enactment of

Point 22 of Resolution 687—fully and without additional conditions." Paragraph 22 lifts the oil embargo without leakage to other Security Council resolutions imposed on Iraq.

While Kozyrev was still in the region, the United States pressed for a quick vote on a Security Council resolution requiring Iraq to pull back its troops from the Kuwait border, and warned that it might attack Iraq with or without the Council's support [*New York Times*, 10/15/94]. Rejecting an appeal by the Russian delegation to delay the vote 48 hours pending the arrival of Kozyrev, **Ambassador Albright risked a Russian veto** and delivered a tough message to Council members: While Washington would prefer to have the Council behind it, it is prepared to take punitive action alone against Hussein. A split developed between Western allies over U.S. plans to establish a zone in southern Iraq below the 32nd parallel from which ground forces would be excluded, similar to the no-flight zone there. The proposal was opposed by France, Russia, and China. However, the United States cautioned that if Iraq failed to comply with the demands of the Security Council, the United States would take all appropriate actions pursuant to Article 51 of the U.N. Charter.

Close to midnight on October 15, the Security Council adopted **Resolution 949** by unanimous vote. Sponsored by Argentina, France, Oman, Rwanda, the United Kingdom, and the United States, the resolution demanded under Chapter VII of the Charter that Iraq immediately complete the withdrawal of all military units recently deployed to southern Iraq to their original positions and never again utilize its military or any other forces in a hostile or provocative manner to threaten either its neighbors or U.N. operations in Iraq. The Security Council met again two days later, October 17, to hear a report from Kozyrev on his just concluded diplomatic initiative. The Council also heard a statement from Deputy Prime Minister Tariq Aziz, who accused the United States and Britain of leading an unjust campaign to deny Iraq economic relief despite what he called his country's cooperation with the United Nations. The meeting highlighted the vastly different approaches used by Washington and Moscow in dealing with Hussein. Russia, supported by France, wants to reward Iraq gradually, if it continues to cooperate with the U.N. commission in charge of eliminating Iraq's weapons of mass destruction. Kozyrev laid out a plan under the terms of which Iraqi formal recognition of Kuwait would be followed a month later by a fixed period of monitoring its weapons programs and a possible Security Council decision to lift the oil embargo. However, the United States and Britain refuse to tie the monitoring regime to a timetable and continue to insist that Iraq comply with all U.N. resolutions pertaining to the Gulf War.

The Security Council refused to link Iraq's belated recognition of Kuwait to any reward and insisted that Iraq must recognize Kuwait's sovereignty, territorial integrity, and borders in the same manner it purported to annex Kuwait: with a statement ratified by the Revolutionary Command Council and by the Iraqi Parliament, published in the Official Gazette, and communicated formally to the Security Council. Baghdad responded formally on November 13, when Iraq's U.N. ambassador, Nizar Hamdoon, transmitted three official documents to the Secretary-General, including a copy of the Official Gazette, which carried the Declaration of the National Assembly "supporting the recognition by the Republic of Iraq of the sovereignty of the State of Kuwait, its territorial integrity, political independence and its borders" as endorsed by the provisions of Security Council Resolution 833 adopted on May 27, 1993 [S/1994/1288]. On February 24, anticipating a showdown in the Security Council over lifting the embargo on oil sales, Clinton dispatched Ambassador Albright on an urgent mission to drum up support to maintain the sanctions regime. In explaining the U.S. position, Albright stated on her return and following a successful Security Council meeting that the Iraqis have to abide by the following: (1) they must tell the United Nations more about their programs of mass destruction; (2) they must return all the property they stole from the Kuwaitis during the war; (3) they must give an accounting of the Kuwaitis that disappeared during the war; (4) they must stop pressuring, torturing, and repressing their people in the north and the south; and (5) they must stop supporting terrorism [MacNeil/Lehrer Newshour interview, 3/13/95].

The issue of Iraq's chemical weapons program—long a sticking point in the debate over sanctions—came to a head in early July. Following years of denial, high Iraqi officials admitted to Swedish diplomat Rolf Ekeus, Executive Chairman of the Special Commission monitoring the elimination of Iraq's weapons of mass destruction, that Iraq had indeed produced offensive biological weapons in 1989–90 just prior to its invasion of Kuwait. In a letter dated July 2, 1995, addressed to the Security Council, Ekeus said that the Iraqis admitted in a meeting in Baghdad that they had produced large quantities of the bacteria that cause botulism and anthrax, but that these had been destroyed prior to October 1990 [*New York Times*, 7/6/95]. The Iraqis were given a month to give the Special Commission full details of the program. The **International Atomic Energy Agency (IAEA)** reported that all the main elements of the IAEA's ongoing monitoring and verification plan had been set in place since September 1994, including the presence in Iraq of resident inspectors. The Agency believes that the overall picture in the nuclear area is satisfactory [S/1995/287].

The United States has come under increasing pressure to relax economic sanctions for humanitarian reasons. The U.S. position is that only Hussein can be blamed for the tragic plight of his people. Reference has been made to Security Council Resolutions 706 and 712, and now to Resolution 986, offering Iraq an opportunity to sell a limited quantity of oil to get hard currency to buy humanitarian supplies. Unanimously approved on April 14, 1995, **Resolution 986 replaces Resolutions 706 and 712.** Under the plan, Iraq would be permitted to sell up to $2 billion worth of oil within 180 days subject to certification every 90 days by the Secretary-General, who must report to the Council on how the income is distributed. Iraq would have to earmark 30 percent of the income to compensate the victims of the invasion of Kuwait and to pay the costs of U.N. monitors overseeing the oil sales and Iraq's compliance with the cease-fire resolution. However, in the first 90 days Iraq would receive only about $650 million because of the cost of repairing the oil pipeline from Kirkuk to Yumurtalik on Turkey's Mediterranean coast. Iraq is also required to set aside $150 million for the Kurdish area in northern Iraq, which means that the net proceeds would fall to about $500 million in the first 90 days. Under the old plan adopted in 1991, the Council offered a one-time sale of $1.6 billion under stricter conditions. Secretary-General Boutros-Ghali welcomed the resolution as a beginning of the end of the sanctions regime.

Ambassador Albright said the sponsors of the resolution had acted at the specific request of a number of Arab, Non-aligned, and European states that shared a common concern about the suffering of the Iraqi people, for which she blamed Hussein's policies. Baghdad formally rejected the resolution, calling the proposal "nothing but a U.S. maneuver to prolong sanctions." According to Iraqi officials, "the resolution seriously compromises Iraq's sovereignty and national unity" [*Middle East International,* 4/28/95]. Regardless of Iraq's negative response, the resolution remains on the table.

In his latest report on UNIKOM, issued on March 31, the Secretary-General reported that the overall situation in the Demilitarized Zone (DMZ) remained generally calm, although there was a period of tension in October 1994 in connection with reports about the deployment of Iraqi troops north of the DMZ [S/1995/251]. The report refers to **U.S. citizens William Barloon and David Daliberti,** who "mistakenly crossed the border from Kuwait into Iraq" [ibid.]. They were sentenced by an Iraqi court to eight years in prison. Without directly involving the United Nations, the United States is relying heavily on France, Russia, and other diplomatic channels to expedite their release. U.S. interests in Baghdad are represented by a Polish diplomat, Ryszard Krystosik. Behind a veil of secrecy, Mrs. Daliberti and Mrs. Barloon met with their husbands in prison in Baghdad in early May. The United States continued to express concern with and opposition to the actions of the Iraqi government. The State Department said that it held Baghdad responsible for the health of the two men [Federal News Service, 5/5/95].

Turkish Action Against Kurds

In the early hours of March 20, about **35,000 Turkish troops** armed with tanks and artillery units and backed by air power, **crossed into Iraq.**

Their aim was to "cause as much destruction as possible" to the bases of the separatist Kurdistan Worker party (PKK), whose guerrillas numbered 2,400 to 2,800. The Turkish Army focused on an area about 40 kilometers wide and stretching the length of the 280-kilometer Iraq-Turkey border. The Air Force carried out attacks deeper into Iraq. Unlike its European allies, the United States has shown some sympathy for the Turkish action. Secretary of State Warren Christopher called Turkey's military moves "**an act of self-defense**," and the United States was the only Turkish ally to call the operation "legitimate." Nonetheless, Washington did call for Turkey's "prompt withdrawal" from Iraq.

During the April 1995 visit to Washington of Turkish Prime Minister Mrs. Tansu Ciller, President Clinton asked her to extend the life of the U.S.-backed **Operation Provide Comfort** for northern Iraq's Kurds. The operation maintains a no-fly zone from a base in Turkey prohibiting Iraqi flights above the 36th parallel. The Turkish parliament must renew the mandate every six months. Fighting among Iraq's Kurdish factions has been blocking relief work and village reconstruction deemed critical to resettling the estimated 250,000 Kurds still waiting for a place to live. The Turkish campaign brought all relief work and reconstruction to a halt in the north. On May 4, six weeks after launching the biggest military operation in Turkey's history, Turkish Defense Minister Mehmet Golhan announced that **all Turkish troops had withdrawn.** The Army will maintain units near the border in the southeast and could cross back into Iraq, should Turkey feel the need.

Efforts by Turkish officials to convince Iraqi Kurds to stop the PKK regrouping appears to be making little progress. Moreover, there are increasing indications that the invasion has not succeeded in crushing Kurdish resistance. Meanwhile Baghdad, supported by the Arab League, cautioned Turkey against any attempt to alter the international borders between Turkey and Iraq. Undoubtedly, the military campaign has focused world attention once more on the Kurds. But if Operation Provide Comfort was to protect the Kurds from Hussein, it did not protect them from their internal differences [*Middle East International*, 3/31/95; *Washington Post*, 4/4/95; *Financial Times*, 5/5/95].

The Arab-Israeli Conflict and the Occupied Territories

As both Israel's Labor-led coalition and the Clinton administration moved closer to national elections in 1996, there was growing concern that chances of making any significant progress in the peace process would evaporate by the summer of 1995. Peace prospects for Israel and Syria were therefore at a critical stage in the spring of 1995. The basic elements for accommodation are well known: complete Israeli withdrawal from the Golan in return for the establishment of normal and peaceful relations. Shortly before his arrival in Washington in May, Israeli Prime Minister Yitzhak Rabin said that while the gaps remained substantial, he hoped that an agreement could be reached within a year and submitted to the electorate in a referendum [*Jerusalem Post International*, week ending 5/6/95].

The Clinton administration invested a good deal of effort in bringing the discussions to their current point. Having reached a strategic decision to come to terms with Israel, **President Hafez al-Assad of Syria is now determined to retrieve all territories lost in the June 1967 war.** On September 10, 1994, in a speech opening the sixth legislative session of the People's Assembly, Assad said: "We want just peace, because we want stability for our region, but the peace we want is one which restores our land to us." Syria has not altered its long-standing demand for a Golan withdrawal to the lines of June 4, 1967, rather than to the international borders, as Israel insists. The difference between the two borders is that by June 4, 1967, Syria had extended its control over El-Hama and the eastern shore of Lake Tiberias—areas that belong to Israel, according to the international border delineated in 1949. However, Israeli officials maintain that discussion of the two borders simply reflects basic differences throughout the years between Israel and Syria and has nothing to do with Israel's position in current negotiations. Rabin's withdrawal map from the Golan has not been revealed, for obvious domestic reasons. The only declared position on this matter was made in September 1994, when he spoke of a "very slight" withdrawal from the Golan, including Druse villages in the north but no Israeli settlements, in return for almost complete normalization [Report of The Foundation for Middle East Peace, 2/95].

The complicated issue of security arrangements has to be dealt with in the face of Syria's refusal to consider interim deals. Rabin has also to contend with the criticism of the Likud opposition of the current peace negotiations and its call for indefinite Israeli control of the West Bank and the Golan.

U.S. Secretary of State Warren Christopher unexpectedly announced on May 24 that Israel and Syria have agreed on the broad terms of security arrangements for the Golan Heights after an Israeli troop withdrawal. Details of the agreement were not disclosed. Specifics were to be worked out by Israeli and Syrian military experts in late June following a trip to the region by Secretary Christopher and Dennis Ross, the U.S. Special Middle East Coordinator. In a statement to reporters, Christopher said: "This is an important development, but there still are significant gaps between the parties, and there is much hard work to be done on the security arrangements and on all the non-security issues." In Tel Aviv, Rabin described the agreement as a "breakthrough in the procedure, but not in the substance" [*New York Times*, 5/25/95]. On June 28, Syria's military chief of staff, Lt.-General Hikmat Shihabi, and his Israeli counterpart, Lt.-General Amnon Shahak, opened negotiations in Washington on security matters. Secretary Christopher attended the opening session as mediator, and was later replaced by Dennis Ross. Following three days of talks the two parties reached a framework of agreement on security agreements. The talks were scheduled to resume in Washington in mid-July, though at a lower level [*Los Angeles Times*, 6/28/95].

It is also possible that an Israel-Syria peace agreement will be reached that **includes a resolution of Israel's occupation of south Lebanon.** Israel is convinced that progress with Syria will clear the way for an agreement on Israel's withdrawal from Lebanon, the curbing of Hizbollah, the extension of Lebanese authority to the international border, and the integration of Israel's proxy south Lebanon army into Lebanon's national forces. Rabin has indicated a preference for an **American military presence in the Golan** to monitor the agreement. The Clinton administration prefers not to discuss the plan prematurely, especially in the face of growing opposition on Capitol Hill to any plan that involves U.S. troops [ibid.].

The **Jordan-Israel peace treaty** signed on October 26, 1994, is a historic achievement with major implications for a comprehensive peace. The treaty was preceded by the Washington Declaration signed by Jordan's King Hussein and Israel's Prime Minister Yitzhak Rabin on the White House lawn in July 1994, officially ending the state of belligerency. The cornerstone of the agreement is mutual cooperation and constructive solutions to common problems. Rabin described the agreement as his greatest achievement, while King Hussein considers it the fulfillment of a historic dream. This achievement was possible because of the Declaration of Principles signed by Israel and the PLO on September 13, 1993, opening the door for Israel to exchange trade and diplomatic relations with many countries.

Because Jordan has a huge Palestinian population, the Palestine dimension is crucial to the future relations between Israel and Jordan. With this in mind, Israel has been watching with concern the growing opposition by Jordanian groups to normalizing ties with Israel [Jewish Telegraphic Agency, 5/5/95]. In an effort to bolster support for the peace treaty in early May, King Hussein invited members of the opposition from both houses for the Jordanian Parliament and told them he intended to implement the accord in letter and spirit. But despite the efforts of both countries' leaders to advance the peace between their peoples, certain developments reflect a different view among many Jordanians, including professional associations, some of which have issued directives against normalization with the Israelis.

On the Palestinian-Israeli track of the peace process, significant developments have taken place, particularly the signing in Cairo on May 4, 1995, of the first implementation agreement of the Declaration of Principles (DOP), namely, the agreement on the Gaza Strip and the Jericho area. Other secondary agreements on early empowerment were also reached. The two parties declared their intentions to negotiate the second implementation agreement on elections, which is of major importance to the Palestinian side, and also on the extension of the self-government arrangements to the rest of the West Bank. Despite numerous delays in the implementation of the DOP, the Palestine Authority had expected Israel to meet the July 1 deadline to reach an agreement on the next phase of the Palestine Authority. Elections were expected to take place within a short time after the redeployment of Israeli forces. However, the July 1 deadline passed without an agreement. Negotiations continued, and Israel and the PLO announced on July 4 that they would sign on July 25 the long-delayed agreement to expand Palestinian autonomy in the West Bank. The key issue believed to be holding up an agreement now was that of security in areas to be held jointly by Israel and the Palestine Authority after the initial redeployment of Israeli forces [*Financial Times*, 7/5/95; Jewish Telegraphic Agency, 7/4/95].

On May 6, Rabin announced that three bases in the West Bank will be partially deployed as a first step of what he calls "pre-deployment." However, the road map for implementing the second phase is full of obstacles. Israel will not withdraw its forces from the major population centers in the West Bank until it is assured that security is maintained. Another attack by suicide bombers from Hamas and Islamic Jihad like the ones that resulted in **the murder of 20 Israeli soldiers in Beit Lid and 22 civilians in Tel Aviv** would undermine any timetable for implementing the second phase of the DOP. The Rabin government's **settlement policy** emerged as a contentious issue between Israeli and Palestinian officials and could undermine the whole peace process. The Rabin government's construction plans for the West Bank and Jerusalem settlements rival, and in some respects surpass, the settlement construction effort of the Shamir government during 1982–92. In late December 1994, Israel caused an international outcry when it expanded the settlement of Efrat near Bethlehem [*Middle East International*, 1/6/95].

In late April 1995, Israel approved the confiscation of 131 acres of Arab land in occupied East Jerusalem. When **the Arab League** called for an emergency meeting of the Security Council, Ambassador Albright said the Council was not the appropriate place to have a discussion about this action. She described the confiscation as a difficult issue that poses problems for the peace process at this time [*Financial Times*, 4/5/95]. Failing to rule out a Security Council debate on the issue, the United States then rejected every conceivable compromise and opted to use its veto on May 17 to defeat a resolution supported by all other 14 members calling on Israel to rescind its expropriation orders [Security Council press release 6043, 5/17/95].

At the request of the European Group, the Arab delegates had toned down their draft, hoping to win at least an American abstention. The rejected text would have held the expropriation to be invalid and in violation of the Fourth Geneva Convention and of previous U.N. resolutions. **The American veto, its first in five years,** followed three days of debate in which at least 40 speakers participated [ibid.]. However, in a surprise move aimed at saving his government, Rabin and his Cabinet decided on May 22 to freeze the confiscation plan. This decision came after two small Arab-dominated parties in the Knesset introduced no-confidence motions that threatened Rabin's government. The decision was welcomed by the PLO and the U.S. State Department. It also led to the suspension of a planned Arab League mini-summit to discuss how to respond to the American veto and the confiscation [*Washington Post* and Jewish Telegraphic Agency, 5/23/95].

Over the past years, the United Nations has significantly enlarged its programs of economic, social, and other assistance to the occupied territories in order to support the implementation of the DOP and to promote peace in the region as a whole. The United Nations is to continue to participate actively in the multilateral negotiations on Middle East regional issues. The World Bank had received donor commitments of $86 million for the U.N. Relief and Works Agency (UNRWA) and $42 million for the U.N. Development Programme for projects that would generate jobs. Having decided to move its headquarters to Gaza from Vienna, UNRWA is expected to assume additional responsibilities related to the functions of the Palestine Authority [A/49/636]. **There is mounting concern over the deteriorating economic state of the Palestine Authority.** The unemployment rate in the West Bank is 50 percent, while in Gaza it was close to 60 percent as of April 1995 [*Jerusalem Post International*, week ending 5/6/95]. Donor countries met in Paris in late April and agreed to provide $60 million toward meeting the Palestinians' budget deficit of $136 million— nearly a third of the total budget of $444 million. The Palestine Authority contends that it had to hire more people for local service jobs because of the hardships created by Israel's closure of the territories. Moreover, many donor countries failed to contribute or conditioned the funding on better spending controls and reporting by the Palestine Authority [ibid.].

At the **U.N. Conference on the Non-Proliferation of Nuclear Weapons (NPT),** Arab countries led by Egypt backed down on the last day and agreed to amend a resolution they had sponsored condemning Israel for its nuclear program and calling on it to join the NPT. According to the *New York Times* of May 12, Clinton personally intervened during the 48 hours preceding final action to win the support of Egypt and other reluctant countries to the indefinite extension of the NPT, which was adopted without a vote on May 11 [General Assembly press release DC/2510, 5/11/95]. To accommodate the Arab countries, the Conference called on all states in the Middle East "without exception" to sign the NPT and accept international controls. The resolution on the Middle East also called upon all states in the region to take steps for the establishment of a Middle East Zone free of weapons of mass destruction.

Libya

Libya's leader, Muammar Qadhafi, is reported to have reorganized his security forces, purged rivals from his inner circle, and set Libya on a course of defiance against the West that will probably endure as long as he remains in power [*New York Times,* 4/20/95]. In press interviews, Colonel Qadhafi now says he will live within the U.N. sanctions regime imposed under Security Council Resolution 748 (1992) for refusing to hand over the two Libyan intelligence officers accused of planting the 1988 bomb that destroyed Pan Am flight 103 over Lockerbie, Scotland, killing 270 people. Resolution 748 imposes diplomatic sanctions, a ban on air travel, and an arms embargo. It also denies Libya access to oil processing and transport equipment. The United States has failed so far to win support for an international embargo on purchases of Libyan oil in an attempt to increase pressure on Libya. Several European countries, especially Italy, Germany, and Spain, are heavily dependent on Libyan oil supplies. Italy has argued that its refineries could not easily be converted to handle crude oil different from that supplied by Libya [*Financial Times,* 3/29/95].

"It will not be easy to achieve, but I think it's a reflection of our commitment to try to put as much pressure on Qadhafi and the Libyan government to turn over those two individuals for trial in the U.S. or the United Kingdom," said Warren Christopher [ibid.]. The Council, which reviews the sanctions every 120 days, extended them for the ninth time on March 30, 1995. At that time Ambassador Madeleine Albright urged the Council to toughen sanctions, but stopped short of proposing an oil embargo.

Coinciding with the U.N. periodic review of sanctions against Libya, the FBI announced on March 24, 1995, a **$4 million reward for the capture of Abdel Basset Ali Megrahi, and Lamen Khalifa Fhima,** implicated in the destruction of Pan Am 103. The bureau also placed the pair, believed to be in Libya, on its 10 Most Wanted List [*Washington Post,* 4/24/95]. Short of turning over the two Libyans to the United States or Britain, Qadhafi has exhausted a variety of tactics as he has sought to obtain the lifting of the three-year-old sanctions. He has offered to make the two men available to an international tribunal in The Hague, has hired lawyers hoping to work out a deal with the families of the victims, and has sought the mediation of the Arab League and the good offices of the U.N. Secretary-General. **France** is also maintaining pressure on Libya for failing to cooperate in the investigation of the bombing of a French jetliner that blew up on September 19, 1989, over Niger, killing all 171 aboard.

With the approach of the annual pilgrimage season known as hajj,

Qadhafi threatened to **defy the U.N. flight ban** and notified Egypt, the Sudan, and Saudi Arabia that he was **sending a plane to Jiddah,** near Mecca, on April 19, 1995, carrying 150 pilgrims. Czech Ambassador Karel Kovanda, who was the Council's President as well as Chairman of the Libya Sanctions Committee for April, called Libya's action a "flagrant violation" of the U.N. embargo. The unauthorized plane left Libya as the Sanctions Committee was in session at Egypt's request [*Washington Post,* 4/21/95]. The Committee hurriedly approved a formula allowing Libyans to make the pilgrimage aboard Egyptian planes, and about 6,000 Libyans were allowed to travel aboard 45 Egyptian flights under strict U.N. conditions.

Saying the United States supported the decision on humanitarian grounds, an administration official in Washington noted that Libyan pilgrims should not be denied the rights to pilgrimage and should not suffer for the actions of their government [ibid.]. This was the first time a U.N. member has requested an exception to the ban. Egypt assured the United Nations that the Libyan plane was denied flight clearance, which meant that Cairo did not violate the U.N. ban. However, a U.S. spokesman declared that the Saudi action in receiving the Libyan plane in Jiddah, in servicing it, and allowing it to take off for Libya violated Resolution 748 [Federal News Service, 4/21/95]. The Sanctions Committee seems to have overlooked this violation.

6. The Former Soviet Union
By Constantine V. Pleshakov

Tajikistan

Two years after the all-out fighting ended in its 1992–93 civil war, tensions remain high in Tajikistan, and particularly on the border with Afghanistan, where more than 840,000 Tajiks out of the total population of 5.1 million sought refuge [*Christian Science Monitor,* 11/4/94]. An economic crisis in this already poverty-ridden land and continued military clashes at the border have had a negative effect on efforts at political stabilization and at repatriating refugees [S/1995/105, 2/4/95].

At the start of the civil war, those opposing what the *Far Eastern Economic Review* characterizes a "hard-line ex-communist regime" [9/15/94] were a loose coalition of liberal, radical Islamic, and regional clan-based groups. But by 1994 these groups were well enough organized to coordinate armed actions and to present an "opposition" position at talks and consultations [S/1994/1363, 11/30/94].

In Russia and in neighboring Central Asian states, the civil war in Tajikistan had been perceived as a threat to regional stability and a prelude to an Islamic fundamentalist sweep through the entire region. (Tajiks, most of them Sunni Muslim, are the only non-Turkic, Persian-speaking people of former Soviet Central Asia.) And, indeed, by 1994, the Tajik opposition was cooperating on a pan-Islamic basis with Iran and Afghanistan, including each country's militant factions, and was receiving military and political support from them. This firmed the resolve of Commonwealth of Independent States (CIS) members Russia, Kazakhstan, Uzbekistan, and Kyrgyzstan—which had established a collective peacekeeping force in Tajikistan the previous year—to prevent Islam as a political force from crossing the Tajik-Afghan border.

In 1992–93 the central Tajik government had yielded control over that border, and even over strategically important junctions within the country, to the (predominantly Russian) CIS forces that had helped turn back the opposition challenge. The military support Russia gave to the Tajik authorities during the civil war (Moscow sent 25,000 troops from the 201st Motorized Rifle Division) was directly aimed at preventing radical, Iranian-style Islamic ideas from spreading through Central Asia [Christian Science Monitor, 11/4/94]. The Russian, Kazakh, and Kyrgyz border forces now in Tajikistan (under Russian command and again mainly Russian) are deployed along the Pyanj River marking the **border with Afghanistan.**

The mandate the CIS gave the collective peacekeeping forces in Tajikistan was to assist in "normalizing" the situation in Tajikistan, beginning with the Tajik-Afghan border; to assist in the delivery, protection, and distribution of humanitarian aid; to create conditions for the safe return of refugees; and to guard the buildings and roads and other infrastructural elements needed to carry these out [S/1994/1363, 11/30/94]. Russian economic aid (in the form of loans amounting to $91 million since February 1994) had the same objective of deterring the growth of Islamic fundamentalism, in this case by helping Tajikistan cope with its economic crisis [Far Eastern Economic Review, 9/15/94].

But even as Moscow was blaming Afghan President Burhanuddin Rabbani and his military commander Ahmad Shah Masud for supporting the Tajik rebels, it seemed displeased at the Tajik government's apparent unwillingness to get involved in serious negotiations with the opposition. At the same time, and confusing matters further, there were reports that Russia and Uzbekistan themselves have "showered support" on General Rashid Dostam, the Uzbek warlord fighting Rabbani [ibid.].

The international community's attempts to reach a political solution of the Tajik crisis began in 1993, some months after the main fighting ended in the civil war. A second round of U.N.-sponsored inter-Tajik talks in Teheran, June 18–28, 1994, bore fruit. Here, in the presence of observers from Afghanistan, Iran, Kazakhstan, Kyrgyzstan, Pakistan, the Russian Federation, and the Conference on Security and Cooperation in Europe (on January 1, 1995, the CSCE was transformed into the Organization for Security and Cooperation in Europe, or OSCE), the two parties were able to work out the terms of a cease-fire and a cessation of "other hostile acts." They also agreed on the need for a mechanism to monitor the implementation of the agreement [S/1994/893, 7/28/94].

On September 17, 1994, the two parties to the inter-Tajik conflict signed at Teheran the **Agreement on a Temporary Cease-fire** and the Cessation of Other Hostile Acts on the Tajik-Afghan Border and within the Country for the Duration of the Talks. Here they pledged to establish a provisional cease-fire and refrain from other hostilities until the referendum on the draft of the new constitution and the election of the president of Tajikistan; to release an equal number of POWs; and to establish a Joint Commission made up of members of both the government and the opposition [S/1994/1080, 9/21/94].

On September 22, 1994, the Security Council "welcomed" the Agreement, and in the course of the next month 15 U.N. military observers arrived in Tajikistan. This **U.N. Mission of Observers to Tajikistan (UNMOT)** was led by Brigadier General Hasan Abaza of Jordan, reporting to Liviu Bota, head of the U.N. office in Tajikistan's capital of Dushanbe. The cease-fire took effect on October 20, following a public announcement by Bota [S/1994/1363, 11/30/94].

The inter-Tajik political dialogue remained extremely fragile, and the CIS countries (especially the most dedicated anti-Islamic fundamentalists, Russia and Uzbekistan) were willing to promote it within the framework of the CIS (mostly Russian) military presence in Tajikistan—a presence that translated into control over the territory of the country. When the CIS Heads of State gathered in Moscow in October, they extended the tour of duty of the collective peacekeeping forces to June 30, 1995, and appointed Russian Major General Vasily I. Yakushev as commander [S/1994/1236, 11/2/94].

The **third round of inter-Tajik** talks on national reconciliation under U.N. auspices took place in Islamabad, Pakistan, from October 20 to November 1, under the gaze of representatives from the host country and the Organization of the Islamic Conference (OIC) as well as from Afghanistan (where the opposition is headquartered), Iran, Kazakhstan, the Russian Federation, Uzbekistan, and the CSCE/OSCE. Overcoming serious difficulties, Tajikistan's government and opposition agreed to extend the cease-fire and refrain from other hostile acts for an additional three months, until February 6, 1995. This was set forth in a joint communiqué signed on November 1, 1994.

At the same time, the two sides signed a Protocol establishing the **Joint Commission to monitor the implementation of the Agreement,** one of the subjects discussed at the second inter-Tajik talks in Teheran the previous June. (The Commission's first meeting was held in Dushanbe on November 14.) Under the terms of the Agreement, the two sides soon undertook to release equal numbers (27) of POWs. The parties agreed to hold the next round of talks in Moscow in early December. On the agenda for discussion would be free and democratic parliamentary and local elections; confidence-building measures, including lifting the government's ban on political parties and movements; and the role of mass media in the process of national reconciliation [S/1994/1363, 11/30/94].

The Joint Commission established under the Teheran Agreement was to be the formal machinery for implementing the Agreement. The U.N. Observer Mission, which is under the exclusive direction of the U.N. Secretary-General, is to act in any way that seems pertinent to the "implementation of the cessation of hostilities," whether at the request of the Joint Commission or on its own initiative [ibid.].

One of the ongoing major objectives of UNMOT is to urge both sides to proceed with their talks; and when the December Moscow round failed to take place, the Secretary-General's Special Envoy for Tajikistan, Ramiro Piriz-Ballon, held consultations with the Tajik government, leaders of the opposition, and senior officials in Moscow and Tashkent, seeking to promote talks. The Special Envoy also spoke with these officials about the desirability of postponing **parliamentary elections** scheduled by the Tajik government for February 26, 1995 [S/1995/105, 2/4/95].

Tajikistan's President Imamali Sharipovich Rakhmonov, under pressure from Moscow to continue the dialogue with the opposition, indicated his willingness to postpone the elections, provided the leaders of the opposition agreed to participate in the rescheduled balloting and to recognize the results [ibid.].

In January 1995 a U.N. team held consultations with the Tajik opposition leaders in Teheran and with high-ranking officials of Iran, but the Tajik opposition expressed no interest in participating in parliamentary elections at this stage, even if postponed for a few months. They did have an interest in registering complaints against the Tajik government and the Russian border forces, accusing both of violating the Teheran Agreement. The opposition also stated that it would not accept Moscow as the venue for the next round of talks, regardless of the previous agreement, unless the Russian Federation met four demands: officially recognize the Teheran Agreement, return to the opposition the weapons and ammunition seized since the Agreement came into force, remove the new checkpoints in the Gorno-Badakhshan area of Tajikistan, and delegate a representative of the border forces to the Russian observer team during the negotiations [ibid., p. 5]. When informed about the results of the consultations, the Tajik government announced that the parliamentary elections would be held as planned.

In mid-December 1994, when the Security Council adopted Resolution 968 supporting international efforts to promote the peaceful resolution of the conflict, the situation in Tajikistan was relatively quiet. Since the end of December, however, Russian border forces have reported a number of attempts by armed members of the opposition to infiltrate Tajikistan from Afghanistan across the Pyanj River. The opposition, for their part, have reported the shelling of Afghan villages by Russian border forces. A particularly serious breach of the cease-fire took place on January 2, 1995, in the Kalaikhumb sector, when opposition fighters ambushed a platoon of the Russian border forces, killing nine Russian soldiers and wounding eight. UNMOT's team at Pyanj reported four shellings by the Russian border forces aimed at Afghani points through January 1995. Also of concern to UNMOT were the broad powers of search and arrest these forces were able to exercise at the border [S/1995/105, 2/4/95].

UNMOT, headquartered in Dushanbe, with a staff now numbering 55, and with field stations at Garm, Kurgan-Tube, and Pyanj, was closely involved in the Joint Commission's work of monitoring the cease-fire between the two parties. The Russian-led collective peacekeeping forces were reluctant to provide the financial and logistical support of the Commission, however—violating the Protocol to the Teheran Agreement and, in the words of the U.N. Secretary-General, depriving the Commission of "the means needed to carry out its tasks" [ibid.].

On February 6, 1995, the U.N. Security Council endorsed the Secretary-General's recommendation concerning the continuation of UNMOT's presence in Tajikistan until March 6. Under-Secretary-General Aldo Ajello held consultations with officials of the Russian Federation, the Tajik government, and the Tajik opposition with a view to resolving the issues of venue, date, and agenda for the elusive fourth round of inter-Tajik talks and to obtain consent to an extension of the cease-fire agreement. The consultations, which took place in Moscow, Dushanbe, and Islamabad, respectively, brought agreement on an extension, if only until April 26, 1995 [S/1995/179, 3/8/95]. The Security Council endorsed on the same day the Secretary-General's recommendation to continue UNMOT's presence in Tajikistan through the April date [S/1995/180, 3/8/95].

On February 10, 1995, the Presidents of Kazakhstan, Kyrgyzstan, Russia, Tajikistan, and Uzbekistan, whose military personnel made up the CIS collective peacekeeping forces, had appealed to the President of the Security Council for a **"reflagging" of the mission.** The CIS summit in Almaty (Alma Ata) in February, they pointed out, had declared once again that there is "no alternative to a settlement of the Tajik conflict through peaceful, political means," and the presence of the CIS collective peacekeeping forces in Tajikistan had the effect of promoting dialogue between the government of Tajikistan and the opposition. Given this obvious commitment to settling the conflict and in recognition of the work yet to be done, they were asking for a "green-light" to establish in Tajikistan "a full-fledged peace-keeping operation" in which the four nations' peacekeepers would serve as U.N. peacekeeping forces [S/1995/136, 2/14/95].

On hand to observe the balloting on February 26—the date chosen by the Tajik government for elections to the Majlis-i Olii (parliament)— were 28 representatives of eight countries (the Russian Federation, India, Afghanistan, Iran, the United States, Belarus, Kazakhstan, and Kyrgyzstan) as well as representatives of the Inter-Parliamentary Assembly of the CIS and Permanent Representative of Tajikistan to the United Nations L. Kayumov. The latter informed the U.N. Secretary-General of the results of the general vote and reported that "In the overwhelming majority of districts, the elections were held on an alternative basis" [S/1995/176, 3/3/95] and "on the basis of a multi-party system, pluralism and free expression of the citizens' will" [S/1995/237, 3/29/95].

The opposition did not share this point of view, and the conflict continued to simmer. In clashes between Tajik opposition fighters and Russian troops at the Tajik-Afghan border on April 9, 25 Russians were killed [*Financial Times*, 4/11/95].

U.N. Under-Secretary-General Ajello's February talks with officials of the Russian Federation, the government of Tajikistan, and the leaders of the Tajik opposition did pay off eventually. The Tajik parties held high-level consultations in Moscow, April 19–26, under U.N. auspices [S/1995/390, 5/12/95], and the national reconciliation process seemed to have been revitalized. In May, in Kabul, came the first meeting between Tajik President Rakhmonov and opposition leader Sayid Abdullo Nuri, bringing a three-month extension of the truce in Tajikistan [*New York Times*, 5/23/95].

On May 22, the government of Tajikistan and the opposition in exile opened the **fourth round of U.N.-mediated talks** in Almaty, Kazakhstan's capital [ibid.]. At meetings that lasted until June, the parties reaffirmed the truce extension [S/1995/460, Annex]. Citing the Kabul and Almaty talks, the Security Council extended the mandate of UNMOT until December 15, 1995 [S/Res/999, 6/16/95].

Georgia

The secessionists of Abkhazia—an autonomous republic within Georgia, where the Abkhaz themselves were a minority during the Soviet era— remain unwilling to work with Georgia's central government at settling such issues as the return of Georgian refugees it ousted forcibly, much less work at a political settlement. The **de facto secession of Abkhazia** continues to create a dangerous precedent in the multiethnic Caucasus.

Fighting broke out in Abkhazia in August 1992, and over the next year the secessionists chalked up a number of impressive victories on the battlefield (an achievement for which the support of some elements of the Russian military is credited) [*A Global Agenda: Issues/49*, pp. 72–77]. The struggle had quickly become an international issue, largely due to the international reputation of **Georgian President Eduard Shevardnadze,** Foreign Minister of the Soviet Union under the presidency of Mikhail Gorbachev and a dedicated opponent of Abkhaz secession. The next 12 months saw U.N. fact-finding missions, appointment of a Special Envoy of the Secretary-General, consolidated appeals for humanitarian aid, the establishment of a **U.N. Observer Mission in Georgia (UNOMIG),** and even a cease-fire agreement. This was broken by the Abkhaz separatists in September 1993; and in mid-October 1993, Shevardnadze appealed to Moscow for help.

Collaborative efforts between the United Nations and the Russian Federation bore fruit during the winter, and on May 14, 1994, the **Agreement on a Cease-fire and Separation of Forces** was signed in Moscow. This was followed by reinforced U.N. efforts to regulate the Georgian-Abkhaz conflict. The two parties agreed to observe scrupulously a cease-fire "on land, at sea, and in the air," refraining from any military action against the other, and to create a sizable security zone (24 kilometers wide) on both sides of the Inguri River and a restricted-weapons zone. It was also agreed that CIS peacekeeping forces would help to maintain the cease-fire [S/1994/583, 5/17/94]. These CIS forces (read Russian troops) were deployed to the area with their CIS peacekeeping mandate intact.

In early June 1994, seeing some chance of settling the conflict, the Secretary-General proposed to expand the tasks of UNOMIG [S/1994/529/ Add.1], which had been established the previous August [S/Res/858 (1993)]. The General Assembly adopted a resolution on financing the mission [A/Res/48/ 256, 6/16/94], and on June 30 the Security Council agreed to extend UNO-MIG's mandate until July 21, 1994, and to expand it according to the Secretary-General's recommendation [S/Res/934, 6/30/94]. According to the **expanded mandate,** UNOMIG was to monitor and verify the implementation of the Moscow Agreement, observe the operation of the CIS peacekeeping force, "verify the regime" of the "security zone" and the "restricted-weapons zone," monitor the restricted-weapons zone and the area in which heavy military equipment withdrawn from the security zone was being stored, monitor the withdrawal of Georgian troops from the strategically important Kodori Valley, patrol the valley regularly, and investigate—and attempt to resolve—reported violations of the Agreement [S/1994/818, 7/12/94].

Security Council Resolution 937 of July 21, 1994, welcomed Russia's peacekeepers **without formally authorizing their dispatch,** and it extended the UNOMIG mandate to January 13, 1995. By that time, Russia had sent a 3,000-strong force with the mandate to reinforce a fragile cease-fire on the Abkhaz border and oversee the return of the 25,000 ethnic Georgians who were forced to flee when the Abkhaz secessionists prevailed in 1993 [*Christian Science Monitor*, 7/22/94].

On October 21, 1994, the Council of CIS Heads of State determined that the mandate of the collective peacekeeping forces in the Georgian-Abkhaz conflict zone would run until May 15, 1995, and could be extended beyond that [S/1994/1459, 12/30/94]. The U.N. Security Council, acting on the CIS decision, extended the mandate of UNOMIG until May 15 as well [S/Res/971, 1/12/95].

Neither the presence of the CIS peacekeepers nor UNOMIG's monitoring had any effect on the stalemate in Abkhazia, including the refugee problem, however, and the Secretary-General's Special Envoy for Georgia convened a round of negotiations in Geneva from February 6 to 7, hoping to make progress toward a comprehensive settlement. The Russian Federation representatives acted as facilitator, and the OSCE and the U.N. High Commissioner for Refugees (UNHCR) sent representatives too.

Still the Abkhaz conflict resisted solution. **Repatriation efforts** remained at a standstill, UNHCR reporting that only 311 refugees had returned under its procedures. This was due largely to Abkhaz resistance, said UNHCR, but also to the deteriorating security situation in the Gali region. UNOMIG was equally unsuccessful in preventing violations of the May 14, 1994, agreement on a cease-fire and separation of forces. Nor were these U.N. forces—now at full strength of 136, with teams based at Otobaya and Ingurges, and operating under the command of the Chief Military Observer, Brigadier General John Hvidegaard of Denmark—able to deter armed groups from entering the security zone [S/1995/181, 3/6/95]. UNOMIG and CIS peacekeeping forces continue their "cooperation," a mandate that could involve exchanges of information, mutual assistance, and joint patrolling [ibid., p. 6].

The CIS presence in Abkhazia has probably been helping to keep the conflict from escalating but has not influenced either party's attitude toward negotiations in any major way. Several CIS (i.e., Russian) soldiers are reported to have been killed or wounded in different incidents in the Gali region, which also have claimed the lives of members of the Abkhaz population [ibid., p. 4]. (UNHCR observed that, by March 1995, conditions in the security zone had deteriorated to the point that the relief supplies delivered to target groups were being looted and the intended beneficiaries placed at risk [ibid., p. 2].)

Following the February talks in Geneva, the government of Georgia and the Abkhaz authorities agreed to consider a "pragmatic timetable" for the voluntary return to Abkhazia of refugees and displaced persons and to take stringent measures to restore "acceptable security conditions" in the areas of return. The Abkhaz side, however, continued to be unwilling to accept a significant number of returnees [ibid.], and the situation in the Abkhazia zone of conflict remained tense, despite a temporary lull in fighting in the Kodori Valley. There were reports of human rights violations against the Georgian population of Abkhazia, UNOMIG contending that these were the acts of armed elements beyond the control of the Abkhaz authorities or the Georgian government [ibid., p. 4]. There is some merit to the suggestion, say observers, since paramilitary units, allied with but not fully controlled by either side, were engaged in the early fighting and remain on the scene. At the same time, both sides have made attempts to reintroduce heavy military equipment and armaments into the security and restricted-weapons zones [ibid.].

In March, the head of the Georgian state, Eduard Shevardnadze, issued a statement to the effect that between March 11 and March 14 more than 500 Abkhaz fighters had burned some Georgian villages of the Gali region, where they executed 24 civilians and captured over 150. He insisted that "the numerous groups of international observers are surprisingly indifferent towards the crimes committed" and that "the neutrality of the commanders of Russian peace-keeping forces is inconsistent with their mandate." Shevardnadze ended with a strong warning: "I wish to warn the Abkhaz separatists: the patience of people is not inexhaustible. The conciliatory position of the United Nations, CIS member States and the Russian peace-keeping forces towards mass crimes and vandalism, genocide and ethnic cleansing committed by the regime of the Abkhaz separatists has its limits" [S/1995/212, 3/21/95].

On May 1, 1995, the Secretary-General reported to the Security Council that his Special Envoy for Georgia had held consultations with officials of the Russian Federation, Abkhaz leaders, and Georgian diplomats. A **draft text that could provide the basis for a Georgian-Abkhaz settlement** was discussed. The Georgian side stated that the draft went as far as it was prepared to go with Abkhaz autonomy. The Abkhaz side insisted on a "union State, in which relations could be determined by horizontal ties between two equal States," effectively dismissing the draft's version of Abkhaz autonomy [S/1995/342, 5/1/95].

On May 12 the Security Council decided to extend the mandate of UMOMIG until January 12, 1996 [S/Res/993].

Armenia and Azerbaijan

The conflict between Armenia and Azerbaijan erupted in 1988 when the Armenian-populated enclave of **Nagorno Karabakh** on the territory of Azerbaijan sought to secede and link up with Armenia. Although Nagorno Karabakh continues to be treated as an separate party to the conflict, the **Armenian military offensive** of 1993–94 left little doubt about who holds the authority and wields the power when it comes to the enclave. That military offensive was highly successful—20 percent of Azerbaijan's territory was occupied—due in part to Azerbaijan's preoccupation with domestic conflicts. The offensive was halted only after considerable international pressure was exerted upon Armenia—largely by Turkey and Iran. Since May 1994 neither side has undertaken any sort of major military action.

By an arguably conservative estimate, the fighting of 1988–94 claimed over 15,000 lives and led more than a million people to flee their homes [*New York Times*, 8/12/94]. Azerbaijan President Heydar Aliev claims that the costs of war have been much higher. As a result of the Armenian aggression, he insists, more than 20 percent of Azerbaijan's territory is still occupied; more than 20,000 have perished among the Azeri population alone; 100,000 people were wounded or maimed and 6,000 taken prisoner; and more than 1 million—about 15 percent of the republic's population—have been driven from their native soil [A/49/764; S/1994/1397, 12/8/94].

An upsurge in the fighting in and around Nagorno Karabakh in April 1994 led to an intensification of peace efforts during May and June 1994. The mediators in this case—**OSCE's Minsk Group** (Germany, the United States, Belarus, France, Italy, Sweden, the Czech Republic, and the Russian Federation) and the Russian Federation on its own part (maintaining its special interest in the area)—managed to obtain agreement to the **cease-fire of May 1994,** still in effect today [A/49/380, 9/13/94], but negotiations appear deadlocked even eight months later.

The loss of a fifth of its territory, the cost of waging war, the economic malaise common to post-Soviet states, and an influx of refugees from Nagorno and other territory occupied by Armenia created a humanitarian emergency in Azerbaijan, and the United Nations began to deliver relief. A U.N. **Consolidated Inter-Agency Appeal for the Caucasus** in 1994 called for $29.3 million to meet emergency needs in Azerbaijan but had netted pledges of somewhat less than $10.5 million by the end of July [ibid.]. Food aid, which is coordinated by the World Food Programme, also fell short. Azerbaijan's estimated needs for the period July 1, 1994–March 31, 1995, came to 28,782 tons, but donors pledged only 12,267 [ibid.]. Efforts were made to place international humanitarian aid for Azerbaijan in a broader, regional framework. To this end, the International Federation of Red Cross and Red Crescent Societies (IFRC) reached an agreement with the Azerbaijan Red Crescent Society and the Iranian Red Crescent Society regarding the management of the camps in southern Azerbaijan, which then housed close to 46,000 displaced persons [ibid.].

Russia's expressed willingness to send peacekeepers to the zone of conflict is explained by some experts as a means of exerting pressure upon Azerbaijan, relations with which have soured since Azerbaijan signed the "contract of the century" with a Western consortium for the extraction of oil from the Caspian Sea [*Financial Times*, 12/7/94]. The Armenian side has never been against the idea of a Russian peacekeeping mission. In fact, in August 1994, Armenian President Levon Ter-Petrosyan declared that Russian peacekeepers would be more apt than anyone else to enforce the peace, to ensure that the forces remained separated, and to guarantee the security of Armenians in Nagorno Karabakh [*New York Times*, 8/12/94].

The Minsk Group of the Organization for Security and Cooperation in Europe continued its attempts at mediating the conflict between Armenia and Azerbaijan, and in December 1994, Sweden and Russia established themselves as co-chairs. They reported at the time that the cease-fire of May 12, 1994, was still largely respected. This finding has been reconfirmed on a number of occasions since.

The Minsk Group has been paying particular attention to the issue of **civilian detainees and POWs.** At a meeting it called in Moscow on February 11, 1995, attended by representatives of the International Committee of the Red Cross and the U.N. High Commissioner for Refugees, the three official parties to the conflict reached preliminary agreement on the "immediate release" of all the wounded, the sick, and those over 50 years of age. The parties also confirmed an earlier commitment to release women and children under 16 and established a special working group on detainees and POWs [S/1995/249, 3/31/95]. On March 27, as a symbol of goodwill, Armenia released six Azeri nationals that its forces had taken hostage [press release, Permanent Mission of the Republic of Armenia to the United Nations, 3/27/95]. There is no assurance, however, of a break in the negotiating deadlock anytime soon. A meeting of the Minsk Group that had been scheduled to take place in Stockholm the previous week was postponed because the positions of the conflicting parties "did not ensure the necessary conditions for constructive talks" [S/1995/249, 3/31/95].

On April 20, the Minsk Group co-chairs reported to the President of the Security Council that the cease-fire in effect since May 12, 1994, was still largely respected, though there had been several recent incidents. They expressed concern, however, at "the lack of concrete progress in the negotiation process" [S/1995/321, 4/20/95].

7. Cambodia
By Frederick Z. Brown

From October 1991 through September 1993, the U.N. Transitional Authority in Cambodia (UNTAC) engineered the perilous passage from war to peace in a country wracked by a generation of violence and domestic insurgency. In May 1993, UNTAC supervised national elections that led to a coalition between the noncommunist National United Front for an Independent, Peaceful, Neutral, and Cooperative Cambodia (FUNCINPEC) and the formerly communist Cambodian People's Party (CPP), with minority participation by the Buddhist Liberal Democratic Party (BLDP). In September 1993, the Kingdom of Cambodia, under King Norodom Sihanouk, was proclaimed and the new Royal Cambodian

Government (RCG) was granted universal recognition by the world community.

A product of the 1991 Paris Agreements on a Comprehensive Political Settlement of the Cambodia Conflict [UN/DPI/1180-0207, 1/92], UNTAC arguably has been the most successful major peacekeeping effort yet undertaken by the United Nations. International organizations, individual donor nations, and scores of nongovernmental organizations (NGOs) have continued to assist the new Cambodian government during its first two years in power. Since 1993 activities of the international community in support of the U.N. peacekeeping effort have fallen into two categories: the creation of a new social order based upon political pluralism, respect for civil and human rights, and reconciliation between former enemies; and the rebuilding of a Cambodian economy virtually destroyed by decades of warfare.

The RCG has gradually assumed primary responsibility for activities in the first area, although it receives key bilateral and NGO support for specific programs. Questions of political toleration, press freedom, and human rights remain highly problematic. Military suppression rather than "reconciliation" with the hard-core Khmer Rouge leadership is clearly the course the RCG has now adopted.

Foreign-assistance programs are concentrated in the second area—economic development—on grounds that rebuilding the physical infrastructure together with economic reform and expansion of the economy are keys to Cambodia's escape from its impoverished condition and to political and broader social stability. The RCG expects to absorb the less committed followers of the Khmer Rouge into Cambodia's mainstream through such measures. The international financial institutions, the U.N. Development Programme (UNDP), and associated U.N. programs are central to the implementation of this effort. The International Committee for the Reconstruction of Cambodia has been an essential venue for the coordination of bilateral and multilateral assistance programs.

The Military Side and the Khmer Rouge

The Khmer Rouge (as the Party of Democratic Kampuchea) signed the Paris Agreements in October 1991 but refused to participate in the subsequent UNTAC peace process. The Khmer Rouge's armed resistance to the RCG has continued to hamper efforts to rebuild some parts of the country. In the spring of 1994 the RCG suffered military defeats at the hand of the Khmer Rouge at An Long Veng and Pailin in Siem Reap and Battambang provinces [see *A Global Agenda: Issues/49*, p. 104]. These defeats were caused less by Khmer Rouge prowess than by the poor leadership, corruption, and professional incompetence of the Royal Cambodian Armed Forces (RCAF), demonstrating the need for a thorough restructuring and retraining of those forces. The implications of the RCAF's ineptness reverberated through the international community.

After Pailin, the RCG appealed for arms, ammunition, and other military equipment, and for training in a range of military skills. The United States, France, Australia, and other foreign governments refused categorically to provide lethal aid. They advised Phnom Penh to reorient and retrain the RCAF and prepare it to take a dual role of security and rural reconstruction. In July and August 1994 the United States supplied trainers to develop the RCAF's demining and road-building skills and provided a modest amount of equipment for these purposes; other donors have followed suit. The United States also sent a team of consultants to Phnom Penh to assist the RCAF in its reorganization planning. France continued the presence of a small group of military trainers, and has provided other forms of nonlethal assistance, as has Indonesia. Australia has assisted RCAF communications capabilities and has begun an infantry training program for RCAF officers. Mine-clearing remained one of the critical aspects of foreign assistance to military and civilian elements of the RCG.

Although donor countries have firmly opposed supplying any sort of lethal assistance, they have been supportive of the reform plan announced by the RCG in October 1994. By mid-1995 the 2,000 general-rank officers had been reduced in number to 199, and colonels from 10,000 to 300. The security forces are still numerous: 200,000 organized in 10 RCAF and 7 police divisions. Strongly encouraged by members of the International Committee on the Reconstruction of Cambodia (ICORC)—a broad coalition of nations and international organizations—the RCG says it plans to scale down its armed forces further and to integrate demobilized soldiers into the civilian economy [*Far Eastern Economic Review*, 3/30/95].

By mid-1995, in the judgment of both the Royal Government and foreign analysts, the Khmer Rouge were militarily weaker than at any time since 1982. The fighting strength of the Khmer Rouge was between 5,000 and 6,000 regular troops, 2,000 holed up in the sparsely populated jungles of the far north and the remainder in the mountainous western provinces of Battambang and Pursat. Khmer Rouge remnants in the southeast were no longer considered a serious threat, and the Khmer Rouge nationally no longer evidenced a political program of significant credibility in the countryside. The rank and file appeared to have lost their ideological fervor, and defections of lower and mid-level cadres have reduced their ranks significantly. Khmer Rouge fighters in whole areas have switched their allegiance away from the hard-core Pol Pot-Tamok leadership in favor of the RCG with the understanding that they will continue to handle the local administration [ibid., 4/27/95]. The government of Thai Prime Minister Chuan Leekpai, after heavy pressure from Western countries, has applied tighter controls on the Thai-Cambodian border and reduced informal assistance the Khmer Rouge may have been receiving from the Thai Army.

For Cambodia, these factors were positive but by no means conclusive. Although weaker, the Khmer Rouge base of hard-core political and military support is apparently intact (with some residual financial resources) and remains dedicated to the destruction of the central government. One top RCG leader, CPP Deputy Prime Minister Sar Kheng, has emphasized that pervasive government corruption and social inequities have provoked widespread indignation among students and the public generally, and that this reality could lead to a resuscitation of Khmer Rouge influence [ibid., 3/30/95].

Internal Politics

On July 2–3, 1994, a theatrical "coup attempt" took place under the ostensible leadership of Prince Norodom Chakrapong and former Interior Minister Sin Song, the same individuals who had led the secessionist movement in the eastern provinces in June 1993 following FUNCIN-PEC's victory at the polls [see *Issues/49*, p. 103]. The affair revealed a split in the CPP's leadership between Second Prime Minister Hun Sen and his rivals for power, Deputy Prime Minister Sar Kheng and President of the National Assembly Chea Sim. Chakrapong was arrested and banished to Malaysia; his colleagues were also arrested and expelled from the country. The consensus after the dust settled was that the "coup" derived from personal rivalries at the highest levels of the CPP and FUNCINPEC. Taken with the Pailin fiasco several months earlier, the July 1994 incident undermined confidence in the Royal Government.

FUNCINPEC politics became further convoluted. First Prime Minister Ranariddh found himself allied with the Hun Sen faction of the CPP for both political and financial reasons. In October, the Royal Government fired Minister of Economy and Finance Sam Rainsy; Minister of Foreign Affairs Norodom Sirivudh resigned in solidarity with Rainsy. The two men voiced a perspective within FUNCINPEC that was different from Ranariddh's, and they enjoyed the sympathy of some FUNCINPEC national assemblymen. As of mid-1995, both men retained their positions as National Assemblymen; Rainsy has given indications that he may form another political party, in which case his seat would be jeopardized. Rainsy had been outspoken in support for human rights and press freedoms, and was responsible for the important 1993 budget bill which sought to rationalize the country's macroeconomic system. The senior leadership of FUNCINPEC was thus divided, with Ranariddh determined to retain his dual positions as FUNCINPEC President and First Prime Minister of the country.

ICORC and Cambodia's Economic Situation

The RCG's relations with the five permanent members of the U.N. Security Council have been generally positive. China and Russia continue to support the principles of the 1991 Paris Agreements, but have played declining roles in Cambodian affairs. Japan, the United States, Australia, France, and other major bilateral donors of reconstruction aid maintain a generally cooperative front when faced with such critical issues as lethal aid, the aborted July coup, and human rights observance. ICORC has been the rallying point for the consolidated development effort, and has reinforced a common approach on issues that are essentially political.

At the third ("nonpledging") meeting of ICORC, March 14–15, 1995, in Paris, Cambodia's macroeconomic policy performance, and the promise of improvement, won endorsement from the members of the Cambodian aid "club." By the time of its initial Paris meeting in 1993, $1 billion had already been committed; by the March 1994 Tokyo meeting, this figure had reached $1.6 billion. According to individual donors, approximately $1 billion has been disbursed as of January 1995. Present at the March 1995 gathering were delegations from more than 30 countries, the European Union, and representatives of UNDP (plus a host of other U.N. agencies), the IMF, the World Bank, and the Asian Development Bank. Although the next ICORC meeting was scheduled for 1997, the participants at this year's meeting agreed that an "alternative format of assistance coordination such as a Consultative Group meeting organized by the World Bank" will replace ICORC in the near future. Further discussions between ICORC members and the RCG on this new format will take place in 1996 [press release, 3rd ICORC meeting, 3/15/95].

In 1994–95, Cambodia was still in the relatively early stages of making a triple transition: from war to peace, from command to market economics, and from state/party control to something approaching a civil administration. Cambodia's annual per capita income remained well under the $200 level, placing it among the poorest countries in the world. Despite an underlying population growth rate of about 2.7 percent annually (1988–93) and the significant number of returnees from Thailand, the increase in real GDP per capita averaged 3 percent annually during that period, and in 1994 reached 5.7 percent. The country's 1995 budget was the equivalent of $423 million (up from $250 million in 1994). The aggregate allotted to defense and internal security—46 percent—remained extremely high.

The RCG continued to respect the fiscal discipline that had been imposed in 1992, a requirement for IMF support and continued confidence of all major financial donors. Macroeconomic factors were favorable. Inflation, which had reached 180 percent in 1992, was brought down to 40 percent by the second half of 1994. In early 1995 inflation had fallen to 18 percent, and by the end of 1995 the RCG expected it to reach 10 percent or lower. The riel–U.S. dollar exchange rate remained fairly stable, trading in the 2,400–2,700 range throughout 1994, though by April 1995 it had appreciated to 2,300 ["Cambodia Rehabilitation Program: Implementation and Outlook," World Bank Report for 1995 ICORC Conference, 2/95].

Human Rights

An important legacy of UNTAC was the growth of Cambodian human rights organizations and nongovernmental organizations (NGOs). After 1993 indigenous human rights networks adjusted to the new political situation and continued their work with support from the U.N. and foreign bilateral programs, which assisted National Assembly members and RCG ministries to write laws and procedures in consonance with international human rights standards. They also assisted in the government's judicial reform process, with the goal of creating an independent judiciary. The human rights organizations ADHOC and LICADO had a combined membership of more than 100,000. Buddhist groups, NGOs seeking empowerment of women, human rights and democracy-promoting NGOs, and even an informal reconciliation movement were raising the consciousness of an increasing number of Cambodians. Yet despite these hopeful signs, in 1994 and 1995 reports of alleged human rights abuses were plentiful, some attributed to the RCAF.

The leadership of FUNCINPEC and the CPP leaned heavily on those members of the National Assembly who expressed views contrary to the government's. Freedom of the press, too, has remained under siege; three newspaper editors were murdered during the past year, and the government's press law promising harsh penalties for loosely construed trespasses has been under consideration for many months [*Cambodia at War*, New York: Human Rights Watch/Asia, 1995].

Cambodia's embattled human rights environment has attracted international attention. Among foreign officials visiting Cambodia in 1994 and 1995 to express concern were Marrack Goulding, U.N. Under-Secretary-General for Political Affairs; Australian Justice Michael Kirby, the Secretary-General's Special Representative for Human Rights in Cambodia; José Ayala Lasso, the newly appointed U.N. High Commissioner for Human Rights; and high-ranking officials from several Western governments. Following his visit, Goulding noted in May 1995 that "there are some disturbing aspects, in particular the unsolved killings which appear to have political motivation, the threats which are alleged to be made against certain political personalities" [*Indochina Digest*, 5/5/95].

The RCG's proposal to close the U.N. Center for Human Rights in Phnom Penh, which had been established in October 1993, was controversial. Prime Ministers Ranariddh and Hun Sen argued that the Center's reports were "no good for investors and donor confidence." After meetings with Secretary-General Boutros Boutros-Ghali in New York and in the wake of blunt criticism from Western governments, Hun Sen announced that the RCG had reversed its position and would permit renewal of the Center's presence through 1996 [ibid., 3/31/95].

Summing Up

As of May 1995 the Secretary-General was still represented in Cambodia by a small office, including military advisors, to carry out the Security Council's mandate "in accordance with the spirit and principles of the Paris Agreements" [S/1994/1182, 10/19/94]. But with a final financial accounting complete, UNTAC itself has stood down [A/49/867, 3/21/95, and other documents in "The United Nations and Cambodia, 1991–1995," UN DPL/1450]. UNTAC was remarkably successful in performing a political legitimation through a fair election and removing Cambodia as a regional irritant. But UNTAC could not heal the grievous wounds of recent decades, let alone reverse centuries of Khmer political attitudes—and in truth this was not its mission. Several fundamental negative trends in Cambodia have defied resolution: a Khmer Rouge insurgency that is weaker but can still inhibit sustained development; perpetual political infighting among the leaders of both FUNCINPEC and the CPP; and a social environment where the few laws that exist are often held in contempt.

Despite indications of interest from foreign investors, projects under discussion or actually being implemented appear inadequate to generate substantial economic development. Moreover, some large logging and other concessions to foreign concerns reportedly ignore environmental and natural resource considerations and could badly affect a sizable piece of the country. Cambodia's labor force is still 80 percent in agriculture, mostly dependent on rice, fish, livestock, and minor crops. While these subsectors offer promise, their development will be a slow process. Soil and water conditions in Cambodia make "green revolution" breakthroughs unlikely. While the population–land ratio is favorably low, much unoccupied arable land can be reopened to settlement and cultivation only if demining efforts can be greatly speeded up.

Cambodia's transport and other economic infrastructure remains deteriorated, severly constraining agricultural, industrial, and tourism development in the short term. ICORC has identified this sector as a prime target for donor programs. While some projects, such as highway repair, are moving quickly into implementation, other areas, such as telecommunications, need an extended period of economic and engineering preparation.

The easier macroeconomic and monetary reforms have already been undertaken but, obviously, must be continued. In the short run, getting

Cambodia's macroeconomic house in order does not have a significant effect on that large fraction of the rural population that is barely monetized. Nor would that sector be affected immediately were an improved investment climate (or banking sector or other institutional developments) to lead to an increase in foreign investment. While macroeconomic change affects the urban population quickly and sets the stage for the viability of many programs having secondary effects on the general population, it has been the ruling political elite—an extremely small group— who have been the main beneficiaries of these macroeconomic gains and from privatization and foreign investment entering the country.

Economically, Cambodia has a reasonable chance of muddling through an extended transition process, if the outside powers and agencies use their substantial near-term leverage in ways that help promote sound economic growth and political maturation along more tolerant, participatory lines. After the extraordinary intrusions of the UNTAC period, there is a fine line between interventionism and a subtler policy that encourages self-reliance and Cambodian "ownership." Conditionality in the delivery of international assistance will continue to be debated, as the March 1995 ICORC meeting demonstrated. With Cambodia's diminished importance as a regional security irritant, an element of "donor fatigue" has set it. It is fair to say that the ability of the foreign aid donors (certainly that of the United States) to sustain a supportive role as this development process unfolds will depend in part on the Cambodian leadership's adherence to the spirit of the 1991 Paris Agreements and to the policy framework defined in the ICORC relationship.

Ending the Khmer Rouge threat once and for all depends not only on military security but also on increasing the size of the economic pie and making a larger slice available to the majority of the population, who are still impoverished. Among the factors that could give the Khmer Rouge a new lease on life are rural poverty; the RCG's weak administrative capability; absence of professionalism in the military establishment; rampant corruption at the highest levels of government; human rights abuses; and the autocratic political attitudes and practices of the leadership of both FUNCINPEC and the CPP.

Personal rivalries in both the CPP and FUNCINPEC could produce a factional realignment during 1996 or 1997 in anticipation of the national elections in 1998. The BLDP's survival is in doubt; its leadership is being cowed or co-opted by the two main parties. To realize any constructive scenario for political change, the concept of a loyal opposition party—in contrast to a revolutionary opposition party—must be broadly accepted by the Cambodian political elites, a concept that still seems very foreign to Cambodia today. What will be crucial in 1998 is the manner in which Cambodian politicians move from the present administration to the next and the extent to which changes occur within the law and the constitution, and with respect for human rights.

II
Arms Control and Disarmament
By Howard A. Moyes

The year 1994–95 witnessed further consolidation of the arms control agenda. On May 12, 1995, after several months of intense lobbying by the United States, the nuclear Non-Proliferation Treaty (NPT) was extended indefinitely by consensus. Only months earlier, Ukraine had signed the NPT, opening the way to full implementation of the START I Treaty between the United States, Russia, Ukraine, Belarus, and Kazakhstan (and possibly also opening the way to ratification of START II). And it was also a year that saw progress on negotiations for a comprehensive nuclear test-ban treaty, with all five nuclear weapon states declaring that they would sign a test ban before September 30, 1996.

Progress was mixed on other arms control issues. Ratification of the Chemical Weapons Convention began to pick up steam. Twenty-eight states had ratified the accord as of June 1, 1995, though still far short of the 65 needed for the convention to enter into force. The 48th General Assembly had expressed the hope of an early 1995 entry date, but many countries are waiting until the United States, Russia, China, and the United Kingdom actually ratify the convention. On a more positive note, there were efforts to strengthen the Biological and Toxin Weapons Convention, notably by negotiating new measures to secure compliance with the accord. A Special Committee met during the year to discuss proposals for transparency measures, including mandatory data exchanges and periodic on-site visits, that could build confidence in the regime. These discussions will continue during the General Assembly's 50th Session.

The U.N. Register on Conventional Arms continued to enjoy widespread support. Over 80 states submitted data on their 1993 imports and exports of major weapons systems, and discussions continue on ways to improve the Register's reporting requirements and expand its scope to include new weapons systems. Still, the Ad Hoc Committee on Transparency in Armaments at the Conference on Disarmament was unable to reach consensus on any changes in the Register for the current term. In Washington, U.S. President Bill Clinton unveiled a new U.S. arms transfer policy, which called for greater transparency in armaments but places few new restrictions on the actual export of U.S. conventional arms.

The 50th Session of the General Assembly is sure to welcome the significant progress made in nuclear arms control during the past year, especially the indefinite extension of the NPT. And it will probably echo the 49th Session's call for the consolidation of arms control and disarmament efforts, particularly in the areas of nuclear testing and chemical and biological weapons, while expressing the hope for progress in new and challenging areas.

1. Nuclear Proliferation and the NPT

After several months of intense lobbying by the United States and others, the **nuclear Non-Proliferation Treaty (NPT)** was extended indefinitely by consensus on May 12, 1995. During the month-long extension and review conference, delegates from Egypt, Mexico, Indonesia, and other developing countries had expressed strong opposition to extending the NPT indefinitely, citing the slow pace and inadequacy of disarmament by the five nuclear weapon states and the continuing refusal of Israel to renounce nuclear weapons and join the NPT as a non-weapon state.

Despite these concerns, the 175 states participating in the conference:

1. Extended the NPT indefinitely.

2. Adopted a consensus resolution calling for all states in the Middle East to accept full-scope safeguards—surveillance and monitoring by the International Atomic Energy Agency on all national nuclear facilities and materials to ensure nuclear technology is used only for peaceful purposes. Egypt had originally pushed a draft of this proposal that made explicit reference to Israel's nuclear facilities, which lack any safeguards, but Cairo backed down at the last minute under intense pressure by the United States.

3. Agreed to replace the five-year review of the NPT's implementation record, especially in regard to nuclear disarmament in the weapon states, with a yearly review cycle to take place over the next five years.

4. Agreed to establish a set of principles to serve as a yardstick in measuring disarmament progress.

The last two of these agreements enable the non-weapon states to exert greater leverage on the weapon states and on those states' disarmament policies even in the absence of an agreement by weapon states to disarm by a given date.

The nuclear weapon states did make **three commitments:**

1. To sign a comprehensive nuclear test-ban treaty (CTBT) by 1996
2. To make "systematic and progressive efforts" to reduce nuclear stockpiles with the "ultimate goal" of eliminating all nuclear weapons
3. To seek "the immediate commencement and early conclusion" of a convention banning the production of fissile materials for weapons purposes [*Washington Post*, 5/12/95].

Largely due to these pledges—and to intense lobbying by the United States—developing states were **unable to attach specific conditions** (among them greater access to transfers of civil nuclear technology that may have potential weapons applications) to the treaty's extension.

In the months leading up to the extension conference, the Non-aligned Movement (NAM), chaired by Indonesia, had demanded comprehensive disarmament measures from the weapon states and had proposed making the treaty's indefinite extension a hostage to these conditions. Egypt, for its part, had announced that it would not support indefinite extension because the NPT "had not lived up to the expectations of its original forefathers" and was "incapable of safeguarding Egypt" [ibid., 5/14/95]. For a time, Egypt supported a Syrian proposal to suspend the conference for a "reasonable period" as a means of pressuring Israel to accept nuclear safeguards.

Another major obstacle to indefinite extension was Mexico. Mexico's ambassador to the conference, Miguel Marin-Bosch, seizing upon a Japanese-sponsored draft resolution (which called on the nuclear weapon states to achieve rapid disarmament), used it as a catalyst for rallying the developing states against indefinite extension of the treaty unless the weapon states agreed to make significant disarmament concessions. But timing was all. Washington, putting the recent peso bailout to advantage, successfully pressured Mexican officials into taking a softer stance at the extension conference.

The major break for the United States and proponents of indefinite extension came when the South African delegation put forward a proposal to both extend the treaty permanently and **strengthen the disarmament review process.** Much to the surprise of many observers, who had feared an impasse, this proposal quickly emerged as the basis for negotiations between the nuclear weapon and Non-aligned states [ibid., 5/14/95]. Within days the conference had reached consensus on the four areas discussed above.

The NPT was extended indefinitely by consensus, not by formal vote, and representatives of eight nations—Egypt, Iran, Iraq, Syria, Jordan, Libya, Malaysia, and Nigeria—took the floor at the end of the conference to voice their unhappiness with the conference and the agreement [ibid., 5/12/95].

Because of such dissatisfaction by a handful of states, and the fact that much of the focus of the conference was on extending the NPT, dele-gates were unable to reach consensus on the second issue before the con-ference: the **adequacy of arms reduction measures by the nuclear weapon states** since the 1990 review conference. Many of the participants did not view this as a major setback, however, since NPT review confer-ences have reached agreement on a final arms control declaration only once, in 1985 [ibid., 5/13/95].

On a related front, the General Assembly passed the by-now peren-nial resolutions calling for **nuclear weapon-free zones** in the Middle East and South Asia; requesting all states in these regions that have not yet done so to join the NPT as non-weapon states; and asking all states to accept International Atomic Energy Agency (IAEA) full-scope safe-guards on their nuclear facilities [A/Res/49/71, 72, and 78]. The 49th Assembly also welcomed the signing by Cuba of the **Treaty of Tlatelolco** on March 25, 1995, further consolidating the nuclear weapon-free zone in Latin America and the Caribbean [A/Res/49/83].

One element that remained in the background of the NPT negotia-tions was the recent progress of the **United States and North Korea** over Pyongyang's nuclear weapons program. The two sides signed an Agreed Framework on October 21, 1994, in which North Korea promised to freeze its nuclear program and remain a non-weapon party to the NPT. In exchange, North Korea would receive two 1,000-megawatt light-water reactors and enhanced diplomatic and economic relations with the United States. The Agreed Framework gave a needed boost to the non-prolifera-tion regime at a time when its future was uncertain at best.

On July 8, 1994, following a visit by former President Jimmy Carter in June, North Korea and the United States agreed on the resumption of bilateral talks after a year's hiatus. In the discussions between Carter and North Korean leader Kim Il Sung, Kim pledged that Pyongyang would ensure the continuity of IAEA safeguards, would not reprocess any spent fuel, and would not refuel its five-megawatt plutonium-production reac-tor. This came just after the U.N. Security Council had begun to consider placing sanctions on North Korea for its refusal to freeze its nuclear pro-gram and its threat to withdraw from the IAEA safeguards regime [*Arms Control Today*, 7–8/94, pp. 20, 25].

North Korea reaffirmed its pledge to freeze its nuclear program on August 12, when the two sides agreed to a "three-stage process" to settle the nuclear dispute. Under this plan worked out by U.S. Ambassador-at-Large Robert Galluci and North Korean chief negotiator Kim Jong U, the first stage would include a restatement by North Korea of the pledges made in June. The second phase of the process would involve "firm assur-ances" by the United States that North Korea would receive two light-water reactors. Once this stage was completed, North Korea would make permanent its current nuclear freeze, end construction of its 50- and 200-

megawatt reactors, seal its plutonium-reprocessing facility, and pledge to forgo the reprocessing of spent fuel. The final phase of the process was less well defined but reportedly included the dismantling of North Korea's reprocessing facility and Pyongyang's acceptance of special inspections at two suspected waste storage sites [ibid., 9/94, pp. 23, 30–31].

Talks between North Korea and the United States continued in Geneva from September 23 to October 21, 1994, at which time both sides endorsed the **Agreed Framework.** This agreement included the following provisions:

1. The United States would organize an international consortium to provide the DPRK with two 1,000-megawatt light-water reactors by the year 2003.

2. The United States would make arrangements to provide North Korea with up to 500,000 tons of heavy oil annually to offset the energy lost by freezing the North's nuclear program.

3. The dismantling of the DPRK's graphite-moderated reactors and related facilities would be completed when the light-water project was completed.

4. Both sides would store safely the spent fuel from the five-megawatt reactor during the construction of the light-water project, would continue to have the IAEA monitor the spent fuel rods, and would explore options to dispose of the spent fuel in a safe manner that would not involve reprocessing in North Korea.

5. Both sides would move toward full normalization of political and economic relations and would work together for peace and security on a nuclear-free Korean peninsula. Formal assurances to North Korea that the United States would not use or threaten to use nuclear weapons came under this heading.

6. North Korea would remain a party to the NPT and allow implementation of its safeguard agreements [ibid., 1–2/95, pp. 20, 26].

On March 9, 1995, the United States, Japan, and South Korea set up an international consortium—the Korean Peninsula Energy Development Organization—to finance the light-water reactors North Korea would receive under the Agreed Framework. The United Kingdom, Australia, Canada, and New Zealand have joined the consortium since. These reactors are expected to cost over $4 billion, with South Korea reportedly paying roughly 60 percent [ibid., 4/95, pp. 19, 28].

This large **South Korean role** created new obstacles to implementing the accord. On April 20, 1995, North Korea abruptly broke off negotiations with the United States, citing a U.S. proposal to list the two light-water reactors as "South Korean-type models," which would credit South Korea with a major role in the design, manufacture, construction, and financing of the project. On June 13, however, North Korea agreed to accept two South Korean-type reactors from the Consortium that were labeled an "advanced version of a U.S. design." North Korea and the United States also agreed that a U.S. firm would serve as the overall program coordinator for the project [*New York Times*, 6/14/95]. The situation on the Korean peninsula is likely to remain at the forefront of proliferation issues during the General Assembly's 50th Session.

Another issue affecting the NPT extension and review conference was a January 1995 **agreement by Russia to sell Iran two light-water reactors** for its Bushehr nuclear facility and a gas centrifuge uranium-enrichment plant. Under Article IV of the NPT, a non-weapon state that has full-scope IAEA safeguards, Iran among them, is entitled to receive nuclear technology designed for civil use. Washington has objected to the Russian move on the grounds that Iran is a "rogue state," one that not only is supporting international terrorist activities but, despite its membership in the NPT, its acceptance of full-scope safeguards, and public declarations about permitting "anytime, anywhere" IAEA inspections of its nuclear facilities, is also covertly pursuing a nuclear weapons program. Although Washington has acknowledged that the Russian light-water reactors would be of no real use in building weapons, it maintains that they could provide the cover for Teheran's acquisition of other technology and materials useful in a weapons program. The enrichment plant, for its part, could be used in manufacturing highly enriched uranium (HEU) that could, in turn, be used in building a nuclear weapon [*Arms Control Today*, 4/95, p. 20].

Iran contends that it wants an enrichment plant to manufacture low-enriched uranium fuel for its light-water reactors. The country does have abundant supplies of natural uranium and, with such a plant, could produce either low or highly enriched uranium. U.S. officials are concerned that Iran would in fact manufacture HEU from the Russian-supplied enrichment facility or, worse, build a duplicate facility at another site and produce non-safeguarded HEU [*Washington Post*, 4/29/95]. In response to the proposed purchases, President Clinton announced that the United States would ban all trade with Iran. The United States also called on its allies Japan and Germany to limit their economic trade with Teheran [ibid., 5/1/95].

At the summit with President Clinton in May 1995, Russian President Boris Yeltsin stated that Russia would not go through with plans to sell Iran the enrichment plant but would proceed with the sale of nuclear reactors to Iran, pending further study of the issue. The reactor sale will be reviewed by a commission led by U.S. Vice President Al Gore and Russian Prime Minister Viktor Chernomyrdin. Secretary of State Warren Christopher had stated before the summit that, if Russia went through with the sale of the two reactors, the United States would like stringent controls placed on the spent fuel from them [ibid., 5/11/95 and 4/7/95]. How this issue is resolved may have a significant impact on the strength of the non-proliferation regime and the right of NPT non-weapon states to acquire nuclear technology and assistance in the future.

2. Nuclear Arms Control

The second major arms control success during the 1994–95 period was the **entry into force of START I** on December 5, 1994. Ukraine's decision to join the NPT in November ended two years of parliamentary maneuvering over this issue and paved the way for the United States and Russia to begin the ratification process for START II. Although Clinton and Yeltsin had hoped to exchange ratification documents for START II prior to the vote on the NPT's extension, the ongoing conflict in Chechnya and Yeltsin's declining support in the Russian Duma (parliament) prevented this on both sides. Nonetheless, the United States and Russia made further progress on reducing stockpiles of fissile materials for weapons and on increasing the transparency of each side's nuclear weapons program.

The cause of **Ukraine's accession to the NPT** picked up much-needed steam when Leonid Kuchma won election as Ukraine's president on July 10, 1994, and President Clinton quickly reaffirmed his pledge to provide Kiev with $700 million in aid upon Ukrainian ratification of the NPT. On October 5, Kuchma formally requested the Rada, Ukraine's parliament, to approve the NPT. He also sent letters to the United States, Russia, the United Kingdom, and France stating that Ukraine's decision to support the treaty had much to do with the willingness of those states to provide Kiev with multilateral security assurances. In the first week of November, Kuchma received formal pledges from the United States, Russia, and the United Kingdom that the assurances would be provided when Ukraine acceded to the NPT, and France agreed to give Ukraine separate but similar assurances [*Arms Control Reporter*, 12/94, pp. 611.B.850–854].

On November 16, after intense pressure by the United States and Russia, the Rada voted 301–8 to accede to the NPT. The legislators, however, attached six conditions to their vote, including Ukrainian ownership of and control over the nuclear weapons on its soil. This was followed by more lobbying from Washington and Moscow, after which Ukrainian leaders agreed to surrender the warheads and President Clinton announced that the United States would provide Kiev with an additional $200 million in aid as a reward for its accession to the NPT.

The START I treaty entered into force on December 5, when the Presidents of the United States, Russia, Ukraine, Kazakhstan, and Belarus exchanged instruments of ratification at the CSCE summit in Budapest [ibid., pp. 611.B.855–858]. The General Assembly welcomed the long-awaited ratification of this treaty [A/Res/49/75L]. Only three months after the treaty entered into force, the U.S. State Department declared that **Belarus, Kazakhstan, and Ukraine** had deactivated or transferred from their territory nearly half of their approximately 3,300 strategic nuclear warheads—a rate faster than START I's seven-year deadline would have suggested [*Arms Control Today*, 4/95, p. 22].

With the entry into force of START I, the General Assembly urged the United States and Russia to take the necessary steps to "bring **START II** into force at the earliest possible date" [A/Res/49/75L]. The ratification process in the United States got a boost when Senator Jesse Helms, a long-time arms control critic and new Chairman of the Senate Foreign Relations Committee, announced his support for the treaty, but the Foreign Relations Committee concluded its hearings on START II on March 29 without taking any action.

One of the reasons for the delay on the U.S. side was the desire of a number of senators to see whether the Russian Duma would ratify the accord. Russian parliamentary elections are scheduled for the end of 1995, and many members of the Duma view support for START II as a domestic political liability [*Christian Science Monitor*, 3/1/95]. Moreover, some Russian legislators and voters believe that START II imposes an unfair burden on their country, since it cuts sharply Russia's land-based, multiple-warhead ICBMs while preserving much of the U.S. submarine-based missile force.

At the September 1994 Clinton-Yeltsin summit, the two leaders did agree that, as soon as possible after START II is ratified, the United States and Russia will deactivate all strategic nuclear delivery systems to be reduced under the treaty by removing their nuclear warheads or taking other steps to remove them from combat-ready status. Yeltsin estimated that the two sides would complete the deactivation process in two years, seven years sooner than allowed by the treaty [*Arms Control Reporter*, 12/94, pp. 614.B.45–46].

The United States and Russia have also made progress on two other nuclear arms control issues. One is the movement toward a **multilateral cutoff in the production of fissile materials for weapons purposes.** On June 23, 1994, Vice President Gore and Prime Minister Chernomyrdin signed an agreement providing, among other things, that Russia will shut down three plutonium-production reactors at Tomsk-7 and Krasnoyarsk-26 no later than the year 2000 and that, in the interim, Russia will not use any plutonium produced in these reactors for weapons purposes. Verification arrangements were also discussed, including on-site inspections of all U.S. and Russian reactors that have produced plutonium for weapons in the past [*Arms Control Today*, 12/94, p. 21].

This bilateral agreement paved the way for a March 1995 consensus resolution in the Conference on Disarmament (CD) calling for the establishment of an ad hoc committee to negotiate a multilateral fissile materials cutoff convention based on the mandate language in the December 1993 General Assembly consensus resolution on this issue. This followed several months of debate in the CD over the scope of a fissile cutoff accord. The Group of 21 Non-aligned countries (G-21) had rejected earlier drafts of a negotiating mandate, primarily because they did not make an explicit reference to existing stockpiles of fissile materials. Such countries as Pakistan and Egypt insisted that a cutoff include a provision covering any fissile materials that have been produced not only by the nuclear weapon states but by India and Israel as well. Pakistan changed its stance in February after receiving assurances that this issue could be raised during the actual negotiations, and the other Non-aligned states soon followed suit. The ad hoc committee is expected to begin its work at the next CD round, which began in May 1995.

The second area of progress was in **reducing U.S. and former Soviet Union stocks of fissile materials** available for use in weapons. One manifestation of this was the secret U.S. operation, code-named "Project Sapphire," that removed roughly 600 kilograms of HEU from Kazakhstan in January 1995—enough fissile material to make more than two dozen nuclear weapons. Kazakh officials told the United States that their government could not provide sufficient safeguards for the material, which was located at the Ulba fuel fabrication facility in Ust Kamenogorsk. The HEU was flown to the United States and taken to the Y-12 plant in Oak Ridge, Tennessee, where it will be blended down to low-enriched fuel and sold to private companies [ibid., 1–2/95, p. 27].

In another development, President Clinton announced in March 1995 that the United States will remove from the **U.S. nuclear stockpile 200 tons of fissile materials (reportedly 30 tons of plutonium and 170 of HEU) and place them under IAEA safeguards.** "This material," he said, "will never again be used to build nuclear weapons" [ibid.]. The United States has called on Russia and the other nuclear weapon states to take similar action. The 50th General Assembly is sure to push for further reductions in fissile material stockpiles and rapid agreement on a fissile cutoff convention.

3. Nuclear Testing

Over the past two years, the Conference on Disarmament and the General Assembly devoted much of their attention to the negotiations on a **Comprehensive Nuclear Test Ban Treaty (CTBT).** In the course of the past year, all five nuclear weapon states pledged to complete a CTBT by September 1996. The General Assembly restated its conviction that "a comprehensive nuclear test ban treaty is the highest priority measure for the cessation of the nuclear arms race and for the objective of nuclear disarmament" [A/Res/49/69].

The General Assembly also expressed its pleasure at the announcement on September 7 that the Conference on Disarmament had adjourned its 1994 session with a **"rolling text" for a CTBT** [A/Res/49/70]. Although this text revealed lack of agreement on many of the substantive issues that must be resolved before the conclusion of a test ban—among them, the scope of the treaty, when it would enter into force, and the means of verifying compliance—it also indicated that there was consensus on less controversial issues, and it raised the hope that a comprehensive test ban would be concluded sometime in 1996 [see *A Global Agenda: Issues/49*, pp. 118–21].

The rolling text appeared as an appendix to a September 5 report from the ad hoc committee of the Conference on Disarmament. The committee had divided it into three parts reflecting the different degree of support for different provisions [CD/12/73/Rev.1]. Into the first section went nine provisions that had "a certain degree of consensus"—these were, in general, the basic treaty articles, such as whether the treaty will be open to all states for signature before its entry into force. Into the second section went "provisions that need more extensive negotiation"—a group that included certain fundamental issues, like the scope of the treaty; which and how many states would have to sign before the treaty entered into force; and means of verification. The third section listed previously issued documents containing various proposals by a number of CD delegations that had yet to be put into the treaty text or had not been discussed thoroughly [*Arms Control Today*, 10/94, p. 20].

A second sign of progress on the CTBT came on January 30, 1995, when U.S. National Security Advisor Anthony Lake announced that the United States would withdraw its highly controversial proposal to allow an "easy exit" from a test-ban accord after ten years. Lake also announced that the current U.S. moratorium on nuclear testing would be extended until a CTBT entered into force, provided this occurred before September 30, 1996. Washington had originally sought a provision that would have allowed parties to withdraw from the CTBT following a review conference ten years after the treaty entered into force. (Under the terms of that provision, a country electing to withdraw would not be required to provide a formal written statement of "the extraordinary events" it saw as jeopardizing its "supreme national interests," provided it gave 180 days' advance notice.) When the United States first proposed a special CTBT withdrawal provision in August 1994, most CD members, including the other nuclear weapon states, opposed it. The G-21 criticized the U.S. proposal too, calling it a "serious setback to the ongoing negotiations" [ibid., 3/95, pp. 27, 30]. U.S. national security and science advisors, the Department of Energy, and the Arms Control and Disarmament Agency urged Clinton to drop the easy-exit proposal, while the Defense and State departments pressed Clinton to stick with it.

The test-ban negotiations were also marked by several **ongoing disputes, most of them between nuclear weapon states.** One contentious issue was the yield limit above which activity would be banned under the treaty. France, for example, pressed for a yield threshold of over 100 tons, Russia for 10 tons, and the United States for one ton. After the Pentagon pressed Clinton to propose a high-threshold yield in exchange for dropping the easy-exit option, the United States decided not to pursue this issue for the time being [ibid.; *Financial Times*, 1/31/95; *Disarmament Times*, 2/95].

Another hotly debated issue was how to verify a CTBT. The United States proposed a "four pillar" verification regime that would include (1) the collection and exchange of data derived from networks of remote sensors; (2) mandatory on-site inspections; (3) "associated measures" involving the exchange of data among parties; and (4) an international implementing body to coordinate the other three pillars. Russia favored a less extensive, and therefore less costly, system of verification. There was likewise no agreement on what the implementing organization should be. Sweden, for example, has proposed the IAEA as the implementing body, but Australia supports the idea of a new organization located (like the IAEA) in Vienna but dedicated exclusively to a CTBT [*Arms Control Today*, 10/94, p. 20; 3/95, pp. 27, 30].

There was also no consensus on the scope of a test ban or on the number and type of states that would have to ratify the treaty before it entered into force. China continues to insist on the right to conduct peaceful nuclear explosions, while France and the United Kingdom push for the right to conduct safety and reliability tests that "may be authorized in exceptional circumstances." On the issue of entry into force, the rolling text indicates three basic approaches: (1) a specified number of states, including, for example, all nuclear weapon states; (2) all CD members or a specified percentage of them; and (3) all states (or a percentage of the states) that have, or once had, nuclear power stations or reactors. Some of these proposals could hold implementation of the treaty hostage to the vote of a single state, even a non-nuclear weapon state [ibid., 10/94, p. 20].

Finally, despite the U.S. and other CD-member appeals to China to stop all nuclear testing, Beijing conducted three underground nuclear tests during 1994–95. This brings to four the number of tests that China has conducted since the other nuclear weapon states began observing an informal moratorium in September 1992, and the People's Republic is reportedly planning two to four more tests before the end of 1995. Some experts believe that China may be rushing to complete additional tests before September 1996 (the target date for concluding the CTBT) as a means of upgrading its nuclear weapons arsenal. Beijing does not have the capability right now to place multiple nuclear warheads on missiles [*Washington Post*, 5/16/95].

The 50th General Assembly is certain to recommend that CTBT negotiations continue in the Conference on Disarmament and that work continue on verification and compliance measures, perhaps to include sanctions against noncompliant states [A/Res/49/69 and A/Res/49/75E].

4. Chemical and Biological Weapons

As of June 1, 1995, 28 of the 159 signatory states had ratified the **Convention on the Prohibition of the Development, Production, Stockpiling and Use of Chemical Weapons and on Their Destruction** (also known as the Chemical Weapons Convention, or CWC). Among these are France, Germany, Mexico, Norway, Spain, Sweden, and Switzerland. Notably absent are the United States, Russia, the United Kingdom, and China. Sixty-five states must ratify the CWC before it can enter into force.

The ratification of the CWC was delayed in the United States because of difficulties in implementing on-site inspections at some of Russia's former chemical weapons production sites. (A number of steps were taken, however, to implement the **1989 Wyoming Memorandum of Understanding between the United States and Russia**. Under the bilateral verification procedures elaborated there, Russian inspectors may—and did—conduct a trial challenge inspection [at the U.S. Pine Bluff site], and a U.S. team conducted inspections [at Russia's Pochep storage area].)

The U.S. delay in ratifying the CWC was also directly related to reports that Russia had failed to declare some dual-use chemical facilities and that Moscow had not terminated development and production of new chemical weapons. Ratification was delayed in Russia largely out of concern about the cost of destroying the country's considerable stockpile of chemical weapons and the costs associated with implementing the verification procedures [*Arms Control Reporter*, 9/94, p. 704.B.572].

In September 1994, a Russian scientist, Vil Mirzayanov, had charged that Russia was developing a class of **binary chemical weapons** (formed by combining two relatively safe chemicals to produce a toxic agent) nicknamed "Novichok" (newcomer) and ten times more toxic to humans than even the deadly nerve gas VX [*Wall Street Journal*, 9/29/94]. These reports prompted 24 Western nations to protest jointly Russia's refusal to allow inspections of all its chemical factories. The United Kingdom, France, and Germany issued separate protests to Moscow. Russian Prime Minister Chernomyrdin responded by saying that Russia "is not concealing or hiding anything" [*Arms Control Today*, 9/94, p. 29].

In testimony before the Senate Foreign Relations Committee, critics of the CWC cited five treaty-prohibited activities for which there are no technical means for detecting noncompliance: (1) clandestine production facilities, which could be small and easily camouflaged; (2) diversion of common chemicals that could be used as CW precursors; (3) production of "non-classical agents"—chemicals not listed on the CWC schedules but of possible use in chemical weapons; (4) secretly stockpiled chemical weapons, agents, or precursors; and (5) the transfer or receipt of chemical weapons or technology.

Testifying on behalf of the CWC were two high-ranking U.S. officials: the Chairman of the Joint Chiefs of Staff and the Director of the CIA. Ratifying the CWC is in the best interest of the United States without Russia's participation in the accord, they said, arguing that even imperfect verification under the CWC is better than no verification at all. It should be noted that if Russia does not become an original ratifying party to the CWC, it will have no say in the Organization for the Prohibition of Chemical Weapons (OPCW, the convention's oversight body) about procedures for implementing it [*Arms Control Reporter*, 10/94, pp. 704.B.578–580].

The 49th General Assembly also saw a replay of the dispute between developed and developing states over the **continuation of export controls on chemical technologies and products**. At the June 1994 meeting of the CWC Preparatory Commission that is paving the way for the OPCW, the Non-aligned Movement called for an end to the Australia Group's ban on exports of dual-use chemical agents. In a statement issued at the conference, NAM members "called upon all developed countries to adopt measures to promote the transfer of technology, materials, and equipment for peaceful purposes in the chemical field and to remove all the existing unilateral restrictions of a discriminatory nature." The African Group too endorsed the removal of export controls outside the CWC. Members of the Australia Group, responding to their call, pointed out that (1) less than 1 percent of export license requests were refused, and these involved substances that could have assisted a weapons program; (2) developing states have the most to gain from these nonproliferation measures, since they are the ones most likely to be the targets of chemical weapons; and (3) much of the trade in chemicals is between developing states, not between developed and developing countries, as many suggest [ibid., 9/94, pp. 704.B.575–576].

There were important developments in the biological weapons area as well. Negotiations on a **legally binding instrument that will provide the means of verifying the Biological and Toxin Weapons Convention** (BWC, in force since 1975 and ratified by 135 states to date) moved one step closer to completion with the establishment of a Special Committee to study the proposals submitted by the Ad Hoc Group of Governmental Experts' Verification Exercise (VEREX) [see *Issues/49*, pp. 127–28]. The General Assembly welcomed the establishment of this committee [A/Res/49/86]. The instrument that emerges will be submitted for consideration by the parties to the BWC.

During the first Special Committee negotiations, some developing countries made it clear they were not eager to negotiate substantive new measures and sought to focus instead on international cooperation and trade in commercial biotechnology, including the elimination of biological export controls. Favoring a more intrusive BWC verification regime were some of the Western Group, particularly France, Germany, the Netherlands, and, to a lesser extent, Australia and the United Kingdom. The United States, Canada, and Switzerland staked out the middle ground by supporting a legally binding transparency regime.

U.S. representatives, some of them skeptical that the BWC can be verified in any useful way, endorsed the idea of negotiating a **transparency regime that would include off-site measures**—for example, declarations of relevant programs, facilities, and equipment—as well as on-site inspections—for example, informational and short-notice visits to relevant facilities and investigations of unusual disease outbreaks or alleged use of biological weapons. Were the U.S. approach to be adopted, the BWC parties would be required to declare treaty-relevant biological research, development, production, and testing facilities. These declarations would be validated through routine on-site informational visits, supplemented by short-notice challenge inspections [*Arms Control Today*, 4/95, pp. 9–12, and *Arms Control Reporter*, 4/94, pp. 701.B.127–128].

The Special Committee, which adopts its decisions by consensus, must also define lists of BW agents and threshold quantities, incorporate existing and further confidence-building and transparency measures into the regime, and define a program for technical cooperation in the field of biotechnology for peaceful purposes. Also on its agenda is the issue of the number of ratifications required before the protocol enters into force. The hope is to make notable progress on at least some of these issues before the BWC review conference scheduled for late 1996.

Whether the "politically binding" **confidence-building measures** established by the 1986 and 1991 BWC review conferences should be replaced by the **new transparency provisions** is a question the Special Committee will have to consider. Currently, all states have the same reporting requirement. If the verification procedures are increased, however, there is a possibility that some states will not sign on, leading to a two-tiered verification regime [*Arms Control Today*, 4/95, pp. 9–12].

The 50th General Assembly is sure to call on all states that have not yet done so to ratify the CWC at the earliest possible date and to finalize negotiation of verification procedures for the BWC.

5. Transparency in Armaments and Conventional Arms Control

After two years of operation, the **U.N. Register of Conventional Arms** continued to have widespread support, although there were continuing problems about discrepancies in the numbers and types of weapons reported by importing and exporting states. (Many of these discrepancies were due to confusion over reporting requirements and to delays in delivering weapons.) The 49th General Assembly welcomed the fact that (based on data received as of September 30, 1994) over 80 countries had submitted data to the Arms Register on their military imports and exports for the calendar year 1993 [A/Res/49/66]. (The submission of data has an informal deadline of September 30 of the following year.) Among those submitting the 1993 data were the six major arms exporters—the United States, the United Kingdom, Russia, France, China, and Germany—and all the parties to the Conference on Security and Cooperation in Europe (CSCE; as of February 1995, the Organization for Security and Cooperation in Europe, or OSCE). Many Middle East and African countries continued to refrain from submitting data on arms imports and exports. Among these were Israel, Saudi Arabia, Egypt, and South Africa [*Arms Control Reporter*, 4/95, p. 707.B.47].

The General Assembly requested the Secretary-General to convene a group of governmental experts in 1997 to prepare a report on the continuing operation of the Register and to **explore ways of expanding its scope and reporting requirements** [A/Res/49/75C]. Whether and how to expand the Register were subjects much debated at the 49th Session.

Reports by the Conference on Disarmament's **Ad Hoc Committee on Transparency in Armaments** and the **Group of Governmental Experts on the Arms Register** issued in late 1994 summarized the positions of members on two issues related to the scope of the Register: adding new categories of weapons, and adjusting current definitions of weapon categories. The committee was deadlocked over national production and holdings, largely because several states had reversed themselves. Some Western nations that originally opposed submitting data in these categories now voiced their support for it, having found that they need not sacrifice secrecy by providing information on their national holdings— and that increased transparency in this regard may have some deterrent value when it comes to potential adversaries. Many G-21 nations also pushed for the addition of national holdings and production, including the research, development, testing, and evaluation of new weapons. Several Western Group states opposed this measure, however, stating that these weapons programs are not under the operational control of their armed forces. In addition, the Western Group maintained that these programs have little military significance and would add little to the Register [*Arms Control Reporter*, 4/95, p. 707.B.46]. Reversing themselves, China, Cuba, India, and Pakistan now argued against including any data on national holdings and production.

Most members of the expert group were willing to support a compromise pushed by Germany, Japan, and the Netherlands in which states could voluntarily submit data on national holdings and procurement in a standardized form, much as they do for the other Register categories. The United States, the United Kingdom, France, and Canada opposed the compromise, however, fearing it would have the effect of postponing indefinitely an expansion of the Register and would weaken the regime by allowing states to decide the type of information they would share. This last group of countries also wanted the commitment to report national holdings upgraded to the same "request" level as arms transfers.

There was also considerable debate in the expert group about including data on the transfer of high-technology components and on national holdings of weapons of mass destruction. Support for these measures came largely from Egypt, consistent with Cairo's drive to create a nuclear weapon-free zone in the Middle East, and also had the support of the G-21 states, including Cuba, Jordan, and Mexico. The G-21 argued that reporting technology transfers with militarily significant applications was an essential step toward genuine transparency. This same group of states sought to include in the Register as well information on the number, type, location, and movement of all weapons of mass destruction. The Western Group opposed including data about these weapons, however, suggesting that their inclusion in the Register would legitimize the existence and transfer of weapons of mass destruction.

Other proposals discussed by the expert group included lowering the tonnage of warships reported in the Register from 750 to 250 tons, adding ground-to-air missiles, eliminating the current 25-kilometer range threshold for missiles, and splitting the reporting of missiles and their launchers into two subcategories [ibid., 4/95, p. 707.B.47, and *Arms Control Today*, 10/94, pp. 8–13]. Participants in the expert group discussion also debated adding small arms and land mines to the Register. Those in favor said this would make the Arms Register more relevant to regions with low participation and in situations in which the major weapons systems currently covered by the Register are not the main problem, such as conflicts in Africa and Latin America.

The group of governmental experts agreed that the Register had operated satisfactorily during its first two years, and the General Assembly has asked the expert group to submit another report in 1997 on the continuing operation of the Register and its further development [*Arms Control Reporter*, 4/95, p. 707.B.48, and *Arms Control Today*, 10/94]. The ad hoc committee, on the other hand, failed to reach consensus on the Register's performance and, in fact, has yet to agree on whether to recommend reestablishing itself in 1995. Many of the G-21 nations said they would not support reestablishing the ad hoc committee until the Conference on Disarmament agrees to expand the scope of the Register [*Arms Control Reporter*, 4/95, p. 707.B.52]. The 50th General Assembly is sure to return to this issue.

The **new U.S. conventional arms-transfer policy,** unveiled by President Clinton in February 1995, was received with disappointment by many in the arms control community, who found few provisions designed to stem the export of U.S. weapons abroad. One critical element of the new policy is to promote transparency in arms transfers, however, and the United States continues to push for the participation in the U.N. Arms Register of a greater number of member states. The United States also took the lead in efforts to expand the Register to include military holdings and procurement through national production. This, it argued, would provide a more complete picture of the annual change in a nation's military capabilities. And Washington continued its **efforts to establish a successor export-control regime to the Cold War-era Coordinating Committee for Multilateral Export Controls (COCOM).** The administration laid out three goals for the new COCOM: increase transparency in transfers of conventional arms and related technology; establish effective international controls; and promote export restraint, particularly to unstable regions and states that are likely to pose a threat to international peace and security [White House press release, 2/17/95].

The Clinton policy also set five **guidelines for U.S. arms transfers in general:** ensure U.S. military superiority over potential foes; help friends and allies deter aggression and defend themselves; promote regional stability "in areas critical to U.S. interests," while preventing the proliferation of weapons of mass destruction; promote peaceful conflict resolution and arms control, human rights, and democratization; and enhance the ability of the U.S. defense industrial base to meet U.S. needs and maintain long-term superiority at low cost. Once a transfer is approved, the President went on to say, the U.S. government will give the U.S. exporter some active support, including the assignment of diplomatic personnel to assist in the marketing efforts of U.S. companies. The administration also announced that it would drop the U.S. prohibition on sales of advanced arms to ten former Eastern-bloc states: Albania, Bulgaria, the Czech Republic, Estonia, Hungary, Latvia, Lithuania, Poland, Romania, and Slovakia. In sum, said the President, "the United States continues to view transfers of conventional arms as a legitimate instrument of U.S. foreign policy when they enable us to help friends and allies deter aggression, promote regional security, and increase the interoperability of U.S. and allied forces" [*Arms Control Reporter*, 4/95, pp. 707.B.51–52, and White House press release 2/17/95].

III
Economics and Development
By George H. Mitchell Jr.

What's wrong with this picture, and why? Scores of guests from around the world have gathered to celebrate 50 years, 50 weeks, or both, of economic successes, yet most are not smiling. Indeed, most have worried looks on their faces. Given a golden opportunity to demonstrate to the world the real and potential benefits of international economic cooperation, their deliberations have become mired in controversy and ultimately end in mutual recrimination. This was the scene at the 50th annual meeting of the International Monetary Fund and the World Bank at Madrid in October 1994. A few months later, quite a few politicians, especially in the United States, where the recovery from the 1991–92 recession had begun and was still going strong at the end of 1994, seemed to be competing in economic doom-saying, despite the fact that, in normal circumstances, incumbent politicians almost naturally accent the positive and hopeful. And so it was that in the second half of 1994 and well into 1995, economics largely—and starkly in the circumstances—lived up to its reputation as a pessimistic science, one convinced that behind every silver lining is a big, dark cloud.

In Madrid, observers from the global media were puzzled and perhaps dismayed by the subdued, anxious, and irritable celebrants. "By rights, it ought to [have been] quite a party . . . ," wrote one puzzled journalist: "For the first time in several years, the finance ministers and central bankers of the Group of Seven largest industrial countries all have growing economies, with barely a hint of inflation to go with it. . . . Who could ask for more?" [*Financial Times*, 10/1/94]. Wrote another, "It has not been a particularly happy 50th birthday for the International Monetary Fund and the World Bank. For all the show . . . , these are troubled giants" [ibid., 10/7/94].

Troubled or not, the IMF and World Bank were busy—along with many senior economic officials from many governments and the managers of a wide range of international agencies. Economic development officials, for example, were preoccupied with trying to do more with less

IMF + World Bank

105

money. Economic planning officials in many developing countries were figuring how to attract (or repel in some cases) foreign portfolio and direct investment, which together form the nucleus of a new development paradigm. Social welfare officials, especially in developing countries, were trying to cope with the negative by-products of market-based economics. Trade officials were adjusting to the existence of the **World Trade Organization**, negotiating the lowering of cross-border barriers to trade in financial services, and coming to terms with, or drafting the terms of reference of, proliferating regional trading associations. And financial officials were grappling with Mexico's crisis while thinking about how to avert or contain such crises in the future.

1. The World Economy: Retrospect and Prospect[1]

1994: Turnaround!

Major economic forecasting groups, somewhat chagrined in 1992 and 1993 by the stubborn refusal of the world economy to meet their optimistic expectations, were greatly pleased, and no doubt relieved, by 1994's impressive results. At 3.7 percent, real (inflation-adjusted) growth exceeded by nearly a full percentage point a number of cautious predictions, some made as late as mid-1994. The advance was attributed to buoyant economic conditions in North America and the United Kingdom, combined with recoveries in continental Europe and continued strong growth in China and Southeast Asia. Moreover, 1994, besides delivering the most vigorous rate of economic activity in several years, also chalked up inflation results that were, in the words of the IMF, "closer to price stability than seen in three decades."

1995: Bumpy, but . . .

Somewhat surprisingly, except when certain major developments in late 1994 and early 1995 are taken into account, world economic growth in 1995 is expected to be, at 3.8 percent, essentially unchanged from 1994. Although one might have anticipated continued vigorous expansion, considering that neither Japan nor most of Europe contributed substantially to global growth in 1994, 1995 is in fact shaping up as a year of adjustment and correction. As the IMF noted, 1994's pace prompted markets and central banks and recovering countries to raise interest rates. And in December 1994, Mexico's foreign exchange crisis triggered a crisis of confidence among investors holding positions in emerging market countries. Then, in early 1995, foreign exchange markets became quite volatile with

---

1. The principal source for this section was IMF, *World Economic Outlook*, 5/95.

respect to the dollar/yen and dollar/deutsche mark exchange rates, with the sharply depreciating dollar having implications for both Japanese export performance and the willingness of the U.S. Federal Reserve to soften its firm stance even in the face of low inflation and slowing output. Still, the IMF remained cautiously optimistic. "For many industrial countries," the Fund contended, "the strong growth momentum seen recently may . . . suggest some upside potential. . . . And for those developing countries that continue to face substantial demand pressures, a moderation of capital inflows may actually help some countries to prevent overheating and, hence, to sustain a satisfactory growth performance."

1996: A Certain Optimism, a Certain Uneasiness

Looking ahead, at mid-1995, to 1996's growth prospects, two contrasting sentiments were noticeable among analysts and policy-makers. One was optimism that, with adjustments and corrections likely to have been made, with so many fundamental economic factors in good shape, and with Japan and some important European economies on the upside of the business cycle, 1996 could not but be a year of strong growth (4.2 percent, according to the IMF). The other sentiment was anxiety or uneasiness on the part of some observers. Their concern focused mainly on U.S. monetary policy (so aggressive that it might fail to produce a "soft landing," that is, a nonrecessionary cooling of the overheated U.S. economy), Japanese macroeconomic policy generally (too restrictive for too long), and the possible reasons for and implications of Western Europe's stubbornly high unemployment rates during a period of economic recovery. And so it was that the outlook for 1996 increasingly took on the character of a coin-toss having major economic and political implications.

The Group of Seven

The economic prospects of the Group of Seven advanced industrialized nations (G-7)—the United States, Japan, Germany, France, Italy, the United Kingdom, and Canada—continue to serve as a bellwether for world economic expectations generally, even though large economies such as China's and Russia's are not included. In both 1993 and 1994 the rapid growth of three North Atlantic G-7 countries—the United States, the United Kingdom, and Canada—more than offset the poor, mediocre, or relatively slow growth of the other four. Especially disappointing during that period was Japan's inability to resume the respectable, if not impressive, growth rates for which it has been so well known, so admired, and, in some instances, so feared. One most welcome source of optimism, however, has been Germany's quick rebound from the recessionary ef-

Table III-1
World Output, 1992–96

(percentage of annual change)

	1992	1993	1994	1995*	1996*
World	2.0	2.5	3.7	3.8	4.2
Industrial Countries	1.5	1.2	3.1	3.0	3.0
Group of Seven	1.6	1.4	3.1	3.0	2.6
United States	2.3	1.2	3.0	3.0	2.7
Japan	1.1	−0.2	0.6	1.8	3.5
Canada	0.6	2.2	4.5	4.3	2.6
European Union	1.0	−0.4	2.8	3.2	3.1
Germany	2.2	−1.1	2.9	3.2	3.3
France	1.2	−1.0	2.5	3.0	3.0
Italy	0.7	−0.7	2.5	3.0	3.0
United Kingdom	−0.5	2.2	3.8	3.2	2.8
Developing Countries	5.9	6.1	6.3	5.6	6.1
Africa	0.8	0.7	2.7	3.7	5.3
Asia	8.2	8.7	8.6	7.6	7.3
Middle East & Europe	5.5	3.7	0.7	2.9	4.7
Western Hemisphere	2.7	3.2	4.6	2.3	3.7
Countries in Transition	−15.3	−9.2	−9.4	−3.8	3.5
Central & Eastern Europe	−11.4	−6.2	−3.8	0.4	3.5
Excluding Belarus & Ukraine	−9.4	−2.0	2.7	3.6	4.3
Russia	−19.0	−12.0	−15.0	−9.0	4.5
Transcaucasus & Central Asia	−17.6	−11.9	−14.9	−5.7	na

*Projected.
Source: IMF, *World Economic Outlook*, 5/95; Table 1, Table A1; also *OECD Economic Outlook*, 12/94, Annex Table 1.

fects of its costly reunification program. Another has been Canada's sustained expansion since the 1991–93 recession.

United States

Overseen by an ever-watchful Federal Reserve Board, the U.S. economy began to slow in the wake of rapid growth (in excess of 4 percent) in the final quarter of 1994. Although the indications of a cooling process seemed to confirm—especially when combined with occasional suggestions of underlying strength—that the Fed was successfully engineering a soft landing, anxiety about the possibility of an imminent recession rose sharply in May and June 1995, so much so that the Fed was reportedly considering a reduction in interest rates to head off a serious slowdown.

Japan

Japan's poor fourth quarter 1994 showing surprised many forecasters, including those at the IMF, who noted that a sharp fall in private consumption, combined with a steep decline in residential investment, had generated almost a 1 percent contraction in real GDP during that period. The IMF found that although Japanese monetary policy has been supportive of the goal of recovery, the surging exchange value of the yen has significantly increased Japanese imports and promises to decrease Japanese exports in the near-to-medium term. The IMF applauded the Bank of Japan's easing of monetary policy at the end of March 1995. A continued accommodative stance is justified, the Fund said, given the stability of prices, the large output gap, and the excessive strength of the yen.

Germany

Germany's recovery has been stronger than many analysts anticipated. Initially export-led, it evolved into a more broadly based expansion as consumer confidence remained high and business fixed investment strengthened. The IMF approved of the Bundesbank's firm but flexible stance, which, the Fund said, had helped to establish the recovery firmly. Despite upward pressure on the mark, continued strong growth may lead the Bundesbank to tighten in late 1995, the IMF acknowledged. Just the same, moderate to strong growth was expected to continue into 1996.

Other G-7 Economies

Much speculation has focused on the future performance of the economies of the United Kingdom and Canada, which have had two of the best growth rates, among the developed countries. Both expansions have been tied to export success. And both have had to be moderated somewhat by their respective monetary authorities. As a result, both economies may grow at a slightly slower rate in 1995 and a noticeably slower rate in 1996.

The French economy has begun to expand steadily. Business and consumer confidence have risen during the post-recession phase. Monetary policy has supported the recovery. However, France's stubbornly high unemployment rate, still in double digits, has greatly detracted from the sense of relief and optimism that might otherwise prevail. Unemployment may have undermined the presidential candidacy of former Prime Minister Edouard Balladur and boosted the chances of the socialist standard bearer. Conservative Jacques Chirac ultimately won the race to succeed François Mitterrand.

In Italy, political turmoil has had negative spillover effects on the economy, which otherwise might have been on a firm trajectory toward recovery. Growth was vigorous in 1994, due largely to export demand and a resurgence of domestic consumption. Unemployment remained high, however, and confidence in the ability of government to manage the economy effectively has been shaken, at least temporarily.

Newly Industrializing Economies of East Asia

In East and Southeast Asia the principal problem was one of too much growth, not too little, for too long. The challenge, therefore, was to engineer a soft landing, especially in China, where anti-inflation policies slowed growth only slightly and inflation soared to over 20 percent in 1994. China's stabilization effort was expected to be more vigorous and more effective in 1995. South Korea, Malaysia, the Philippines, and Thailand recorded high rates of growth that seemed likely to continue, even though inflationary pressures may, before long, elicit countercyclical measures.

The Transitioning Economies of Eastern Europe and the Former Soviet Republics

According to the IMF, most countries in transition have now embarked on serious stabilization and reform efforts. Those that undertook reform efforts sooner—Poland, the Czech Republic, and the Baltic states, for example—have begun to record increasingly positive growth rates. Those that postponed reform measures have either just begun to bottom out or are still declining under the weight of inevitable adjustment measures. Hungary continues to struggle, as does Russia. The latter's prospects brightened, however, even as its performance during the second half of 1994 weakened, said a number of analysts, including some influential ones at the IMF, because, appearances notwithstanding, Russia has turned the corner and—Russian politics permitting—is destined to emerge as an important market economy.

Other Developing Regions[2]

The economic prospects of Western Hemisphere developing countries worsened as a result of a "contagion effect" created by Mexico's financial crisis. Mexico, of course, suffered a direct and serious setback. However, by June 1995 a fairly rapid return to stability seemed likely. Chile, which was virtually unaffected by the "Mexican effect," is expected to enjoy continued solid growth as it anticipates membership in the North American Free Trade Agreement. Brazil, which has embarked on a major market reform program, also is expected to record some successes, especially in its fight against inflation. Argentina, apparently, may suffer more than any other large Latin American economy because of the alleged resemblance, in investor eyes, of its economy's structure to Mexico's.

Africa's prospects are considered bright, relative to the continent's experience during the 1980s. The IMF attributes the improvement to the

---

2. See also World Bank, *Global Economic Prospects and the Developing Countries*, 4/95.

adoption of structural reforms and stabilization programs in a number of countries, including Ghana. Among the larger sub-Saharan economies, however, disappointment is the byword. The Zairean economy has been crushed by political turmoil. Nigeria's economy has suffered for the same reason, as have others. And South Africa, while its economic prospects are greatly promising, is shrouded in uncertainty as to precisely when the constellation of political, economic, and social conditions necessary for sustained economic growth will emerge.

Developing countries of the Middle East and southern Europe experienced rather slow growth (0.75 percent) in 1994. A major contributor was a severe financial crisis in Turkey during the first half of 1994. Turkey's prospects remained uncertain at mid-1995. The oil-exporting countries in the area were expected to contribute to stronger regional growth in 1995, if oil prices firmed as expected. The dollar's decline might have adverse implications, however, since international oil transactions are denominated in that currency.

2. Economic Development

Loans and Grants to Developing Countries[3]

Measured in 1992 dollars and exchange rates, total net resource flows to developing countries increased in 1993 by 10.5 percent, or $18 billion, to $171 billion. In 1993 dollars the increase was $12 billion and the total $167 billion. Of the latter amount, $42 billion came from private or nonofficial sources: $35 billion in foreign direct investment and $7 billion in private flows on market terms. Private flows—which, when bank loans are included, have since 1992 exceeded official flows, and which constitute the core of what the Development Assistance Committee of the Organization for Economic Cooperation and Development (OECD) has labeled "the new development paradigm"—are discussed in greater detail in Section 5 below.

At 1992 prices and exchange rates, **official development finance (ODF)** declined in 1993—though marginally—for a third consecutive year, to $69.9 billion from $70.4 billion in 1992. In 1993 dollars the total was $68.5 billion. The drop was attributable mainly to cutbacks in foreign aid budgets by several donor governments under economic or political pressure, or both, to reduce budgetary outlays. Bilateral aid fell sharply, although multilateral aid actually increased. And while private flows compensated to a large extent for the reductions in official financial support for economic development, differences in distribution and impact could

---

3. Unless otherwise noted, material in this section is drawn from the OECD Development Assistance Committee's (DAC) *Development Co-operation, 1994.*

be observed. Sub-Saharan Africa, specifically, suffered because of its relatively greater dependence on ODF and its relative unattractiveness to private flows. On a more positive note, 62 percent of ODF in 1993 took the form of grants, which by definition do not increase recipients' debt load and debt-servicing obligations.

Official development assistance (ODA)—which, as the principal component of ODF, refers to grants or loans that are undertaken by the official sector at concessional financial terms, with the promotion of economic development and welfare as the main objective—fell by an unexpectedly steep 8 percent in current dollars and 6 percent in constant (1992) dollars between 1992 and 1993. Among the reasons cited were recessionary influences in donor countries, budget cutbacks, and conditions in some recipient countries that thwarted some flows. The ODA of the Development Assistance Committee (DAC) members as a percent of GNP fell in 1993 to 0.30 percent—the lowest level in two decades—from 0.33 percent the previous year. While the DAC was optimistic that the change was not indicative of a downward trend, political events in the United States in late 1994 and early 1995, discussed below, suggested otherwise. The largest donors in dollar terms in 1993 were Japan, at about $11 billion, and the United States, at about $9.5 billion. They were followed principally by France ($8 billion) and Germany ($7 billion). Once again four European countries—the Netherlands, Denmark, Norway, and Sweden—were at or above the U.N.'s target of 0.7 percent of GNP. Eight countries, led by France, were at or above the OECD/DAC's 1992 average of 0.33 percent. The United States, at 0.15 percent, ranked lowest among the 21 DAC members.

Stretching Shrinking Development Dollars: The "Best Practice" Norm

According to the new DAC Chairman, James H. Michel, who has succeeded Alexander R. Love, both bilateral and multilateral donors have, for various reasons, focused increasingly on **"aid effectiveness"** and **"development results."** Aid effectiveness, Michel noted, was the theme of the Development Committee of the International Monetary Fund and the World Bank at its October 1994 meeting. One of the most pressing reasons for undertaking to make development assistance more efficient and effective is the shrinkage of available official development resources. In short, it is imperative that development agencies, programs, and personnel do more with less. Other reasons include a recognition that it is not reasonable to deal with complex disasters in a reactive manner; the growing demands by parliaments, the media, and the public for the demonstration of tangible results from aid; and a long overdue desire to capture and apply the "lessons" of "successful" development. It is with respect to the

Table III-2
Selected Overseas Development Assistance Indicators

A. Sources of ODA, 1993

Country	US$ amount (billions)	Percent of GNP
Japan	11.26	0.26
United States	9.72	0.15
France	7.92	0.63
Germany	6.95	0.37
Italy .	3.04	0.31
United Kingdom	2.91	0.31
Netherlands	2.52	0.82
Canada	2.37	0.45
Sweden	1.77	0.96
Denmark	1.34	1.03
Spain	1.21	0.25
Norway	1.01	1.01

B. Geographical Distribution of ODA in 1982–83 and 1992–93
(percentage of total ODA*)

Period	Sub-Saharan Africa	Oceania	Asia	North Africa and Middle East	Latin America and Caribbean	Southern Europe
1982–83	27.9	3.5	33.3	21.4	11.7	2.2
1992–93	37.3	3.0	29.4	12.3	11.4	6.3

*Including forgiveness of certain export credit and/or military non-ODA debt.
Source: OECD, Development Assistance Committee (DAC), *Development Co-operation, 1994;* Chart IV-1 and Table 39.

latter that the term "best practice" has come into common use among development agencies. As the DAC report observes, it is "through evaluation of both successes and failures [that] valuable information is obtained which can be fed back to planners and managers to improve future operations."

Market-Driven, but Flexible, Development: The New Paradigm

According to Michel, while the end of the Cold War regrettably did not produce a windfall of resources for economic development, it did allow—if it did not produce—a greater convergence of views between industrialized and developing countries about such "basic" issues as political and economic stability, good governance, popular participation, investing in people, reliance on market forces, and concern for the environment. This set of values, combined with greater accommodation of differences among cultures and societies, has created a "new paradigm" or model of economic development. In this new philosophical framework, "Distinctions between East and West, North and South, donor and recipient should become less significant. . . ." It is envisioned that developing countries' political will, institutional capability, and public support for development will combine with coherent and coordinated policies of industrialized countries to transform underdeveloped areas of the world.

This new paradigm came under close scrutiny in the wake of Mexico's December 1994 foreign exchange crisis. As a result of the crisis, the North-South consensus underpinning the new development paradigm was shattered, although it may one day be reestablished. It might be said that contemporary international economic development history has become divided into two periods—Before Mexico and After Mexico.

Before the Mexican crisis, conventional wisdom held that developing countries could accelerate their rate of economic growth simply by relaxing trade and capital controls, launching privatization schemes, and creating at least semisophisticated securities markets. Foreign investors—both portfolio and direct—would rush into the new market seeking relatively high returns, even at relatively high risk. Rapid growth would follow, assuring high returns and perhaps less risk for future investors. The capital-importing country would undergo a dramatic economic and perhaps even social transformation, ultimately joining the ranks of newly industrializing, if not fully developed, economies.

After Mexico there were a number of interpretations of the event's meaning. Many in the developing world felt that their worst suspicions of foreign investors had been confirmed. Many observers in developed countries, however, blamed the Mexican government. Others directed criticism at the U.S. government and the International Monetary Fund. Six months after the crisis began, developing countries, as discussed in Section 5 below, remain wary of foreign portfolio investors in particular. The Mexican government has stood behind its promise to make adjustments, and it is beginning to reap some rewards. And, as discussed in Section 4 below, the United States and the IMF have reached basic agreement concerning the management of future Mexico-style crises.

External Debt

The "end" of the 1980s international debt crisis brought an end neither to the development crises facing many less- and least-developed countries, nor—happily—to the analysis of such countries' plight and possible escape routes. For example, in August 1994 the U.N. Secretary-General issued a report on the developing country debt situation as of mid-1994 [A/49/338, 8/26/94]. The report drew attention to the fact that between 64 and 72 countries still face a debt crisis, even though progress, mainly in Latin America, caused aggregate debt indicators to improve significantly during the past decade or so. "In Africa," the report noted, ". . . the situation . . . is considerably worse than in the early 1980s. Indeed, payment arrears of Africa continue to soar."

"It is in no one's benefit," the report continued, "if the situation drags on." What is necessary is for all debt-crisis countries to be helped by the international community onto a definitive reform track to achieve a critical mass of debt reduction that would restore debt-servicing capacity, strengthen the confidence of domestic and international investors, and induce a positive new inflow of resources.

World Summit for Social Development

Leaders from 117 countries met in Copenhagen, Denmark, March 6–12, 1995, at a World Summit for Social Development. Known variously as the Poverty Summit or the Social Summit, the conference was the first time that the international community gathered to express a clear commitment to eradicating the causes and consequences of absolute poverty [UNDP *Update*, 2/13/95]. At the meeting a political consensus was reached in support of ending global poverty, lessening joblessness, and promoting social integration. The resulting **Copenhagen Declaration and Programme of Action,** though nonbinding on governments, is expected to help guide concerned governments in creating more socially equitable and just societies. The Declaration and Programme include calls to eradicate poverty, increase ODA, reduce or cancel debts to poorer nations, strive to reach a foreign aid spending target of 0.7 percent of GNP, allocate 20 percent of ODA to basic social programs (as part of a "20:20 compact," developing countries would allot the same percentage of their budgets to such programs as well), promote gender equality, improve international and regional cooperation, and fight illiteracy [ibid., 3/27/95].

UNCTAD IX/Africa 1996

At the conclusion of its two-week session on March 31, 1995, the Trade and Development Board reported the adoption of the theme "promoting growth and sustainable development in a globalizing and liberalizing world economy" for the **ninth session of the U.N. Conference on Trade and Development (UNCTAD IX),** which will be held in Africa in 1996. According to UNCTAD, the conference will examine that theme with a view toward maximizing the development impact of globalization and liberalization on the world economy while minimizing the risks of marginalization and instability. Four topics will receive special attention: development policies and strategies in an increasingly interdependent world economy in the 1990s and beyond; promoting international trade as an instrument for development in the post-Uruguay Round world; promoting enterprise development and competitiveness in developing countries and countries in transition; and UNCTAD's future work.

Coordination of U.N. Development Policy and Programs

On June 27, 1994, Secretary-General Boutros Boutros-Ghali designated the Administrator of the U.N. Development Programme, James Gustave Speth, to assist the Secretary-General in improving the coordination of U.N. operational activities for development. The Secretary-General said he decided to act after following with interest the deliberation of the Economic and Social Council (ECOSOC) concerning the need to increase the effectiveness of U.N. development and international economic cooperation operations. The Secretary-General asked Speth, who is the U.N.'s highest ranking American, to pay special attention to ensuring policy coherence and enhancing coordination with the United Nations itself, especially among Headquarters departments, the regional commissions, and the funds and programs of the United Nations [ibid., 8/15/95].

Separately, the Group of 77, speaking for 132 developing-country members of the United Nations, issued a statement of support for UNCTAD as "the sole entity in the U.N. system that deals with development questions in a comprehensive manner." In its February 22, 1995 declaration, the G-77 stated that developing countries had received enormous assistance from UNCTAD since its inception, and that UNCTAD still had the central role of assuming responsibility for working out coherent approaches to development problems, given its expertise and the inputs drawn from governments, the private sector, and elsewhere. UNCTAD, the group said, should be given the opportunity and the resources to play its full role and must be a permanent feature of the U.N. system.

Untying Aid

In 1992 members of the DAC and participants in the OECD-based Arrangements on Officially-Supported Export Credits agreed to strengthen restrictions on the use of tied aid—that is, economic development assistance that is conditional on procurement in the donor country. Since the introduction of the new measures ("the Helsinki Package"), there has, according to the DAC, been "a dramatic shift" in the pattern of notifications by donor governments. A "steep rise" has been observed in the proportion of untied aid credits in notifications. To the degree that donor governments are not evading the Helsinki disciplines—or, in other words, that aid notified as untied is exactly that—these notifications suggest that those disciplines or guidelines are working.

Dramatic Developments in U.S. Politics

The mid-term congressional elections in the United States brought an unexpectedly dramatic shift in the balance of power between the Democratic and Republican parties and, simultaneously, in the balance of emphasis between domestic and international concerns in U.S. public policy. The Democrats lost control of the House of Representatives for the first time in 40 years. They also lost control of the Senate, something they had regained in 1986 after losing in 1980. Of course, a Democrat, President Clinton, remained at the head of the Executive Branch. However, it was immediately evident, given the scope of the Republican victory, that Clinton would be greatly constrained in his ability to adopt domestic and even foreign policies disliked by the Republicans in Congress.

Although the Republicans' 1994 platform, known as the **Contract with America,** focused mainly on domestic concerns, it broadly implied that the level and scope of U.S. international activity would be reduced, especially with respect to U.N. peacekeeping and other operations, and with respect to international economic development assistance or foreign aid. Both of these prospects generated considerable anxiety among both foreign and domestic supporters of U.S. international leadership. President Clinton vowed to maintain, to the best of his ability, the capability of the U.S. government to influence both political and economic developments abroad. But the undeniable weakness of his position vis-à-vis Congress was a source of consternation for all internationalists.

For example, the Administrator of the U.N. Development Programme, James Gustave Speth, speaking in New York in March 1995, reminded his American audience that trade and private investment are not sufficient to ensure economic development. "The policies the U.S. adopts today . . . with regard to ODA," he said, "are defining decisions for the United States" [Address, Council on Foreign Relations, New York, 3/22/95]. And following the May 1995 DAC meeting in Paris, Chairman Michel, speaking for the Committee, expressed support for the Clinton administration's efforts to protect the U.S. foreign aid budget and expressed deep concern that cuts in U.S. foreign aid could seriously jeopardize international economic development efforts. A Japanese delegate urged other industrialized-country governments not to give in to "donor fatigue" [*Financial Times*, 5/5/95].

Nevertheless, in early June 1995 both the House of Representatives and the Senate prepared to confront the President with legislation implying deep reductions in U.S. peacekeeping and international development programs. Whether the President would be in a position to force modifications in the legislation remained uncertain.

Promoting Sustainable Development: The View from the DAC

The importance of the role of donor countries, the largest of which are members of the OECD's Development Assistance Committee, or DAC, in promoting sustainable development generally and the goals and objectives of Agenda 21 (adopted at the 1992 U.N. Conference on Environment and Development) probably cannot be exaggerated. DAC members have committed themselves to comply with the **Forest Principles** and the **Conventions on Climate Change, Biological Diversity, and Desertification.** To this end they have undertaken to cooperate with the **U.N. Commission on Sustainable Development.** The Committee maintains a focus on the all-important "new and additional financial resources" issue and plays a key role in modifying approaches to development cooperation to make them more compatible with the imperatives of sustainability. While helping donor countries better understand the challenge of sustainable development, the DAC also attempts to enhance developing countries' capacities in environmental areas.

Infrastructure for Development

The World Bank, in its *World Development Report 1994*, focused on the infrastructure needs of developing countries. While applauding a dramatic increase in infrastructure services in developing countries since about 1980, the Bank observed that a billion people in the developing world still lack access to clean water and nearly two billion lack sanitation. Coping with future challenges with respect to infrastructure—facilities for transport, power, water, sanitation, telecommunications, and irrigation—will require, the Bank maintained, not only plotting needed investments but tackling inefficiency and waste and responding more effectively to user demand. The Bank's principal recommendations for making infrastructural investments more efficient and effective include the wider application of commercial principles to service providers, the broader use of competition, and the increased involvement of users where commercial and competitive behavior is constrained.

Coping with the By-Products of Structural Adjustment and Market-Based Economics

As economic liberalization has become an increasingly irresistible force in national and international economic thinking and planning, many state and nonstate actors have become increasingly concerned about the economic and social consequences of structural adjustment and market-based economics for the most vulnerable people and communities in liberalizing countries. This concern, already substantial before, was intensified after the Mexican economic crisis of December 1994. As discussed in Section 5 below, a recurrent theme in the aftermath of the Mexican crisis has been the two-edged nature of foreign portfolio investment and the consequent need for capital-importing states to be aware of their vulnerability to rapid and substantial outflows of foreign portfolio investment, sometimes sparked by "irrational" beliefs on the part of foreign portfolio investors.

In anticipation of the World Summit for Social Development, the **U.N. Research Institute for Social Development** hosted, in January 1995, a three-day seminar to debate the challenges posed by global free market reforms and the implications of economic restructuring for social policy. In a statement [SOC/4325], the Institute noted the arguments of critics and defenders of structural adjustment and market-oriented reforms generally. "Officials from developing countries and non-governmental organizations in particular have criticized structural adjustment programs for undermining social policies on health, housing, unemployment and poverty," the explanatory statement began. "They have often argued that the leading international financial agencies and development organizations in the industrialized world have forced inappropriate programmes on countries in exchange for debt relief. Advocates of free market reforms, on the other hand, have tended to blame individual governments for their own failures to alleviate poverty, noting that the amount of foreign aid and debt relief accorded a given nation does not correlate historically with either successful economic development or effective social relief programmes." Looking toward a solution, the Institute's Director, Dharam Ghai, said: "It is clear that a reversion to past policies cannot provide an answer to these problems, so we must create a new set of institutions that are compatible with both free markets and social welfare."

Separately, UNCTAD, while expressing firm support for structural adjustment as a viable means for developing countries to remain competitive as the world economy becomes more global and trade liberalization continues, recommended that developing countries adopt a systematic and open approach to the process and that developed countries, in taking account of the implications of their policies for developing countries, "create substantial new room for expansion of production and trade in developing countries and countries in transition in sectors where [such countries] have gained a comparative advantage" [TAD/1784, 4/6/95].

World Labor Report/1995

The consequences of economic reform for employment and social welfare also figure prominently in the **International Labour Organisation's (ILO)** eighth annual *World Labor Report*. In a chapter called "Privatization, Employment and Social Protection," the report notes that, worldwide, the pace of privatization activity increased dramatically between 1990 and 1995, and especially so in those developing countries where state-owned enterprises once played an important role in the national economy. According to the report, the impact of privatization on employment has proven very difficult to measure, while its impact on social protection depends on a number of particulars, including whether workers remain in employment with a privatized company or are retrenched and the nature of the social security schemes that cover those who are still employed after the privatization process. On balance, the report observes, workers' social protection has tended to deteriorate as a result of privatization, but their losses have been offset to some degree by wages that have tended to rise.

The report addresses other major contemporary employment issues as well. One is the problems and prospects for older workers as the world's population, especially in the industrialized countries, ages faster than it grows. Although population aging may be viewed as progress of a sort—it is, after all, a sign of prosperity and of great social achievement; and it is not unreasonable to expect that societies may benefit from the accumulated experience and skills, and maybe even the wisdom, of older workers—there is still ample basis for economic, social, and political apprehension. "A major concern," the report states, "is the increasing old-age dependency on the economically active population. . . . Some observers are alarmed [that] this could lead to inter-generational conflict . . . , greater migratory movements or . . . increasing relocation of industries to countries with an abundant younger labor force."

A second issue is changing relationships between public authorities and other economic actors. The report's analysis starts with the premise that even though it is theoretically possible to imagine that governments could leave the conduct of industrial relations to workers and employers, it is, in practical terms, impossible for them to do so. In such circumstances there are two distinct dangers: one is that government will play too small and the other that government will play too large a role. The developed countries seem to tend toward the former risk while the developing countries tend toward the latter.

Another issue discussed at some length is the timely and important one of retraining workers displaced as a result of globalization, liberalization, and technical advances—three factors that in recent years have brought dramatic and transforming change to production and marketing activities in almost every country. According to the ILO report, displaced workers are those with a stable employment history who have been laid off with little chance of being recalled to jobs with their former employer or even in their old industry. While such workers may be relatively young and productive, there may be no jobs to match their skills in a rapidly evolving economy. The challenge for government and business is to retrain and redeploy such workers so as to avoid wasting their competence, abilities, and productivity. Workers, of course, seek to prevent being laid off, to achieve career advancement when they are employed, and to get a new job if unemployed. Yet the costs and complexities associated with retraining are often staggering, and changes in occupational demand continue even as retraining takes place. Three models of retraining have been identified: the Japanese (within the enterprise), the Swedish/German (under a hierarchical institutional structure), and the American (ad hoc). All must grapple with the high costs of retooling workers, however. And, in this regard, certain solutions have been offered. One is for the financing to be done independent of the provision of training. Another is performance-based contracting, under which training institutions are compensated according to completion and placement rates of trainees.

3. Trade and the Trading System

International Trade 1994

The **World Trade Organization (WTO)**, which came into being as expected in January 1995, reported in April that the volume of world trade increased 9 percent in 1994, the largest annual increase since 1976. The value of world trade in goods rose 12 percent, reaching the $4 trillion level for the first time and marking a sharp reversal of 1993's 0.8 percent decline. The WTO attributed 1994's rapid growth to a sharp economic recovery in Western Europe and continuing expansion of trade in Asia, North America, and Latin America [AFX News, 4/4/95]. More specifically, six East Asian countries—Hong Kong, Malaysia, Singapore, South Korea, Taiwan, and Thailand—recorded a combined export growth rate of 15 percent. Western Europe's exports increased by 9 percent, compared to 1.5 percent in 1993.

Table III-3
World Trade, 1990–94

(annual percentage change in export volumes)

	1990	1991	1992	1993	1994
World	4.5	2.9	5.1	3.8	9.4
Developed Economies	5.4	2.8	4.2	1.5	8.6
United States	7.3	7.6	7.4	4.6	11.4
Japan	5.8	2.4	1.6	−1.1	1.0
Germany	2.2	−1.7	0.6	−6.0	8.9
Developing Economies	6.2	7.1	9.6	9.0	10.4
Africa	6.5	2.3	1.0	4.2	0.1
Asia	7.8	12.8	12.3	11.0	13.4
Western Hemisphere	6.8	4.3	6.2	8.9	9.4

Source: IMF, *World Economic Outlook*, 5/95; Tables A22, A23, A24.

The International Trading System

WTO Report on Regionalism and Trade

In April 1995 the Secretariat of the newly established World Trade Organization released a study concerning the implications of proliferating regional economic arrangements for the world trading system [WTO, "Regionalism and the World Trading System," Geneva, 4/95]. The study considered (1) whether postwar regional integration agreements have tended to complement or undermine the objectives of the world trading system, and (2) whether the WTO's rules and procedures are equal to the task of ensuring that regional and multilateral approaches to integration are mutually supportive. The report concluded in these respects that regional and multilateral integration initiatives are complements rather than alternatives in the pursuit of more liberal and open trade, but that the multilateral rules concerning regional integration—especially Article XXIV of the General Agreement on Tariffs and Trade—have rarely been enforced. The report recommends, among other things, an improved ex ante examination process, clarification and strengthening of the rules, and improved transparency and surveillance.

Developing Countries and the Uruguay Round

In late 1995, UNCTAD released a pessimistic assessment of the Uruguay Round agreements from a developing country standpoint [Manuel R. Agosin, "Developing Countries and the Uruguay Round: An Evaluation and Prospects for the Future," *UNCTAD Bulletin* 29, 11–12/94]. In the opinion of the analyst, "The results of the Uruguay Round do not represent a good deal for developing countries." The evaluation found the Uruguay Round result deficient in several areas, including market access, safeguards, and (potentially) dispute settlement.

Strengthening International Organizations in the Area of Multilateral Trade

In its Resolution 48/54 [12/10/93], the General Assembly asked the Secretary-General to prepare an updated report concerning institutional developments related to the strengthening of international organizations in the area of multilateral trade. In September 1994 the Secretary-General recommended, in "Strengthening International Organization in the Area of Multilateral Trade" [A/49/363, 9/6/94], that "Existing *de facto* co-operation arrangements between the United Nations and GATT should be strengthened to reflect the new context created by the establishment of the WTO." He also recommended that cooperation arrangements between UNCTAD and WTO be enhanced.

Japan, the United States, the European Union, and the WTO

In late spring 1995 a simmering dispute between the United States and Japan concerning the latter's import treatment of foreign-origin autos and auto parts threatened to erupt into a trade war. As threats of retaliation against Japan for refusing to concede to U.S. demands for market-access assurances escalated into a U.S. decision to impose about $6 billion in punitive tariffs on Japanese luxury automobiles exported to the United States, expressions of grave concern about the direction of international trade relations and the fate of the fledgling WTO were heard around the world, though especially in the European Union and at the Geneva head-quarters of the WTO. The EU expressed anxiety that a bilateral U.S.-Japan settlement would operate to the detriment of European automakers. The WTO and its supporters, on their part, feared that any WTO ruling concerning the dispute might be ignored by one or both of the parties, effectively smothering the WTO in its infancy [*New York Times*, 6/14/95]. As of mid-June, bilateral consultations between Japan and the United States, under WTO auspices, were continuing, although prospects for an agreement were dim. But on June 28, just hours before the U.S. sanctions were to take effect, U.S. and Japanese negotiators announced that a compromise had been reached.

U.N. International Symposium on Trade Efficiency

In connection with a trade-efficiency initiative launched in 1992 at UNC-TAD VIII, some 700 delegates from 138 countries participated in a seminar on trade efficiency at Columbus, Ohio, October 17–21, 1994. The symposium was part of a larger **World Summit on Trade Efficiency**, involving a private sector-focused Global Executives Trade Summit, a Global Summit for Mayors, and a World Trade Efficiency and Technology Exhibition. The symposium was opened by Secretary-General Boutros-Ghali and closed by U.S. Commerce Secretary Ron Brown. The symposium adopted the Columbus Ministerial Declaration on Trade Efficiency, which calls for measures to increase efficiency in international trade, reduce transaction costs and barriers, and improve the participation of poorer countries in rapidly expanding trade and communications networks [TAD/1769, 10/24/94].

4. International Monetary Relations

The International Monetary Fund's 51st year got off to an inauspicious start as the 50th anniversary celebrations, held in Madrid, Spain, were marked by controversies and ended in open disagreement between and among major developed and developing-country members. Then, about three months later, in December 1994, things got worse. The Mexican peso, freed by the Mexican government, lost 40 percent of its value against the U.S. dollar in a matter of two weeks or less. A very large rescue package was assembled, though not without substantial domestic and international controversy, by the United States and the IMF.

The Mexican crisis forced the IMF and its leading members, the United States and the European Union, to prepare better for future "Mexicos." Media reports in the spring of 1995 declared that multilateral agreement was near with respect to establishing improved early warning systems, surveillance mechanisms with "teeth," and an emergency credit line on which the Fund could draw in emergencies [*Financial Times*, 4/26/95, 4/27/95; *Boston Globe*, 6/11/95].

The bracing challenges to international monetary management not only spilled over into the new year, they seemed to multiply. Between January and April 1995, foreign exchange markets were roiled by market shifts in the dollar/yen and dollar/deutsche mark exchange rates. The dollar declined by 17 percent against the Japanese currency and 10 percent against the German currency. And the resulting turmoil and implications for trade flows and macroeconomic policies led to mutual recriminations among the principal states involved. The IMF declined to enter the fray directly, preferring instead to find all parties, plus market speculators, at fault to some degree. Japan should ease monetary policy, the Fund said, while the United States should tighten. Apparently neither followed the Fund's advice.

Separately, the European Union recorded a roller-coaster-style ride of downs and ups in connection with its ambitious plan for **economic and monetary union (EMU),** including eventual adoption of a single European currency to be known as either the ecu as France prefers or the franken as Germany prefers, or neither as the United Kingdom prefers.

5. Foreign Portfolio Investors, Transnational Corporations, and the Global Economy

As mentioned in Section 2 above, private flows have exceeded official flows to developing countries and helped generate a "new development paradigm," even if that paradigm may not have survived the Mexican crisis. As has been widely reported, total private capital flows to developing countries almost quadrupled between 1990 and 1993. Among private capital flows, foreign portfolio investment or FPI (which involves the purchase of financial instruments offered for sale by host-country firms or agencies) was, at least until the Mexican crisis of December 1994, increasing at a much faster rate than foreign direct investment or FDI (which involves the establishment of production facilities in the host country). However, as described below, foreign direct investment has itself resumed a very respectable rate of increase, while foreign portfolio investment slowed noticeably before, and considerably after, the Mexican crisis. In April 1995 a new Washington-based think tank, the Institute for International Finance, predicted that net private sector capital inflows to Latin America would total just $1.3 billion in 1995, compared with more than $60 billion in 1994 and more than $75 billion in 1993 [*Financial Times*, 4/21/95].

Foreign Portfolio Investors in the World Economy: Saviors, Swindlers, or Simply Unsentimental Speculators?

The Mexican foreign exchange crisis inflicted substantial losses on foreign-owned portfolio and direct investments in Mexico. Severely "burned" investors either abandoned Mexico entirely or postponed investment plans indefinitely. Deprived of anticipated inflows of investment-related foreign exchange, the Mexican economy went into a tailspin. An international rescue effort was mounted, led by the U.S. government, which was concerned not only about U.S. investors' losses and future behavior but the rather large amount of political capital invested in Mexico by two U.S. administrations, one Republican and one Democratic. The Mexican government adopted a severe austerity program in an effort to slow the peso's free-fall and the outflow of both foreign and domestic capital seeking safe havens abroad. Instead of heading upward on the development escalator, Mexico was suddenly and rapidly heading downward.

Mexico's rise and fall prompted many observers in developing countries to change their view of foreign portfolio investors from saviors to swindlers. This impression was verified, in the eyes of quite a few developing-country commentators, when foreign portfolio investors began, in the wake of the Mexican crisis, to withdraw their investments not only from Mexico but also from other Latin American developing countries with economic situations quite unlike Mexico's.

The U.S.-IMF rescue plan also attracted a fair amount of criticism in U.S. congressional and public opinion and in the European Union. Many critics shared the view that the foreign portfolio investors involved in Mexico were swindlers. The United States and IMF held to the view, and eventually pressed it with success on the world's major economic state-actors, that foreign investors are neither saviors nor swindlers but simply unsentimental speculators responding to the various forces that move markets. Their investments may be useful to recipient countries, but the investors did not invest for humanitarian purposes and cannot be expected to maintain their positions in the face of disadvantageous conditions, no matter how "irrational" the forces that created those conditions.

It appears, therefore, that the Mexican crisis may represent less a change in development paradigm than in states' appreciation of the vagaries of foreign portfolio investment in particular. As UNCTAD noted in its "Trends in Foreign Direct Investment":

> Portfolio equity investment flows are typically of a more speculative nature and respond quickly to higher returns offered elsewhere and to higher risks in the host economy as perceived by foreign investors. As a result, portfolio equity investment tends to be more unstable than FDI and reacts faster to transient financial shocks. . . .

Or, as the IMF noted with great understatement in its May 1995 *World Economic Outlook*, "The surges in capital flows to developing countries have complicated policymaking. . . ."

Transnational Corporations in the World Economy: Trends in Foreign Direct Investment[4]

After falling by 4 percent between 1991 and 1992, total outflows of foreign direct investment from all source-countries rose by a respectable 5 percent to $193 billion in 1993 and are expected to have increased again in 1994, by 6 percent to $204 billion. "The FDI recession of 1991–1992," UNCTAD declared, "has ended." The recovery in outflows was concentrated in the United Kingdom and the United States, however. French, Japanese, and German outflows continued to decline in 1993, although all except German outflows were expected to be positive in 1994.

As usual, developed countries were not only the principal exporters but also the principal importers of foreign direct investment. Developed countries took in $107 billion, or 58 percent, of total inflows of FDI in 1993 and about $117 billion, or 57 percent, of total inflows in 1994. Among the developed countries, the United States experienced a strong and rapid recovery of inflows in 1993, following on a major decline in 1992. Inflows to Western Europe and Japan fell in 1993.

Developing countries enjoyed a record-high level of inflows of foreign direct investment—$71 billion in 1993 (an amount that represented a 36 percent increase over 1992 and that was expected to climb an additional 13 percent to $80 billion in 1994). However, only one developing country—China—received more than 80 percent of the increased amount of FDI to developing countries in 1993. This fact highlights a persistent pattern: the ten largest developing host countries have tended to absorb 65 to 80 percent of total inflows to developing countries. They accounted for 81 percent in 1993. In contrast, flows of FDI to the 47 least-developed

4. Source, unless otherwise indicated, is "Trends in Foreign Direct Investment," UNCTAD, TD/B/ITNC/2, 2/21/95.

Table III-4
Inflows and Outflows of Foreign Direct Investment, 1982–94

Type of Country or Actual Country	Billions of dollars							Share of total (percentage)					Growth rate (percentage)				
	1982–86 (average)	1987–91 (average)	1990	1991	1992	1993	1994 (est.)	1982–86 (average)	1987–91 (average)	1992	1993	1994 (est.)	1982–86 (average)	1987–91 (average)	1992	1993	1994 (est.)
Inflows																	
Developed	42	143	177	120	100	107	117	77	82	64	58	57	24	1	−16	7	9
Developing	13	30	32	39	52	71	80	23	17	33	39	39	−0.4	13	32	36	13
Central & E. Europe	0.02	0.6	0.3	2	5	6	7	0.03	0.4	3	3	3	3	278	91	22	23
All	55	174	209	161	157	184	204	100	99	100	100	99	17	4	−3	17	11
Outflows																	
France	3	20	35	24	31	21	25	5	11	17	11	12	17	27	31	−34	21
Germany	6	18	29	23	16	15	15	10	10	8	7	9	35	26	−32	−3	−1
Japan	7	35	48	31	17	14	18	13	18	9	7	8	34	12	−44	−20	32
U.K.	10	28	19	16	19	26	27	19	15	11	13	13	24	−16	21	33	5
U.S.	11	28	30	31	41	58	56	20	15	22	31	28	22	73	−0.3	7	6
All Source-Countries	55	192	239	191	194	193	204	100	100	100	100	100	25	9	−4	5	6

Source: UNCTAD, "Trends in Foreign Direct Investment," TD/B/ITNC/2, 2/21/95, Tables 4 and 5.

countries have remained exceedingly small—$500 million, or 0.7 percent, of flows to all developing countries in 1993.

Central and Eastern Europe enjoyed above-average inflows in 1993 (22 percent) and, probably, 1994 (23 percent). However, those rates of growth are far below the spectacular rates recorded in 1989–92. In addition, the base or stock of foreign direct investment in Central and Eastern Europe is, at $14 billion at the end of 1993, comparatively small. And that amount is rather unevenly distributed, with the Czech Republic, Hungary, and Poland accounting for most of it. Rapid growth in foreign direct investment in Central and Eastern Europe appears to have been hindered by economic recession in Western Europe and the stop-go nature of many of the economic reform programs in the formerly planned and state-dominated economies.

Multilateral and Regional Arrangements and Agreements Relating to Transnational Corporations

Since the collapse in 1987 of the ten-year-long effort to conclude a multilateral voluntary code of conduct for transnational corporations and host and home governments under U.N. (Economic and Social Council) auspices, interstate discussions about the rules of the foreign investment "game" have been conducted mainly in bilateral, regional, and plurilateral settings. Such was the case in 1994–95. Of course some states, including Brazil and India among quite a few others, have undertaken unilateral programs of investment liberalization and, as a result, have been attracting substantial amounts of new foreign direct, and in some cases portfolio, investment. Others, however, have demonstrated a greater readiness to join in plurilateral agreements. For example, in November 1994 the 18 members of the **Asia-Pacific Economic Cooperation forum (APEC)** agreed on the text of a nonbinding code on foreign direct investment [*Financial Times*, 11/11/94]. Then, in early 1995, spokespersons for the European Union and the United States began to express support for a broad-based international investment agreement [ibid., 1/19/95; *Wall Street Journal*, 2/1/95]. However, the EU and the United States were unable to agree on an appropriate forum for negotiating such an agreement. The EU strongly preferred the more universal World Trade Organization, while the United States expressed a strong preference for the more intimate and manageable Organization for Economic Cooperation and Development (OECD), even though the OECD adopted investment guidelines about 20 years ago.

Separately, UNCTAD called for international negotiations to curb incentives for foreign direct investment ["Incentives and Foreign Direct Investment," TD/B/ITNC/Misc.1; also *Financial Times*, 4/13/95]. As competition for foreign direct investment has become more intense, the UNCTAD report maintained, would-be host states (and subnational units) have resorted to an ever increasing variety of incentives. These incentive programs threaten to "raise the cost of attracting foreign direct investment, to the detriment of poorer countries, and increase the risk of distorting investment flows." Multilateral negotiations, UNCTAD argued, could aim to cap the value of incentives and overall government spending on them, or to eliminate the most inefficient incentives.

Transnational Corporations in the U.N. System

As reported in *Issues/47* and *Issues/48*, the Secretary-General decided early in his tenure to terminate the U.N. Centre on Transnational Corporations as an autonomous unit. The U.N. Commission on Transnational Corporations was retained, however, as the locus of U.N. activities concerning international investment shifted to the Department of Economic and Social Development in the Secretariat.

Many U.N. members, especially developing countries, were critical of the reorganization because of the apparent downgrading of U.N. interest in the activities of multinational enterprises. The Secretary-General reconsidered and made UNCTAD the focal point of investment-related activities. In December 1994 the General Assembly, in approving a report of the Second Committee [A/49/726], expressed support for the Secretary-General's actions, made the Commission on Transnational Corporations a commission of the Trade and Development Board, and renamed it the Commission on International Investment and Transnational Corporations.

IV
Global Resource Management

1. Environment and Sustainable Development
By Gail V. Karlsson

The debate over the meaning of sustainable development continues as the international community works to breathe life into a variety of treaties and institutions that grew out of the U.N. Conference on Environment and Development (UNCED or, more familiarly, the Earth Summit), held in Rio in 1992. Sustainable development was also a key topic at two more recent U.N. conferences: the International Conference on Population and Development (Cairo, September 1994) and the World Summit for Social Development (Copenhagen, March 1995).

One major element of the sustainable development debate involves the relationship between economic growth and environmental protection. Many poorer countries stress the development side—usually couched in terms of economic growth—to meet the needs of growing populations. They are concerned that environmental considerations will be used by industrialized countries to place conditions on aid and impose limits on growth—a sort of "green" colonialism that consigns them to a permanently unequal economic status. Environmentalists, however, fear that the developing countries, in their pursuit of economic growth, do not sufficiently recognize the severity of threats to the global environment.

The developing countries constantly berate the industrialized countries for failing to fulfill long-standing commitments to increase official development assistance (ODA), but most donor countries seem unlikely to do so. Without such assistance, however, developing nations will not readily accept limitations on their exploitation of natural resources to fuel economic growth, viewing these limitations as an encroachment on sovereignty. Alternative financing mechanisms to support sustainable development, such as international taxes, have also met with resistance on sovereignty grounds.

These themes—financing, sovereignty, and the tension between economic growth and environmental protection—have echoed throughout international meetings on sustainable development issues during 1994–95.

From the debate at those meetings it appears that the term "sustainable," whether applied to development, use of natural resources, livelihoods, or communities, means different things to people of different economic status.

The treaties that emerged from the Earth Summit at Rio (on climate change, biological diversity, and desertification), as well as negotiations on forest management and preservation of fish stocks, represent significant attempts by the international community to reach consensus on the means of addressing specific environmental concerns. But the potential of Rio—to forge a new era of common respect and responsibility for a shared planet—has not yet been realized, hampered by political disputes and economic disparities.

Biodiversity

The first meeting of the parties to the **Convention on Biological Diversity** was held in the Bahamas, November 28–December 9, 1994, only 11 months after the treaty entered into force. Opened for signature during the Earth Summit in June 1992, the biodiversity treaty had collected 167 signatures and 107 ratifications by December 1994 [E/CN.17/1995/7, p. 18]. The signatories to this Convention pledge to conserve, use sustainably, and share the benefits of the world's wealth of biological diversity. The speed with which governments have ratified it may be based on varied expectations of financial benefit.

The Convention requires balancing a state's sovereign right to exploit biological life-forms within its national borders against the need to conserve planetary resources. Countries with substantial biological resources hope to reap considerable income from their indigenous genetic materials. Indeed, according to one estimate, the poor countries supply as much as $30 million worth of medicinal plants, herbs, and other biological resources to drug and cosmetic companies each year, most of them based in the United States and Europe [New York Times, 4/23/95]. Many developing countries thus look at the subject of biological resources and the conservation of biodiversity from an economic development perspective and not primarily from an ecological one.

In the Bahamas, the **Conference of the Parties** to the Convention on Biological Diversity agreed on a program of work for the next few years. Their primary focus will be on efforts to conserve threatened species and on negotiations concerning the terms on which foreign companies will be allowed access to genetic resources. Given widespread concern about the handling of biologically modified living organisms, the conference decided to convene an ad hoc panel of experts to consider the need for a protocol on biosafety [E/CN.17/1995/7, p. 20]. It also set up the **Subsidiary Body for Scientific, Technical and Technological Advice** called for by the Convention—the first meeting is scheduled for Paris in September 1995—and agreed to ask the Convention secretariat to consider the possibility of creating a clearinghouse mechanism to promote technical and scientific cooperation [ibid., p. 19]. The U.N. Environment Programme will supply the secretariat for the Convention, but there is no agreement on where that office will be located.

After much discussion, the Conference of Parties decided to ask the **Global Environment Facility (GEF)** to continue operating as the Convention's financing mechanism on an interim basis. At issue was whether the GEF, after a restructuring process called for by the Convention, had achieved sufficient transparency and would be responsive enough to the countries it would assist in implementing the treaty. Many developing countries doubted the adequacy of the restructuring measures undertaken, but agreed to defer decision on the GEF's status until the next meeting of the parties (scheduled for November 1995) following a review of other financing options. Other difficult, outstanding issues include a definition of sustainable use, the means of securing rights and benefits for indigenous peoples and local communities, and appropriate measures for providing the intellectual property protections required by developed countries.

As recommended by the conference, the U.N. General Assembly adopted December 29—the date on which the Biodiversity Convention entered into force—as the International Day for Biological Diversity [A/Res/49/119].

Climate Change

Economic development issues were also central to negotiations on implementing the **Framework Convention on Climate Change,** the other treaty opened for signature at the Earth Summit. The Climate Change Convention entered into force in March 1994, and the first conference of the treaty parties took place a year later in Berlin. When the meeting opened on March 28, 1995, 127 countries had ratified the Convention.

The Climate Change Convention is **designed to stabilize greenhouse gas concentrations** at a level that would prevent dangerous interference with the world's climate system. Accumulations of greenhouse gases, which trap radiation from the sun in the Earth's atmosphere, contribute to changes in weather patterns and rises in global temperatures. Atmospheric concentrations of such greenhouse gases as carbon dioxide, methane, and nitrous oxide are the result of widespread use of fossil fuels for energy and transportation, particularly in industrialized countries. Reflecting the industrialized countries' greater responsibility for greenhouse gas accumulations, the Climate Change Convention commits them to adopt measures "with the aim of" reducing their carbon dioxide emissions to 1990 levels by the year 2000. Although developing countries agreed in general to help protect the atmosphere, the Convention does not ask them to make any specific emission-reduction commitments, despite the fact that rapid economic growth has led to increased emissions in some newly industrializing regions.

The major topic of discussion and debate at the **Berlin meeting of the parties to the Climate Change Convention** was the adequacy of existing commitments to prevent dangerous accumulations of gases. Responding to recent scientific projections, many countries saw a need to establish additional emissions limitations, which would apply after the year 2000. Some also expressed doubt that the industrialized countries were making sufficient efforts to meet their current commitments.

The Intergovernmental Negotiating Committee on Climate Change, meeting for the last time in February 1995, considered a draft protocol that required developed countries to reduce their emissions of carbon dioxide by the year 2005 to at least 20 percent below 1990 levels and established timetables for controlling emissions of other greenhouse gases [A/AC.237/L23, p. 4]. The draft, introduced by the Alliance of Small Island States (AOSIS), reflected these nations' growing concern about rising sea levels and increasingly violent storms—themes presented at the **Global Conference on Sustainable Development of Small Island Developing States,** held in Barbados in the spring of 1994. It said nothing about obtaining commitments from developing countries to reduce emissions as well. Germany created a stir by proposing a protocol that did suggest limitations on the emissions of certain more advanced developing countries [A/AC.237/L.23/Add.1]. Developing countries objected to any proposal that would shift responsibility from the industrialized countries for dealing with the consequences of their own pollution or that might restrict economic growth in developing countries.

A month later in Berlin, after extensive negotiations, the parties to the Climate Change Convention adopted a document that asks an ad hoc group of states to formulate a protocol or other legal instrument covering a period beyond the year 2000 [FCCC/CP/1995/L.14], to be submitted to the conference of parties in 1997. The **protocol would ask the developed countries to strengthen their commitment to emissions reductions** by meeting certain quantified objectives within a designated period of time, but the developing countries would not be asked to make any new commitments themselves [*Earth Negotiations Bulletin*, 4/10/95, p. 5; hereafter *ENB*]. The AOSIS countries, feeling the need for urgent action, were disappointed that their draft protocol was not adopted. The oil-producing countries, however, concerned about efforts to reduce the consumption of fossil fuels, registered formal objections to the conference document and held up agreement on the rules of procedure for voting on protocols, perhaps with the intention of blocking future agreement on such an instrument [ibid., pp. 10–11].

Another contentious issue at the Berlin conference was the Convention's provision for **joint implementation efforts,** under which one country could fulfill part of its commitment to limit climate change when it supplies money or technology that helps to reduce emissions of greenhouse gases in another country. Some developing countries argued that the industrialized countries might try to use such transfers to avoid making emission reductions at home. In the end, the Conference of Parties agreed to a pilot, voluntary joint implementation program. It stipulates that any such project should result in measurable long-term environmental benefits that would not have occurred otherwise, and that no emissions reduction credits will be given during the pilot phase [ibid., p. 6]. Reports on the pilot program will be prepared by two subsidiary bodies—on implementation and on scientific and technical advice—established by the Convention. These two bodies are to begin work in Geneva in October 1995.

The Conference of Parties to the Climate Change Convention agreed on locating the **permanent secretariat in Bonn** and on calling the next meeting before October 1996. The parties also agreed to keep the GEF on, for the interim, to provide financing for countries that need help in implementing the Convention.

Desertification

The **Convention to Combat Desertification** is intended to address a problem that affects fragile dry lands and threatens the livelihoods and food security of over 900 million people. Conditions are especially serious in Africa, 66 percent of which is desert or dry land and where 73 percent of the agricultural dry lands are already affected [U.N. press release DPI/SD/1581, 10/94]. Negotiations on the Desertification Convention were concluded in June 1994, and it was opened for signature that October. Although the Convention is not expected to enter into force until 1996 (after ratification by 50 countries), the **International Negotiating Committee on Desertification (INCD)** adopted a resolution in June 1994 recommending urgent action in Africa during the interim period [resolution 5/1]. Since then African governments have come together to establish subregional coordinating structures, some resources have been mobilized for implementing national action programs, and public-awareness campaigns are getting under way [ENB, 1/20/95].

The Desertification Convention notes that physical, biological, political, and socioeconomic factors contribute to widespread land-management problems, and it seeks international cooperation to address them in the form of technology transfers, scientific research, information collection, and financial resources. It also advocates a **bottom-up approach,** emphasizing the importance of participation by local people familiar with land conditions.

The 49th General Assembly decided to preserve the INCD during the ratification period to prepare for the first session of the Convention parties and promote measures that would aid in implementing the June 1994 interim resolution on Africa [A/Res/49/234]. At a January 1995 meeting in New York, the INCD established two working groups. One of these will designate a permanent secretariat and identify an organization to house the "global mechanism" called for in the Convention but yet to be defined. Developed countries have in mind a coordinating facility, while developing countries hope this mechanism will have a funding role [*ENB*, 1/20/95, pp. 4–9]. (Article 4 of the Convention calls for mobilizing substantial resources for affected developing countries but does not call for a commitment of new and additional resources.) The second of the INCD working groups will organize scientific and technical cooperation and implementation procedures [ibid., p. 4].

The role of the **interim secretariat** was also a subject of debate at the January INCD meeting. The developing countries favored an activist body that could begin to coordinate implementation plans and build public awareness of the desertification treaty and its goals. Any less of a mandate, they feared, would diminish the importance of a Convention that, unlike the climate change and biodiversity treaties, which address global conditions, applies mainly to the poorer countries [ibid., pp. 9–10]. Emphasizing the importance of the bottom-up approach, the developed countries recommend that the interim secretariat serve as a facilitator, not as a new international bureaucracy [ibid.].

Given the importance of local participation in implementing the Convention, education and publicity were important topics of discussion as well. The 49th General Assembly proclaimed **June 17** the **World Day to Combat Desertification and Drought** [A/Res/49/115]. The INCD decided to meet again in August 1995 in Nairobi.

Forests

The issue of a forest treaty was revisited in April 1995 when the U.N. Commission on Sustainable Development (CSD) reviewed countries' progress in implementing the **general principles on forestry** adopted at the Earth Summit and in implementing Chapter 11 of Agenda 21 on combating deforestation. Although forests have been a primary focus of policy debates about sustainable development, the governments represented at the Earth Summit were unable to reach agreement on a treaty on sustainable forest management. Discussions of forests involve many of the conflicting elements that make up the sustainability debate: demands for market-driven economic growth, trade liberalization, and more equitable distribution of economic opportunity; growing recognition of the importance of ecosystems in preserving global biodiversity and climate conditions; assertions of national sovereignty; empowerment of rural and indigenous communities; and recognition of the impact of both overconsumption and poverty in the rapid destruction of ecosystems.

Forest protection is also a key issue in the other environmental treaties. **Deforestation** contributes to desertification, to the Earth's decreased capacity to absorb carbon dioxide, and to a loss of biodiversity. Forests also provide homes and livelihoods for indigenous peoples and are sources of food, fuel, medicine, and a variety of products.

Tropical timber is covered by an **International Tropical Timber Agreement (ITTA),** concluded in January 1994 and opened for signature that April but not yet in force. (This ITTA is the successor to the 1983 ITTA, which expired on March 31, 1994.) Despite an emphasis on sustainable use and management, the ITTA is essentially a commodity agreement **designed to facilitate the tropical timber trade.** It recognizes the sovereignty of states over their natural resources and seeks to promote industrialization, employment opportunities, and export earnings through increasing the amount of tropical timber processed. Responding to the tropical countries' charge that the ITTA was one-sided in its requirements for sustainable use, the consumer countries made a formal commitment to ensure the sustainable management of their own forests by the year 2000 in a separate agreement attached to the ITTA document.

As the appointed task manager for the CSD review of forest management, the **U.N.'s Food and Agriculture Organization (FAO)** prepared a report containing various proposals, including an exploration of the **possibility of turning the forest principles into a legally binding instrument** [E/CN.17/1995/3, p. 34]. The FAO report also suggested preparation of an agreement on a harmonized set of criteria and indicators for sustainable forest management [ibid., p. 33].

Discussion of forest issues, including the FAO report, dominated the meeting of the **CSD Working Group on Sectoral Issues,** February 27–March 3, 1995. The group recommended that the CSD consider setting up an intergovernmental panel on forests to assess the work done to date and propose further action [ENB, 3/6/95, p. 11]. At the CSD plenary in April 1995, the Commission established an open-ended **ad hoc Intergovernmental Panel on Forests** to consider, inter alia, the need for other instruments or arrangements to strengthen compliance with the forest principles, including legal arrangements and mechanisms covering all types of forests. The panel will also examine the underlying causes of deforestation, development of indicators for sustainable forest management, and full-cost valuation of forest products [ENB, 5/1/95]. It will submit a progress report to the CSD at its fourth session, in 1996, with conclusions and recommendations to come in 1997.

Fish Stocks

Marine fisheries are another arena in which unchecked commercial exploitation has destroyed habitats and wiped out entire species. Despite international efforts to protect marine resources through the provisions of the **U.N. Convention on the Law of the Sea (LOS)**, fish stocks have been sharply depleted throughout the world's oceans. (The LOS Convention entered into force only in November 1994, but its provisions on management of coastal waters have been observed for many years.)

The LOS Convention defines **exclusive economic zones (EEZs)** for coastal states extending 200 miles offshore. About 80 percent of the world's fish stocks are located within these zones. Even within areas controlled by only one country, overfishing and unsustainable practices have destroyed commercial fishing bases. By the beginning of the 1990s, according to FAO reports, about 69 percent of the world's commercial fish species were fully exploited, overexploited, or rebuilding after depletion [*Earth Times*, 4/15–29/95, p. 5].

On the high seas, and in relation to **fish that migrate among EEZs and from EEZs into the high seas,** the LOS Convention requires that all fishing states cooperate in fishery conservation and management. Because of growing pressures on global fish resources and intense conflicts between the fishing fleets of various countries, the Earth Summit recommended establishing a **Conference on Straddling Fish Stocks and Highly Migratory Fish Stocks** to elaborate on the LOS Convention provisions on these fisheries and promote their implementation. The final result of the conference is expected to take the form of a **binding agreement** that establishes a better means of ensuring compliance with conservation and management measures. At the fourth substantive session of the "fish stock conference," held in New York, March 27–April 12, 1995, negotiators were still dealing with a number of controversial issues but were expected to reach consensus at their final session, July 24–August 4, 1995.

At its 49th Session the General Assembly expressed deep concern about the effect of unauthorized fishing in zones under national jurisdiction [A/Res/49/116], highlighted wasteful fishing practices that destroy nontarget fish and other species [A/Res/49/118], and deplored noncompliance with the 46th Assembly's resolution [A/Res/46/215] establishing a global moratorium on large-scale driftnet fishing on the high seas [A/Res/49/436].

Related U.N. Conferences: Population, Social Development, and Women

Many of the pressures on the natural environment addressed in the environmental treaties are related to population growth. Increasing populations in poor countries overwhelm fragile ecosystems, while people in wealthy countries consume a disproportionate and unsustainable amount of natural resources. The September 1994 International Conference on Population and Development in Cairo addressed, in part, the relationship of population to environmental protection and to sustained economic growth. The "principles" section of the **Programme of Action adopted at Cairo** affirms that human beings are at the center of the concern for sustainable development [principle 2], reiterates that the right to development is a universal and inalienable human right [principle 3], identifies sustainable development as a means of ensuring human well-being and emphasizes the need to eliminate unsustainable patterns of production and consumption [principle 6], calls on all nations to eradicate poverty, characterizing this an indispensable requirement for sustainable development [principle 7], and finally, requires that sustained economic growth be broadly based, offering equal opportunities for all [principle 15].

Despite adoption of these principles, some complained that the Population Conference did not give sufficient attention to the connections between population and environmental issues, particularly the environmental impact of consumption and wasteful production patterns in industrialized countries [*ENB*, 9/14/94, p. 11]. Some participants also observed that the Programme of Action's promotion of "sustained economic growth in the context of sustainable development" [ibid., p. 5, in reference to par. 3.22 et al.] placed too much emphasis on improved socioeconomic conditions as the key to reducing population as well as overcoming poverty and environmental degradation, citing their fear that unregulated economic growth will destroy already devastated ecosystems and bring even greater poverty in the end.

That debate continued in Copenhagen, at the World Summit on Social Development (the Social Summit) in March 1995, where some developing countries argued that the Social Summit was intended as a forum for discussing poverty and unemployment, not environmental issues. Focusing on their need for sustained economic growth, these countries resisted until the last minute the insertion of references to sustainable development. The final negotiated language of the **Social Summit Declaration** attempts to integrate the social, economic, and environmental elements that define sustainable development:

> We are deeply convinced that economic development, social development, and environmental protection are interdependent and mutually reinforcing components of sustainable development, which is the framework for our efforts to achieve a higher quality of life for all people. Equitable social development that recognizes empowering of the poor to utilize environmental resources sustainably is a necessary foundation for sustainable development. We also recognize that broad-based and sustained economic growth in the context of sustainable develop-

ment is necessary to sustain social development and social justice [A/Conf.166/L.3/Add.1, 3/10/95, p. 2].

Education and empowerment of women are other aspects of sustainable development linking the Population Conference and the Social Summit as well as the September 1995 World Conference on Women in Beijing. Current research indicates that investments in the education of girls and women contribute to sustainable development through higher economic productivity, lower birthrates, improved health and nutrition, and stronger families and communities. The Declaration of the 1995 Copenhagen Summit acknowledged that women carry a disproportionate share of the burdens of coping with poverty, social disintegration, and environmental degradation [par. 16(g)], and it recognized that empowering people, particularly women, to strengthen their own capacities is both a main objective of development and its own best resource [par. 26(o)]. The Beijing Women's Conference will take a further look at the role of women in the development of sustainable and ecologically sound consumption patterns and natural resource management.

Role of U.N. Agencies in Sustainable Development

The **Commission on Sustainable Development** is the primary U.N. forum for defining and promoting sustainable development and for overseeing the follow-up to Earth Summit agreements. There is considerable overlap, however, in the responsibilities of the CSD and those of the other U.N. agencies involved with the environmental treaties and conference agendas, particularly the U.N. Environment Programme (UNEP) and the U.N. Development Programme (UNDP). The CSD is not an operational agency, and its formal activities between annual meetings are limited to those of ad hoc working groups. Every year the CSD examines certain general issues affecting all the specific environmental topics covered in Agenda 21, the broad program of work adopted at the Earth Summit. Such general matters include financial resources, technology transfer, science, education, trade, and the roles of major social groups in implementing Agenda 21. Each year the CSD also reviews a certain number of the specific environmental topics listed in Agenda 21. Those addressed by the CSD at its April 1995 session were land management, agriculture, desertification, mountains, and biodiversity. The primary focus, however, was on forest management and assessment of the need for a binding treaty on that topic. In 1996 the CSD will consider another cluster of special environmental topics, including the atmosphere, oceans, and seas and coastal areas.

UNEP was established in 1972 to monitor the world's environment and stimulate the conservation and environmental protection efforts of governments and other institutions. It provides technical advice, coordinates scientific research, and disseminates environmental information, among other activities. UNEP also plays important roles in facilitating the environmental treaties and in managing the Global Environment Facility. Yet since the Earth Summit and the establishment of the CSD, UNEP's overall mission has been somewhat murky. It has been called the environmental conscience of the United Nations, but one of the principal messages of the Earth Summit was that environmental, economic, and social issues are inextricably linked. The CSD was created to focus on those linkages.

At the April 1995 CSD meeting, UNEP Executive Director Elizabeth Dowdeswell described UNEP as "the source of knowledge about the world's environments, a voice that complements the work of the CSD by bringing the environmental perspective to the discussion" [*UNEP Bulletin*, 4/27/95, p. 3]. Under her direction, UNEP has in fact been undergoing a reassessment and a restructuring. It has adopted an issue-oriented approach to environmental protection, focusing on four areas: sustainable management and use of natural resources, sustainable production and consumption patterns, reduction of health threats from hazardous chemicals and industrial waste, and examination of the environmental consequences of the globalization of trade [*Earth Times*, 4/30–5/14/95, p. 17]. It also plans a program on international law aimed at providing a framework to facilitate the implementation of Agenda 21.

Recently UNEP, with its small staff and budget, has begun cooperating more closely with **UNDP**, a large operational agency with offices in many countries. UNDP already provides financial assistance for sustainable development projects through its Capacity 21 program, and cooperation with UNEP will strengthen its ability to provide scientific information and technology assistance to developing countries. During the April 1995 CSD meeting, UNEP and UNDP signed two new partnership agreements, one to help combat desertification, the other to increase the flow of information to developing countries through coordinated computer networking programs [U.N. press release DEV/2059/HE 890, 4/28/95].

Another U.N. entity created after the Earth Summit and complementing the work of the CSD is the **High-level Advisory Board on Sustainable Development,** an independent group of experts established to advise the U.N. Secretary-General and through him the CSD, the U.N. Economic and Social Council, and the General Assembly. At the Advisory Board's third session, held in New York in October 1994, it expressed concern about the lack of progress in implementing the social and economic changes required for sustainable development. The experts decided they should concentrate on defining issues needing the attention of the CSD and the U.N. system [E/CN.17/1995/25, 2/16/95, p. 3].

The report issued by the Advisory Board highlights the importance of food security, mutually reinforcing trade and environment policies, and educational strategies demonstrating that sustainable development is about "enhancing quality of life, not merely material wealth" [ibid., p. 21]. It also issued a strong plea for a campaign to mobilize public opinion in favor of transferring to sustainable development the resources now spent on arms [ibid., p. 25].

Financing Sustainable Development

Despite promises made at the Earth Summit to provide developing countries with new and additional resources for sustainable development, the level of financial aid to developing countries has actually fallen [ibid., p. 3]. The accepted target for **official development assistance (ODA)** by donor countries is 0.7 percent of gross national product. Only a few industrialized countries have met this target.

When the **CSD's Ad Hoc Intersessional Working Group on Finance** met in March 1995, it discussed a variety of **alternative measures for financing sustainable development,** among them user charges for activities with adverse environmental impacts, removal of subsidies encouraging overuse of energy and natural resources, "green" taxes, and tradable emissions permits. During the meeting, developing countries tended to focus on the need for financial assistance and expressed the fear that discussion of innovative economic instruments—though intended as ways of raising the necessary funds—would lead donors to postpone the fulfillment of current funding commitments [*ENB*, 3/13/95, p. 13].

The CSD itself, meeting a month later, expressed "great concern" at the decline in ODA and recommended the use of official development funds "to leverage additional domestic and external financial resources through various innovative schemes," such as joint ventures and venture capital funds [E/CN.17/1995/L.11, 4/26/95, p. 2]. It accepted the proposal of the Working Group on Finance for a study on the feasibility of imposing environmental user charges on air transport and encouraged pilot projects on internationally tradable carbon dioxide-emission permits [E/CN.17/1995/ 11, 3/29/95, p. 11].

In its decision on financial mechanisms, the CSD urged the international financial institutions to integrate the economic, social, and environmental goals of sustainability into their development projects from the moment of inception and to continue to increase financial flows for sustainable development [E/CN.17/1995/L.11, 4/26/95, p. 3]. The **World Bank,** the major source of funding for development projects, will consider innovative ways to mobilize resources for sustainable development at its third Annual Conference on Environmental Sustainable Development in September 1995.

The World Bank, together with UNEP and UNDP, manages the Global Environment Facility that (at least on an interim basis) operates the financial mechanisms of the biodiversity and climate change treaties. The GEF is also responsible for funding certain extra costs incurred by developing countries for projects that provide global environmental benefits. The CSD observed that the $2 billion replenishment of the GEF in 1994 was a minimal first step and noted that there would have to be other replenishments at later dates to meet the GEF objectives [ibid.].

In general, the financing of sustainable development is expected to come from a country's own public and private sectors, but this is virtually impossible in countries whose financial resources are being drained to service a huge external debt. The 49th General Assembly encouraged reductions in bilateral official debt of the poorest and most heavily indebted developing countries [A/Res/49/94], and the Copenhagen Declaration of the World Summit for Social Development went further, offering a commitment to assist Africa (and least-developed countries elsewhere) through such solutions as cancellation of bilateral debt and debt-relief measures on the part of the international financial institutions [A/Conf.166/L.3/Add.1, 3/10/95, p. 16].

Trade and Environment

The potential impacts of increased trade liberalization on social and environmental conditions have been the subject of considerable international debate. The World Summit on Social Development was convened primarily to address the widening gap between the winners and losers in the new global economy, and the conference Declaration directly confronts the effects of globalization on sustainable development:

> Globalization, which is a consequence of increased human mobility, enhanced communications, greatly increased trade and capital flows and technological developments, opens new opportunities for sustained economic growth and development of the world economy, particularly in developing countries. . . . At the same time, the rapid processes of change and adjustment have been accompanied by intensified poverty, unemployment and social disintegration. Threats to human well-being, such as environmental risks, have also been globalized [A/Conf.166/L.3/Add.1, 3/10/95, p. 3].

The CSD's High-level Advisory Board on Sustainable Development had previously asserted that a large proportion of the resources for sustainable development will have to come from increased trade and greater market access for poorer countries but had cautioned that, without stronger measures for environmental protection, international trade liberalization could promote economic growth beyond environmentally sustainable levels [E/CN.17/1995/25, 2/16/95, pp. 15–16]. Sustainable development, said the Board, will require not only growth "but a sea change in the quality of growth to make it less raw material and energy-intensive" and far more equitable. It will take "measures that allow for the limitation of population growth and respect for the rights of future generations." It will also require "measures to reduce the consumption of raw materials and energy in the developed countries" while "allowing space for the developing countries to expand their use of those commodities" [ibid., p. 15].

Regarding the role of the new **World Trade Organization** in coordinating trade and environment issues, the Advisory Board recommended that the new WTO Trade and Environment Committee grant observer status to the CSD and that the Committee be served by an interim secretariat unit staffed by UNEP, UNDP, the U.N. Conference on Trade and Development (UNCTAD), and FAO to "bolster" its efforts. The Board also urged a policy of openness by the WTO itself with regard to meetings and dispute-settlement mechanisms [ibid., pp. 18–19].

UNCTAD is the designated task manager assigned to report to the CSD on trade and environment issues, and it has already worked with UNEP on a joint program to assess the environmental impact of trade policies. At its April 1995 session, the CSD stressed the need for continued close cooperation in the work of the WTO, UNEP, and UNCTAD. It encouraged these groups to supply technical and other assistance to help mitigate the **effects of such measures as eco-labeling and packaging and recycling requirements on the trade competitiveness** of developing countries and countries with economies in transition [CSD draft decision, 4/28/95, p. 4].

The WTO Committee on Trade and Environment has already met to consider product standards and packaging, labeling, and recycling requirements as well as the effect of environmental measures on the market access of developing countries [UNEP magazine _Our Planet_, vol. 7, no. 2 (1995), p. 30]. Developing countries worry that such requirements as eco-labeling that are based on environmentally friendly production methods could give rise to "green protectionism," further restricting their exports to industrialized countries. Others fear that countries with lax environmental standards will have a competitive advantage in the global marketplace, creating pressures to reduce environmental standards at a time when higher standards are urgently needed.

Consumption and Production Patterns

At its April 1995 meeting the CSD reaffirmed the Agenda 21 conclusion that "the major cause of the continued deterioration of the global environment is the unsustainable pattern of consumption and production, particularly in industrialized countries, which is a matter of grave concern, aggravating poverty and imbalances" [E/CN.17/1995/L.12, 4/27/95, p. 1]. It adopted a work program designed to assess the efficacy of altering production and consumption patterns through the **full internalization of**

environmental costs [ibid., pp. 4–5], involving such government measures as emission charges, taxes on environmentally unfriendly products, deposit/ refund systems, and tradable permits. Internalization of costs could help to combat undervaluation of natural resources, which leads to overuse and environmental destruction.

Emphasizing the responsibility of all stakeholders in society, the CSD urged businesses to provide information on the environmental life-cycle impact of their products, and recommended national public-aware-ness campaigns and education programs to encourage households to adopt sustainable life-styles [ibid., p. 3]. Eco-labeling schemes are one means of informing consumers about the environmental impacts of products, since most are unaware of the consequences of their consumption habits. UNCTAD has been examining eco-labeling issues, with a view toward increasing the participation of developing countries in setting criteria about production processes and the use of raw materials.

UNEP's **"Cleaner Production" initiatives** are intended to help governments and industry develop policies for reducing industrial pollution and facilitating the transfer of cleaner production technologies [E/CN.17/ 1995/13, 3/20/95, p. 35]. The transfer of technologies to promote cleaner production and enhance energy efficiency is a key factor in sustainable development, helping newly industrializing countries avoid some of the environmentally destructive side-effects of economic development.

Energy consumption is, in fact, a critical area in which transfers of appropriate technology could not only help to accelerate economic development but could also serve to reduce deforestation, desertification, pollution of ecosystems, and climate change. Today, the per capita consumption of fossil fuels is nine times greater in the industrialized countries than it is in the developing ones [ibid., p. 8], and for all the advances in energy efficiency, the global demand for commercial energy is expected only to grow. About two-thirds of that additional energy demand is likely to occur in the developing countries [ibid., p. 9]. In many developing countries, **subsidies** for electricity and use of fossil fuels lower energy prices artificially, leading to excessive consumption.

The **U.N. Committee on New and Renewable Sources of Energy and on Energy for Development** concluded at its meeting in 1995 that **"technological leapfrogging"** is the best option for development strategies:

> A number of technologies for increasing energy efficiency are not only available but also economically advantageous at today's energy prices. The priority is to accelerate the dissemination of these technologies by improving information, enhancing education, promoting capacity-building, removing regulatory, technical and legal barriers, facilitating credit, promoting the market mechanism and, when necessary, adapt-

ing or developing technologies to make them suitable to local conditions [E/1995/25, E/C.13/1995/2, 4/6/95, p. 11].

In its February 1995 report, the Committee recommended to the CSD that UNDP, the GEF, and the World Bank launch a global initiative to bring power to rural areas via such renewable technologies as photovoltaics, wind, and minihydro [ibid., p. 5]. UNDP itself recently adopted an energy strategy that emphasizes energy efficiency, renewables, and the substitution of low or no-carbon-based fuels for high-carbon-based fossil fuels [E/CN.17/1995/13, 3/20/95, p. 34]. The Renewable Energy Committee also suggested establishing a special U.N. institution to advance energy for sustainable development.

Substantial changes in patterns of consumption, of goods as well as of energy, cannot be achieved without partnerships among governments, international organizations, industry, and other major sectors of society. The CSD plans to invite workers' groups, trade unions, and businesses to its 1996 meeting to present case studies of partnerships in the workplace and case studies of environmental management policies in small and medium-sized enterprises [E/CN.17/1995/L.10, 4/26/95, p. 1].

The CSD's High-level Advisory Board has concluded that **education** is the most important factor in ensuring the involvement of all members of civil society in the sustainable development process [E/CN.17/1995/25, 2/16/95, p. 23]. That education, it said, must incorporate a long-term perspective, "recognizing that in 40 years the world will have to achieve a fundamental reconfiguration of resources." Education should also address specific problems of the environment, such as the use of water and energy. "The future custodians of the Earth must be given the practical knowledge for those tasks" [ibid., p. 21].

2. Food and Agriculture
By Martin M. NcLaughlin

World food issues are dealt with directly by three U.N. agencies: the Food and Agriculture Organization (FAO), the International Fund for Agricultural Development (IFAD), and the World Food Programme (WFP). Indirectly the problem is also a focus of the World Health Organization (WHO), the U.N. Environment Programme (UNEP), the U.N. Development Programme (UNDP), the U.N. Children's Fund (UNICEF), the U.N. High Commissioner for Refugees (UNHCR), and of course, the World Bank Group, the regional banks, and the International Monetary Fund (IMF).

Moreover, although the topic of food and agriculture is not often addressed directly by the General Assembly or by the Economic and Social Council (ECOSOC), it regularly appears as a subtheme or counterpoint in their consideration of many other related topics—especially the disruption of societies by civil conflicts and disasters. It also constitutes a significant element in many of the U.N.'s current series of international conferences, e.g., on Environment and Development (Rio, June 1992), on Human Rights (Vienna, June 1993), on Population and Development (Cairo, September 1994), and on Social Development (Copenhagen, March 1995).

The World Food Situation

In the fall of 1994 the Secretary-General submitted to the General Assembly an overall report entitled *Food and Agricultural Development* [A/49/438, 9/27/94, hereafter referred to as *Report*] in response to the General Assembly's resolution of two years earlier [47/149, 12/18/92] requesting a report on world food production. This is the first comprehensive report in this area in many years (other than FAO documents and the annual reports of the World Food Council, submitted through ECOSOC), and one that was well received [A/Res/49/103, 1/30/95].

Its basic thrust appears in the report's introduction:

> Given recurrent and chronic shortfalls in food production in a large number of food deficit areas, as well as the ever-increasing pressure of population growth, the inter-linkages between sustainable agricultural development, the environment and international trade are likely to remain at the top of the international agenda during the 1990s.

The decline in the food supply in 1993 (1.2 percent in production and 2.7 percent in per capita food supply) did not bode well for the remainder of the decade, and the report's outlook for the near future was for slow progress at best (0.1 percent). The report noted a lack of progress in Africa, despite an increase of 3.2 percent in production; a decline in the growth rate of agricultural trade; developing countries as a group becoming net agricultural importers; and reduced output of grains and fish [Report, par. 8–16]. Agricultural imports continued to exceed exports, by about 9 percent in 1992; and industrialized-country imports of agricultural, fishery, and forest products exceeded those of developing countries by 23 percent that same year [Table II.2].

In the short run, however, some of the pessimistic forecasts in the report have not been borne out. According to FAO, the total output of cereal grains increased by 3 percent in 1994, to 1.953 billion metric tons [Food Outlook, 1–2/95], almost to the record high (1.966 billion tons) of 1992. Even in most sub-Saharan African countries, where per capita food production has generally not been keeping up with consumption, output improved; the exceptions were countries affected by conflict—notably Angola, Burundi, Liberia, Rwanda, and Sudan. Northern Africa and the Sahelian region of West Africa had good harvests and showed promising crop futures, but the prospects in southern Africa remained uncertain.

A cereal production drop in Central America was balanced by increased harvests in South America, and on the whole the situation in Asia was favorable. There was some concern, however, about such populous countries as Bangladesh, China, and Indonesia, where weather conditions seriously affected harvests; and Australia had its worst cereal harvest since 1972—50 percent less than the year before. Crops in Eastern Europe, the former Soviet Union, and the European Union declined across the board. Still, an increase of nearly a third in the North American harvest made up for these reductions and probably will prevent deterioration in global cereal stocks.

Food Aid

While long-term sustainable development must be the ultimate answer to the problems of the food and agriculture system, food aid continues to be the first line of defense. The Secretary-General's report noted that "the total volume of food aid reached the record level of 17.1 million tons in 1993" [par. 34]. Nevertheless, it was felt that it was still necessary to appeal for continuing high levels, especially in view of immediate needs in Sudan [A/49/376, 9/12/94], Mozambique [A/49/387, 9/16/94], Rwanda, [A/49/516, 11/14/94], Somalia [SOM/64 WFP/1004, 1/9/95], and parts of the former Yugoslavia [WFP/1009, 2/16/95]. It should be noted that nearly 10 percent of the food aid was provided by the U.N./FAO World Food Programme, which purchased three-fourths of its share (1.1 million tons) from developing countries [WFP/1003, 1/3/95].

The report's assessment of the impact of the new GATT agreement suggests that one aspect of it will be to reduce food aid, particularly as food stocks decline as the surpluses that sustained them are reduced. In fact, the amount of food aid provided in 1994 was significantly less than in 1993, and the United States, the largest food aid provider, announced plans to cut its annual total almost in half—from 4.47 million tons to 2.5 million tons [New York Times, 4/1/95]. A month later the *Times* reported a plea from the WFP Director for an increased contribution of food "to help hundreds of thousands of refugees from . . . 25 crises involving 24.3 million people."

Agriculture in the Global Economy

But food aid, as nearly everyone in the development field recognizes, only buys time; it cannot solve the problem of chronic hunger, or food insecurity, which affects a minimum of 800 million people [FAO, *Agriculture Toward*

2010, C 93/94, 11/93]. The irony of this hunger lies in the fact that every year the world produces enough food to provide an adequate diet for everyone on the planet—nearly 2 billion tons in 1994 [*Food Outlook*, 1-2/95]; but every year this food fails to reach that 800 million people, mainly women and children, who have not achieved what the FAO calls "food security"—the ability to grow or buy the food they need. The World Bank has pointed out [*The World Food Outlook*, 11/93], reflecting the FAO's *Production Yearbook* [1993 and other years], that the world food supply situation will likely continue to improve; therefore, "the focus must be on alleviating poverty." FAO's 1993 publication *The State of Food and Agriculture* generally echoes this optimistic forecast about agriculture, though it is predicated on whether overall recovery persists and commodity prices for developing-country exports remain relatively firm.

Of the nearly 2 billion tons produced, the industrialized world accounts for about 800 million tons (two-fifths); nearly half of the rest is rice, a major staple of people in the developing world. Only about 200 million tons (10 percent of the total)—mostly wheat, maize, and other feed grains, but not rice—enters the international market. Of this, 5 percent is donated as food aid; the rest is consumed by people and animals in the country or region where it is grown. The developing countries have only 10 percent of that export market, but they account for 40 percent of the imports [*Report*, par. 81].

Forty percent of total cereal consumption, mainly maize—plus most of the soybeans, the major nongrain trade crop—did not reach the tables of the poor, because it was fed to animals; neither did most of the products (meat, milk, and eggs) of the animals that consumed those crops. Nevertheless, the total world harvest continued to be large enough to provide all the world's population an adequate (not minimal) diet, were they to have access to it by either production or purchase.

In addition to its generally dim view of global food security prospects for the remainder of this century, the Secretary-General's report also notes that external commitments to and disbursements for assistance to developing-country agriculture have declined in recent years [ibid., par. 43], and that the concessional component of such assistance has also dropped. This is despite a general recognition that most poverty in developing countries is in rural areas, and that improvement in the quality of life (i.e., development) in those countries must begin with agriculture.

Because food self-sufficiency is not an immediate prospect for most of what the report calls LIFD (low-income food-deficit) countries, international trade in food assumes very great importance. Yet trade in agriculture, which "has been traditionally characterized by a considerably lower degree of multilateral discipline and market access commitments than those governing trade in industrial products" [UNCTAD, *Trade and Development Report 1994*], was one of the most controversial areas of negotiation in the

Uruguay Round, which led to the new GATT agreement. In the end, agreement was achieved only by allowing significant exceptions to the new rules for the industrialized exporting nations. Despite efforts to soften likely adverse impacts of the new GATT on the poor countries, the report is not optimistic about the prospects: If production in the exporting nations decreases and their imports increase, world market prices could rise beyond the ability of poor countries to pay for imports. Also, reduced government activity in supporting prices could lead to less government stockpiling and thus to a reduction in global food stocks and in reserves for food aid. Moreover, the effort to develop domestic policies acceptable under the agreement [MTN/FA II-AIA-3, pp. 17–22—Final Act, 12/15/93] may not be affordable by the poor countries [*Report*, par. 86].

The developing countries also face a dilemma in the new World Trade Organization into which GATT has been incorporated: that is, will a sharp reduction of industrialized countries' export subsidies, which have largely frozen the developing countries out of their "natural" market in the North, outweigh the enlarged threat to their agriculture from penetration of their markets by the highly capitalized, resource-depleting agriculture of the traditional exporters? It would seem that the LIFD countries' prospects are bleak under any currently conceivable scenario.

Agriculture and Development

Trade in agricultural products is generally associated with two major issue areas: development and the environment (a connection that has come to be more broadly recognized and better understood since UNCED—the 1992 U.N. Conference on Environment and Development). On the development side, when production is geographically separated from consumption, the levels of both may change—generally to the disadvantage of poor people. Per capita production and consumption are both higher in the industrialized exporting countries, and the processing of food (packaging, transport, marketing, etc.) requires nonrenewable resources. Moreover, because the production of agricultural goods strains the resource base more than consumption does, the exporter is more responsible than the consumer for environmental stress [ibid., par. 108–10].

Intensive irrigation in the exporting industrialized countries depletes water tables, painfully built up over centuries, at a rate 100 times faster than they can be replenished. Capital-intensive agriculture tends to inundate the land (and the lakes and streams) with toxic chemicals rather than making use of regenerative processes and natural manures and predators. It uses soil-compacting, land-depleting heavy equipment to plant, cultivate, and harvest crops and then processes that harvest into new, "attractive" products with mostly nonbiodegradable packaging.

The bulk of agricultural research funding is devoted to temperate-zone agriculture, often to new processed (mostly fast) foods and to capi-tal-intensive technologies designed to increase production that is already surplus. This is done at the expense of making photosynthesis more effi-cient (it is currently only about 5 percent efficient); maintaining crop and species diversity; developing pest-resistant, drought-resistant, disease-re-sistant seeds; and working with peasants to improve traditional agricul-ture. At the same time, the Consultative Group on International Agricul-tural Research (CGIAR) now says that demand is increasing faster than yields for a dozen major crops on which people depend for sustenance [CGIAR press release, 2/6/95].

The Secretary-General's report to the General Assembly is supple-mented by his report to ECOSOC, *Integrated approach to the planning and management of land resources* [E/CN.17/1995/2, 2/2/95], which was pre-sented to the Third Session of the Commission on Sustainable Develop-ment, April 11–28, 1995. Citing Chapter 10 of Agenda 21, this report defined the task of land-use planning as follows: "to facilitate the match-ing of land resources and land uses at every level in such a way that the satisfaction of human needs and human rights is maximized on a sustain-able basis. A balance must be struck between the need to increase produc-tion and raise living standards and the need to preserve the environment . . ." [par. 5].

This later report, prepared by the FAO, further documents the envi-ronmental degradation resulting from some agricultural practices and adds its support to the growing consensus on sustainable development. It underscores the linkages among abandonment of traditional labor-inten-sive conservation practices, increased irrigation, soil degradation, deple-tion of tropical forests, destruction of natural habitats, reduction of water resources, adverse effects on human health, political instability, poverty, hunger, and migration. "During the period 1988–1993," the report states, "per capita food production actually declined in 99 countries, one-third of which are in sub-Saharan Africa" [p. 11]. Although the report acknowl-edges "the enormous potential in the ability of local groups to plan and manage their own resources" [par. 72b] and the central role of women in this respect [par. 68], its overall conclusion, or warning, is grim:

> Unless a significantly more effective approach to land resources man-agement is adopted now, a possible scenario could include a large in-crease in poverty, hunger, social instability, war, greatly increased mi-gration from resource-poor environments to more favorable ones, together with almost complete destruction of the remaining natural en-vironment and possible modifications to the world's climate which will cause social upheaval and political unrest on a vast scale. These are not things which may happen some time in the far distant future. They are already starting to happen, and the process may intensify exponentially

over the next five or six decades unless appropriate action is taken. [par. 12]

Just a few months earlier the Secretary-General's report to the General Assembly had ended with a section on "Sustainable Agricultural Development, International Trade, and the Environment." It acknowledged that agriculture's expanded acreage and increased yields continues to feed a world population that has doubled in the past 50 years, but warned that:

> There is strong evidence that the requirement for ever-increasing agricultural output as well as for employment and income of the growing population dependent on agriculture, particularly in developing countries, cannot be accommodated in an environmentally sustainable manner with present agricultural practices and trends. . . . Although there is not necessarily a conflict between production increases and sustainability, in practice the quest for ever-increasing quantities of food has often led to unsustainable production methods and environmental degradation. [par. 91 and 93]

A report of the U.N. Administrative and Coordinating Committee's Subcommittee on Nutrition (the Committee consisting of all department and agency heads) underscores this basic thesis:

> Our continuing concern about undernutrition and household food security leads us to conclude that agricultural research and investment will have their greatest impact on reducing hunger if they are planned specifically to take account of both the changing geographical and socio-economic characteristics of hunger in the world and poor people's perceptions of their malnutrition-related problems. . . . In the present analysis of the world food problem, household access to food remains one of the most urgent food problems for the foreseeable future. [ACC/1994/18, 7/25/94, Annex III]

Conclusions

As noted in the 1994–95 edition of this publication and elsewhere [e.g., *The Hunger Report: 1993*], hunger has reemerged on the international development agenda. The World Bank has published a report of its November 30– December 1, 1993 conference in Washington, D.C. [*Overcoming Global Hunger*, ESD Proceedings No. 3, 1994], and hunger was a significant topic at the U.N. conferences in Cairo and Copenhagen, mentioned earlier. While there seems to be a clear consensus that the answer to global hunger is sustainable development, even conferences that include "development" in their titles tend to focus on the specific element with which it is paired—e.g., environment (Rio) and population (Cairo)—rather than on a global economic system that benefits the wealthy at the expense of the poor. Even the World Summit on Social Development, whose report [A/Conf.166/L.3/Add.1, 3/

10/95] reiterates the sustainable development consensus, shies away from such analysis.

In part, this may stem from the imprecision of the word "sustainable," which permits widely varying interpretations. The concept became the mantra of environmental policy with the publication of the Brundtland Report [*Our Common Future*, 1987]. Later it became the watchword for development policy. The 1995 World Summit for Social Development seems to have allowed "sustainable development" to become "sustainable economic development," which suggests little more than maintaining the current global economic order, with all its imperfections, but without seriously considering other possible economic and social arrangements.

The increased concern of the General Assembly and ECOSOC about the food and agriculture system and about world hunger, as well as the interest of the U.N.'s specialized and other agencies and the international community, is a reminder that the kind of anxiety that led to the 1974 U.N. World Food Conference can be revived without another global meeting. But it seems clear that the problems will not be resolved by concentrating on agriculture alone or seeking a solution solely in the concept of sustainability.

There are manifest and growing obstacles inherent in the international system: the enormous debt overhang of the developing countries (nearly $2 trillion, according to the 1995 *World Debt Tables*), of which Mexico is a current poignant example; the decline in official development assistance in 1993 by 8 percent in total value and by 9 percent in percentage of GNP [Development Assistance Committee of the OECD, *Development Cooperation*, 1995]; the disastrous social consequences of the indiscriminate application of structural adjustment conditionality on poor nations in the interest of restoring their credit worthiness; the worsening terms of trade as the accelerated international mobility of capital abrogates the "law" of comparative advantage; the growing weakness of nations in the face of the globalization of investment and production; the persistent refusal of world leaders to accord to women the justice they demand and deserve, when it is clear that without gender equity there will be no real development; and the increasing indifference of the industrialized nations to the developing countries as Cold War rationales for paying attention to them fade. Clearly, the U.N. system will have much work to do in this area as the world moves into the final years of the 20th century.

3. Population
By Craig Lasher

World population currently stands at 5.7 billion and is increasing at nearly 90 million annually. Actions taken during the remainder of the decade will determine the size and pace of population growth into the next century. Projections produced for the **International Conference on Population and Development (ICPD),** held in Cairo, September 5–13, 1994, place world population at 7.9 billion to 11.9 billion in 2050. Effective implementation of the goals and objectives—and meeting the expanded financial commitments—of the ICPD's 20-year Programme of Action would result in a world population below the U.N. "medium projection" of 9.8 billion people in the year 2050 [A/Conf.171/13]. But under any of these scenarios, demographic factors pose serious environmental, security, and development challenges to the international community.

Two major international conferences that flanked the ICPD—the U.N. Conference on Environment and Development (UNCED, June 1992) and the World Summit on Social Development in Copenhagen (the Social Summit, March 1995)—extended the discussion of population issues into new areas and will have an impact on the U.N.'s response to global population problems as well as on whether the international community marshals the necessary political will and financial resources to stabilize world population. The Fourth World Conference on Women in Beijing in September 1995 will reprise reproductive and health issues at the heart of the population debate.

The Conference Preparatory Process

The 1994 gathering in Cairo was the fifth in a series of population conferences convened by the United Nations at ten-year intervals. The first two were purely technical meetings, while the two subsequent meetings (Bucharest, 1974) and (Mexico City, 1984) set goals and made recommendations for governments on population issues. ICPD reviewed progress toward stabilizing world population and prepared a new plan of action for the coming two decades.

To prepare for the 1994 conference the United Nations convened meetings around the world at which experts considered population policies and programs and such relationships as population and women, population and environment, demographic structure and international migration, and family planning, health, and family well-being. Five regional conferences (for Asia and the Pacific, the Arab states, Latin America and the Caribbean, Africa, and Europe and North America) were organized jointly with a variety of institutions [A/Conf.171/PC/2]. For these meetings each national delegation was to prepare a report on its own country's situation. The recommendations developed by the expert groups and the regional conferees were to provide the basis for the final document to be agreed to at Cairo.

At the second of the Preparatory Committee meetings, held in New York in 1993 (PrepCom II), the country delegations began the process of formulating actionable recommendations for that ICPD document. The United Nations encouraged **the involvement of nongovernmental organizations (NGOs)** in this process and helped to organize a separate NGO meeting to coincide with the official conference. Observers note that the level of NGO participation was exceptionally high for a U.N. conference and that the influence of these organizations on the Programme of Action was profound [Lori Ashford, "New Perspectives on Population: Lessons from Cairo," *Population Bulletin*, 3/95]. More than 500 NGOs were in attendance at the final Prep-Com, and NGOs were represented on several country delegations. Both the PrepComs and the Cairo conference itself were official U.N. meetings, however, and only country delegations could participate in the formal negotiating sessions.

One highlight of PrepCom II was the announcement of dramatic changes in **U.S. population assistance policy.** The U.S. position, said the head of the American delegation, is "to support reproductive choice, including access to safe abortion," and he noted that the "abortion issue should be addressed directly with tolerance and compassion, rather than officially ignored while women, especially poor women, and their families suffer" [*New York Times*, 5/12/93].

A major subject of controversy was the extent to which the conceptual framework for the conference action agenda should be modified to address broad development and health issues. Efforts to dilute the focus on concrete actions to stabilize population led to objections from several official delegations, including representatives of India, Bangladesh, and Indonesia. In commenting on the annotated outline prepared by the ICPD secretariat following PrepCom II, the **General Assembly** reaffirmed the "need to maintain the centrality of population issues in the final document of the Conference" [A/Conf.171/PC/2].

At PrepCom III in April 1994, delegates of over 180 countries joined in negotiations to finalize the exact wording of the action program, working with a draft document prepared by the ICPD Secretariat after Prep-Com II [A/Conf.171/PC/5]. The main drama at this final preparatory meeting was provided by **the Vatican's efforts to change the conference document.** The Vatican (formally, the Holy See) has permanent observer status at the United Nations, which gives it the right to participate in all negotiations but not the right to vote. The PrepCom process, which sought consensus through negotiation, enabled the Vatican to exercise considerable influence, even though its view were usually in the minority. The draft text the delegates adopted at PrepCom III bracketed some 200 phrases and definitions yet to be agreed upon—prominently "reproductive rights," "fertility regulation," "safe motherhood," and "sexual and reproductive health." Most had been singled out by the Holy See and a variety of predominantly Catholic countries (namely, Argentina, Benin, Guatemala, Honduras, Malta, and Nicaragua) and several Muslim countries [Susan W. Cohen and Cory L. Richards, "The Cairo Consensus: Population, Development and Women," *Family Planning Perspectives*. For further details of the preparatory process see *A Global Agenda: Issues/49*, pp. 185–90].

The Cairo Population Conference

As foreshadowed by the debates during the preparatory process, the ICPD will probably be remembered most for the religious controversies that dominated the conference proceedings. In addition to efforts by the Vatican and its Catholic allies to weaken language on abortion and reproductive rights in the Programme of Action, a number of Muslim countries opposed language they perceived as undermining **traditional Islamic values.** Nonetheless, the final document was adopted by broad consensus and fundamentally changes the international community's approach to population issues [A/Conf.171/13]. The Programme of Action incorporates a richer and more comprehensive view of global population problems, and appropriate policy responses to them, than do the documents adopted at Bucharest and Mexico City [United Nations, *Population Newsletter*, 12/94, pp. 5–8]. It recognizes the importance of family planning but also sees social investments in health and education as key to creating a favorable climate for voluntary fertility decline and eventual global population stabilization. Universal access to family planning and reproductive health services is one of the document's **quantitative goals;** additional goals relate to education for girls and reduction of infant and child mortality. The need to improve the status of women by effecting a change in the roles of men and women is a theme of the entire document.

A further difference from the documents of previous conferences is the discussion of **family planning within an overarching ethical and policy framework of broader reproductive health and rights.** The Cairo document emphasizes that family planning programs should respond to the needs of individuals, and that governments should not impose demographic targets or limits on family size. Also groundbreaking is the Cairo document's offering of new concepts and strong language on the need for **education in sexuality and contraceptive services for adolescents,** on the need to **prevent unsafe abortion and female genital mutilation,** and on the importance of **improving the quality of reproductive health care.**

Some 15,000 people converged on Cairo for the official conference and the simultaneous NGO forum, among them approximately 3,700 delegates representing 179 nations, 7 delegations with official observer status [*ICPD 94*, 9/94], 4 prime ministers, 4 presidents, and 5 vice presidents. Security was very tight, and despite threats by extremist elements of the Egyptian fundamentalist movement, there were no incidents of violence during the conference.

At the opening plenary sessions, Prime Ministers **Gro Harlem**

Brundtland of Norway and **Benazir Bhutto of Pakistan** set the tone of the conference. Brundtland, arguing from a pragmatic perspective, stated that "morality becomes hypocrisy if it means accepting mothers suffering or dying in connection with unwanted pregnancies and illegal abortions, and unwanted children living in misery." Bhutto, who forcefully rejected abortion and emphasized the sanctity of the family and of traditional cultural and religious values, nonetheless went on to give a strong endorsement to family planning [*Washington Post*, 9/6/94].

Under pressure from domestic fundamentalist groups, several **Muslim political leaders** had canceled their plans to attend the conference, including the Prime Ministers of Bangladesh and Turkey (both women) and President Suharto of Indonesia. Saudi Arabia, Sudan, Lebanon, and Iraq boycotted the conference entirely [*New York Times*, 9/6/94], but other Muslim nations decided to participate, with the aim of ensuring that Islamic values were reflected in the final document. Iran, Egypt, and Pakistan eventually played key roles in reaching a compromise on sensitive language.

Different cultural and religious views of women's role in society were at the heart of many of the controversies at the ICPD. Feminist groups, who supported expanded health and educational opportunities for women, charged that the Holy See and Muslim governments opposed the idea of providing such opportunities because these would give women greater autonomy. Muslim countries were especially concerned about gender issues related to inheritance, which they perceived as conflicting with Islamic law, and about language on education in sexuality and contraceptive services for adolescents, which they viewed as legitimizing sexual activity outside marriage [Cohen and Richards, p. 274]. These cultural and religious differences were compounded by linguistic misunderstandings. Ambiguous language on "marriages and other unions," which raised Muslim concerns about homosexuality, was ultimately deleted. References to sexual health and rights also led to cross-cultural problems and were dropped as well. Making for still other problems was the difficulty of translating English terms like women's "empowerment" and "reproductive health" into the U.N.'s other official languages.

Official debate and negotiations took place in the Main Committee, chaired by Dr. Fred Sai, a Ghanaian physician and president of the International Planned Parenthood Federation (IPPF). But much of the real work was carried out in "informal" sessions of the committee, from which the media were excluded, and in numerous working groups, which conducted their search for compromise language behind closed doors.

In what appeared to be a strategic decision by the ICPD secretariat to discuss the most contentious issues first, the Main Committee began by considering Chapter VII ("Reproductive Rights and Reproductive Health") and Chapter VIII ("Health, Morbidity, and Mortality") [*ICPD 94*,

9/94, p. 5]. The discussion promptly unraveled over one paragraph of the over 100-page document—Chapter VIII, paragraph 25, which deals with **abortion.** In fact, the draft document had supplied alternative texts, one emphasizing the need to reduce deaths from unsafe abortion and the other incorporating strong language against the decriminalization of abortion. At the halfway point, with the Holy See and a small number of allies refusing to compromise on paragraph 8.25, the meeting came to a virtual halt [*New York Times*, 9/7/94]. The deadlock was broken only when a working group, chaired by Pakistan, negotiated new language that was acceptable to virtually all delegations, including many of the Vatican's allies. The Holy See refused to accept the compromise language but agreed to allow debate to proceed on other unresolved issues.

With the decision of the committee to borrow from the 1984 Mexico City conference document the statement that "abortion should never be promoted as a method of family planning," the Vatican announced that it was dropping its prior objection to the term "family planning," which it now considered to be defined in such way as to exclude abortion [*Washington Post*, 9/10/94].

With this subtle but important shift, the Vatican no longer blocked consensus on the need to make family planning more widely available. It also acknowledged that serious problems are connected with rapid population growth. But the delegation of the Holy See made clear that it remained opposed in principle to modern contraception, sterilization, and the use of condoms, including their use to prevent HIV/AIDS infection.

Even as these debates went on, there were informal negotiations and meetings of working groups to finalize the 15 other chapters of the Programme of Action. Rapid progress was made by the Main Committee in the closing days of the conference. On September 13, the final day, the plenary formally adopted the **conference document—a comprehensive, 20-year strategy for addressing population and development issues—** and a number of countries presented their **reservations and comments** on several chapters [A/Conf.171/13]. Some Muslim states noted that they could not be bound by any part of the document that was inconsistent with Islamic law. When all the chapters were discussed in the plenary, 13 countries had offered their general reservations about the final Programme for the record. Ten countries—most of them with predominantly Catholic populations—eventually filed written reservations.

The Holy See, which had refused to endorse the documents adopted at Bucharest in 1974 and Mexico City in 1985, surprised the gathering by announcing its desire "in some way to join the consensus even if in an incomplete and partial manner" [Reuters, 9/13/94]. It then signed on to six of the Programme of Action's 16 chapters dealing with general principles rather than with specific actions.

Since the final document was adopted by consensus of all the official delegations present, all interested parties were able to claim victory. The more liberal countries, as well as women's and family planning groups, were pleased by the overall progressive tenor of the document. The Holy See and the more conservative nations and groups could claim that they had thwarted a conspiracy aimed at undermining the traditional family and making access to safe abortion a worldwide right [*New York Times*, 9/18/94].

Although the continuing focus on the problem of unsafe abortion had its positive side, the lengthy debate on this subject took attention away from the broad goals of the conference and left **no time for other vital issues.** The relationship between population, the environment, and sustainable development was barely discussed, for example (language on these issues had been largely resolved prior to the conference). Critical issues of implementation and follow-up to the conference, the problems of HIV/AIDS, and the role of men in family planning also received scant attention at Cairo.

One of the most significant aspects of the conference was the **avoidance of major North-South conflicts,** although some tensions did arise in the discussion of Chapter X ("International Migration") [*New York Times*, 9/11/94]. The industrialized countries that receive significant numbers of international migrants refused to agree to an international legal "right" to family reunification, while the "sending countries" pushed for the strong language. The compromise language finally adopted referred to the "vital importance" of family reunification. Major conflict between developing and industrialized countries was avoided primarily because the conference preparatory process and the document clearly recognized that both excessive consumption in the wealthier countries of the North and rapid population growth in the poorer South contribute to global population problems.

Another major issue that remained unresolved prior to Cairo involved estimates of future **resource requirements** to address global population problems and the failure to secure **funding commitments** from both donors and developing countries [Reuters, 4/25/94]. Initial opposition from some European countries reflected a perception that the draft Programme of Action's call for a large increase in funding for family planning but a far smaller amount for women's reproductive health undermined the broad approach to population policy outlined in the document. Although the ICPD secretariat significantly increased the cost estimates for reproductive health initiatives, final agreement was not achieved at Prep-Com III. As a result, the entire section on "Resource Mobilization and Allocation" in Chapter XIII ("National Action") was bracketed by the European Union and remained unresolved going into Cairo. The European countries also resisted a specific target for donor assistance to population activities and bracketed language calling for 4 percent of official development assistance to be spent on population activities.

In Cairo, agreement was reached in principle that roughly $17 billion will be needed in the year 2000 and $22 billion in 2015 for both family planning and broader reproductive-health programs. **Current worldwide spending on population** is believed to total about $5 billion from all sources, including donor assistance, the expenditure of developing-country governments, and Southern "consumers." The document calls for donor countries to increase their share of the expenses of family planning and reproductive health services from a quarter to a third of the total. Several donor countries did announce plans to increase population assistance, but most donor countries and developing countries made no new pledges at Cairo. Developing and donor countries were also reluctant to commit themselves to specific goals for social sector-spending, deferring discussions to the Summit for Social Development in Copenhagen [*New York Times*, 9/12/94].

Implementation of the Cairo Programme of Action

The ICPD Programme of Action is not binding on member states but is likely to have a profound influence on population policies and programs around the world. To make this influence felt will require follow-up mechanisms to hold governments accountable for implementing the program and to measure their progress toward meeting its goals. It will also require an increase in funding for family planning and reproductive health—and for the social sector generally—by both donor and developing countries. "Without resources," stated **Dr. Nafis Sadik, Executive Director of the U.N. Population Fund (UNFPA)** and Secretary-General of the conference, "the Programme of Action will remain a paper promise" [*ICPD 94*, 9/94, p. 3].

The **prospects for increased donor assistance** for population programs do not appear promising, however [*Earth Times*, 12/31/94]. The donor community convened in Paris in November for a special meeting on population and development organized by the **Development Assistance Committee (DAC) of the Organization for Economic Cooperation and Development.** The United States and a few other countries stressed the importance of moving ahead purposefully with implementation of the Cairo program. Japan, Germany, and the United Kingdom had pledged significant increases in funding in the days leading to the Cairo conference, but no other DAC members made any new commitments to increase population assistance at the DAC meeting. A major disappointment was the continuing lack of interest on the part of France, Italy, and Spain, all of which have large development assistance budgets.

The United Nations has moved quickly to reorganize itself, the better to help implement the Cairo agenda. The **General Assembly** devoted three plenary meetings in November to consideration of the report of the

Cairo conference [A/Conf.171/13]. All the speakers who addressed the plenary session, which spanned two days, endorsed the achievements of the conference and applauded the Programme of Action's emphasis on the need to empower women and on a comprehensive approach to family planning and reproductive health. Most of the plenary statements had to do with implementing the program—prominently, resource allocation and institutional arrangements for supporting and monitoring follow-up [*ICPD 94*, 11/94].

A consensus resolution of the General Assembly, negotiated by the Second (Economic and Financial) Committee and sponsored by Algeria for the Group of 77 developing countries and by China and Indonesia for the Non-aligned Movement, dealt with ICPD implementation [A/Res/49/128]. It emphasizes the importance of enhanced cooperation and coordination by all relevant agencies, organizations, and programs of the U.N. system and outlines a three-tiered intergovernmental mechanism, consisting of the General Assembly, ECOSOC, and a **revitalized Population Commission,** to play the central role in this process. In recognition of the broader approach to population issues endorsed in Cairo, the Population Commission has been **renamed the Commission on Population and Development** and will meet annually instead of every two years. At its high-level session in June 1995, ECOSOC planned to assess the capabilities and comparative advantages of the U.N. system and other intergovernmental bodies, make recommendations on necessary institutional changes, and consider the question of establishing a separate executive board for the UNFPA [ibid.].

At the request of the U.N. Secretary-General, UNFPA Executive Director Sadik will chair an **interagency task force,** composed of high-level officials from key parts of the system, to ensure a common and integrated strategy within the U.N. system. Through the U.N. Administrative Committee on Coordination, all U.N. agencies and organizations will be exploring ways to promote implementation of the Programme of Action. The Consultative Committee on Programme and Operational Questions (also chaired by Sadik) will attempt to ensure that organizational missions are mutually supportive and that there is a minimum of duplication [*ICPD 94*, 11/94, p. 5].

UNFPA is the most active of the U.N. agencies in following up on the ICPD. Immediately after the conference it convened four regional consultations with representatives of Africa, Central and Latin America, the Arab states and Europe, and the countries of Asia and the Pacific [UNFPA press release, 12/15/94]. UNFPA's technical and geographic divisions have been charged with reviewing all its country programs for conformity with the principles of the Programme of Action. The 167 national reports on population and development submitted in preparation for the Cairo conference have been synthesized and issued as a report [A/49/482].

UNFPA has established an **internal Task Force on ICPD Implementation** to take over many of the functions of the ICPD secretariat. The duties of the task force include coordination within UNFPA; communication of developments in the General Assembly, ECOSOC, and other U.N. bodies; and integration of the Programme of Action in country programs, in cooperation with personnel working in the field. The task force has a two-year mandate [UNFPA press release, 12/21/94].

Population at the Social Summit, and Beyond

Despite the obvious links between demographic factors and poverty and unemployment, the final document of the **World Summit for Social Development** makes only passing reference to population growth. It does not state directly that family planning is a means of empowering women and integrating them into the development process. And there is only an oblique reference to reproductive and child health "consistent with the International Conference on Population and Development" in the section on primary health in Chapter II. (The Holy See and several national delegations had made repeated attempts to reopen and weaken the language on reproductive rights and the family approved at Cairo in September, and this language was the negotiated compromise for the document of the Copenhagen Summit in March.)

Although the Cairo conference had deferred until Copenhagen any serious discussion of goal-setting for social sector-spending, once March rolled around the donor nations were still unwilling to make increased financial commitments. The so-called **"20:20 compact"** established at the Social Summit is only a voluntary target [for details on the preparations and outcome of the Copenhagen meeting, see Chapter V, "Social and Humanitarian Issues—The World Summit for Social Development"].

In the spring of 1995, at the last preparatory committee meeting before September's **World Conference on Women,** the Holy See and a small group of countries (among them Argentina, Benin, Ecuador, Guatemala, Honduras, Malta, and Sudan) also attempted to renegotiate ICPD language on reproductive rights for inclusion in the Beijing Platform of Action. The Vatican also proposed for the Platform "a conscience clause" that health workers could invoke when refusing to provide or recommend medical services to which they object on moral grounds [for details on the preparations and agenda for Beijing, see Chapter V, "Social and Humanitarian Issues—The Status of Women"].

Beijing not only presents the possibility of a retreat from the language agreed to at Cairo, however, but may also serve to **reopen debate about U.S. funding for UNFPA** and for population programs in general. As the basis for its decisions to withhold funds from UNFPA over a decade, the U.S. Agency for International Development (AID) claimed that the organization was co-managing **China's population program** and that the Chinese program relied on coercive abortion and involuntary sterilization. The Clinton administration resumed funding of UNFPA, to which the United States contributed $14.5 million in 1993, and $40 million in 1994. Congress had appropriated $50 million for 1995, but the fate of the year's contribution remains in doubt as leaders of the new Republican majority act on their vow to reduce U.S. involvement in the United Nations and anti-abortion activists press the United States to withdraw its contribution from UNFPA because of UNFPA's program in China. (UNFPA continues to point out that it does not support abortion in China or anywhere else in the world, and it denies the charge that it "manages" China's program in any way.)

U.N. Population Awards

The winners of the U.N. Population Award for 1995 are the **Inter-African Committee on Traditional Practices Affecting the Health of Women and Children (IAC)** and **Dr. Halfdan Mahler,** Secretary-General of the International Planned Parenthood Federation (IPPF) [UNFPA press release, 3/13/95].

An Ethiopian-based NGO founded in 1984, the Inter-African Committee targets the custom of female genital mutilation, traditional practices relating to childbirth and child marriage, social and nutritional taboos, and adolescent pregnancy. The IAC conducts research, engages in public education and media outreach, and trains nurses and birth attendants. There are active IAC committees in 23 African countries.

Mahler, Secretary-General of IPPF since 1989 and a former Director-General of the World Health Organization (1973–88), is being honored for his distinguished career in public health and his strong leadership in the field of population and family planning. At WHO he promoted the concept of primary health care, of which family planning and reproductive health were important components, and he helped to establish the Special Programme of Research, Development and Research Training in Human Reproduction. At IPPF, he has increased public awareness of global population issues and played an important role in building the international consensus that emerged at the ICPD in Cairo.

4. Law of the Sea, Ocean Affairs, and Antarctica
By Lee A. Kimball

The 1982 **U.N. Convention on the Law of the Sea (LOS Convention)** entered into force on November 16, 1994 (exactly one year from the day the 60th country to ratify it had deposited documents to this effect at the

United Nations). Some four months before, the General Assembly had adopted an **agreement modifying the LOS Convention**'s controversial provisions on mining the deep seabed beyond national jurisdiction. The Agreement was the result of four years of informal consultations, convened by two Secretaries-General, among states that were already parties to the LOS and some (including such industrialized nations as the United States and Germany) that were not. The Convention and the Agreement are to be interpreted and applied as a single instrument [A/Res/48/263, Annex. See, too, *A Global Agenda: Issues/49*, pp. 197–98].

Resolution of the deep-seabed mining issue opened the door to ratification by the industrial countries that had resisted doing so. By May 1995, Germany, Australia, and Italy had ratified the Convention and the new Agreement, and nearly all of the industrialized nations had signed it. The **United States** signed the Agreement on July 29, 1994, and on October 7 forwarded it *and* the Convention to the U.S. Senate for advice and consent [Treaty Document 103–39, U.S. Senate]. The intentions of the present Congress, elected after that date, are unclear.

The 49th General Assembly treated the Convention's entry into force as a historic event, a triumph of international relations. Secretary-General Boutros-Ghali traveled to Kingston, Jamaica, for the ceremonial opening of the International Seabed Authority (ISA). And the United States, for the first time since adoption of the Convention in 1982, was a supporter (and sponsor) of the annual LOS resolution in the General Assembly, which passed easily [A/Res/49/28].

The next stages of Convention implementation occur on two different tracks. The first involves implementing the Convention's deep-seabed mining provisions, including establishment of ISA, the autonomous organization made up of all contracting parties to the Convention that will administer deep-seabed mining. Its first plenary Assembly met in Kingston, November 16–18, 1994, in keeping with the Convention requirement that it meet on the day the Convention enters into force. The schedule called for two substantive sessions in Kingston in 1995: February 27–March 17 and August 7–18.

The second track involves the implementation of the Convention's remaining provisions, including the assignment of roles and responsibilities to the **Secretary-General.** The job of convening the contracting parties to elect the 21 members of the International Tribunal on the Law of the Sea (Annex VI of the Convention), to be located in Hamburg, Germany, and the 21 members of the Commission on the Limits of the Continental Shelf (Annex II of the Convention) falls to the Division for Ocean Affairs and Law of the Sea (DOALOS) in the U.N. Legal Office, which serves as de facto secretariat and has already arranged two such meetings at the United Nations in New York. The first (November 21–22, 1994) considered the requirement that Tribunal members be elected within six months of entry into force of the Convention. It was decided to postpone elections until August 1, 1996, to give still other countries time to ratify the Convention and participate in the process [SPLOS/3, 2/28/95]. (The members of the Continental Shelf Commission must be elected by May 15, 1996.)

At the May 15–19, 1995, meeting in New York, the states parties to the LOS Convention adopted their own rules of procedure and considered the practical administrative and financial arrangements for establishing and carrying out the work of the Tribunal—the "central mechanism" of the Convention's "compulsory dispute-settlement system" [U.N. press release SEA/1483, 5/12/95]. A third meeting is scheduled for November 27–December 1, 1995, to consider the Tribunal's draft budget [SEA/1485, 5/19/95].

The U.N. **General Assembly** is charged with reviewing developments in international ocean law and policy that give expression to and elaborate on the LOS Convention's provisions, and it receives an annual report on these matters [see A/49/631 and Coor.1]. The 49th Session requested that the Secretary-General have ready for the 51st Session an additional, special report on the "impact" of the entry into force on U.N. system instruments and programs [A/Res/49/28].

The omnibus LOS resolution of the 49th General Assembly stressed the importance of ensuring a uniform, consistent, and coordinated approach to implementing the treaty provisions, and urged competent international organizations, as well as development and funding institutions, to pay particular attention to the needs of developing states for technical and financial assistance. The resolution also called for a strengthened system of collection, compilation, and dissemination of information relevant to the implementation of the LOS Convention and for collaboration among international organizations on an integrated system of databases. It gave the Secretary-General ongoing responsibility for establishing special facilities for the maps, charts, and geographic coordinates concerning national maritime zones that are to be deposited by states.

During the debate on the LOS at the 49th Session, many delegates noted the important functions carried out by **DOALOS** and the high quality of its reports and studies. Some expressed concern that discussions on LOS Convention-related matters might be dispersed among the committees of the Assembly, urged that DOALOS continue to consolidate its role as a focal point in preparing materials and meetings related to the Convention, and urged too that it be given the **resources and organizational structure** to meet the new demands placed on it.

The International Seabed Authority

The ISA is functioning on a provisional basis, pending ratification of the 1994 Agreement by 40 states (which must include five developed states).

Served by a core staff in Jamaica, its initial administrative expenses will be supplied by the regular budget of the United Nations ($776,000 for 1995) [U.N. press release SEA/1460, 2/23/95]. As of April 1995, well over 100 nations had agreed to apply the Agreement on a provisional basis.

Elections to the Authority's **36-member Council** and its subsidiary technical organs were not completed at the Assembly's first substantive meeting in February. The delay was a result of differences over how to constitute the five categories of membership in the Council: major consumers of the minerals found in manganese nodules, major investors in deep-seabed mining, major net exporters of the same minerals, developing states representing special interests, and equitable geographic distribution. The February meeting did adopt rules of procedure for the Assembly, with elections expected in August 1995, including elections for a secretary-general of the ISA.

Since commercial mining operations are unlikely until well into the 21st century, the Authority's role for the time being is to review trends relating to mining and to monitor the exploration and training activities of the **"pioneer" miners.** At the August 1994 meeting of the Preparatory Commission for the Authority and the Tribunal it was decided to waive certain fees applicable to pioneer investors, and to defer pioneer obligations to carry out specified exploration activities, pending demonstrated activity on the part of any contractor. On August 2, 1994, the Commission registered the Republic of Korea as a pioneer investor [LOS/PCN/L.115/ Rev.1, 9/8/94].

The Commission has been meeting since 1983 to prepare for the establishment of the Authority and the Tribunal. Its final report on deep-seabed mining aspects was presented to the inaugural ISA Assembly at its first meeting, in November 1994. Its final report on preparations for the Tribunal was presented to the November meeting of contracting parties. The Commission will expire at the end of this first Assembly's third meeting, in August 1995.

The comprehensive LOS Convention has already begun to function as the framework for international ocean law and policy, as witness the development of a number of agreements and **activities that were spawned by the U.N. Conference on Environment and Development** in Rio of 1992.

1. **The U.N. Conference on Straddling Fish Stocks and Highly Migratory Fish Stocks, and Related Fishery Matters.** The Conference's spring meeting (a second, and final, session was scheduled for July 24– August 4, 1995) produced a revised draft Agreement for the Implementation of the Provisions of the LOS Convention relating to the conservation and management of these stocks [A/Conf.164/22/Rev.1, 4/11/95]. This takes the same form as the binding agreement on deep-seabed mining and, like that

mining agreement, is intended to be interpreted and applied with the Convention. The Agreement is expected to be finalized in August.

If the Agreement is widely endorsed by both coastal and distant-water fishing states, it will represent a significant step forward in interpreting and elaborating the LOS Convention's general obligations. It requires that the development of fisheries be firmly grounded in scientific evidence, and it strengthens reporting and observation schemes so as to do a better job of monitoring and enforcing conservation and management measures affecting these stocks. While the draft Agreement deals with only two categories of fish stocks, a related initiative undertaken by the U.N.'s Food and Agriculture Organization (FAO) is intended to lead to the adoption in 1996 of a **Code of Conduct for Responsible Fishing** for all fisheries and aquaculture [COFI/95/2, 11/94]. The Code is voluntary and will reflect and complement the Agreement. As technical guidelines for implementing the Code are completed, they may have considerable influence on national practices and international programs as well as on regional fisheries agreements. The binding 1993 FAO Agreement to Promote Compliance with International Conservation and Management Measures by Fishing Vessels on the High Seas is an important element of the Code.

The General Assembly adopted four resolutions on fisheries in 1994. One calls attention to progress in the U.N. Fisheries Conference [A/Res/49/121; see also the report on the conference, A/49/522, 10/14/94]. Another resolution calls on states parties to fulfill their LOS Convention obligations by ensuring that the fishing vessels of their own country do not fish without authorization in zones that are under the jurisdiction of another country. The same resolution requests development assistance organizations to aid developing countries in improving their ability to monitor and control fishing activities, and it calls for a report to the 50th General Assembly on steps taken and problems encountered in carrying out these measures [A/Res/49/116]. A third resolution of the 49th Session calls for further effort to minimize waste in fisheries, including discards of by-catch of nontarget fish and nonfish species, and that these issues be elaborated in the work of the U.N. Fisheries Conference and in the FAO Code of Conduct [A/Res/49/118]. In the fourth resolution on fishing [A/Res/49/436], states are urged to ensure the effective application of the moratorium [A/Res/46/215] on large-scale pelagic driftnet fishing on the high seas [see also the report on large-scale pelagic driftnet fishing, A/49/469].

2. **The U.N. Environment Programme (UNEP) intergovernmental meeting on Protection of the Marine Environment from Land-Based Activities** (Washington, D.C., October 23–November 3, 1995). More than three-quarters of marine pollution (whether from coastal and watershed sources or airborne) originates on land—its industry and agriculture, its households and urban development, and the sediment result-

ing from erosion and construction. Efforts to implement LOS Convention obligations on land-based sources are being given fresh impetus by the 1995 UNEP meeting. Following preparatory meetings in December 1993, June 1994, and March 1995, the conference is expected to adopt a global program of action and, possibly, a legally binding convention on persistent organic pollutants that reach the marine environment. The institutional mechanisms for follow-up to this meeting are critical, including linkages with the UNEP regional seas programs, bilateral and multilateral development agencies, and the many sources of data and expertise for dealing with the problem. A clearinghouse mechanism has been proposed, and governments are deliberating on the appropriate intergovernmental mechanism to review progress, address critical and emerging issues, and set priorities. The conference is to (1) identify approaches to land-based pollution that can be tailored to particular economic and/or geographic circumstances, (2) identify areas requiring, and the opportunities for, international cooperation, and (3) establish criteria for development and technical assistance projects [UNEP Governing Council Decision 17/20].

The **Global Environment Facility (GEF)** has been singled out as a source of funding for such initiatives to reduce coastal and marine degradation—helping to establish a link between the GEF and the concerns of the LOS Convention. The GEF has identified land-based sources as the main cause of such degradation and as one of the four major concerns of its program on "international waters," both marine and freshwater (the other three are physical habitat degradation, introduction of nonindigenous species, and excessive exploitation of resources) ["Scope and Preliminary Operational Strategy for International Waters," GEF/C.3/7, 2/95]. The GEF has also been sought as a funding mechanism for the Programme of Action for Small Island Developing States (below) and for implementation of the U.N. Fisheries Conference Agreement.

3. **The Global Conference on the Sustainable Development of Small Island Developing States** (Barbados, April 26–May 6, 1994) [see Report of the Conference, A/Conf.167/9]. After reviewing the results of feasibility studies conducted in 1994, the General Assembly invited UNEP to develop a technical assistance program and related information network for the states concerned [A/Res/49/122]. It went on to ask the Commission on Sustainable Development (CSD) to review progress on the Conference's Programme of Action at the CSD's 1996 session and again in 1999, and it requested the Secretary-General to establish a "clearly identifiable support entity" within the Secretariat's Department for Policy Coordination and Sustainable Development, reporting back to the General Assembly's 50th Session on actions taken by U.N. organs to implement the Programme of Action [ibid.].

4. **The U.N. Commission on Sustainable Development review of Agenda 21's provisions on oceans and coasts** (chapter 17). The Subcom-

mittee on Oceans and Coastal Areas of the Inter-Agency Committee on Sustainable Development, established to follow up on UNCED, is charged with preparing reports on U.N. system activities supporting chapter 17. The reports, and an analysis of the effectiveness of such activities, will be reviewed at the Commission's 1996 session.

The LOS Convention contemplates enlisting still other bodies—prominently the International Maritime Organization, UNESCO's Intergovernmental Oceanographic Commission, the FAO, and UNEP—to provide technical advice and assistance. And it assigns them specific responsibilities for identifying the experts who will sit on special arbitration panels in their respective fields of competence: navigation, including vessel-source pollution; marine scientific research; fisheries; or marine environment [Annex VIII of the LOS Convention]. Numerous other global and regional organizations also have a role in supporting implementation of the Convention [see *The Law of the Sea: Priorities and Responsibilities in Implementing the Convention,* Part II (IUCN, 1995)]. Many groups are already acting on their responsibilities toward the LOS Convention and taking the opportunity to advance its goals [see A/49/631].

Antarctica

For the first time since 1985, the members of the **General Assembly reached consensus** on "the question of Antarctica," adopting a resolution on the subject without a vote [A/Res/49/80]. They welcomed the regular reports provided to the Secretary-General on the meetings and activities of the countries engaged in Antarctic research pursuant to the 1959 Antarctic Treaty and its associated instruments [A/49/370], and they recognized the Antarctic Treaty as furthering the purposes and principles of the U.N. Charter.

The General Assembly went on to urge the Antarctic Treaty parties to invite the Executive Director of UNEP (designated by the Secretary-General to follow Antarctic matters) to attend their meetings. Relevant U.N. agencies have been invited to participate as expert organizations in Antarctic Treaty meetings for several years. UNEP made its first appearance at the 1994 meeting. Successive resolutions of the General Assembly have urged the treaty parties to invite the Secretary-General to attend treaty meetings, and by recognizing the special competence of UNEP, the treaty parties have, de facto, invited the participation of the Secretary-General's designated representative on Antarctic matters. (The Antarctic agenda item will not be reconsidered by the Assembly until 1996.)

The 19th **Antarctic Treaty Consultative Meeting** (XIX ATCM) took place in Seoul, Republic of Korea, May 8–19, 1995. The Group of Legal Experts charged with preparing an annex to the **Protocol on Liability** met in The Hague in November and was scheduled to meet again during the first week of the Seoul ATCM. Ratification of the 1991 Protocol on Environmental Protection has proceeded at a glacial pace. Twenty-six parties to the Antarctic Treaty must ratify the Protocol before it enters into force. There were 14 by the spring of 1995, five more than the previous year [*Issues/49*, p. 199].

The 13th annual meeting of the **Commission of the Convention for Conservation of Antarctic Marine Living Resources (CCAMLR)** took place at headquarters in Hobart, Australia, October 26–November 4, 1994. CCAMLR's precautionary approach to the initiation of new fisheries and the maintenance of existing fisheries—requiring the development of an information base sufficient to inform decisions—continues to set the pace for global fisheries management, in particular the U.N. Fisheries Conference discussed earlier.

Reported incidents of **illegal fishing** during the 1993–94 season led the Commission to consider means of improving compliance with the Convention through such devices as vessel transponders. A review of further studies and reports on **marine debris** led it to reaffirm the importance of educational placards on ships as well as to call for additional beach surveys. The Commission also agreed on further measures to reduce **incidental bird mortality** due to longline fishing, in particular through contacts with other fishery organizations responsible for fisheries adjacent to the CCAMLR area; on explanatory documents for use by the fleets of Commission members; and on placing additional observers on fishing vessels to report on incidental mortality of seabirds.

A new model for **krill management** was considered, one that could justify higher fishing limits for future krill harvests. Since the current catch rate is well below that permitted under the present model, the Commission recommended no changes to existing conservation measures. Commending the efforts of its Scientific Committee in devising assessment methods and models that incorporate scientific uncertainty into management actions, the Commission agreed to continue this work [Report of the XIII Meeting of the Commission].

In May 1994 the International Whaling Commission (IWC) established a **sanctuary for whales in the southern ocean** aimed at putting an end to commercial whaling. Japan and Russia, having filed formal objections to the sanctuary measure within the time IWC rules allow, are not bound by it.

V
Social and Humanitarian Issues

1. The World Summit for Social Development
By Gail V. Karlsson

The World Summit for Social Development, held in Copenhagen in March 1995, was the first U.N.-sponsored meeting to focus on the social and economic needs of individuals, families, and communities, and the first to explore the unique opportunities for social justice and social development offered by the end of the Cold War. Over 100 heads of state attended this discussion of the structural causes of poverty, unemployment, and social exclusion—profound problems affecting every country of the world.

Though couched in terms of **"people-centered sustainable development,"** the Social Summit concentrated on fundamental economic issues. The current worldwide enthusiasm for free markets, economic growth, and globalization of trade presents dramatic new opportunities for some people but has also intensified the despair of those who are excluded from the global marketplace. More than a billion people live in absolute poverty today, lacking sufficient food, clean water, sanitation, education, and health care. A large proportion of them are the women and children of the least-developed countries. The negative effects of globalization are not confined to the poorest countries, however. Economic divisions are also widening within the industrialized countries as they adjust to global transformations of the world economy. This growing gap between rich and poor threatens the peace both within and between countries.

Despite a new international commitment to the goal of eradicating poverty in the world, **few concrete plans emerged** from the Social Summit negotiations. All political leaders are opposed to poverty and unemployment, of course, yet none can offer global solutions to these problems. The issue of economic injustice in world markets is by no means a new topic for the United Nations and, since the end of the Cold War, has become further complicated by the needs of countries trying to move from planned economies to open markets. The poorest countries continue to struggle with overwhelming debt burdens, trade barriers, low commodity prices, and onerous structural adjustment programs. At the same time, many of the industrialized countries have themselves suffered recession, economic restructuring, and ballooning budget deficits, with resulting social tensions, shrinking governmental resources, and diminished funds for foreign aid.

One of the main controversies during Social Summit preparations was **the relationship between economic growth and social progress.** Draft documents emphasizing the importance of "sustained economic growth" to combat poverty and unemployment were criticized by some for failing to recognize the shortcomings of the global market system in meeting human needs. Environmentalists were alarmed that an undue emphasis on job creation and economic growth represented a retreat from the Rio Earth Summit's commitment to "sustainable development." Developing countries responded that the industrialized countries had failed to live up to their obligations to provide money and technological resources for sustainable development and so should not attempt to impose further constraints on economic development in poorer countries.

At the last minute, negotiators achieved a reluctant consensus on the need for "sustained economic growth in the context of sustainable development" as a basis for social development and social justice [A/Conf.166/L.3/Add.1, 3/10/95, p. 2]. In addition, they agreed on the need to "promote dynamic, open, free markets, while recognizing the need to intervene in markets, to the extent necessary, to prevent or counteract market failure, promote stability and long-term investment, ensure fair competition and ethical conduct and harmonize economic and social development" [ibid., p. 9].

One recommendation that attracted widespread support was the promotion of small enterprises, cooperatives, and self-employment opportunities through better access to credit, technology, training, and technical assistance, especially for those currently excluded from formal employment markets. The **Social Summit declaration** reaffirmed that "empowering people, particularly women, to strengthen their own capacities is a main objective of development and its principal resource" [ibid., p. 7].

Negotiators of the Social Summit **Program of Action** recognized that "nothing short of a renewed and massive political will at the national and international levels to invest in people and their well-being will achieve the objectives of social development" [A/Conf.166/L.3/Add.7, 3/10/95, p. 1]. That political will was not clearly evident when the heads of state arrived in Copenhagen. The U.S. delegation played a significant diplomatic role in negotiating the language of the Social Summit documents but lacked the public support of **President Bill Clinton,** who was reluctant to be seen as supporting global welfare programs. His absence tended to marginalize the Social Summit. Vice President Al Gore, who appeared in the

President's place, acknowledged that the proper role of government in addressing poverty, both at home and abroad, is currently the subject of intense political debate in the United States. Also absent from the summit were Boris Yeltsin of Russia, himself preoccupied with internal conflicts and an uncertain political position, and John Major of Great Britain.

Among the most visible participants were **Hillary Clinton,** who spoke out on behalf of women and children; France's departing President **François Mitterrand,** who was influential in arranging the Social Summit and attended despite ill health; and Cuban President **Fidel Castro,** who used this platform to denounce hegemony and neoliberal economic policy and then joined Mitterrand for a visit in Paris. Although the leaders of the Nordic countries held an impressive joint press conference with South African President **Nelson Mandela,** they merely reaffirmed their general interest in assisting the newly democratic South African government but made no new commitments to it.

There were, however, some **new debt-relief initiatives** announced in Copenhagen. Prime Minister **Poul Rasmussen of Denmark** led the way by announcing the cancellation of $118 million in developing-country debt. Austria followed with another $100 million debt cancellation, but other countries failed to agree to outright debt forgiveness. The official Program of Action [A/Conf.166/L.3/Add.3, 3/10/95, p. 7] refers to the terms of bilateral debt forgiveness agreed upon in the "Paris Club" in December 1994, which require recipient countries to undertake structural adjustment programs. The Program of Action also invites the international financial institutions to consider alleviation of the multilateral debt burdens of low-income countries, measures the World Bank and International Monetary Fund (IMF) have been reluctant to take (and in fact continued to resist during Social Summit discussions).

On **International Women's Day,** which was celebrated during the week of the Social Summit, Hillary Clinton announced a **modest U.S. initiative** that would allocate $100 million over a ten-year period to provide enhanced educational opportunities for girls and women in Africa, Asia, and Latin America, under the leadership of local women's groups. Almost a billion people in the world are illiterate, two-thirds of them women, and she pointed out that investing in education for girls generates higher economic productivity, improved health, lower birthrates, and stronger families and communities. The United States sponsored a commitment on education, which was added to the official summit declaration in Copenhagen.

The Social Summit Program of Action urged the donor countries to meet the previously agreed target of 0.7 percent of gross national product for overall official development assistance, a commitment few except the Nordic countries have fulfilled. Since it was clear from the outset that the Social Summit would not immediately generate new and additional financial resources for poverty relief and social development, however, a good deal of attention was paid to **reallocating existing financial resources.** Some delegates argued that existing resources are sufficient to eradicate absolute poverty but that different choices have to be made, nationally and internationally, about how to distribute the funds.

The 1994 *Human Development Report* issued by the U.N. Development Programme (UNDP) proposed an agenda for the Social Summit that included a **"20:20 compact"** calling for developing countries to devote at least 20 percent of their budgets to basic human needs, such as nutrition, safe drinking water and sanitation, primary education and health care, family planning, and access to credit for self-employment projects. According to the report, developing countries spend an average of only 13 percent of their national budgets on such concerns, less than half of what they spend on military matters [p. 7]. Since some of the poorest countries would need financial assistance in supplying basic human needs, donor countries were asked to allocate the same percentage—20 percent—of their bilateral aid (up from the current average of 7 percent) for human priority concerns.

Even though the 20:20 compact required no new money, it did not win widespread acceptance at Copenhagen and in the end was endorsed only as a **voluntary commitment** by interested countries. Many countries objected to the whole idea of setting specific mandatory budget targets as well as to imposing further conditions on development assistance.

Throughout the Social Summit preparatory process, developing governments and nongovernmental organizations (NGOs) repeatedly complained about "conditionality"—the **structural adjustment programs** these nations must undertake to qualify for World Bank and International Monetary Fund loans. The programs imposed by these international financial institutions have led to reduced government spending on social programs in some developing countries, bringing only greater hardships for the poorest citizens, particularly women and children. NGO groups attending the Social Summit staged a hunger strike during the conference to call attention to these concerns. NGO activists at the parallel Social Development conference disrupted a World Bank panel discussion to deplore the Bank's lending practices, chanting "50 years is enough."

In Copenhagen, the international community made its first **specific commitment** to ensure that structural adjustment programs promote social development goals and protect the most vulnerable segments of society [A/Conf.166/L.3/Add.1, 3/10/95, p. 17]. The World Bank, the IMF, and the other international financial institutions were urged to give higher priority to social sector-lending and to improve policy dialogues with affected countries in order to reduce the negative impact of structural adjustment programs [A/Conf.166/L.3/Add.7, 3/10/95, p. 9].

The Social Summit Program of Action further suggested that the

U.N. Economic and Social Council (ECOSC
vative ideas for generating funds [ibid.]. One
possibilities was the **tax on internation**
gested by James Tobin, winner of the N
Many of the overall foreign exchange ‹
trillion per day, are purely speculative, sec.
rate fluctuations and international interest rate
velopment Report, p. 70]. Speculative currency transactions
in exchange markets, with an adverse effect on national
[ibid.]. Tobin suggested a worldwide tax rate of 0.5 percent on
tions to discourage speculative capital movements, with the
made available for "international purposes." Even a tax of 0.05 per
during the period 1995–2000 could raise $150 billion per year [ibid., p. 9].

The "Tobin tax" has recently generated a significant amount of interest at the United Nations. Such an instrument has the potential to help stabilize financial markets while creating a steady flow of funds for global development, peacekeeping, environmental protection, and other international initiatives without further burdening national budgets. It would also relieve some of the current political tensions between donor and recipient countries. In Copenhagen the idea of a currency speculation tax was endorsed by French President Mitterrand and Norwegian Prime Minister Gro Harlem Brundtland as well as by a number of developing countries. It was strongly opposed by the United States, however, which views the tax as an interference with an efficient free market system.

Despite wistful allusions to the peace dividend, there was little serious discussion of **funding social development by reducing military budgets** or arms expenditures. Given the numerous post-Cold War outbreaks of regional and ethnic conflict, hopes for speedy disarmament have not materialized. Global military spending has declined somewhat, chiefly because of budgetary pressures in the industrial countries, but these same countries have major economic incentives for continuing arms sales. Some 86 percent of current arms supplies come from the five permanent members of the Security Council. The Social Summit declaration was weak on shifting resources from military budgets to human development, recommending nothing more than "appropriate" reduction of excessive military expenditures, global arms trading, and investment for arms production and acquisition, "taking into consideration national security requirements" [A/Conf.166/L.3/Add.1, 3/10/95, p. 19].

The **relationship between poverty and unfavorable terms of trade** was also touched upon only lightly in Copenhagen. The Social Summit declaration included international commitments to fully implement the Uruguay Round of multilateral trade negotiations, to monitor the impact of trade liberalization on developing countries, and to improve market access for developing countries and countries with economies in transi-

20]. Serious discussion of trade issues was deferred to the meet-
newly created World Trade Organization (WTO). The Program
n encouraged the U.N. General Assembly to strengthen coordi-
between the United Nations, the international financial institu-
, and the WTO, and to invite the WTO to consider how it might
tribute to the social development program [A/Conf.166/L.3/Add.7, 3/10/95,
2].

Within the U.N. system, the **General Assembly** has the primary policy-making role on matters relating to the follow-up to the Social Summit. In 1996 it will review international progress on eradicating poverty,
and in 2000 it will hold a special session to access the overall outcome of
the Social Summit [ibid., p. 9]. **ECOSOC** is charged with overseeing system-
wide implementation of the Social Summit recommendations.

The Social Summit cannot, however, be assessed in isolation. It is
part of a continuing series of U.N.-sponsored conferences intended to
define international goals for the next 50 years. Vice President Al Gore
characterized these conferences on environmental, economic, and social
issues as **"town meetings of the globe"** through which individual citizens, nongovernmental organizations, and governments are working together to generate a new consensus about the kind of world in which
we want to live. Cynics have denounced these meetings as wasteful and
ineffective, yet they are part of an ongoing process that is designed to
create an international civil society capable of meeting the challenges of
global interdependence.

2. Human Rights
By Felice D. Gaer

Fifty years after the founding conference of the United Nations, human
rights activists draw inspiration from those nongovernmental representatives who served as "consultants" to the U.S. delegation and worked with
such extraordinary creativity and persistence to inscribe human rights in
the U.N. Charter as one of four purposes of the new world body. And
there is inspiration to be derived too from those similarly dedicated private individuals and government representatives who, during the Cold
War, helped develop a body of principles and action-oriented mechanisms
that promote and protect those rights worldwide. Despite the enormous
political changes in the world since the end of the Cold War in 1991, there
is no less a need at the United Nations for creativity and persistence on
behalf of human rights.

Gross violator states and a coterie of others uncomfortable with the
very idea of external scrutiny of human rights still labor assiduously to
keep the U.N.'s action-oriented human rights mechanisms small, ineffec-

tive, and marginalized from field operations and hands-on programs of the world body. Failing that, these governments attempt to portray the U.N.'s emphasis on eradicating torture, arbitrary arrests, summary executions, religious persecution, and discrimination against women and minorities as illegitimate or "imbalanced." Governments that actively champion human rights causes and the many well-informed and courageous nongovernmental human rights organizations (NGOs) face sizable challenges as they seek to strengthen the effectiveness of the United Nations in defending human rights. The U.N. General Assembly's 50th Session has an opportunity to reaffirm the importance of human rights as a core purpose of the world body, and to bolster and strengthen the advances made since the Charter was signed. With the post-Cold War advent of field operations in human rights as part of the U.N.'s multifaceted peacekeeping, humanitarian, and post-conflict peace-building programs, there is also a dramatic opportunity to put human rights principles into practice in U.N. missions worldwide.

At the heart of this effort is the hard work of identifying and publicly stigmatizing countries in which there are gross patterns of human rights abuse. For it is through the **"mobilization of shame"** that the human rights community has been most effective in curbing human rights violations. The United Nations is a political body, after all, and both the General Assembly and Commission on Human Rights are composed of representatives of government. For years, and particularly during the Cold War, the choice of which countries were to be criticized publicly by the Commission on Human Rights had less to do with the intensity of the abuses themselves than with the politics of the Organization and its member states. Thus, the first special human rights teams investigated violations in South Africa (1967), Israel (1968), and Chile (1975), the politically stigmatized member states of their day. Even today, the Commission on Human Rights and the General Assembly cannot criticize important countries for their human rights abuses because the political support is lacking and the votes are not there. Despite years of NGO reporting on atrocities in Iraq, for example, Baghdad was first cited for human rights abuses only *after* the Gulf War, in 1991. Myanmar (Burma), Sudan, and Zaire came up for public scrutiny in the 1990s after years of "consideration" in confidential sessions under the "1503" procedure. Global television news reports led the Commission to hold the emergency sessions on former Yugoslavia (1992) and Rwanda (1994).

Individuals (alternatively called "experts," "special representatives," or "special rapporteurs") have been appointed by the Commission on Human Rights to investigate allegations of human rights abuses and report back. The United Nations has appointed rapporteurs on Afghanistan, Cuba, Equatorial Guinea, Haiti, Iran, Iraq, Burma, Sudan, Zaire, and now former Yugoslavia and Rwanda; and it has designated "experts" to examine and offer advice about conditions in El Salvador, Guatemala, Somalia, Togo, and Cambodia, among others.

The 1995 session of the Commission on Human Rights saw **the formal end of U.N. scrutiny of South Africa's human rights situation after some 27 years,** following democratic nonracial elections and the inauguration of Nelson Mandela as President, marking the formal end of apartheid. Yet political changes were not enough to see Commission scrutiny ended elsewhere. The Special Rapporteur on the Occupied Territories, Switzerland's former President René Felber, stating that "human rights will have the most chance of being enforced once the [peace] process has been completed" [E/CN.4/1995/19], proposed that his post be ended because of the changed circumstances in the Middle East and his conclusion that "the solution to the problem [of human rights abuses] lies elsewhere than in simply reporting facts." (Felber had been the first official of the U.N. Human Rights Commission permitted to visit Israel since the 1970s and the beginning of U.N. scrutiny.) Several NGOs and some government delegates accused Felber of having insulted the very purpose of the Commission, which (they argued) is to examine human rights, not political processes. The Commission went on to adopt its **standard five separate resolutions critical of Israel,** and one U.S.-sponsored resolution that speaks positively of the Middle East peace process. Felber resigned his post, and a new rapporteur is to be appointed, for an indefinite term.

Precisely because of the politics often surrounding the criticism of countries responsible for gross violations of human rights, major efforts have been made to establish effective **U.N. human rights machinery able to examine and respond to violations independently, impartially, and wherever they occur.** In the late 1970s the Commission on Human Rights established a regionally balanced, five-person Working Group on Forced or Involuntary Disappearances. Report after report of "disappearances" in Argentina prompted concern, but the inability to gather enough political support to name Argentina in a resolution led to the tactical decision to create a body capable of examining "disappearances" *everywhere.* This global approach turned out to be a strategically brilliant breakthrough that led to the creation of about a dozen similarly conceived **"thematic mechanisms":** a working group on **arbitrary detentions** and a series of experts, or "special rapporteurs"—on **summary executions, torture, religious intolerance, freedom of expression, violence against women, sale of children, independence of the judiciary, the internally displaced, mercenaries,** and **contemporary forms of racism.** Each of these is able to act urgently to inquire into individual cases of threatened or existing abuses, and to examine the conditions affecting the right under scrutiny in countries throughout the world. Persons appointed to these bodies serve as **unpaid independent experts,** not as representatives of government. At the 1995 **Commission on Human Rights,** the three-year mandates of many of these reporting mechanisms were renewed, despite some efforts to curtail the thematic mechanisms severely because of dissatisfaction by many developing countries with the exposure of their reported abuses in the annual reports of the investigators. Those mechanisms extended for three more years are the rapporteurs on torture, executions, and mercenaries; the representative on the internally displaced; and the working groups on arbitrary detention and disappearance.

Powerful countries, particularly those serving on the Commission, have long escaped the ignominy of a public condemnatory resolution, but now even they sometimes may be the subject of investigative missions by thematic rapporteurs, consensus statements, and attempts to adopt resolutions. In 1995 the Special Representative on Torture examined **Russian prisons,** the Special Representative on Religion went to **China and Tibet,** and the Special Representative on Contemporary Forms of Racism examined **racial discrimination in the United States.** Although none of the permanent five Security Council members have been the subject of Commission resolutions, the chairman did read out a mild statement—based on consensus—regarding the **Soviet Union's use of excessive force in the Baltic republics (1991)** and a statement on the **Russian Army's "disproportionate use of force" in Chechnya** (1995, see below). Efforts to censure China since the suppression of the 1989 democracy movement and the **Beijing massacre** have not succeeded to date, although in 1995 the United States and the European Union achieved the unprecedented first defeat of China's usual procedural shield—a motion to shelve even discussion of the subject by taking "no-action" (the equivalent of a "tabling" motion in U.S. parliamentary procedure). When the Commission voted on the substance of the resolution, Russia and others changed their vote, making for a tally that came one vote shy of formally identifying China as an abuser of human rights.

A **Cuban-led effort to condemn the United States,** which had permitted the Special Rapporteur on Racism to visit the country, fell flat: Only three of the Commission's 53 member countries (China, Cuba, and Sudan—themselves the subjects of intense scrutiny for human rights abuses) voted in favor of a much watered-down text.

In the course of 1994–95, the thematic mechanisms of the Commission did send rapporteurs on field missions to a number of countries that have not been the subject of official scrutiny, with public reports issued on each:

- **Indonesia,** where the destination of the Rapporteur on Summary and Arbitrary Executions was East Timor [E/CN.4/1995/61, Add.1]
- **Colombia,** which received a visit from both the Special Rapporteur on Torture and the Special Rapporteur on Summary Executions [E/CN.4/1995/111]

- **Vietnam and Bhutan,** both of which received missions from the Working Group on Arbitrary Detention.

Another means of citing countries has been through the so-called **"1503" confidential procedure.** In 1995, for the first time, **Saudi Arabia** was cited on the basis of NGO communications alleging widespread human rights violations and will remain under scrutiny until further review in 1996. The Commission also decided to keep under confidential review **Chad, Armenia,** and **Azerbaijan.**

The European Union, strongly backed by NGOs, made a formal bid to censure **Nigeria,** where a military dictatorship seized power in 1993 after elections it didn't like and where repression has grown, but solid opposition from the African members of the Commission defeated the attempt.

The U.N. General Assembly also holds the power of the purse, but governments committed to zero-real growth budgets remain unwilling to allocate adequate **funds** for ongoing programs, much less for the dozen or so thematic and country rapporteurs established since 1991. The United Nations agreed to allocate $28 million in 1995 alone for the war crimes tribunal on the former Yugoslavia, for example, yet provided a total of only $18 million for the entire **U.N. Centre for Human Rights**—the U.N. Secretariat's main human rights arm—which acts as the secretariat for six treaties, the Commission and Subcommission on Human Rights, and special rapporteurs for 26 separate country and thematic issues. This last group must take action on more than 10,000 complaints annually and investigate and report on a long list of other topics. **As mandates are added they remain "unfunded,"** so that most country or thematic rapporteurs are assigned less than one staff assistant to help investigate, prepare, and submit urgent case inquiries and to assist in the preparation of their reports.

The High Commissioner

The newest development affecting U.N. human rights programs is the establishment in April 1994 of the post of U.N. High Commissioner for Human Rights, created by the General Assembly in 1993. The **High Commissioner, José Ayala Lasso of Ecuador,** will present his second report to the General Assembly at the 50th Session. That report is expected not only to reflect his latest travels and achievements but also to assess the implementation of the Vienna Declaration and Programme of Action adopted at the **1993 World Conference on Human Rights** and reveal the results to date of the mandated restructuring of the U.N. Human Rights Centre.

The long-awaited creation by the General Assembly of the post of

U.N. High Commissioner for Human Rights has raised hopes that the U.N.'s capacity to respond to and curtail serious violations of human rights will improve dramatically. The High Commissioner's mandate is extremely broad, however, and the demands on the first occupant of this post are great.

The notion of establishing the post of High Commissioner, which dates from early in the life of the United Nations, was revived by the Vienna-based World Conference on Human Rights in 1993. Many human rights activists sought a skilled and vigorous champion of human rights able to integrate human rights concerns into U.N. field operations, such as the peacekeeping, peacemaking, and humanitarian assistance programs of the United Nations, as well as to coordinate the U.N.'s entire spectrum of programs on human rights through regular interaction with the U.N. Development Programme (UNDP), the U.N. Children's Fund (UNI-CEF), the World Health Organization (WHO), the International Labour Organisation (ILO), and others. Advocates of a High Commissioner have always looked for an office with the independent authority to dispatch envoys on fact-finding missions and speak out publicly—and independently—about his findings. In the post-Cold War world, proponents also sought a High Commissioner who could request the Secretary-General to bring to the attention of the U.N. Security Council (long resistant to discussion of human rights anywhere but in South Africa and Israel) any serious violations of human rights that appeared to threaten international peace and security. Still others—prominently, states that are among the gross violators of human rights—vigorously opposed any innovation that would strengthen the U.N.'s human rights activities, and most vigorously when it came to the idea of empowering anyone to conduct on-site investigation or take these issues to the Security Council.

The mandate given the High Commissioner is less specific and less activist than suggested in early proposals, but its very vagueness allows a committed human rights leader to shape the post in the direction suggested by its most avid proponents. Under his initial mandate, the **High Commissioner's specific responsibilities** consist of making recommendations to U.N. bodies for the promotion and protection of all rights, including the right to development; playing "an active role" in the elimination and prevention of violations of human rights around the world; providing overall coordination of human rights activities throughout the U.N. system; enhancing international cooperation in human rights, including the provision of technical assistance; coordinating education and public information programs in human rights; and rationalizing, adapting, and strengthening U.N. human rights machinery. He is based in Geneva but maintains an office in New York.

For the High Commissioner to make a difference in people's lives, he must have the ability to respond promptly to human rights violations wherever they occur. To do so will require, at a minimum, that the High Commissioner monitor the fulfillment of human rights obligations and respond to violations through, inter alia, effective fact-finding, public reporting, and securing relief and redress for victims of violations, including efforts to establish a means of making those responsible for gross abuses accountable for those abuses.

At the tactical level, there has long been considerable agreement that the most effective way to halt violations is to place them under such a bright spotlight that the government itself will agree to stop the abuses. This is something the nongovernmental human rights sector has done a better job of demonstrating than has the intergovernmental one. Publicity may also have the result of triggering other behavior-modifying pressure, such as unilateral or regional economic linkages or sanctions.

The High Commissioner has begun a **reform and restructuring of the U.N. human rights program**—a program that grew up in the Cold War years, when even the words "human rights" were anathema to some governments. During 1995 there were reports from the U.N. Inspector General's office and elsewhere about operational tensions between the new office of the High Commissioner and the offices of the Centre for Human Rights directed by an Assistant Secretary-General for Human Rights. In mid-1995 it was reported that the U.N. central offices had requested a "unity of action" between the two: the High Commissioner to provide overall supervision of the policies of the Centre, the Assistant Secretary-General to serve as day-to-day manager of the Centre.

Nongovernmental human rights organizations, which helped develop the strategy of establishing global "mechanisms" to take action against human rights violations (and which in turn have provided most of the specific information on complaints to these U.N. human rights mechanisms) look to the High Commissioner to take the lead in marshaling the entire strength and potential of the human rights movement against gross violations of human rights ["The Promise of the U.N. High Commissioner for Human Rights," statement adopted after the Consultation with the High Commissioner, organized by the Blaustein Institute of New York and the Carter Center of Atlanta, June 4–6, 1995].

NGOs have been concerned that situations may arise in which governments responsible for human rights violations seek to play off the efforts of the High Commissioner against the efforts of working groups or rapporteurs. Urging the High Commissioner to safeguard against such stratagems, the NGOs have recommended that his visits to member states be substantive and meaningful, that they be part of a coordinated strategy, with appropriate follow-up, and that he draw upon the full range of assets of the human rights community, including NGOs within and outside the country. Such concern surfaced after the **High Commissioner's early visit to Cuba** (to which he did not take the Human Rights Commission's Special Rapporteur on Cuba), to **Colombia** (where NGOs reported no evidence of his having sought to back up or implement the recommendations of the reports of the Rapporteurs on Torture and Summary Executions), and to **India** (in whose troubled Kashmiri region ancient temples were destroyed only days after he had traveled to the area). Many nongovernmental human rights organizations are calling on the High Commissioner to speak out publicly about violations, arguing that his preference for a confidential approach on his country visits is less than effective when there is no threat (or reality) of public criticism or any timetable for follow-up action.

In short, there is concern in the human rights movement that the High Commissioner has begun his tenure so quietly. He undertook more than 20 country visits in his first 14 months in office but began with Austria and Switzerland, effectively signaling that the visits were matters of routine diplomacy, aimed at fostering support for human rights rather than at looking into human rights violations. And, in fact, the High Commissioner has spoken of exploring the possibility of using "cooperation" through diplomatic channels to address human rights problems in place of the traditional tools of investigation, public reports, and stigmatizing violators.

In his public appearances, such as those during an official visit to Washington in June, the High Commissioner **asked to be judged by the concrete results of his actions,** not by the volume of his public remarks. Among the "results" cited by U.N. officials are events following the High Commissioner's visits. Cited in the Cuba case are the release of prisoners, ratification of the Convention against Torture, and plans to establish a chair of human rights at the University of Havana. Human rights activists have been quick to point out the *continuing* infringements of human rights and freedoms on the island as well as in other countries in which results are said to have followed a visit by the High Commissioner. Clearly Ayala Lasso will have to consolidate and develop his programs, strategy, and style during the remainder of his four-year term.

Among the **initiatives the High Commissioner could take to strengthen the capacity of the United Nations to protect human rights** is to submit a monthly report to the Security Council, or conduct monthly informal consultations with it, advising the members of urgent situations that warrant attention because they threaten international peace and security. If he establishes his presence (and his office) in New York, the High Commissioner could report and make recommendations to the General Assembly as well as to the governing councils of the specialized agencies and the international financial institutions. He could begin to energize the Commission on Human Rights and call on governments to convene in emergency session, such as the one held on former Yugoslavia and (during his own tenure) on Rwanda. He could interact regularly with top officials in New York and be included in the Secretary-General's regular "cabinet" meetings with the heads of political affairs, peacekeeping, and other departments.

In a hint of the leadership the High Commissioner could bring to the U.N.'s action on human rights, Ayala Lasso not only opened the 1995 session of the Human Rights Commission in Geneva but presented a substantive report drawing attention to his efforts on Chechnya, former Yugoslavia, and Rwanda. In a body accustomed to set speeches, the High Commissioner engaged in a lively discussion—using a question-and-answer format—with delegations during the official meeting time.

In his first year in office the High Commissioner also made important innovations in the areas of emergency response to human rights violations, field monitoring, and preventive activities. These must be consolidated and advanced significantly to be effective, in large part because they are so new and the Centre for Human Rights has never launched large emergency response operations on its own.

Ayala Lasso took up his appointment as High Commissioner on April 5, 1994, and on April 6 the plane carrying the Presidents of Rwanda and Burundi was shot down, setting off violence and genocide within Rwanda. The High Commissioner visited the area in May, calling for a special emergency session of the Commission on Human Rights, and established a human rights monitoring mission in Rwanda (which, as of June 1995, had some 120 monitors on the ground). Critics have pointed to the monitors' lack of training, operational experience, and vehicles or communications equipment, and the High Commissioner has acknowledged that the Centre for Human Rights lacks the experience and capacity for launching such missions. He has called for measures to address these shortcomings on a permanent basis.

In his first report to the Commission on Human Rights [E/CN.4/1994/ 98, par. 32], Ayala Lasso identified the following three **long-term needs for securing support to prevent further human rights violations in rapidly deteriorating situations:**

1. Logistical assistance capacity on a standby basis to provide material, communications, and other support for emergency or preventive field missions.

2. Establishment and maintenance of an international roster of specialized staff to be available at short notice for human rights field missions (investigation teams, field officers, legal experts, and the like).

3. Increased contributions to the Voluntary Fund for Technical Cooperation.

The fact that the Centre for Human Rights has no such operational field capacity at present not only makes clear that the U.N. human rights programs lack a field orientation but also underscores the point that such programs have been starved for resources—human and financial. If the U.N. human rights programs, and the High Commissioner in particular, are to play a major role in combating gross violations of human rights, they will need the resources and political support to do so. In the opinion of many human rights advocates, the General Assembly can provide no more important support to the cause of human rights than to enhance the High Commissioner's capacity to combat abuses, which also means rendering greater financial assistance to the thematic mechanisms and the Special Rapporteurs.

Country Situations

In the post-Cold War era the U.N. Human Rights Commission is no longer limiting itself to ritualized and redundant resolutions but has begun to expand its scrutiny of human rights situations, has convened its first emergency sessions in history (on former Yugoslavia in 1992 and on Rwanda in 1994), has dispatched monitors to the field (initially to Yugoslavia and Rwanda, and several new ones in 1995), and under the leadership of the High Commissioner is exploring various new forms of emergency response and preventive mechanisms.

Of the many country situations under scrutiny by the U.N.'s human rights bodies and likely to be addressed at the 50th General Assembly, a few of the entrants stand out as particularly important because they are new, or because the scale of abuses is particularly severe, or because new kinds of mechanisms (including monitors and war crimes tribunals) have been established by the United Nations to address them.

Chechnya

The Russian government's indiscriminate bombing of civilians in the northern Caucasus republic of Chechnya was on the minds of delegates as they convened for the 51st session of the Commission on Human Rights, from January 30 to March 11, 1995. In his opening address to the Commission, High Commissioner Ayala Lasso reported that he had "contacted the Russian authorities to express my concern over human rights violations and violations of humanitarian law" and offered assistance to end them and ensure that human rights would be part of any peace talks. All eyes were on the Russian delegation: Its leader since 1992 has been **Sergei Kovalev**, head of the Russian parliament's human rights committee and, as the session began, his country's commissioner of human rights.

Kovalev, who had traveled to Grozny and reported extensively on the atrocities he had seen, emerged in the Chechnya crisis as the foremost critic of the Russian government's policy. Nonetheless, Russia's top leaders decided to send him back to the Commission as head of delegation. Kovalev's arrival some days after the meeting had begun electrified the delegates, who had already heard from famed Russian dissident **Elena Bonner** on the human rights situation in Chechnya. (Bonner, the widow of Andrei Sakharov, had appeared as a representative of the New York-based International League for Human Rights with which both she and her husband have been associated.)

The European Union, with the Germans in front, took the lead in seeking some action by the Commission on Chechnya. The Islamic Conference also played an active role.

For all the evidence marshaled of extensive violations, negotiations on the form and content of a Commission statement, and its probable follow-up, took nearly a month. It was not until February 27 that a text was agreed upon by all parties—including the Russian government—and a **chairman's statement** (in place of a resolution) read out. The statement called for an immediate cease-fire and unhindered humanitarian aid deliveries to civilians; expressed deep concern over the disproportionate use of force by the Russian armed forces and the human rights violations that had occurred "before and after" the onset of the current crisis; called for all individuals who had committed violations to be brought to justice, and called for a dialogue, based on conditions set forth in the statement. The statement went on to request free access to Grozny and nearby areas by the High Commissioner for Human Rights and others, asked the High Commissioner to continue his dialogue with the Russian government to secure respect for human rights in Chechnya, and called on the High Commissioner to cooperate with the Organization for Security and Cooperation in Europe (OSCE), which had already sent an investigative mission (whose travels and ability to interview key army officials had been restricted). To ensure that there would be proper follow-up, and despite the fact that this was a statement without binding force, the Secretary-General was asked to report on the situation at the 1996 Commission. The statement did not specify the agenda item.

When Kovalev addressed the Commission on the subject of Chechnya on March 6, 1995, he described the events there since December 1994 as **a "tragedy" for Russia.** After outlining the challenge posed to the Russian government's authority and stability by Chechnya's illegal armed forces, he went on to describe Moscow's decision to try to resolve the situation by the massive use of armed force as "a mistake" and "inappropriate." The thousands of deaths, he said, were the "price that the civilian population had to pay for the mistakes of politicians," and he called for legislation in Russia to govern the use of armed force in internal conflicts. Kovalev criticized "attempts made by officials to mislead public opinion" on the actual situation in the conflict area, and called for strengthening the freedom of the press.

The Commission chairman's statement, Kovalev said, is "exactly what is needed at this point in time" because Russia itself agreed to fulfill certain obligations and expressed a willingness to cooperate with the Commission and other international organizations. Kovalev concluded by expressing the hope that Russia's delegation would be able to report positive results of this interaction and advances toward democracy when it appeared at the 1996 Commission.

It took several months more until, at the end of May 1995, a mission was dispatched by the High Commissioner for Human Rights with explicit government permission to conduct an on-site investigation of human rights abuses in Chechnya. Russia's own review of its overall human rights performance is scheduled for delivery at the July 1995 meeting of the **Human Rights Committee,** the supervisory body of the International Covenant on Civil and Political Rights. Whether the 50th General Assembly will take further action on Russia's human rights practices vis-à-vis Chechnya will depend on the nature of the High Commissioner's findings, the situation itself, and whether any member states initiate further action before the Commission meets.

Rwanda

High Commissioner Ayala Lasso took up his post in Geneva on April 5, 1994. The airplane returning the Presidents of Rwanda and Burundi from a regional summit was hit by Tutsi rebel fire outside Kigali Airport the very next day, triggering **the mass killings of Tutsis by Hutus.** The High Commissioner undertook a personal mission to Rwanda in mid-May and issued statements from its capital during the visit. Amnesty International proposed and Canada formally initiated the request that led to the convening of an **emergency session of the Commission on Human Rights** in late May. This was the second time an emergency session had been convened to address the situation in a single country—the first had to do with former Yugoslavia—and the Commission established the same kind of machinery it had established in that case: a **Special Rapporteur** with wide authority to investigate and monitor human rights.

The Rapporteur, René Degni-Ségui, traveled to Rwanda in late June accompanied by two other Special Rapporteurs, on torture and executions, respectively. The latter, Bacre Waly Ndiaye of Senegal, had conducted an earlier investigation into executions in Rwanda and, in August 1993, had issued a report that warned of the consequences of allowing those who had already carried out planned waves of killings to go unpunished and raised the issue of genocide regarding the earlier wave of killings [E/CN.4/1994/7/Add.1]. The Commission's member states had not even discussed his earlier report, leaving Rwanda solely for consideration under the Commission's 1503 confidential procedure.

After the June 1994 field mission, Degni-Ségui concluded that it **was appropriate to use the term "genocide" to describe what had happened in Rwanda** and, having set forth this international definition, reported on the **existence of a plan of genocide** replete with specific targets that became official policy and resulted in the massacres themselves [E/CN.4/1995/7]. He called on the United Nations either to establish a new international criminal tribunal to judge the evidence in all cases in Rwanda or to extend the jurisdiction of the international tribunal set up to prosecute war crimes in former Yugoslavia.

On July 26, 1994, Secretary-General Boutros Boutros-Ghali reported that he had established a **Commission of Experts** to investigate and reach conclusions on violations of international humanitarian law, and particularly genocide, in the Rwanda case. (A similar commission had been created for former Yugoslavia—as in the case of Nazi Germany—as a precursor to the war crimes tribunals.) The new Commission was seated in Geneva, and top U.N. officials made efforts to ensure a good working relationship between the Experts Commission and the Special Rapporteur on Rwanda.

After his second trip to Rwanda, in July, following the rebel Tutsi RPF victory over the Hutu government, Degni-Ségui reported authoritatively as Special Rapporteur that the **mass exodus of Hutus from Rwanda to Zaire** was not spontaneous but, rather, "forced" and "planned." Associating himself with the August 2 appeal by the High Commissioner for Human Rights for voluntary funds to establish an on-site human rights mission, Degni-Ségui recommended establishing immediately a **U.N. monitoring mission** of 20 staff members, eventually to reach 150–200, to monitor the return of refugees, investigate the massacres, and provide a setting of confidence for the reconstruction of the country [E/CN.4/1995/12].

Following his October 1994 visit, the Rapporteur revealed the existence of further evidence that the 1994 genocide was planned—mass graves and documentation of who was specifically responsible for issuing the orders, sometimes including lists of those to be killed. The Rapporteur then stated in his public report that the human rights monitoring mission's investigations had "not yet really begun," noting that the first observers did not arrive until August 4 and that, as of October 22, only 37 of 147 agreed-upon observers had taken up their duties at Kigali. The reasons for the delay were an **"absence of material and logistical facilities"**—vehicles, communication radios, and "provisional instructions." Degni-Ségui, clearly furious, noted that this lack of resources explained why **the monitoring mission's initial staff members resigned,** and he suggested that unless matters improve promptly, others might resign as well. These logistical problems plagued efforts to get the investigations started.

The High Commissioner has also tried to work with a variety of U.N. agencies, both peacekeeping and humanitarian, to establish field monitors in Rwanda and technical assistance programs in neighboring volatile Burundi. But these efforts have been plagued by continued bureaucratic inaction, inefficiency, financing problems, lack of trained staff, and the absence of any operational capacity (whether within the U.N. system as a whole or the Centre for Human Rights) to establish human rights monitors in an emergency situation.

In November 1994 the Security Council established an **International Criminal Tribunal for the Prosecution of Persons Responsible for Genocide and Other Serious Violations of International Humanitarian Law Committed in the Territory of Rwanda between January 1, 1994, and December 31, 1994** [S/Res/955, 11/8/94]. The new Tutsi-dominated Rwandan government voted against the resolution, stating that it was for the creation of such a tribunal but not one that covered so short a time period. Since the mandate covered calendar year 1994 only, the current Rwandan government argued, no one could be prosecuted for the past government's "pilot projects" preceding the 1994 genocide. Expressing doubts that the proposed tribunal was well enough staffed for so monumental a task, it registered its displeasure at the fact that **perpetrators would be imprisoned outside Rwanda** and that the international tribunal **forbade the death penalty.** In such circumstances, those who had fled to Zaire but who "planned [genocide] might escape capital punishment" while those within Rwandan jurisdiction would "bear the brunt of the punishment" [U.N. press release SC/5932, 11/8/94].

Although the location of the tribunal has been established (it will be seated outside Rwanda, in the city of Arusha in neighboring Tanzania), the judges selected, and funds said to have been allocated, the tribunal had yet to begin functioning as of May 1995.

In May 1995 came reports that tens of thousands of Rwandans suspected of war crimes, including genocide, had been imprisoned but that no investigators had begun the work of interviewing them or determining who should be held for trial and who freed. Many other suspects were said to be at large outside the country. Reportedly, the funding and staffing of the tribunal were moving very slowly, again because of bureaucratic impediments at U.N. Headquarters.

In January 1995, Degni-Ségui submitted a succinct and precise summary of his findings on the Rwanda massacres to the Commission on Human Rights, pointing out the planning of the massacres, their extent and horrific nature; the causes of the genocide and its perpetrators; and the kinds of human rights abuses that are being committed after the hostilities, related to then forced exodus of refugees and displaced persons; and continuing insecurity within Rwanda. Among his recommendations to the United Nations were the establishment of "an international force responsible for ensuring security in the camps" in Zaire for refugees and displaced persons and "arrangements for repatriation" to Rwanda in safety [E/CN.4/1995/71]. In mid-May 1995 came press reports of mounting abuses in the refugee camps around Rwanda by former Hutu officials and armed leaders, and a report by the U.S.-based Human Rights Watch exposing the **rearmament of the Hutu forces** suspected of the 1994 genocide by the governments of Zaire, France, and South Africa [Human Rights Watch Arms Project, "Rwanda/Zaire: Rearming with Impunity," 5/95].

For all the problems encountered thus far, the substantial U.N. emergency responses to human rights abuses in Rwanda and former Yugoslavia are unique in the Organization's history and were possible only in the post-Cold War era.

Burundi

Following his visits to examine the massacres in Rwanda in May 1994, the High Commissioner for Human Rights began to establish an **"advisory services" human rights program** in Burundi, as a preventive measure and a complement to his activities in Rwanda. Agreements were signed in September 1994 [see E/CN.4/1995/66 for more on human rights in Burundi]. In 1994 the Commission on Human Rights had responded gently to **Burundi's inter-ethnic massacres of fall 1993,** which followed an attempted coup d'état, by demanding an end to the violence, welcoming efforts of the U.N. **Secretary-General's Special Representative to Burundi** to set up an inquiry, and urging the Burundi authorities to examine and bring to justice those responsible for the violence. This did not happen. In the meanwhile, events in neighboring Rwanda spun out of control. Again in 1995, with the sponsorship of 15 African member states and acting by consensus, the Commission strongly condemned the "brutal and violent break in the democratic process" in Burundi. This resolution supported the **creation of a commission of inquiry into the October 1993 coup attempt and the massacres that followed** and now encouraged the stationing of human rights experts and observers throughout the country. Because the Burundi delegation itself made the request, the resolution called for the **appointment of a Special Rapporteur,** who took up the post in mid-1995. The rapporteur can be expected to report his findings—assigning responsibility for past killings as well as for the current waves of killings reported in Burundi in mid-1995—at the 1996 Commission on Human Rights.

The Former Yugoslavia

In August 1992, after the international media released pictures of emaciated prisoners behind barbed wire accompanied by reports of depravity and torture as part of a policy of "ethnic cleansing" in Bosnia-Herzegovina, the U.N. Commission on Human Rights convened its **first-ever emergency meeting in response to a human rights crisis.** At that meeting in Geneva, the 53-member Commission appointed former Prime Minister of Poland Tadeusz Mazowiecki as **Special Rapporteur on former Yugoslavia** and dispatched him immediately to the region.

Underlying these efforts was the expectation that once an accurate account of human rights violations had been obtained, reported, and publicized, the United Nations could, at a minimum, bring sufficient pressure against the offending parties to stop the violations. In this case, the U.N. efforts to gather evidence of abuses and "mobilize shame"—the traditional tools of human rights advocacy—may have diminished some vicious abuses but did not help to end the war. Still, as a result of the massive publicity campaign conducted through the media, some prisons were emptied (after a time), many ex-prisoners were permitted to leave for safety abroad or in neighboring Croatia, and, according to the war crimes Commission of Experts, certain abuses (notably rape as an instrument of "ethnic cleansing") diminished substantially.

In appointing a Special Rapporteur at an emergency session, the Commission on Human Rights dramatically **advanced the scope and means of U.N. human rights monitoring employed by the U.N. Centre for Human Rights.** From the outset, the Special Rapporteur was authorized to take measures, utilize personnel, and act in ways that would cut across the normally restrictive human rights investigatory mandates that the U.N. Commission had established (often with great difficulty) to that point. Mazowiecki was authorized to utilize the **combined expertise** of the U.N.'s other independent human rights experts (on torture, executions, the internally displaced); and, in fact, two such experts accompanied this "country special rapporteur"—a U.N. first—on an urgent fact-finding mission. Mazowiecki's reports (16 were issued between August 1992 and May 1995) are even sent to the Security Council, which has long rejected any receipt or consideration of human rights findings on the grounds that they should be discussed only in the Human Rights Commission.

Mazowiecki recommended—and the General Assembly eventually agreed to—the **first-ever deployment of Commission human rights field monitors to the country under scrutiny,** where they would reside and examine human rights on a continuing basis. A handful of these monitors were sent in 1993 and remain there still. The monitoring force has never increased in size.

Yet, for all these breakthroughs (vigorous reporting, an abundance of recommendations, and an unprecedently high level of support, including $500,000 in voluntary contributions from the United States) and staffing in Geneva and the field (eight persons), the Rapporteur spoke in 1994 of the **slowness of other U.N. agencies,** among them the Security Council, to take measures aimed at stopping or preventing further rights abuses. The very lack of responsiveness, he argued, illustrates the weakness of U.N. human rights rapporteurs.

No one could expect a single human rights investigator, however prominent, with a mere handful of staff to *resolve* a conflict as complex as that in Yugoslavia, particularly when the investigator was appointed a full year after the fighting erupted in Croatia (the first and one of the principal theaters of that conflict) and four months after ethnic cleansing's worst atrocities ravaged Bosnia (another major battlefield). The Special Rapporteur's authoritative findings, active intervention, and targeted recommendations, however, should have clarified the responsibilities of the respective parties to the conflict and led still other U.N. bodies and personnel to employ at least some of the strategies for protecting individuals under their guard from further atrocities and "ethnic cleansing."

The **lack of sensitivity to human rights issues by other U.N. agencies** engaged on the ground in former Yugoslavia, particularly the large peacekeeping force UNPROFOR (which to this day has assigned only one or two staff members to address human rights issues)—and the **lack of coordination among those agencies to report on or act to prevent human rights abuses**—means that the world body is not taking its own expert advice. It has failed to utilize human rights reporting and information to protect victims of abuse in Bosnia and neighboring states, failed to prevent further atrocities, and failed to maintain the U.N.'s own credibility as an impartial international force committed to upholding U.N. principles, whether of nonaggression or of human rights.

Although it has not been possible for Mazowiecki to change the policies of the great powers—much less change the policies of the ex-Yugoslav parties—his reporting and related interventions have kept the human rights issue in front of the policy-makers even when they would have been happier to ignore it. In 1994–95, for example, he issued a major report on the control of the press and media in all the countries of the region, issued a report on the ethnic cleansing and other abuses continuing in Bosnian Serb-held Banja Luka, and examined reported abuses in Western Slavonia after Croatian forces had invaded the area and caused Serbs to flee. In fact, Mazowiecki often serves as **the U.N.'s earliest spotter of human rights problems** and is often the first to speak out publicly against them.

Mazowiecki's field staff have been barred from conducting investigations in Serbia and in Bosnian Serb-occupied parts of Bosnia-Herzegovina, allegedly on the grounds that his (unwelcome) reporting of abuses is biased. Yet his reporting suggests, if anything, his reluctance to use the terms "ethnic cleansing" or "torture" about the Bosnian Serbs. **Absent too is any reference to "genocide,"** a word used by virtually all U.N. bodies (save the Security Council).

In December 1994, following former **U.S. President Jimmy Carter's mediation mission to Bosnia,** U.N. officials obtained written assurances from all parties that U.N. monitoring missions—including those in human rights—would be permitted into the area. Hoping to take advantage of this promise, the High Commissioner for Human Rights convened at the beginning of February 1995 a meeting of all U.N. agencies active on the ground in those countries, with a view to setting up a **monitoring mission,** first in the Bosnian-Croat Federation and eventually through the entire Republic of Bosnia and Herzegovina. He received lukewarm responses from those other U.N. departments—peacekeepers and peace negotiators among them—but nonetheless continues to explore the prospect of an expanded monitoring mission able to protect people within the country, investigate abuses, and bring perpetrators to account.

Most of the burden of bringing to justice those responsible for war crimes and crimes against humanity falls to the **International Criminal Tribunal on the Former Yugoslavia,** headquartered in The Hague. Named as Prosecutor was **Justice Richard Goldstone** of South Africa, whose staff began in late 1994 to issue indictments of some prison camp guards and other suspected perpetrators. So bold and independent was Goldstone that he even asked for a delay in local Bosnian legal proceedings against Bosnian Serb leader Radovan Karadžić because Karadžić was a suspect in the tribunal's own investigations. To date the tribunal has had to struggle to obtain adequate financial support for investigations and witness protection, which is essential if victims are to feel confident enough to come forward to testify, as the cases will be witness-driven.

Both the 1994 General Assembly and the 1995 Commission on Human Rights **altered the mandate** of Mazowiecki so that it no longer specifically referred to the **Former Yugoslav Republic of Macedonia (FYROM),** a potential powder keg to which the United Nations has sent its first preventive deployment of peacekeepers (made up of U.S. and Scandinavian troops) and which Mazowiecki previously monitored. Despite ongoing tensions between the Macedonian and Albanian populations in FYROM, the Commission resolutions appear to have decided to concentrate solely on Croatia, Serbia, and Bosnia. This may be rethought at the 50th General Assembly.

Iraq

Since his mandate was established four years ago, **Special Rapporteur for Iraq** Max van der Stoel has issued nine reports totaling some 500 pages and detailing a wide range of human rights abuses. In his 1995 report [E/CN.4/1995/56] he identifies **the overarching problem in Iraq as the concentration of political power in a few hands**—and those of the President of the Republic in particular. His report focuses on the 600 Kuwaitis and nationals of other countries who are alleged to have disappeared during the Iraqi occupation; on the situation of the Marsh Arabs; on the legal application of cruel and unusual punishment, such as amputations, branding, tatooing, and the cutting off of ears; on political killings; and on infringements on the rights to food and health care. The Iraqi government has replied at length to the Special Rapporteur's questions, but he characterizes these responses as "denial, excuse, or obfuscation."

Van der Stoel has been **unable to dispatch human rights monitors to an on-site field location in Iraq** because the government does not give him permission to do so, **or even on its border** because of a lack of funding or approval by the Secretary-General. But relying on the Commission's toothless and fundless authorization to have monitors in the first place, the Special Rapporteur has sent personnel from the Human Rights Centre to London, Kuwait, Iran's southwest province of Khuzestan, and Beirut on information-gathering missions [ibid.]. At the 49th General Assembly, the resolution on Iraq was much more specific: The Assembly "welcome[d] the sending of human rights monitors to the border between Iraq and . . . Iran and call[ed] upon the government of Iraq to allow immediate and unconditional stationing of human rights monitors throughout the country, especially the southern marsh area." As of June 1995 they had not been dispatched.

In a 31–1–21 vote (Sudan dissenting), the 1995 Commission on Human Rights [Res. 1995/76] condemned "massive and extremely grave violations of human rights . . . resulting in an all-pervasive order of repression and oppression which is sustained by . . . widespread terror." At the 49th General Assembly the vote on human rights in Iraq had been 114–3–47 (Iraq, Libya, and Sudan dissenting; Libya and Iraq are not on the Commission at present). The number of abstentions in both votes indicates that the odium surrounding Iraq in 1991 has been wearing off, albeit gradually.

The High Commissioner reported in mid-1995 that he had been invited, and that he expected, to visit Iraq on one of his country visits. Whether he will report publicly, back up the Rapporteur, or obtain permission for the Rapporteur to visit remains to be seen.

Iran

Both the Commission and the General Assembly received from Reynaldo Galindo Pohl, **Special Representative on Iran,** another annual report on human rights conditions in that country. The 51st Commission's resolution, adopted by a vote of 28–8–17, sharply criticized Iran's **repressive human rights practices** and made specific reference to the government's support of death threats against author Salman Rushdie, to discrimination against the Baha'i minority, and to harassment of Protestants. The Special

Representative had also criticized the executions (carried out by stoning or hanging) that follow summary trials, the practice of amputations, the torture used to extract confessions, and the discriminatory laws against women.

The Special Representative has not been permitted to visit Iran for many years. In June 1995 it was reported that a new Representative would soon be appointed. It was also reported that the High Commissioner for Human Rights has received an invitation to visit Iran. As with Iraq, close observers believe this may be a test case of whether the High Commissioner consults with and backs up the recommendations of the special rapporteurs and representatives, and whether he can obtain access to the country for a firsthand investigation.

Haiti

The 1995 Commission on Human Rights welcomed the **return of democracy to Haiti** and condemned the human rights violations of the de facto military regime that had seized power from President Jean-Bertrand Aristide. The Commission noted the large **international human rights observer mission in Haiti,** set up jointly by the United Nations and the Organization of American States, but, curiously, made no mention—positive or negative—of the multinational peacekeeping force that had come to the island with U.N. authorization in fall 1994. Although the **Special Rapporteur for Haiti,** Marco Bruni Celli of Uruguay, called for the Human Rights Centre to continue its own human rights monitoring of violations in Haiti, the Commission requested only the **appointment of an independent expert to furnish technical assistance in human rights to the government and to monitor human rights,** but not under Commission agenda item 12 (gross violations). For years the Commission has bounced examination of Haiti from its agenda item on advisory services (with the government's approval only) to the agenda item on gross violations (which carries a certain opprobrium).

Sudan

The U.N.'s **Special Rapporteur on human rights in Sudan,** Gaspar Biro of Hungary, presented detailed reports on conditions in that country to both the General Assembly [A/49/539] and the Commission on Human Rights [E/CN.4/1995/58] and is expected to do so again at the next session of each body. At the 1994 Commission, the Sudanese government made such **personal attacks** against Biro—in Sudanese papers and speeches also distributed at the United Nations—that the Chair of the Commission was called on to criticize the Sudanese government publicly and defend the rapporteurs of the Commission from such threats. Biro has not been permitted to visit Sudan again, and his letter of request has gone unanswered. His reports to the Assembly and Commission, based on information from representatives of U.N. agencies, international NGOs, and Sudanese organizations and refugees with whom he visited in Uganda, Kenya, and Egypt, cite **extensive rights abuses.** Among these are extrajudicial executions; disappearances, torture, and arrests in the northern part of Sudan; and atrocities and violations of the laws of war in the south, including indiscriminate civilian bombing, land mines, and forced evacuation.

The Rapporteur has been particularly critical of the **extensive abuses against women and children,** and the Commission in turn has called on Sudan to end policies or practices that "support, condone, encourage, or foster the sale of or trafficking in children," that separate children from their families, or that subject children to forced internment, indoctrination, or other cruel treatment. Biro also writes about the problems of street children and the practice of slavery and slavery-like practices in Sudan.

The 1995 Commission expressed its concern over the human rights violations and its outrage over the **use of military force to disrupt relief supplies.** It deplored the government's lack of cooperation with the Special Rapporteur and called on Khartoum to "ensure that the Special Rapporteur has free and unlimited access to any person in the Sudan with whom he wishes to meet, with no threats or reprisals." (A number of persons who met with Biro on his 1993 mission were imprisoned afterwards.) The Rapporteur had asked and the 1995 Commission on Human Rights recommended that Biro begin to consult with the Secretary-General on **"modalities leading to the placement of monitors"** in areas that would improve information and verification of reports about Sudanese human rights conditions. This language is essentially the same as that used for Iraq, and suggests that the Special Rapporteur's human rights monitors could be similarly located just outside the country's borders or travel elsewhere for information, depending on the judgment of the Rapporteur. This would enable the investigators to obtain more thorough and more timely information, primarily from refugees. The Commission resolution on Sudan was adopted by a 33–7–10 vote.

Cuba

Cuba has been the subject of scrutiny by the Commission since the late 1980s. Only the government's skill at manipulating U.N. procedures kept a special rapporteur (rather than a representative or other special investigative envoy) from being appointed until 1992. The Cuban government refuses to permit any visits by the **Rapporteur,** Carl Johan-Groth of Sweden. Both the General Assembly and the Commission have called on Havana to permit Groth into the country [A/Res/49/200; Commission resolution 1995/

66], to no avail. A breakthrough seemed imminent in late 1994, when High Commissioner for Human Rights Ayala Lasso was invited and traveled to Cuba. Human rights groups have expressed disappointment that "he offered no public comment on the government's repressive human rights record or even its refusal to allow a visit by Cuba's special rapporteur on Cuba" [Human Rights Watch 1995 World Report, xviii]. Amnesty International, expressing concern about the large number of political prisoners and summary trials, commented further: "While Amnesty International regards the visit . . . of the High Commissioner . . . as an important step, this is no substitute for the government reversing its policy of non-cooperation with the Commission's recommendations" [Amnesty International Document IOR 41/11/94, 12/94]. In February 1995, U.S. Ambassador to the Commission Geraldine Ferraro told the Commission that some of Cuba's actions are designed to "block the Commission from addressing rather serious human rights abuses." She was referring, inter alia, to the fact that Cuba had kept Groth from speaking at the Commission session in Geneva on the date originally scheduled for the presentations by all special rapporteurs. As a result, the Special Rapporteur had to return to Sweden and make a second journey to Geneva at a later date to introduce his report. The 1995 Commission adopted another in a **continuing series of resolutions critical of Cuba's human rights practices.** It also asked Groth to present an interim report to the 50th General Assembly.

Cuba struck back at the United States for sponsoring this resolution by drafting and introducing a Commission resolution as a follow-up to the report of the **Special Rapporteur on Racism,** Maurice Glele-Ahahanzo of Benin, who had been invited by the United States to examine at firsthand the American situation and the country's means of addressing such issues. The Cuban resolution would have deplored "continued violation, on racial grounds, of the human rights . . . of . . . Afro-Americans, Hispanics, Asians, and indigenous people" and called on the United States to invite the Special Rapporteur back, take measures to prevent racist and discriminatory propaganda, and report to the General Assembly on its actions. This draft received only three votes in favor: from Cuba, the Sudan, and China (the last two also subjects of Commission resolutions drafted and advanced by the United States). Thirty-two states voted against the draft and 18 abstained.

Harassment of Human Rights Defenders

Governments often attempt to intimidate and direct reprisals against private individuals and groups that cooperate with or submit information to U.N. human rights bodies. To deter this, the Commission on Human Rights has for several years adopted resolutions criticizing such actions, issued reports of specific cases alleging harassment, and installed a "prompt intervention" procedure to protect any persons so threatened. In 1995 the U.N. report to the Commission stated that "all the alleged victims were private individuals or members of non-governmental organizations which were or had been sources of information about human rights violations for United Nations human rights bodies." This report identifies harassment of local human rights defenders in **Guatemala, Colombia, Mexico, Argentina, Honduras, Peru, Rwanda, Myanmar, Zaire, and Iran.**

Human Rights of Women

One of the significant developments in the 1993 Vienna World Conference on Human Rights was the acknowledgment that the human rights of women are part of the mainstream of universal human rights. At the Commission on Human Rights this led to the 1994 appointment of a **Special Rapporteur on violence against women,** Radhika Coomeraswamy of Sri Lanka, who delivered her first report at the 1995 Commission. Her report details the abuses women face throughout the world—in the family, in the community, in refugee camps, and from their own governments. The Rapporteur—the first woman to hold such a position—stated that "in most societies, crimes of violence against women are invisible" and that "the greatest cause of violence against women is government inaction . . . a permissive attitude, a tolerance." Coomeraswamy recommended that women have full access to free and fair courts in bringing cases of violence to justice and that women be given support and rehabilitation following any abuse; that police, armed forces, and law-enforcement officials be provided with specialized training in gender-related issues and international standards; and that populations be educated about ways to prevent violence against women and other abuses of the rights of women [E/CN.4/1995/42].

The Commission on Human Rights has also made considerable strides toward the **integration of women's rights into the mainstream of U.N. human rights activities.** At the Commission's 51st session in 1995, some 30 resolutions referred either to specific abuses affecting women or to the need to pay special attention to gender-related aspects of such abuses as torture and internal displacement and of such rights as free expression and religious freedom. It came as something of a surprise when, as the Commission was nearing a close, the Chinese delegation began to call for the withdrawal of the pending consensus resolution on "integration of women's rights" into the mainstream of U.N. human rights activity. The Chinese delegation contended that this was to prejudge an issue that would be taken up at the **World Conference on Women,** for which Beijing was to serve as host in September 1995.

Eventually, Beijing's delegates were persuaded to support the resolution, although not before weakening somewhat the language that called on various U.N. officials to arrange for the Commission's special rapporteurs to attend the Beijing conference so that they would make the contacts and obtain the gender awareness needed to integrate these issues into their work. Chinese objections were also responsible for moderating a call by the Commission for making the human rights of women a separate topic on the Beijing conference agenda.

Human Rights Operational Activities

Geneva-based human rights reporting has been supplemented recently by **New York U.N. Headquarters-conceived-and-run human rights operations in the field.** Such programs began when the United Nations launched human rights monitors or education operations as part of multifaceted peacekeeping activities in El Salvador and Cambodia and later sent a human rights monitoring mission to Haiti. These human rights monitoring and protection missions have opened the door to a variety of on-site U.N. human rights field operations in conjunction with still other peacekeeping activities, in humanitarian emergencies, and as part of development activities. New human rights field operations are now in place in former Yugoslavia, Rwanda, and Guatemala. The 1995 Commission requested that field monitors be located in such places (inside or outside the country under scrutiny) that they will be able to aid the information flow and verification processes connected with the mandates of the Special Rapporteurs on Iraq, Sudan, and Zaire.

In this new generation of U.N. field activities, **nongovernmental organizations concerned with human rights** continue to play their traditional role as outsider advocate-critic. Human rights NGOs have issued a bevy of reports critiquing U.N. peacekeeping mandates—including their planning, performance, training, and track record—as well as the Organization's relationships with domestic human rights NGOs in carrying out such missions. The critiques are premised on the assumption shared by all the vocal critics among NGOs that human rights factors must be central to the design and execution of peacekeeping mandates.

Amnesty International has developed a set of **human rights principles to be followed when designing peacekeeping operations.** Those principles call on U.N. peacekeepers not simply to remain silent or serve as indifferent witnesses but to receive proper training in human rights principles and protection strategies, to be ready to uphold international law—and to adhere to it themselves.

The fact that the Centre for Human Rights has virtually no field staff experience or capacity at present means that much has to be done to design and develop such a capacity. It can be expected that, just as the Centre's mechanisms have **depended on the NGOs** for information, so too will they depend on them for personnel and ideas in field operations—particularly those operations set up to address emergency situations.

Several of the top officials engaged in running the U.N. human rights operations in El Salvador and Haiti today were enlisted from the ranks of international human rights NGOs. As yet, however, **local NGOs** have not been tapped for the U.N. monitoring teams, and the U.N. is criticized for failing to consult with them and, indeed, ignoring them for the most part. International human rights NGOs are likely to remain the principal source of personnel for future U.N. human rights monitoring missions.

Since the Vienna World Conference on Human Rights, the U.N. Human Rights Commission and such operational programs as the U.N. Development Programme, UNICEF, and the U.N. High Commissioner for Refugees have been giving a higher priority to the development of advisory services for human rights. One result is that human rights NGOs may well face the prospect of becoming "insiders"—working through and with the United Nations to achieve what has not been achievable in the past (or even desirable to many governments): **the delivery of legal services** that help victims bring their complaints before courts and seek redress and remedies. It remains to be seen whether international and national NGOs will wish to join in this aspect of the U.N.'s work and whether, if they do take part, it will directly affect their independence, impartiality, and outspokenness.

The arrival of so many **new national NGOs** on the U.N. human rights scene has also raised questions about consultative status with the Commission and about the participation by NGOs at the Commission on Human Rights and its subsidiary body, the Subcommission on Prevention of Discrimination and Protection of Minorities. Already the Subcommission has rearranged its agenda so that country "situations" are taken up at the start of its four-week session. Typically, NGOs have done their lobbying about country situations throughout the session, since it is by being specific about abuses in particular places that pressure can be brought for change. Such a focus has distracted the Subcommission members from considering the important studies carried out by expert members of the Subcommission and other generic issues about standard-setting. The Commission on Human Rights has also been discussing reform of its agenda and working methods, although so far to no avail. Time pressures did effect a change in 1995: Because of a decision to curtail meetings on the occasion of the Muslim holiday Ramadan, the Commission's Malaysian chair reduced by half the speaking time allotted all participants, whether governments or NGOs. Some governments are exploring whether this would be an effective means of further diminishing NGO activity and government "speechifying" at the proceedings, with the aim of allowing genuine on-the-record debate and discussion among member governments. Some NGOs have proposed that when new national NGOs and the representatives of single-issue organizations come to the Commission, they be required to discipline themselves, grouping their statements and speaking in coalition with others. Other NGOs argue that it is the governments whose speeches have grown in number and length, and that to curtail the NGOs' ability to bring public pressure to bear on the governments present will diminish these groups' effectiveness in promoting human rights.

There is no doubt that human rights NGOs have grown in size, have grown more professional, and have established themselves in all regions of the globe. Nor is there any doubt that the information they report receives greater acceptance by the public and the media, and wider use within the U.N. system. As their number and impact grow, however, some of the gross violator states struggle even harder to deny the NGOs access to and legitimacy in the U.N. system.

Looking Back on 50 Years

Reflecting on the accomplishments of the United Nations in human rights over the past 50 years, it is instructive to realize that time and again it was the **nongovernmental sector** that provided the key strategic, technical, and organizational leadership for developing human rights norms and procedures. Concerned governmental representatives have carried the NGO proposals forward.

In fact, the initiative to turn the U.N. Charter into an instrument concerned with promoting respect for the human rights of individuals came from many of the 42 American organizations invited to serve as "consultants" to the U.S. delegation at the San Francisco founding conference of the United Nations. Their conviction that respect for human rights and the dignity of the individual was essential to peace and to preventing conflict arose not merely out of deep-seated American values but also from a realistic assessment of contemporary events—the failure of interwar treaties that were aimed at protecting a few minorities in a few countries, and a world war stoked by hatred and dehumanization. Convinced that only if the rights of all people were protected would the rights of particular minority (and ethnic and religious) groups be protected and future conflicts avoided, the consultants—led by Judge Joseph Proskauer and Jacob Blaustein of the American Jewish Committee, working closely with Frederick Nolde of the Federal Council of the Churches of Christ, James Shotwell of the Carnegie Endowment for International Peace, and Clark Eichelberger of the American Association for the U.N. (a UNA-USA predecessor)—persuaded the official American delegation and other drafters of the Charter to make the new world body different from the League of Nations by **including human rights among its primary purposes.**

Well before the San Francisco conference, several of these consultant organizations had advocated development of an "international bill of rights" and begun to lobby for it, using techniques that would become familiar to NGOs that work at the United Nations to promote human rights. For example, on March 20, 1945, the American Jewish Committee's representatives, Proskauer and Blaustein, presented the proposal directly to President Franklin D. Roosevelt and obtained from him a favorable response; they published in the newspapers a petition signed by 1,300 prominent people; and they formed a coalition with other consultants on this and other provisions of the Charter. One result of their efforts is that **the Charter calls for a Commission on Human Rights by name.**

On May 2, 1945, a week before the Nazi surrender (and even as the concentration camps were being liberated), U.S. officials told the NGO advocates in San Francisco that human rights would not, after all, appear in the Charter and that there would be instead some vague references to humanitarian, economic, and social programs. Proskauer, Blaustein, and colleagues sprang into action. Working much of the night, they prepared a detailed memorandum arguing that human rights are essential not only to domestic life but to international peace as well, and they proposed specific language on human rights, arguing for the precise spots in the Charter at which to insert it. In the course of the next morning, representatives of all the consultant organizations present in San Francisco were pressed to sign the memorandum. Among the signatories were such civic groups as the National Association of Manufacturers, the Chamber of Commerce, the National Council of Farmer Cooperatives, the American Bar Association, the National Association for the Advancement of Colored People, and the League of Women Voters. During the afternoon of May 3, all the "consultants" met with U.S. Secretary of State Edward Stettinius and an assistant. Here, Nolde made the specific proposals and Proskauer, as his autobiography relates, revealed the passion—and strength—of the petitioners:

> I said that the voice of America was speaking in this room as it had never spoken before in any international gathering; that that voice was saying to the American delegation: "If you make a fight for these human rights proposals and win, there will be glory for all. If you make a fight for it and lose, we will back you up to the limit. If you fail to make a fight for it, you will have lost the support of American opinion—and justly lost it. In that event, you will never get the Charter ratified." [*A Segment of My Times*, New York: Farrar, Straus, 1950, p. 225]

Stettinius explained that he hadn't realized feelings were so intense on the subject. He declared himself convinced, and then worked to convince not only the U.S. delegation but also the others in the big four

[ibid.; Sidney Liskofsky, *American Jewish Yearbook* (1945–46), Philadelphia: Jewish Publication Society, pp. 491–92; Clark M. Eichelberger, *Organizing for Peace*, New York: Harper and Row, 1977, pp. 268–73; *New York Post*, 5/4/45; *San Francisco News*, 5/16/45]. The rest is history.

3. Refugees and Internally Displaced Persons
By Christina M. Schultz and Heidi R. Worley

In the past 50 years the world's refugee population has increased markedly. Moreover, the increasing number of asylum seekers lacking refugee status and the estimated number of internally displaced persons suggest that the overall number of uprooted persons is far greater than ever before [UNHCR, *UNHCR At A Glance*, 3/1/95]. Refugee issues have become increasingly difficult because of broader emergency complications. In the past five years there have been significant changes in the manner in which the international community responds to emergencies—changes that stem from the evolution of the traditional concepts of protection and the increasing requirement of humanitarian operations to function in or near combat zones.

The 1951 Convention Relating to the Status of Refugees and its related Protocols in 1967 were developed to address the needs of persons fleeing a country of origin because of a well-founded fear of persecution based on race, religion, nationality, membership in a particular social group, or political opinion. The Convention and Protocols, supplemented by regional commitments in both Africa and Latin America, have failed, however, to cover all displaced populations in need. The complexity of contemporary emergencies has enlarged the focus of efforts to include the countries of origin. In cases like Rwanda, the nature of the political and ethnic tensions has resulted in genocide and a mass migration that strains the capacities of the refugee system.

The Evolving Nature of U.N. Response to Refugee Crises

Shifts in the post-Cold War landscape, characterized by the revival of historic animosities and ethnic tensions, have led to an increasing number of complex emergencies, an increasing number of people affected by them, and a change in the nature of population displacements. The lead agency in the U.N. system charged with providing assistance and protection to refugees is the **U.N. High Commissioner for Refugees (UNHCR)**. UNHCR was established in 1951 with a mandate to seek durable solutions for affected refugee populations through repatriation programs, integration in the host communities of the country of first asylum, or resettlement in a third country.

The activities of UNHCR have changed dramatically since the 1950s, when refugees were primarily individuals fleeing communist repression in

Eastern Europe. Then UNHCR focused on long-term integration, since repatriation was neither feasible nor politically desirable. In the 1960s and '70s the process of decolonization in Africa led to flight motivated by violence and economic hardship, and characterized by large-scale movements rather than by individuals escaping persecution. UNHCR was committed to providing long-term assistance and protection in asylum countries, but most of the refugees of this period eventually returned home once independence and stability were achieved in their countries.

In the late 1970s and early '80s, Cold War rivalries polarized developing countries. Arms acquisitions during this time led to a proliferation of regional and internal conflicts, resulting in large-scale displacements and a doubling of the number of refugees from 1970 to 1990. UNHCR focused on asylum, but the sheer numbers and the complexity of political situations surrounding their flight drained the capacities of receiving countries. Millions of refugees were left in overcrowded camps without clear repatriation options.

With the end of the Cold War, the challenges to the humanitarian community, marked by an increasing reluctance to grant asylum and widespread internal displacement, have directed greater attention to the situation in the countries of origin than in the past. For the first time ever, UNHCR efforts have been supplemented by armed humanitarian intervention to ensure the delivery of relief supplies. In Somalia and in the former Yugoslavia, U.N. forces were deployed to airlift supplies to besieged civilians and to secure food distribution after the failure to negotiate safe passage.

UNHCR maintains its commitment to programs in countries of first asylum, but today, wherever possible, it also delivers assistance and lends its protection to internally displaced persons as well. At the same time, there have been increased possibilities for repatriation as conflicts in Southeast Asia, Central America, and Southern Africa are resolved. In 1993, UNHCR repatriated 370,000 Cambodians, and it is currently in the final stages of a program to return 1.5 million Mozambicans from six asylum countries.

Emphasis on prevention and attention to early warning prompted UNHCR to create the post of **Director of Policy Planning and Operations** in 1994. This decision marked a move toward a more proactive approach to its early response and preparedness activity. Also in 1994 the High Commissioner for Refugees, **Sadako Ogata,** called for greater attention to the prevention and solution of refugee problems by strengthening the U.N.'s commitment to preventive diplomacy and mediation efforts, greater respect for and monitoring of human rights, and better linkages between relief and development.

Institutional Collaboration

Although the role of the U.N. as a systemwide coordinating body in complex emergencies is constantly being debated, there has been a trend toward the growth and sophistication of its overall institutional capacity. The creation in April 1992 of the **Department of Humanitarian Affairs (DHA)** as a focal point for coordinating the emergency relief activities of the United Nations was a landmark decision creating a new model of interagency coordination [A/Res/46/182, 12/19/91].

The DHA, directed by an Under-Secretary-General who would serve as **Emergency Relief Coordinator,** assigns responsibilities to U.N. operational agencies in complex emergencies, particularly in situations where mandates overlap or where no U.N. agency has a clear mandate to act. The Emergency Relief Coordinator also works closely with governments of both donor and recipient countries in facilitating a comprehensive response to humanitarian emergencies. The **Inter-Agency Standing Committee (IASC)** is the mechanism for strengthening this coordination of emergency humanitarian assistance. The Committee is chaired by the Emergency Relief Coordinator and is composed of the executive heads of the operational U.N. agencies, the International Committee of the Red Cross (ICRC), and intergovernmental and nongovernmental organizations [General Assembly, "Summary Record of the 26th Meeting," 11/10/94].

In emergency situations, UNHCR collaborates with other key U.N. agencies in an effort to respond to the multiple needs of civilians. Chief among these agencies are the U.N. Children's Fund (UNICEF) for child welfare needs, the World Food Programme (WFP) for food delivery and distribution, the World Health Organization (WHO) for health assessment and essential drugs, and the U.N. Disaster Relief Organization (UNDRO), which is under the auspices of DHA. UNHCR operated as the lead agency in the former Yugoslavia and in northern Iraq in 1991. In 1992 and 1993 in Somalia, UNHCR's assistance was through cross-border operations, while WFP and UNICEF were the key U.N. agencies engaged within the country [John G. Sommer, *Hope Restored? Humanitarian Aid in Somalia 1990–1994*, Refugee Policy Group, 11/94]. More recently, UNHCR has been working in Rwanda in close cooperation with DHA.

UNHCR has also worked with multinational U.N. military and relief forces in several operations: UNPROFOR in the former Yugoslavia, ONUMOZ in Mozambique, UNTAC in Cambodia, ONUSAL in El Salvador, and UNREO in Rwanda. UNHCR increasingly collaborates with human rights bodies, including representatives of the U.N. Commission on Human Rights when monitoring is necessary in a conflict situation, and with the U.N. Development Programme (UNDP) in the field in post-conflict situations to address the need for reintegration and development assistance. It also coordinates with international and local NGOs—such as the International Committee of the Red Cross, which possesses specialized skills and operations—as preventive instruments or once an emergency is under way.

Since its establishment, UNHCR has collaborated with over 200 NGOs in relief or legal assistance programs, and it maintains contact with close to 1,000 NGOs involved with refugees [UNHCR, *State of the World's Refugees, 1993*]. To better facilitate this collaboration, UNHCR, in coordination with the International Council of Voluntary Agencies (ICVA), sponsored a series of consultations known as **Partnership in Action (PARINAC)**. PARINAC regional conferences have involved some 400 NGOs, and have taken place in Caracas and Kathmandu in 1993 and in Tunis, Bangkok, Addis Ababa, Budapest, Oslo, and Washington in 1994.

At its 49th Session the General Assembly adopted a set of 14 resolutions designed to strengthen the coordination of humanitarian and disaster relief efforts throughout the U.N. system. Most of the resolutions dealt with wars and natural disasters in specific countries, but others set priorities and responsibilities for tasks aimed at the improvement of operations within DHA. Important among the resolutions is the management of a **central emergency revolving fund,** which provides resources for emergency action. The fund functions as a stop-gap measure while awaiting government contributions to larger consolidated appeals for disaster relief. The second major issue addressed by the Assembly was coordination at the field level. The Secretary-General has approved the appointment of a humanitarian coordinator for each emergency, who would take overall responsibility for field-level decisions.

Complex Emergencies

There are today over 20 complex emergencies facing the international community in which assistance and protection to refugees, internally displaced persons, and other war-affected populations are needed. According to one definition, a complex emergency is "a humanitarian crisis in a country, region or society where there is a total or considerable breakdown of authority resulting from internal or external conflict and which requires an international response that goes beyond the mandate or capacity of any single agency and/or the ongoing U.N. country program" [Meeting of the Department of Humanitarian Affairs' Inter-Agency Standing Committee, 12/9/94]. Other organizations use somewhat different criteria to distinguish a complex emergency from other types of emergencies. Most would agree, however, that a complex emergency generally has more than one disruptive root cause, including civil conflict, the collapse of the state, food insecurity, macroeconomic collapse, and mass population movements. These situations tend to last beyond six months and tend to require massive international assistance.

The term "complex emergency" has been applied to the Kurdish displacement during the Gulf War, the ongoing conflict in the former Yugoslavia, and the catastrophe within Rwanda. The term is also applicable to the situations in El Salvador, Haiti, Sudan, Somalia, Cambodia, and Afghanistan.

Under the Emergency Relief Coordinator, DHA is the agency responsible for ensuring that an expedient and well-coordinated humanitarian assistance approach is taken in new complex emergencies. DHA was restructured in August 1994 in order to strengthen its capacity for such emergencies. The **Complex Emergency Division (CED),** centered in New York, includes a Rapid Response Unit as the focus of DHA response in the initial phase of an emergency. The **Complex Emergency Support Unit,** based in Geneva, is responsible for providing liaison and support services.

The number of complex emergencies has been increasing steadily since the end of the Cold War, and the massive number of people being uprooted—as well as the problem of carrying out so many relief missions simultaneously—overwhelms the capacity of the international system to cope with their needs. This raises questions of how the international community will proceed with its current humanitarian response. However, there exists a range of options to meet the challenges of complex emergencies and the subsequent recovery process. These include "national prevention and preparedness policies, preventive diplomacy, conflict resolution, peace-keeping and human rights initiatives, use of military assets, dovetailing relief and development funding, programmes for the rehabilitation of war-torn societies, national food security policies, and capacity building programmes" [Report by Michael Priestley, Senior DHA consultant to Peter Hansen, Under-Secretary-General, DHA, 9/21/94, p. ii]. UNHCR, for example, operates emergency response mechanisms and procedures that did not exist in 1990. The increased operational capacity of UNHCR and UNICEF during emergencies, and WFP's growing emphasis on relief, are evidence that the U.N.'s institutional capacity for direct service delivery is expanding.

Internally Displaced Persons

Beyond the increasing number of refugees looms a growing group of people who have suddenly or unexpectedly fled their homes but have not crossed the border of their own country. They, like refugees, have been forced to flee as a result of armed conflict, internal strife, systematic violations of human rights, or natural or man-made disasters [E/CN.4/1992/23, 2/14/92]. These are the world's more than **30 million internally displaced persons,** who now outnumber refugees. However, because they are within the territory of their own country, they most often do not have access to the assistance and particularly the protection that would normally be given to refugees.

The appointment by the Secretary-General in July 1992 of a **Representative on Internally Displaced Persons** created a focal point within the U.N. system (at the request of the Commission on Human Rights) to summon attention to the needs of the displaced. The Representative has a specific mandate to monitor the problems of internal displacement and to focus on both protection and assistance. In his 1995 report to the Commission, the Representative reported on his visits to nine countries and made recommendations regarding the compilation and evaluation of existing legal norms, identification of gaps and formulation of guiding principles, and establishment of an information center as well as recommendations for institutional responsibility. At its 1995 session the Commission voted to extend the Representative's mandate for a three-year period.

The Inter-Agency Standing Committee serves as a vehicle for coordination in emergencies. In 1992 the IASC established a **Task Force on Internally Displaced Persons.** In December 1994 the IASC approved a 1993 decision that the Under-Secretary-General of DHA will serve as the entry point to receive requests for assistance and protection on actual or developing situations of internal displacement. This decision represented a move on the part of operational agencies toward better coordination of their efforts on behalf of the internally displaced [*Internally Displaced Persons: The Next Stage*, Inter-Agency Standing Committee, 7/5/93].

While assistance to internally displaced persons is not required under its mandate, UNHCR has played a critical role to this end in Mozambique, Cyprus, the Horn of Africa, Sri Lanka, Iraq, and the former Yugoslavia. UNHCR has become increasingly involved in situations of internal displacement at the request of the Secretary-General or the General Assembly. In 1993, UNHCR adopted criteria for its involvement with the internally displaced where there is a direct link with its activities for refugees and where there is a significant risk that the internally displaced will become a refugee problem. The U.N. Development Programme also helps coordinate relief for the displaced, working closely with governments, local representatives of donor countries, and U.N. agencies in the field [A/Res/44/136, 2/27/90].

Voluntary Repatriation and Return

Since the end of the Cold War, UNHCR has been optimistic that the conditions that cause an exodus would improve, thus allowing thousands of refugees to return home safely. The agency has promoted voluntary repatriation as the most desirable of the three durable solutions, and has facilitated repatriation whenever possible [UNHCR, *Voluntary Repatriation: Principles and Guidelines for Action*, Inter-Offices Memorandum, No. 5, 2/10/87, p. 1]. In 1992, UNHCR declared the start of the "decade of voluntary repatriation." Although the number of refugees has gone from 19 to 23 million in the past year, almost 7 million refugees, from countries such as Afghanistan, Cambodia, El Salvador, Angola, and South Africa, have returned home since the beginning of this "decade" [Cuny and Stein, "The Contemporary Practice of Voluntary Repatriation: Repatriation during conflict reintegration amidst devastations," *Report on 1992 International Study of Spontaneous Voluntary Repatriation*, 1994, p. 2]. The High Commissioner for Refugees has described the large-scale returns and the prospects for additional mass repatriations as "immensely satisfying." Today, the agency's primary concern is to deal with problems that "continue to plague countries of origin and that, if not contained, could undermine the impetus to return."

According to UNHCR's mandate, the agency can promote repatriation only when conditions are favorable for the refugees' return. This usually involves the signing of a tripartite agreement among UNHCR, the country of origin, and the country of return, and the assurance of the refugees' complete safety and socioeconomic integration. Repatriation by refugees without international support, however, is far more common than the more formal return process organized by UNHCR. Over 90 percent of all repatriation takes place by this so-called "spontaneous repatriation," although the decision of refugees to return home on their own is anything but spontaneous [Cuny, Stein, and Reed, *Repatriation During Conflict in Africa and Asia*, Dallas: The Center for the Study of Societies in Crisis, 1992, p. 15]. High Commissioner Ogata has acknowledged the "limited" role UNHCR can play in monitoring and protecting the safety of returnees after repatriation, and she has appealed to human rights agencies to "consider how their own monitoring mechanisms might be employed to complement UNHCR's efforts to promote the safety and dignity of returnees" ["Statement to the Fiftieth Session of the U.N. Commission on Human Rights," 2/9/94]. In select situations, UNHCR and human rights monitors have monitored the return of internally displaced persons.

While the prospects for the repatriation of refugees are promising in some cases, the conditions for internally displaced populations continue to deteriorate. The 30 million internally displaced persons in 1994 represent an increase of about 20 percent over the previous year. The number of uprooted people has clearly increased at a startling rate, leaving a larger overall vulnerable population. Because human rights law is only selectively applicable to situations of internal conflict, internally displaced persons are not always protected under these laws in emergency situations.

Asylum

The U.N. system has been instrumental in delivering assistance to mass movements of uprooted populations throughout the world. However, it has had relatively little impact on the conditions for securing asylum, particularly in industrialized countries. The Convention and Protocols on refugees define a person's fundamental right to seek asylum and not to be forcibly returned to a country where he or she fears persecution. Article 14 of the Universal Declaration of Human Rights provides that "everyone has a right to seek and enjoy in other countries asylum from persecution." National asylum policies nevertheless remain the prerogative of individual states. International law governing the right to asylum continues to allow states considerable freedom of interpretation in opening their doors to asylum seekers. While many refugees prefer resettlement, Western governments often view this option as the least desirable of the three durable solutions. This can be seen in the growing emphasis on preventing the movement of people across international borders and in the trend in both Europe and North America toward restrictive asylum policies and practices.

This shift toward more rigorous standards for granting asylum appears to be a response to the increasing number of asylum seekers around the world. The period between 1990 and 1993 saw a rise from 320,000 to 560,000 asylum applicants in the European Community. This flood of asylum seekers, along with economic and social problems within Europe, has reinforced xenophobic attitudes and prompted restrictive policies in many countries that were previously committed to protecting those fleeing human rights violations. In June 1993, Germany enacted amendments designed to deny the right to seek asylum to persons traveling through "safe third countries" or who come from "safe countries of origin." Because all countries surrounding Germany can currently be called "safe," no person entering the country by land has the right to claim asylum in Germany. Similar measures discouraging asylum seekers have been put in place in France. Airports have been declared international zones where French law does not apply, and the French Constitution has been amended to deny refugee claims to those people who have been refused this status in other European Community states.

North American countries have likewise been following this trend. Canada has increased "external control" measures, such as Operation Shortstop, that may prevent refugees from entering Canada. In the United States asylum adjudication has been a topic of heated debate since reform efforts in 1990 and in response to anti-immigrant sentiment and the continuing rise in asylum applicants. Asylum for refugees, however, has still not been given priority in the context of overall immigration policy and enforcement. U.S. levels of resettlement have not significantly declined, but they are currently inadequate to meet the needs of the growing numbers of uprooted persons.

Until the passage of the Refugee Act of 1980, Washington defined refugees as only those fleeing communist countries. Over the past two decades the United States has had to respond to a number of immigration emergencies, most notably from Haiti, Cuba, Central America, Eastern Europe, and Indochina. U.S. refugee policy, however, is still deeply embedded in the framework of the Cold War and remains focused on certain groups, especially Indochinese and Russian asylum seekers. As a result, the U.S. policy of picking up Cubans and Haitians at sea and returning them to their country of origin without a fair hearing sends a message to the international community that it is acceptable to ignore international law in dealing with an immigration emergency. In addition, in-country processing in Cuba and Haiti jeopardizes an asylum seeker's right to flee persecution and seek protection.

There is concern that future levels of resettlement will decrease if refugee resettlement policy is not reevaluated. The optimum answer would be to eliminate, through development and democratization efforts, the crises that cause people to flee their homes. In the meantime, more effective policies and mechanisms are needed to deal with the growing numbers of uprooted people facing persecution and continued displacement.

Relief, Reconstruction, and Development

Traditionally, relief and development have been regarded as separate fields. The international humanitarian aid community has begun to address the relief-to-development continuum by recognizing that disaster assistance itself is a continuum rather than a set of stages (preparedness, relief, and rehabilitation). This focus means that traditional concepts of disaster management need to be expanded to include resumed sustainable development, and that the aim of activities in the continuum must move from relief to rehabilitation/reconstruction to sustained development at the earliest possibility.

UNDP is the U.N. agency charged with development capacities. Increasingly, UNHCR has cooperated with UNDP to address the gaps between relief and development. UNDP maintains a humanitarian program in New York that has special responsibilities in emergency situations, manages funds from the Special Programme Resources (SPR), serves as a liaison with headquarters of field units, and organizes with DHA. The United Nations has focused on the relief-to-development continuum in several ways ["The Roles of DHA and UNDP in Linking Relief and Development," *IDS Bulletin*, vol. 25, no. 4, 10/94]:

- Training under a joint UNDP/DHA Disaster Management Training Programme (DMTP) with follow-up done by U.N. Disaster Management Teams (DMTs).
- Designating the 1990s as the **International Decade for Natural**

Disaster Reduction (IDNDR), setting such targets for the year 2000 as preparation of comprehensive national assessments of risk from natural hazards; preparation of mitigation plans at national and/or local levels; and ready access to local, national, regional, and global early warning systems.

- Using resources in selected countries to provide technical cooperation in strengthening disaster preparedness and disaster mitigation systems, so as to reduce the vulnerability of populations to disasters.
- Developing DHA as the focal point for systematic pooling, analysis, and dissemination of early warning information.

The General Assembly resolution establishing DHA calls for emergency assistance to be provided in ways that will be supportive of recovery and long-term development and makes the Under-Secretary-General for Humanitarian Affairs responsible for actively promoting the smooth transition from relief to rehabilitation and reconstruction. UNDP has been active in helping to design longer-term development programs in favor of refugee reintegration and rehabilitation in Eritrea, Ethiopia, Mozambique, and Somalia, and, with DHA, in organizing appeals for resource mobilization. An example of this approach is the UNDP Development Programme for Displaced Populations, Refugees and Returnees in Central America (PRODERE).

Special Populations

Among the most significant and high-risk groups within refugee and internally displaced settings are women and children. In fact, approximately 80 percent of the world's 53 million refugees and displaced persons fall into this category. This figure indicates that particular emphasis must be placed on the unique protection needs of uprooted women and children. However, the needs of these groups are often overlooked in camp design, documentation, protection, access to food and appropriate health care, and opportunities for education, skills training, and economic activities.

Uprooted women face particular hardships at all stages—from flight to the eventual resolution of their situation. A policy on refugee women has been called for since 1980 by U.N. conferences on the status of women, and has been identified by successive High Commissioners as one of UNHCR's highest organizational priorities. Knowledge of the factors particular to women assisted the UNHCR in developing the **Policy on Refugee Women,** introduced in 1990, and the **Guidelines on the Protection on Refugee Women,** completed the following year. These guidelines have assisted refugee workers in planning and implementing activities to address some of the special problems refugee women face.

While UNHCR has made efforts to implement and institutionalize this policy with the potential of effectively and systematically addressing the needs of women and girls, more far-reaching progress is needed. In March 1995 the **Guidelines on Sexual Violence** were adopted, and it was hoped that the U.N. World Conference on Women in September 1995 would highlight the conditions of refugee and displaced women as well as provide the impetus for action to protect their human rights.

Half of most refugee populations are persons under age 15, who require special attention. UNHCR has recognized the need to improve and enhance the protection and care of refugee children. In October 1993 the agency adopted a **Policy on Refugee Children,** which was endorsed by the UNHCR Executive Committee. This policy is an update of the UNHCR Guidelines on Refugee Children, first published in 1988. Its purpose is to provide for the special care, protection, and assistance that children need.

The General Assembly has also begun to pay special attention to the needs of unaccompanied minors. Primary focus is being given to reuniting these children with their families and protecting them from further harm and exploitation. Children who need particular care are those who have been used "as soldiers or human shields in armed conflict" and those who have been recruited in military forces.

4. The Status of Women
By Erin Meyer

The **Fourth World Conference on Women** (the Beijing Conference), September 4–15, 1995, is the culmination of several years of preparation by U.N. bodies, governments, nongovernmental organizations (NGOs), and grass-roots groups at five regional preparatory meetings, international conferences, and official and unofficial gatherings of many sizes and in many venues [for background see *A Global Agenda: Issues/49*, pp. 239–42]. The aim has been to assess the progress made since the **Third World Conference on Women** (the Nairobi Conference) in the summer of 1985 and "to hasten the removal of remaining obstacles to women's full and equal participation in all spheres of life, to protect women's human rights and to integrate women's concerns into all areas of sustainable development" [U.N. press release WOM/812, 3/13/95]. That integration process was given a definite boost by successive U.N.-sponsored international conferences—on Environment and Development (Rio, 1992), Human Rights (Vienna, 1993), and Population and Development (Cairo, 1994)—and at the World Summit on Social Development (Copenhagen, March 1995).

As delegates began packing their bags for Beijing, however, several old battles (e.g., on the "universality" of human rights and the definition of "reproductive health") were being refought. In fact, the final draft of the Conference's "Platform of Action," which would be voted on at Beijing, had even more brackets signaling disagreement about words and concepts than did the previous draft. As one NGO leader explained the Beijing process: "It is about people making the claim, moving the agenda forward, even if it takes a generation to do that. Teaching women that life does not have to be the way it is right now is the catalyst" [*Christian Science Monitor*, 4/19/95].

Participants in the Beijing Conference on Women rally under the banner "Equality, Development, and Peace," three **"priority themes"** established at the First World Conference on Women (Mexico City, 1975) and embellished during the **Decade for Women (1976–85).** A mid-decade conference in Copenhagen (the Second World Conference) designated Education, Employment, and Health as important subthemes. The Third World Conference (Nairobi) approved by consensus the **Forward-looking Strategies for the Advancement of Women to the Year 2000,** whose 371 paragraphs continue to serve as the U.N.'s official guide to national and international action in this arena.

Appraising the success of the ten-year-old Nairobi Strategies, the **Commission on the Status of Women (CSW)** found that "most of [them] have not been achieved," and it went on to identify a dozen critical areas requiring immediate attention. Those 12 supplied the outline of the final draft Platform of Action that CSW—the 45-member intergovernmental commission serving as the main preparatory body for Beijing—drew up at its 39th annual session, March 15–April 4, 1995 [International Institute for Sustainable Development, *Earth Negotiations Bulletin*, 4/10/95; hereafter *ENB*]. The bracketed words and phrases (and occasional paragraph) in this draft were to be negotiated by the official government delegates at Beijing.

One of the most heated debates had to do with **"gender,"** a word that appears throughout the text and caused no such stir when employed in other U.N. documents over the years. Arguing for the use of "gender" (in preference to "sex") in the Beijing Platform, former Member of Congress Bella Abzug stated at the CSW session that the word "sex" conveys a biological fact while "gender" expresses "the reality that women's and men's roles and status are socially constructed and subject to change" [InterAction's Commission on the Advancement of Women, *Mobilizing for Beijing '95*, Spring 1995; hereafter *MFB '95*]. U.N. members Guatemala, Honduras, Ecuador, Benin, Sudan, Libya, Egypt, and Malta demanded further clarification of the term, apparently out of fear that "gender" could accommodate "the perspectives of homosexual, bisexual, and transsexual persons" [ibid.]. Raising alarm about such a "hidden/unacceptable agenda" [*ENB*] have been conservative U.S. and Canadian Christian organizations. Australia, the United States, Chile, and Cuba countered that the term was nonnegotiable because already agreed upon at preparatory meetings. Hoping to head off deadlock at the conference, Austrian delegate Irene Freudenschuss suggested a **Contact Group** to search for "a common understanding of the word . . . within the context of the document" [*MFB '95*]. The group, chaired by Namibia, will report its findings to the conferees in Beijing.

The text was not the only preconference controversy. Four months before opening day, the host country announced that the **NGO Forum**—a "parallel event" traditionally held in proximity to the official conference—would have to move some 30 miles out of town because of structural problems at the original site. Representatives of nongovernmental organizations, many with expertise in conference-related fields, make their presence and opinions known to delegates at press conferences and public demonstrations and by lobbying official delegates and distributing materials. Of China's 11th-hour attempt at isolating these groups, one conference organizer remarked: "No host government has tried to control them like this" [*New York Times*, 5/11/95].

An "NGO Forum Mission" traveled to China in mid-May to inspect alternative sites, none of which had nearly the advantages of communications technology and proximity of the initial site [ibid.]. The Chinese government, however, continued to insist on the remote site [*ibid.*, 5/25/95] and U.N. Secretary-General Boutros Boutros-Ghali sent a high-ranking U.N. official to Beijing to speak with the government. According to a compromise reached on June 8, the Forum will have a satellite site near the official conference, giving accredited NGOs a small base from which to lobby government delegates ["Dear Friends" fax from NGO Forum on Women, 6/9/95].

China had also agreed to provide a visa to anyone holding credentials for the NGO Forum, but the U.N. Secretariat for the Women's Conference (perhaps to preempt such a move by China itself) recommended that NGO credentials be denied to representatives from (among others) Taiwan, Tibet, and some U.S.-based groups concerned with human rights in China. No reason was given at the time [fax letter from Human Rights Watch to the U.N. Secretary-General, 3/16/95].

The Vatican too attempted to block the participation of some NGOs—Catholics for Free Choice, USA, and sister groups in Mexico, Brazil, and Uruguay, on the grounds that they "publicly opposed the position of the Catholic Church" [U.N. press release WOM/834, 4/10/95]—but it was unsuccessful in this bid. (The U.S. Mission to the United Nations called for the establishment of an international committee to review denials of admission and insisted that the reasons for rejection be made public. The U.N.'s Economic and Social Council [ECOSOC] was asked to provide such a review at its next substantive session, in July 1995 [A/Res/49/243].) In mid-March the Commission on the Status of Women gave a definite nod to 1,326 NGOs, which were then eligible to participate actively in the NGO Forum, in company with the NGOs that regularly enjoy consultative status with ECOSOC [U.N. press release WOM/834, 4/10/95].

The Platform for Action

A **Beijing Declaration**—the traditional statement summing up the conference's main theme and pledging to create an "enabling environment" and take action toward achieving conference goals—was scheduled to be negotiated by the official government delegates on the spot [*ENB*].

The delegates would already have in hand the CSW final draft (cum brackets) of the Platform for Action, with its recommended actions in the 12 "priority" areas (labeled A–L) in which reality has fallen short of Nairobi's expectations. These recommendations are addressed, variously, to national and local governments, bilateral donors, international financial and development institutions, the private sector, NGOs, and academic and research bodies. The 12 priority concerns (a number of whose headings wear brackets too), and some of the main points of discussion and debate in each category, are noted below [*ENB* is the source of headings and most quotations from the draft Platform; U.N. press release WOM/834, 4/10/95, and *MFB '95* are the sources of still other details and of quoted commentary].

A. "The persistent and increasing burden of **poverty** on women." Noting the effects of this condition on women's economic, social, political, and cultural status, the section recommends government analysis of development policies and programs from a gender perspective and the allocation of public monies to promote economic opportunities for women and their access to resources. There are also recommendations for programs to, for example, ensure the equal distribution of food to boys and girls in the same household. A proposal on debt reduction, bracketed by the United States and the European Union, calls upon such multilateral financial institutions as the World Bank and the International Monetary Fund to cancel or reduce "the foreign debt burden of developing countries to help them finance development programmes which include the advancement of women."

B. "Unequal access to and inadequate **educational opportunities.**" Noting that education is "an essential tool for achieving the goals of full equality, development and peace," the Platform calls for "equal access to basic education" and to "scientific and technological training"; "gender-sensitive curricula"; "use of mass media as an educational tool"; and equal access to "resources for education." There are brackets around the year 2000 as the target date for achieving literacy among the world's women; around a phrase citing the impact of "the lack of sexual and reproductive education" on women and men; and around a call to respect cultural and religious diversity in educational institutions.

C. "Inequalities in **access to health** and related services." Language agreed upon less than a year before at the Cairo Conference on Population and Development was bracketed in the draft Platform for Beijing.

This included two definitions—"reproductive health" and "reproductive rights"—and all references to "unsafe abortion," "sexual health," "contraceptives," and "the right of women to control their own fertility." The Holy See has suggested an amendment, vigorously opposed by the NGO Health Caucus, that would establish an "international conscience clause," which health professionals and facilities could invoke when refusing to provide or recommend services on moral or religious grounds. The draft Platform goes on to recommend action "increasing women's access throughout the life cycle to appropriate free or affordable and good quality health care" and strengthening "preventive programmes that address threats to women's health."

D. "**Violence** against women." The document attributes this problem to the "historically unequal power relations between men and women" based on cultural patterns that perpetuate women's lower status. It calls upon governments to "adopt measures to modify the social and cultural patterns of men and women, and to eliminate cultural practices based on stereotyped roles for men and women." Governments are also urged to provide well-funded shelters and support, counseling, and legal aid for victims of violence. Brackets surround the clause that defines as violence against women such acts as "terrorism, forced sterilization and forced abortion, coercive/forced use of contraceptives, female foeticide/prenatal sex selection and female infanticide." Also controversial are the recommendations to eliminate "patterns of media presentation that generate violence" and to supply resources to heal female victims of the violent results of "prostitution and trafficking."

E. "Advance peace, promote conflict resolution and reduce the impacts of **armed or other conflict** on women." The drafters include under this rubric acts of terrorism, torture, rape, and displacement. Agreed-upon language in the introduction calls for "the promotion of an active and visible policy of mainstreaming a gender perspective into all policies and programs addressing armed or other conflicts so that before decisions are taken an analysis is made of their effects on women and men, respectively." Another of the few unbracketed portions of this section calls upon governments and organizations to condemn the "systematic practice of rape and other forms of inhuman and degrading treatment of women as a deliberate instrument of war and ethnic cleansing."

Bracketed are all references to "forced pregnancy" and "foreign occupation" as well as calls for "promoting the elimination of all weapons of mass destruction, especially nuclear weapons," and for taking "measures to alleviate the negative impact of economic sanctions on women and children."

F. "Inequality in women's access to and participation in defining **economic structures and policies** [and the productive process itself] [economic potential and independence of women] [gender equality in the economic structures, policies and in all forms of productive activity]." There was consensus on the recommendations that governments "enact legislation to guarantee the rights of women and men to equal pay for equal work or work of equal value" and "ensure that policies related to trade agreements do not aggressively affect women's new and traditional economic activities." There was also agreement that states should begin to take a look at unremunerated work in family businesses and on family farms, but there was no mention of housework or child care in this category. Agreement had yet to be reached on laws granting parental leave and parental benefits to both men and women, and on such matters as applying labor laws and social security provisions to part-time jobs and jobs performed in the home.

G. **"Inequality between men and women in the sharing of power** [family responsibilities] and decision-making at all levels." Still to be negotiated in the introduction were references to "the functioning of democracy" as well as to "unbalanced power relations between women and men within the family." Bracketed in the subsequent recommendations were references to monitoring (and ensuring) the full participation of women in decision-making positions of all varieties as well as a reference to policies aimed at achieving gender parity in employment by the year 2000.

H. "Insufficient **mechanisms at all levels to promote the advancement of women.**" One set of brackets in the introduction embraces a reference to the limited resources allotted two of the U.N.'s most important mechanisms in this arena: the CSW and CEDAW (acronym for both the **Convention on the Elimination of Discrimination against Women [1979] and the Committee of experts** that monitors government compliance with the Convention). Among the bracketed portions of this section were recommendations to two other U.N. bodies, the **International Research and Training Institute for the Advancement of Women (INSTRAW)** and the **U.N. Development Fund for Women (UNIFEM)**. (How the Beijing Conference treats such mechanisms is expected to influence the General Assembly's decision—during the 50th Session—on the proposed merger of INSTRAW and UNIFEM [A/Res/49/160].

Also bracketed under the "mechanisms" heading were the paragraphs that speak of "mainstreaming a gender perspective into all policies" (to be promoted through the collection of data) and "legal reform with regard to the family."

I. "Lack of awareness of and commitment to [internationally and nationally] recognized **human rights** of women. [The enjoyment of [all] [universal] human rights by women]." Bracketed in addition to the definition of human rights were introductory passages referring to "systematic discrimination against women" and "women in vulnerable circumstances." Bracketed too was the statement that "gender-based violence, and all forms of sexual harassment . . . including those resulting from cultural prejudice . . . are incompatible with the dignity and worth of the human person and must be eliminated." Noncontroversial was the call for national programs to educate about human rights and programs to publicize the means available to redress violations of such rights.

J. "Inequality in women's access to and participation in all communications systems, especially **the media,** and their insufficient promotion of women's contribution to society [mobilize the media to portray women's contribution to society] [responsibility of the media for the impact of their content on women] [women and the media]." Gender-based stereotyping is among the topics addressed here, to be redressed (among other recommendations) by an increase in the number of programs for and by women. There were no provisions, however, for ensuring the participation of women in developing "professional guidelines and codes of conduct" to promote a nonstereotypical image of women. A bracketed proposal suggests establishing another set of guidelines and codes to discourage the media (and advertisers) from portraying women in pornographic and degrading ways.

K. "[Lack of adequate recognition and support for] [promote] [women's contribution to **managing natural resources** and safeguarding the environment] [women and the environment]." This section acknowledges an essential role for women in the "development of sustainable and ecologically sound consumption and production patterns and natural resource management." Bracketed in the introduction are references to "the sustainable pattern of consumption and production, particularly in industrialized countries," on the one hand, and to "the relation between poverty and environmental degradation," on the other. Governmental action to reduce risks to women from known environmental hazards received a thumbs up as did an "analysis of the structural links between gender relations, environment and development."

L. "[Persistent discrimination against and violation of the rights of] [survival, protection and development of] **the girl child.**" Bracketed text in the introduction included references to "the rights and duties of parents; reasons that boys have fared better than girls in education, including customary attitudes, child labor and teenage pregnancies; responsible sexual behavior and sexual education; and trafficking in human organs and tissues."

The draft Platform's additional sections on **institutional and financial arrangements** note that lack of resources "contributed to the slow progress . . . in implementing the Nairobi Forward-looking Strategies." Still, there was little in the draft document to suggest that governments would allocate sufficient resources to increase the pace of implementation after Beijing. The editors of *Mobilizing for Beijing '95* foresee the Platform of Action becoming "a key political tool for governments and NGOs alike" in the cause of "mobilizing the resources and political will necessary for achieving greater power and equality for women."

The U.N. Secretary-General was asked to prepare for the 50th Session of the **General Assembly** a report "on follow-up to the Fourth World Conference on Women, taking into consideration the recommendations made at the Conference" [A/Res/49/161].

5. Drug Abuse, Production, and Trafficking
By Adam Williams

The **U.N. Decade against Drug Abuse (1991–2000)** reached its midpoint in 1995, and the International Narcotics Control Board's (INCB) latest annual report on the world drug situation describes an uphill battle against a $500 billion-a-year industry in the production, trafficking, and sales of illicit drugs [E/INCB/1994/1]. Spearheading the global response to this industry is the **U.N. International Drug Control Programme (UNDCP)** with a budget of $190,641,600 for the biennium 1995–96 [U.N. press release SOC/NAR/705, 3/24/95]. In 1992 the General Assembly adopted a **System-Wide Action Plan on Drug Abuse Control** to harmonize the efforts of **UNDCP,** the umbrella agency for U.N. drug-control activities; **INCB,** the independent body of experts that monitors the efficacy and implementation of drug treaties and reports to ECOSOC any leakages from illicit manufacture to illicit use; and ECOSOC's **Commission on Narcotic Drugs (CND,** the intergovernmental, policy-making organ for international drug control).

In December 1994 the General Assembly reaffirmed the importance of that cooperation in mounting "a global response to a global challenge"—the theme of the Decade against Drug Abuse [A/Res/49/168]. As an integral part of this process, UNDCP worked to form partnerships and strengthen linkages with both member state law enforcement agencies and nongovernmental organizations. In pursuing what UNDCP Executive Director Giorgio Giacomelli characterizes as a "balanced approach to drug control"—one aimed at curbing both drug supply and drug demand—UNDCP has taken some well-publicized recent initiatives that reflect a new emphasis on demand reduction.

Helping to widen participation in this cause was a UNDCP-sponsored **Non-Governmental Organization (NGO) World Forum on Drug Demand Reduction.** For four days in December 1994, 436 representatives of national and international NGOs met in Bangkok to explore "the reduction of drug demand in the context of overall social development" and appealed for "more effective coordination among groups seeking to reduce illicit demand" [U.N. press release SOC/NAR/688, 12/16/94].

UNDCP also teamed up with the International Olympic Committee for a **"Sport against Drugs"** program, presenting sports as a means for reducing illicit demand for drugs among youth. Professional athletes from every continent were on hand for the inaugural conference in February 1995 [U.N. press release SOC/NAR/690, 2/15/95]. In the same month, UNDCP and the European Union launched a collaborative demand-reduction project for Asia and the Pacific region. During 1995 the two groups will be spending a combined $281,000 to support two demand-reduction expert forums in that region [U.N. press release SOC/NAR/692, 2/17/95].

But if the U.N.'s Decade against Drug Abuse has reached the halfway mark, the end of the battle is nowhere in sight, and new forces are entering the lists. Giacomelli warns that "the opening-up of trade world-wide [symbolized by GATT and NAFTA] has made it easier for drug smugglers." One effect is that "countries which previously had no drug problems now face a growing number of addicts" [*World Chronicle*, 11/2/94]. In this new climate it is **no longer possible to distinguish between producing, transit, and consumer states.**

Pakistan, for example, a long-time producer and exporter of heroin, now has "3 million addicts, of which 1.5 million are heroin addicts," says UNDCP [ibid.]. The situation will likely worsen, since this year's "bumper crop" of opium poppies is expected to push Pakistan and Afghanistan ahead of South Asia's Golden Triangle as the world's major heroin-producing area [*Far Eastern Economic Review*, 12/15/94]. Production and abuse of drugs is on the rise in the Golden Triangle too, with profound consequences for health and social welfare. Burma is one that will feel the sting. The UNDCP reports that 74.3 percent of all tested drug users in the country are HIV positive [ibid., 7/21/94].

In Eastern Europe there is growing concern too over **new drug trafficking channels** that exploit "lax controls and desperate cash needs" [*Christian Science Monitor*, 10/20/94]. European delegates to the regional meeting of the **Heads of National Drug Law Enforcement Agencies (HONLEA)** in February worried that the trafficking channels would leave trails of drug abuse, as they have elsewhere, and urged states to combat money laundering through new legislation. Lowering the standard of proof for prosecution of laundering offenses was one suggestion. The meeting also recommended that law enforcement agencies establish "watch lists" of persons, vessels, and flights most likely to be transporting cocaine and to share these lists with other data banks [U.N. press release SOC/NAR/689, 2/9/94].

There also seems no abatement in the **corruption and official complicity** that contribute to the success of the drug industry. In Mexico, for example, federal police agents are suspected of engineering the disappearance of several tons of confiscated cocaine [*New York Times*, 4/19/95]. In Colombia an army colonel was caught running a police ring that charged $1,300 for each kilo of cocaine allowed to pass through airport inspection [ibid., 8/

14/94]. The U.S. State Department criticized Colombia's government for "weak legislation, corruption, and inefficiency" [ibid., 3/2/95], and shortly after, Senator Jesse Helms sponsored a bill linking U.S. trade benefits to improvements in Colombia's fight against traffickers [ibid., 6/11/95].

The persistence of drug production and corruption in Colombia owes much to the fact that roughly as many peasants (300,000 families) make their living growing coca, marijuana, or opium poppies as make their living growing coffee, the country's main licit agricultural export [ibid., 8/14/94]. In Pakistan's case, says the *Far Eastern Economic Review*, heroin-export earnings are equivalent to "about 20% of the country's legitimate commodity exports" [12/15/94].

Nonetheless, UNDCP does enjoy significant cooperation from a number of Latin American and other key governments in the struggle against drug trafficking. Peru, which is the largest producer of semirefined cocaine and where 200,000 families grow coca leaves, recently made its largest cocaine and opium seizures ever, indicted a general of the army for protecting cocaine shipments, and dismantled a major drug-trafficking group [*New York Times*, 1/23/95]. Brazil's President, Fernando Henrique, signed an agreement with the Rio de Janiero State government to "keep the army rooting out the drug trade," and the next day Rio police tracked (and killed) one of the city's "most ruthless drug gang leaders" [*Christian Science Monitor*, 1/23/95]. In June 1995, Colombia's government too struck against the country's major drug-trafficking organization, cornering a leader of the Cali cartel (exporters of most of the cocaine that reaches the United States) and pledging new blows to come. U.S. and domestic pressure was credited for the move [*New York Times*, 6/13/95]. Pakistan's Prime Minister, Benazir Bhutto, has responded to growing international pressure to control the country's drug industry by conducting the government's "largest raid" on a drug factory, extraditing 12 alleged drug barons to the United States, and creating a Special Anti-Narcotics Task Force made up of 1,200 soldiers [*Far Eastern Economic Review*, 12/15/94].

In an effort to facilitate such drug-control activities for national governments, UNDCP unveiled a new **electronic information system** in March 1995 at the 38th annual session of the CND. The new system is designed to improve both the access of national drug-control authorities to UNDCP databases and the sharing of information between U.N. agencies and governments. To ensure that the databases are comprehensive, UNDCP and the World Customs Organization will adopt compatible terminologies for the identification of illicit drugs and for those otherwise licit **precursor chemicals** used in the manufacture of narcotic drugs [U.N. press release SOC/NAR/705, 3/24/95].

UNDCP has also begun to elicit multinational cooperation where such a goal has been traditionally most illusive: on the high seas. Acting on a decision of the CND, UNDCP Secretary-General Giacomelli established a 35-member **Working Group on Maritime Cooperation against Drug Trafficking.** The group met for four days in September 1994 and again in February 1995 to discuss "cooperation among States' parties in identifying, boarding, and searching suspicious ships, as well as in conducting whatever arrests and seizures might be called for" [U.N. press release SOC/NAR/680, 8/3/94].

Speaking at ECOSOC's 1994 Substantive Session, Giacomelli advocated that the **World Bank** and the **International Monetary Fund** become involved in a whole range of development activities aimed at deterring drug cultivation and production. Although the World Bank traditionally has been involved in supporting crop-substitution programs to discourage drug cultivation, most of these programs have failed because the proceeds from the alternative commodity could not match the profits from cannabis, poppy seeds, or coca. Giacomelli reported that "Peasants were generally open to accepting less income provided there was a guarantee of better social and educational facilities in the community" [U.N. press release ECOSOC/5541, 7/12/94].

The 1994 annual report of INCB endorsed the view that universal adherence to the three major international drug treaties would strengthen them immeasurably. As of April 1995, 150 states had ratified the **1961 Single Convention on Narcotic Drugs** (six more than in the previous year); 134 were parties to the **1971 Convention on Psychotropic Substances** (up 11); and 108 states and the European Union were parties to the **1988 Convention against Illicit Traffic in Narcotic Drugs and Psychotropic Substances** (up 19) [faxed communication from UNDCP, 5/10/95].

The report stressed the need for more countries to accede to the 1971 convention concerning international trade in many psychotropic substances, and especially states that are home to major pharmaceutical houses, prominently Austria, Belgium, and Switzerland. This would help to close loopholes in international control measures and make it easier to police the sale of benzodiazepines (tranquilizers that can be fatal when used with heroin or cocaine). Responding to the INCB call, Switzerland announced on March 23, 1995, that it intends to adhere to that Convention [*A Global Agenda* interview with the Swiss Observer Mission, 5/10/95]. Africa, with 14 countries not yet party to any of these treaties, remains the weakest link in the international effort to halt drug abuse, production, and trafficking.

On UNDCP Secretary-General Giacomelli's crowded speaking schedule was an address to the March 1995 meeting of the CND, where he noted that the drug-control program's resources continue to fall far short of need [U.N. press release SOC/NAR/695, 3/14/95]. The **International Day against Drug Abuse and Illicit Trafficking,** traditionally June 26, is intended to focus global attention on the work of drug control and presents an opportunity for UNDCP to strengthen partnerships with (and solicit funds from) governments and NGOs.

6. Other Social Issues

Children and Youth
By Anne Witt-Greenberg

The **U.N. Children's Fund (UNICEF)**, winner of the Nobel Peace Prize in 1965, approaches the millennium with a new leader and a variety of challenges—institutional and international. Its **long-time Executive Director, James Grant,** a dedicated and effective advocate for the world's children, resigned shortly before his death in January. The European Union conducted a vigorous campaign to win the directorship for a European, but in the end the U.N. Secretary-General selected U.S. Peace Corps Director **Carol Bellamy** for a post traditionally held by an American. The EU had pointed out that, jointly, its members contribute almost twice the sum contributed by the United States, which pays a quarter of UNICEF's budget.

One of the tasks facing Bellamy, noted the *New York Times* in reporting the appointment, is to "restor[e] confidence in an agency dogged by low morale and allegations of poor management oversight" [4/11/95]. An interim assessment by the firm of Booz-Allen and Hamilton, which is conducting a management study of UNICEF, noted some "disturbing forces" in the funding environment as well: "Some major donor nations are reducing contributions substantially" and "overall growth in government donations is slowing down" [E/ICEF/1994/AB/L.12].

One of the latest challenges for the Children's Fund is to anticipate, and meet, the ever-expanding **emergency needs** of its highly vulnerable constituency—infants, children, and their mothers. UNICEF's 1994 Annual Report notes that "the scale and scope" of emergency operations "increased substantially in 1993, with more than 25 per cent of the organization's resources devoted to assistance in 64 emergency countries, compared with 54 the previous year."

In 1994 those receiving humanitarian assistance included an estimated 7 million young refugees as well as the millions more who were displaced within the borders of their own countries [U.N. press release ICEF/1819, 1/31/95]. **"Short-duration country programmes,"** such as those in a number of East and Central European countries and in Eastern and Southern Africa, attempt to fill an immediate need for food, medicine, clothing, and shelter.

The 48th General Assembly asked the U.N. Secretary-General to name an expert who, enlisting the cooperation of UNICEF and the Centre for Human Rights, would study the **problems of children during armed conflicts,** including children who themselves take up arms [A/Res/48/157]. Among the trends noted by the U.N. Secretary-General in his progress report [A/49/643] on the study ("Promotion and Protection of the

Rights of Children") is that civil wars now kill more children than combatants—claiming 2 million young lives in the past decade—and that children are sometimes the targets of war, in violation of every international
treaty governing the conduct of war. By estimate of Bosnia's Prime Minister, some 17,000 of these children were victims of the conflict in former
Yugoslavia [U.N. press release SOC/4363, 3/13/95]. Nearly a quarter (300,000 plus)
of the 10-year total occurred during Rwanda's civil war alone [UNICEF Fact
Sheet #1, 1/18/95]. This figure does not include the estimated 80,000 Rwandan
children orphaned by war or unable to find their parents [ibid.], and additional numbers who suffered rape and other sexual abuse, with their high
risk of exposure to AIDS.

A follow-up to UNICEF's emergency aid in the **Rwandan theater
of war** are programs for demobilizing some 4,000 soldiers aged 10 to 16,
for educating and developing their vocational skills, and for integrating
them into the life of the community and often into foster families as well
[UNICEF Fact Sheet #33–34, 1/18/95]. The Children's Fund, in cooperation with
the U.N. **Commission on Human Rights,** has also finalized an agreement with the country's Ministry of Justice on the protection of juvenile
prisoners, including a number who have been accused of genocide—the
first such indictment in history [Fact Sheet #6, 1/18/95]. A Trauma Recovery
Programme, part of UNICEF's project on Children in Especially Difficult Circumstances, attempts to address the immediate psychosocial
needs of war-affected Rwandan children and their families [Fact Sheet #33–34,
1/18/95]. A similar program for youngsters caught up in the wars of **former
Yugoslavia** sparked the publication of *I Dream of Peace,* a collection of
writings and drawings now available in ten languages [*U.N. Chronicle,* 6/94].
The U.N. High Commissioner for Refugees' computerized "Operation
ReUNITE" is collecting and distributing information about children separated from their parents in this theater of war [ibid.]. UNICEF, for its part,
has been collecting deserted and lost children along the Rwandan path to
hoped-for refuge in Zaire, Tanzania, and Burundi [Fact Sheet #5, 1/18/95].

UNICEF's **traditional programs** take a far longer-range view of
health and welfare than these emergency programs, addressing problems
that are endemic to poor and developing countries but susceptible to solution, and helping to establish inexpensive, community-based services to
sustain the gains already made. This involves the Fund in a variety of areas
related to child and maternal health, nutrition, education, safe water and
sanitation, and inevitably human rights. UNICEF's reputation for "getting the job done" has much to do with the development of community-
based services, the close working relationship with other specialized U.N.
bodies, its cultivation of national governments, and the willingness of a
wide variety of nongovernmental organizations to enlist in campaigns that
benefit children.

One legacy of James Grant's 14-year tenure at UNICEF is the 1989

U.N. Convention on the Rights of the Child, which affirms the necessity for government measures to protect and care for this particularly vulnerable population and sets the standard to be met. Signed quickly by many countries of the world, the Convention had been ratified by 171 of them by May 1995 [U.N. Secretariat, Office of Legal Affairs]—up from 157 in March 1994. (Only on February 16, 1995, did the United States put its signature to the Convention—an action described as a tribute to Grant [*Global Child Health News & Review*, vol. 3, no. 1, 1995]—and the Clinton administration has yet to indicate when it plans to inaugurate the process of ratification.)

At the U.N.-sponsored **World Summit for Children in 1990,** heads of state and government agreed to upgrade the priority they give to children's needs and to meet certain goals by the year 2000: "a one-third reduction in under-five mortality rates, the halving of child malnutrition, the achievement of 90% immunization coverage, the control of major childhood diseases, the eradication of polio, the halving of maternal mortality rates, a primary school education for at least 80% of children, the provision of safe water and sanitation for all communities, and the making available of family planning information and services to all who need them" [UNICEF, *State of the World's Children 1994*]. The agreement took the form of a **Plan of Action,** to be adapted to national circumstance. UNICEF's annual *State of the World's Children,* and its even more recent annual report on the *Progress of Nations* toward meeting child health and welfare goals, continue to monitor developments in the field.

Reviewing the progress made since the World Summit for Children, UNICEF reports that more than 100 of the developing nations, accounting for over 90 percent of Third World children, are making "significant practical progress" toward maintaining or increasing immunization levels; that measles deaths are down 80 percent from preimmunization levels; that polio has been eradicated in the Western Hemisphere; that iodine-deficiency disorders and vitamin A deficiency are in retreat; that the increased use of oral rehydration therapy for diarrheal diseases is preventing more than a million child deaths a year; and that UNICEF's Baby Friendly Hospital Initiative to encourage breastfeeding is receiving wider community support. It also reports more money for primary education and a lower teacher-student ratio than in the past [*State of the World's Children 1995*].

The official monitor of national progress in implementing the Convention is the 10-member **Committee on the Rights of the Child,** whose formation was dictated by the Convention itself. At semiannual meetings, this committee of experts (who serve in their own capacity and not as representatives of government) reviews the reports submitted by states parties on the fulfillment of their duties under the treaty; Colombia, Denmark, Jamaica, the Philippines, Poland, and the United Kingdom were discussed at the ninth session [U.N. press release HR/4121, 1/30/95]. The formal observations made by the Committee regarding these reports are considered among its most valuable contribution to the cause of children [A Global Agenda: Issues/49, p. 245]. Recognizing that country reports are potentially valuable educational and political tools, the Committee advocates greater involvement of national, local, and grass-roots organizations in preparing them [U.N. press release HR/4116, 1/30/95].

The states parties to the Convention themselves, meeting in annual session in February 1995, "decided not to allow the Federal Republic of Yugoslavia (Serbia and Montenegro) to participate in its current meeting," as proposed by Bosnia. The Federal Republic's representative argued that "denying the legitimate right of the Federal Republic to participate in the meeting would imply the suspension of its obligations arising from the Convention." Several supporters of the proposal said that they were simply "reject[ing] the Federal Republic's claim to automatic succession to the international rights and obligations" of the former Yugoslavia [U.N. press release HR/4121, 2/21/95].

Speaking at the start of a year that would see two major international conferences linking development and human rights issues, UNICEF's then Acting Director Richard Jolly noted that only a "holistic social approach" can offer much assurance that children's lives will be protected [*U.N. Development Update*, 1–2/95; *World Chronicle*, 1/16/95]. To this end the Children's Fund has sought a substantial role in preparations for each of **the decade's global conferences**—on environment and development (Rio, 1992), human rights (Vienna, 1993), population and development (Cairo, 1994), social development (Copenhagen, March 1995), and the status of women (Beijing, September 1995). Deputy Executive Director of UNICEF Operations Karin Sham Poo was on hand for the Economic Commission of Europe's Fall 1994 High-Level Regional Preparatory Meeting for the Beijing Conference, for example, and spoke of the Fund's "strong resolve to help end" all forms of discrimination against women. This commitment to work toward the **empowerment of women** at all stages of life indicates a shift from UNICEF's traditional emphasis on women as mothers and the nurturers of children [UNICEF Division of Information, "The 'Apartheid of Gender' Must End," 10/17/94].

Something of this holistic perspective on tackling problems in the developing world, as well as practicality, informs the close working relationship between UNICEF and the World Health Organization (WHO), the U.N. Development Programme, the U.N. Population Fund, the U.N. High Commissioner for Refugees, the International Labour Organisation (ILO), and the U.N. Educational, Scientific and Cultural Organization (UNESCO), to name some of UNICEF's "natural" partners.

The need for partnership is particularly apparent in countries with a large population of "**AIDS** orphans"—a phenomenon whose effects are most keenly felt in sub-Saharan Africa today but are expected in other developing regions in days to come. A recent WHO-UNICEF study to anticipate the problems of the nations so affected cites health, shelter, education, unemployment, and other areas that will draw down these countries' already limited budgets for national development [WHO/UNICEF staff working paper, "Action for Children Affected by AIDS," 1994].

A special ally in the fight against child prostitution—and thus against the rising rate of HIV infection in some of Asia's poorest countries—is the **Special Rapporteur for the Sale and Trafficking of Children** appointed by the U.N. Commission on Human Rights. His recent report on "AIDS and Child Rights—the Impact on Thailand" recommends changes in Thai law and policies to protect from abuse and discrimination the growing number of children affected by AIDS [UNICEF, *First Call for Children*, 1–3/95]. Statistics gathered by UNICEF in 1994 indicate that as many as a million children throughout Asia are involved in the sex trade under "conditions that are indistinguishable from slavery" [*Freedom Review*, 9–10/94].

The ILO, for its part, continues to look into the entire subject of **child labor,** and in a recent study examined the distorting effect of "sensationalist reporting" about "child sex." It argued for a better understanding of the dynamics surrounding the employment and career paths of young people, especially girls [ILO, *In the Twilight Zone*, 1995].

In Paris, coinciding with the fifth anniversary of the Convention on the Rights of the Child (and with California's Proposition 187 denying undocumented immigrants access to public education and most health care), UNESCO Director-General Federico Mayor called upon governments to resist discriminatory policies that deny a child's fundamental right to an **education.** Discrimination against any group of youngsters is not only irreparably damaging to them and to society as a whole, he said, but "would also constitute a grave offense against the conscience of humanity." Statistics gathered by this Specialized Agency indicate that more than 129 million children between the ages of 6 and 11, and more than 276 million adolescents between 12 and 17, were not enrolled in school when the Convention on the Rights of Children entered into force in 1990. And nearly half of the children who did enroll in school dropped out before completing four years of basic education [*UNESCO Presse*, 11/23/94]. One of the joint UNESCO-UNICEF endeavors in the days since is the development of a "classroom in a box." First intended to serve the children of war-torn Somalia in 1992, it was refined in the refugee camps of Djibouti and tested nationally in Rwanda [*UNESCO Sources*, 11/94].

Education for girls—to enhance their skills, improve their self-esteem, and help put an end to the discrimination against them—was spotlighted at the January 1995 session of the Children's Rights Committee and recommended as a strategy for the Beijing Conference Platform of Action [U.N. press release HR/4116, 1/24/95].

Youth

Education, vocational skills, and self-esteem are also the means, and ends, of the U.N. programs for persons in the 15 to 24 age group. Responsibility for those who are making the passage to adulthood falls to the small **"youth unit"** of ECOSOC's Department of Policy Coordination and Sustainable Development, which works at developing national responses to their problems and at ensuring that youth-related concerns are integrated into national development strategies. Youth make up a third of the population of the developing regions [*Women on the Move*, no. 7, 1995].

International Youth Year (IYY) 1985 gave birth to a **draft World Programme of Action for Youth Towards the Year 2000 and Beyond,** and with the approach of the tenth anniversary of the IYY, the General Assembly spoke of getting down to the business of adopting the Programme [A/Res/49/152]. It requested the Commission for Social Development "to consider further the draft and, as a matter of priority," submit it to the Assembly through ECOSOC [ibid.].

A subsequent resolution of the 49th Assembly requested the U.N. Secretary-General to recommend "specific programs aimed at encouraging school attendance through various means" in consultation with UNICEF and other appropriate bodies. These suggestions will be considered at the 52nd Session, in 1997 [A/Res/49/154].

With the aid of UNICEF, the International Institute for Sustainable Development, and the preparatory body for the March 1995 Social Summit in Copenhagen, youth were given a literal "voice" at the gathering—via Internet. This innovative, interactive project in cyberspace appealed for users with the call "Let the leaders of the world know what you think" [*Global Child Health News & Review*, no. 1, 1995]. A concerted effort at the regional level to integrate youth's concerns into the actual planning for the September 1995 Beijing Conference on Women may well have "raised the profile" of this constituency regionally, and perhaps even globally [*Women on the Move*, no. 7, 1995].

Aging
By Kestrina Budina

The situation of older persons has been a concern of the United Nations since early in its history, and the General Assembly has proclaimed 1999 the International Year of Older Persons (IYOP) [A/Res/47/5]. The past five decades have witnessed dramatic changes in the demographic structure of the world population due to the continued decline in mortality and fertility levels and the increases in life expectancy. In fact, **the elderly have become the fastest-growing population group** in the world—from 200 million (or 8 percent of global population) in 1950 to a projected 1.2 billion (or 14 percent) in 2025. This population was evenly distributed between developing and developed regions in the years 1950–75, but by the turn of the century, 62 percent of the world's over-60 population will be living in developing countries (an estimated 72 percent, or 1.4 billion people, by 2025) [United Nations, *The World Ageing Situation 1991*, p. 15].

The radical change in the demographic structure of the world community requires a fundamental change in the way each society organizes its affairs and the development of practical strategies to integrate the older person into society. Health and nutrition, housing and environment, national infrastructure, family care, social welfare, income security, employment, and education are among the many issues of concern to an aging population that governments must address. In his contribution to *Prospects in Ageing*, Alexandre Sidorenko noted that a U.N. program on aging developed over the years to "coordinate a global response" to the graying of populations "in cooperation with States Members of the UN and NGOs" [J.L.C. Dall et al., eds., New York: Academic Press, 1992]. Today, the office of the **"sub-program on ageing"** in the New York-based **Division for Social Policy and Development** serves as a specialized secretariat for the General Assembly, ECOSOC, and the Commission for Social Development and has links with several U.N. offices, programs, and funds concerned with the subject.

The Vienna **World Assembly on Aging** in 1982 directed world attention to aging-related issues and agreed to an **International Plan of Action on Aging.** In 1991, the 46th Session of the U.N. General Assembly adopted the **"U.N. Principles on Older Persons"** aimed at promoting the independence, participation in society, care, self-fulfillment, and dignity of this population. On the Vienna Plan's tenth anniversary in 1992, the General Assembly adopted a **Proclamation on Aging** that urged the international community to address the challenge of demographic change [A/Res/47/5].

The Plan's tenth anniversary was also the occasion for the Secretary-General's **Global Targets on Aging,** in which he outlined strategies for integrating aging into national and international development plans [A/47/339]. The **International Conference on Population and Development,** (Cairo, September 1994) and the **World Social Summit** (Copenhagen, March 1995) made general recommendations for improving the opportunities of older persons "to achieve a better life" [Copenhagen Declaration (unedited text), 3/20/95]. Both conferences saw a need for the development of appropriate mechanisms to increase the self-reliance of older people and improve social-support systems, both formal and informal, including systems to buttress **family care** for older relatives.

The 1982 Plan of Action had noted that "respect and care for the elderly, one of the few constants in human culture everywhere in the world, reflects a basic interplay between self-preserving and society-preserving impulses which has conditioned the survival and progress of the human race" [par. 27]. Today, that care often passes to strangers.

Demographics are part of the reason. In the Western and Northern Europe of 1950, for instance, there was an average of four women aged 40 to 59 (the potential caregivers) for every person 75 or older. By 1990 this ratio had diminished to approximately two potential caregivers for every 75-year-old [E/ECE/RW/HLM/3]. In the developing world the ratio between caregivers and the elderly is expected to decrease as well. The *Far Eastern Economic Review* uses China as an example. In the China of 2030, according to World Bank estimates, the number of those available to care for each person of retirement age will be 2.3, down from the current 6. Here, pension protection is largely an urban phenomenon; family is still the main source of support for the older people of rural areas. But as more young people leave the countryside, this informal system is sure to weaken [3/2/95].

Given such migration—not to mention emigration, eroding family ties, and shrinking family incomes—much of the burden and expense of caring for the elderly falls to society. For aging populations, income-security after retirement is now a major concern; and for the government, the financing of adequate social security systems is a major policy challenge. The change in demographic trends since the 1960s, when the social security systems of many developed countries were devised, has forced the industrialized countries to consider major reforms of those systems. Some countries are considering extending the legal retirement age "to encourage old-age independence" [A/49/482] and offer retraining programs so that the skills of the older people do not become outdated. In this way retirement is postponed and the day of payout is delayed. Many governments are also attempting to establish community-based personal-care systems for the elderly. A number of developing countries are taking similar steps in anticipation of a graying population [ibid.].

The situation of the graying population in the so-called **"countries in transition"** presents a unique challenge—one taken up by an expert group meeting that was called in response to a General Assembly recommendation that the United Nations provide advisory services to countries in the process of development, change, and transition [A/Res/46/91]. The meeting was also viewed as part of the preparations for the March 1995 Social Summit. These experts identified the special needs of the countries of East and Central Europe, where the state had been the sole source of social benefits for 50 years, and where economic instability has reduced the ability of the family to provide personal care. According to the meeting report, the primary challenge for these governments is "achieving a balance between measures of economic liberalization and social adjustment to transition" [EGMEU/1994/R.2, p. 5]. The United Nations is currently providing advisory services to integrate programs for the aging into the development plans of this region.

Recognized as particularly vulnerable in all regions are **elderly women,** who live longer than men and yet have fewer resources and "societal entitlements" [A/50/114]. The 49th General Assembly called attention to the need to identify and evaluate older women's activities, especially those not often recognized as having economic value [A/Res/49/162]—this in recognition of the finding that, by 2025, there will be 604 million elderly women over the age of 60, up from 208 million in 1985. The Assembly asked the Secretary-General to let it know how the resolution is being implemented when he issues his report on "Advancement of Women" at the 50th Session. The Fourth International Conference on Women (Beijing, September 1995), is expected to take up the special problems of this group.

As directed by the 48th General Assembly [A/Res/48/98], the Secretary-General has set out a conceptual framework for the preparation and observance of IYOP, whose main objective is to promote the Principles on Older Persons that the General Assembly adopted in 1991. Noting that "society needs to accord equal importance to the challenges of each stage of the life cycle," the Secretary-General said that a suitable slogan for '99 would be a "society for all AGES"—one that releases "the potential of all for the benefit of all" [A/50/114].

Disabled Persons
By Daretia J. Austin

A World Programme of Action Concerning Disabled Persons to the Year 2000 and Beyond was one outgrowth of the **International Year of Disabled Persons 1981.** Another was the **U.N. Decade of Disabled Persons (1983–92),** which sought to direct further attention to the needs of a global population estimated at more than a half-billion [United Nations, *The United Nations Decade of Disabled Persons: A Decade of Accomplishment 1983–92,* 1992]. A year after the Decade's close, an ad hoc working group completed, and the General Assembly approved, a set of **"Standard Rules on the Equalization of Opportunities for Persons with Disabilities."** The Rules, or principles, provide an actual framework for national policies that will integrate disabled persons into the economic, political, and social life of their nations [*A Global Agenda: Issues/48,* pp. 264–66, and *Issues/49,* pp. 249–50], and the Secretary-General went on to appoint a **Special Rapporteur,** Bengt Lindqvist of Sweden, to monitor government implementation of those Rules. (Lindqvist, a member of Parliament, had been the first blind Cabinet minister in his country's history.)

In November 1994, the Special Rapporteur sent a questionnaire to U.N. member states, requesting information on their progress to date, and has characterized as "very disappointing" the number of responses received (25 from member states and four from nongovernmental organizations). Lindqvist's first report to ECOSOC's Commission for Social Development in April 1995, read in draft, observes that U.N. questionnaires on disability matters do not elicit much response. He goes on to point out, however, that countries have been asking for advice on implementing the rules and often require assistance in doing so. Unfortunately, Lindqvist noted, there is little "possibility" that U.N. Advisory Services will have more than a "very limited" ability to assist member states in the monitoring process [draft report of the Special Rapporteur to the Commission for Social Development, 34th session, 4/95]. A ten-member panel of experts established by the major NGOs in the disability field will lend a hand in this area by reviewing, advising, and providing feedback and suggestions on implementing and monitoring the Rules [United Nations, *Standard Rules on the Equalization of Opportunities for Persons with Disabilities*, 1994]. It held its first meeting in February 1995.

The U.N. Department for Policy Coordination and Sustainable Development's Social Policy and Development Division, which houses the **subprogram on disabled persons,** has been helping to establish national committees on disability and holds regional training seminars [A/49/435]. The United Nations publishes the Standard Rules in its six official languages and in English, French, and Spanish Braille [ibid.]. Other sources offer Czech, Finnish, Icelandic, Japanese, Korean, and Swedish translations.

The U.N.-sponsored global conferences of the past several years have devoted attention to disability-related issues, most recently the **Social Summit** (with particular regard to employment and social integration) and the **Beijing Conference on Women** (where "gender and disability issues intersect" the conference's 12 priority themes [ibid.]). On the occasion of the International Year of the Family (IYF) 1994, the Year's ad hoc secretariat issued a paper on "families and disability."

A program to prevent accidents and disabilities is the **joint undertaking** of the U.N. Development Programme, the U.N. Children's Fund, and the World Health Organization. IMPACT (the International Initiative Against Avoidable Disablement) attempts this through "integrated approaches to strengthening the health and development sectors at the community level" [ibid.]. Such preventive measures as immunization and proper nutrition are the essentials of UNICEF's own "mid-term plan for childhood disability" (1994–97).

The 48th **General Assembly** had asked the Secretary-General to give disability issues "higher priority . . . within the programmes of work" of the United Nations and requested a report on "the development of a plan of action to implement the long-term strategy to further the implementation of the World Programme of Action" of 1982 [A/49/435]. His report cum action plan [A/49/605] was considered by the 49th Session, which called upon governments to take these strategies into account as they implement the World Programme of Action [A/Res/49/153]. The Secretary-General will report on developments on these fronts at the 52nd Session, in 1997 [ibid.].

Human Settlements
By Daretia J. Austin

The U.N. Conference on Human Settlements (HABITAT II; Istanbul, June 3–14, 1996), dubbed **"the City Summit,"** will be the last major U.N.-sponsored international assembly of the 20th century. Human habitats are defined by the Nairobi-based **U.N. Centre for Human Settlements (UNCHS, or Habitat)** as "the physical articulation of the social, economic and political interactions of people living in communities" [UNCHS, "Profile Brochure," n.d.], and organizers see HABITAT II as the culmination of the series of development-related world gatherings that began with the Conference on Environment and Development (UNCED, or Earth Summit) of 1992. In fact, **Agenda 21,** UNCED's action plan, contains specific proposals for improving the social, economic, and environmental quality of human settlements, rural as well as urban. Part of the preparations for HABITAT II has been to assess the progress made in linking shelter policies with such specific concerns as land-use planning and management and energy-efficient technology.

The Nairobi Centre's programs on human settlements, guided by a **Global Strategy for Shelter to the Year 2000 (GSS)** [A/Res/43/180], supply a range of government needs—from technical assistance in developing the legislative and institutional capacity for implementing the GSS to help in carrying out specific shelter projects. In each case, the emphasis is on enlisting the effective and ongoing participation of the national business sector, nongovernmental organizations, local communities, and individual households.

The intergovernmental entity responsible for setting UNCHS policies and for "coordinating, evaluating, and monitoring" the implementation of GSS [A/Res/43/181] is the **U.N. Commission on Human Settlements,** which meets biannually in the spring. At its 15th session, April 24–May 1, 1995, the Commission adopted 13 resolutions dealing with such matters as children's housing rights and policies regarding assistance to refugees and displaced persons [press release HAB/97, 5/9/95].

It was the Commission that had approved the themes of HABITAT II: "adequate shelter for all" and "sustainable human settlements in an urbanizing world" [A/49/37]. A U.N. human rights body that is contributing to HABITAT II notes the emergence of a "third theme"—the **development of standards for fulfilling the right to adequate housing** [E/CN.4/Sub.2/1994/20]. One controversial element of that standard-setting process has to do with **security of tenure** [*Earth Times*, 2/28–3/5/95]—that is, freedom from "arbitrary eviction, expropriation or relocation, in the absence of an alternative acceptable to those affected, notwithstanding the type of housing inhabited" [E/CN.4/Sub.2/1994/20].

Concurrent with the Commission on Human Settlements' spring meeting was the second substantive session of the Preparatory Committee (PrepCom II) for HABITAT II, which continued work on the **Plan of Action** that will be voted on by the governments represented at the Conference [press release HAB/95/30, 5/5/95]. The Plan will have a section on "best practices," supplying information about programs that have been successful in addressing problems of urban living. A 1995 conference in the Municipality of Dubai, United Arab Emirates, will explore successful programs of both developing and industrialized countries. PrepCom III—the final meeting before Istanbul—is scheduled for February 1996 and will be held in New York.

The **Special Rapporteur on the right to housing** of the U.N. Subcommission on Prevention of Discrimination and Protection of Minorities, addressing ECOSOC's Committee on Economic, Social, and Cultural Rights in May 1995, expressed concern about one aspect of the draft plan for HABITAT II that had emerged from PrepCom II. The very right to adequate housing could be eclipsed at the upcoming conference, said Rajindar Sachar, if some PrepCom participants continued to downplay the importance of economic rights when championing political and civil rights [U.N. press release HR/4165, 5/17/95].

World Habitat Day, traditionally the first Monday in October [A/40/202A], put the spotlight on home and family in 1994 in recognition of the International Year of the Family [UNCHS brochure for World Habitat Day 1994]. As of spring 1995 there had been no announcement of the theme for the next "Day."

The 50th **General Assembly** will have before it a report of preparations for HABITAT II. A discussion of that report is on the agenda [A/Res/49/109].

Crime
By Adam Williams

Today the perpetrators, the proceeds, and the detritus of crime cross national borders at record pace. A growing pool of profit from illegal activity, currently estimated at $1 billion, is "washed" through the world's financial markets every day, feeding the aspirations of domestic criminal groups to become global contenders [U.N. press release SOC/CP/100, 3/1/94]. Aiding in this effort, Secretary-General Boutros Boutros-Ghali has noted, are many otherwise beneficial developments, such as new information and transportation technologies, relaxation of border controls, and the move toward freer trade [SOC/CP/141, 4/28/95]. Recent trends in transnational crime, and the means of upgrading the ability of national law enforcement agencies and legal systems to combat them, were the subject of three U.N.-organized international conferences between the summer of 1994 and the spring of 1995. The culmination of the three was the quinquiennial U.N. Congress on the Prevention of Crime and Treatment of Offenders in May 1995.

At the first of these conferences—on **Laundering and Controlling the Proceeds of Crime,** held in Courmayeur, Italy, in June 1994—representatives of 45 countries devised national strategies for countering money laundering, among them identification of new kinds of businesses that are acting as launderers, adoption of new laws to require reporting of "suspicious transactions" [DPI/1644/CRM-95-93315-4/95-6M], and limitation of bank secrecy [*Development Update*, 9–10/94]. These recommendations were submitted to the **World Ministerial Conference on Organized Transnational Crime,** which met in Naples during November 1994 [ibid.].

The Naples conference, a three-day event organized by the Vienna-based Crime Prevention and Criminal Justice branch of the United Nations and attended by representatives of 140 nations, was the highest-level gathering ever called by the world body on the issue of transboundary crime. Among the participants were three presidents, three prime ministers, and, representing the United States, Deputy Attorney-General Laurel Robinson. Among the subjects discussed were strategies for addressing both the expansion of transnational crime into new areas (money laundering, trade in nuclear technology, and transport of illegal immigrants) and the challenges of improving cooperation among state governments and among law enforcement agencies [U.N. press release SOC/CP/134, 11/22/94].

The conference promulgated a **Naples Political Declaration and Global Plan of Action,** which the 49th General Assembly seconded, urging states to implement its provisions [A/Res/49/159]. The Action Plan calls for multinational cooperation in the struggle against organized crime, specifically the harmonization and strengthening of national legislation for dealing with complex criminal activities. It endorses the Courmayeur conference recommendation that national governments adopt legislative and regulatory measures to limit financial secrecy, and it goes on to call for international cooperation to "facilitate extradition" [A/49/748].

In the interest of improving technical cooperation between states in combating cross-border crime, described as "an instrument for . . . destabilizing democratic institutions" [SOC/CP/141, 4/28/95], the Naples conference welcomed Italy's own promise to organize and finance a "task force" to examine the feasibility of creating an **international training center for law enforcement and criminal justice personnel** [SOC/CP/139, 11/28/94]. (No report on Italy's project had been made available by the following spring.) A similar project is being undertaken by the United States, which announced in April 1995 that it would set up an FBI international police training academy in Budapest [*New York Times*, 4/17/95]. A new cooperative European police agency and data-sharing network, called Europol—described as having "wider powers than Interpol"—was expected to gain final approval from European leaders in June [*Christian Science Monitor*, 5/3/95].

The main goal of the Naples Action Plan—improving global cooperation to combat global crime syndicates—was the first item on the agenda at the **Ninth U.N. Congress on Prevention of Crime and the Treatment of Offenders,** in May 1995, attended by the delegates of 138 governments as well as by representatives of 15 intergovernmental and 48 nongovernmental organizations and 22 U.N. agencies and programs [SOC/CP/159, 5/8/95]. Discussions at the ten-day gathering in Cairo fell into four categories, as decided at regional preparatory meetings: "international cooperation and practical assistance for strengthening the rule of law; action against national and transnational economic and organized crime, and the role of criminal law in the protection of the environment; management and improvement of police and criminal justice systems; and strategies for preventing urban crime, violent criminality, and juvenile crime" [SOC/CP/140, 4/24/95]. The Ninth Congress was not only the first to take place on the African continent and the first in the Arab world but also the first to add to the traditional debate format a series of informal workshops for devising strategies to combat specific types of crime [SOC/CP/159, 5/8/95].

Egyptian President Hosni Mubarek opened the meeting with a speech on **terrorism,** which he characterized as "one of the most violent manifestations of organized crime" and one that "shakes the foundations of all stable societies" [SOC/CP/142, 5/1/95]. The topic resurfaced at many points during the conference, and the Congress passed a resolution, cosponsored by Egypt and Turkey, unequivocally condemning terrorist acts, organized crime, and linkages between the two. Several delegates, most of them representing countries of the Middle East, objected to the resolution on the grounds that it failed to make a clear distinction between terrorism and acts of self-defense or national liberation [SOC/CP/159, 5/8/95].

The Congress also adopted an omnibus resolution dealing with matters as various as **eco-crimes** and **juvenile delinquency.** In the former case, it called on states to consider "enacting penal provisions, establishing special investigative bodies or appointing a special prosecutor to address criminal activities resulting in damage to the environment" [ibid.]. Turning to urban and juvenile crime, the Congress called for the development of domestic projects to address juvenile delinquency, especially in the case of homeless children. (Another resolution, on "children as victims and perpetrators of crime," calls for universal prohibition of child pornography and adherence to the principle that depriving child offenders of their liberty will be used only as a last resort.) Concerned about the number of urban and juvenile crimes committed with guns, the Congress sought "urgent measures to regulate firearms" [ibid.].

In a separate resolution addressing **"violent criminality,"** the delegates called for the enactment of laws to deal with violence against women and for sanctions against the practice of genital mutilation as well as against rape and sexual abuse [SOC/CP/158, 5/8/95].

Turning to the general topic of **international cooperation** in its omnibus resolution, the Crime Congress asked states to "facilitate transnational criminal investigations" by exchanging evidence, sharing records, locating persons, serving subpoenas, and carrying out inspections and seizures [SOC/CP/159, 5/8/95]. A separate resolution requests states to report their views on the desirability of elaborating a **convention against organized transnational crime** [ibid.]. Such a treaty might include arrangements for cooperation among legal systems and among law enforcement agencies as a means of coordinating action against (e.g.) money laundering. In the same cause, the Congress passed another resolution that called for the convening of an expert group to create model legislation on extradition and related forms of international cooperation [ibid.].

The Congress submitted its recommendations (and ten resolutions) on the prevention of crime and treatment of offenders to **ECOSOC's Crime Commission,** scheduled to meet May 30–June 9, 1995. The 50th General Assembly will review the report of the Commission, and will also decide whether to allocate the extra funds to upgrade the U.N. crime prevention and criminal justice program to division status, in accordance with a request of the Naples Declaration [A/Res/49/159].

The actions of the 50th Session will have significant bearing on the scope of activities that the U.N. crime prevention program can undertake in the coming years, but it is the decisions of national governments to implement the U.N. resolutions they have issued on crime prevention that will have the greater effect on reducing transnational crime. During the closing days of the Crime Congress the U.S. Department of Justice signed an agreement to assist the U.N. crime branch in setting up the **U.N. Online Crime and Justice Clearinghouse** (UNOJUST)—a contribution to strengthening the multilateral effort to upgrade law enforcement and criminal justice systems around the world [U.N. press release CP/CAI/28, 5/6/95].

VI
Legal Issues
By José E. Alvarez

Recent developments at the United Nations confirm a trend that has been evident for some years, and particularly since the end of the Cold War: Despite dwindling financial and other resources, U.N. organs, including the Secretariat, take an expansive view of their mandate to "maintain international peace and security." According to the Secretary-General's annual Report on the Work of the Organization, "maintaining peace" also means restoring respect for human rights, promoting democratization, and encouraging economic development. That report, essentially an "agenda for development," attempts to give coherence to the myriad tasks of the Organization, including those on its rich and challenging legal agenda. Among the items on that agenda are the prospective trials of alleged perpetrators of war crimes in the former Yugoslavia and Rwanda (the first to be conducted by an international tribunal since World War II); a draft proposal for a permanent international criminal court; new treaties to protect U.N. peacekeepers and regulate the use of cross-boundary rivers and streams; and the binding decisions of an activist Security Council increasingly concerned with "second-generation" peace operations as well as with the consequences of economic sanctions for both the target and other parties. Most of these developments, and the institutional reforms that may be needed to accommodate some of them, will be taken up at the 50th Session of the General Assembly.

1. The International Law Commission

The 46th session of the International Law Commission (ILC), established to assist the General Assembly in the codification and progressive development of international law, was one of the most productive in history. Meeting in Geneva, May 2–July 22, 1994, the 34-member Commission completed a second draft of a statute for an international criminal court, a second reading of articles on nonnavigational uses of international watercourses, and a first draft of a discrete portion of its articles on liability for injurious consequences arising out of acts not prohibited by international law. It also began a second reading of articles for a Draft Code of Crimes against the Peace and Security of Mankind, considered aspects of state responsibility (for international crimes, for one), and appointed rapporteurs to consider two new topics, **the law and practice relating to reservations to treaties and state succession and its impact on the nationality of natural and legal persons** [see A/49/355 for texts of the Draft Statute and proposed articles on international watercourses and international liability; A/49/10 for the ILC's annual report; and A/Res/49/51 for the Assembly's approval of this report and the ILC agenda].

The ILC's greatest achievement was the extraordinarily quick redraft of its 1993 **Draft Statute for an International Criminal Court** [see *A Global Agenda: Issues/49*, pp. 258–62]. The Draft Statute has been modified in light of considerable comments by governments [see A/CN.4/458 and Adds.1–8, A/CN.4/457] as well as recent experience with the war crimes tribunals for the former Yugoslavia and Rwanda [see Peace and Security section below]. Although the proposed 18-member International Criminal Court would be created by treaty and not by the Security Council (unlike the Yugoslav and Rwandan ad hoc tribunals) and would have a relationship agreement with the United Nations, the new draft streamlines the court's proposed jurisdiction and emphasizes that the new court would supplement but not displace national jurisdiction for international crimes [for text of the second draft, along with ILC commentary, see A/49/10, pp. 23–161; see also A/C.6/49/SR.16]. Although many states had sought to convene a diplomatic conference immediately to conclude a treaty incorporating the proposed statute, the 49th Assembly opted instead for an ad hoc committee, open to all members, that would review the new draft and report to the 50th Session [A/Res/49/53]. That committee, which met for the first time from April 3 to 13, 1995, has had the benefit of further government views [see, e.g., A/AC.244/1] and agreed to meet again, on August 14–15, to finalize its recommendations to the 50th Assembly. If the General Assembly convenes a diplomatic conference leading to the conclusion of the proposed treaty, the ILC will have accomplished within the space of three sessions what has eluded others for decades: the creation of a general, permanent criminal court at the international level—a development whose consequences could be as revolutionary as those wrought by the introduction of human rights into international law after World War II [see, e.g., B. Ferencz, *An International Criminal Court: A Step Towards World Peace*, Dobbs Ferry, N.Y.: Oceana Publications, 1980].

Under the revised statute, the International Criminal Court would have **jurisdiction over two types of crimes,** which it goes on to enumerate: (1) four crimes under general international law (genocide, aggression, serious violations of the laws and customs applicable in armed conflict, and crimes against humanity) [article 20(a–d)] and (2) "exceptional serious crimes of international concern" established under specific treaties identified in an annex [article 20(e)]. Among the treaty crimes identified in the annex are war crimes enumerated in the Geneva Conventions and Protocol I; crimes defined in the Apartheid, Torture, and Hijacking and other antiterrorism multilateral conventions; and, most controversial of all, international drug trafficking (as defined in the U.N. Convention against Illicit Traffic in Narcotic Drugs and Psychotropic Substances). The court would not have jurisdiction to try all crimes under these conventions but only those reaching a certain threshold of gravity, as determined by the court [see article 35]. And the court would not, contrary to the first draft, have the broad discretion to "define" new crimes under "general international law," which would now enable it to avoid an undefined, uncertain, and controversial jurisdiction base [compare *Issues/49*, pp. 259–60].

Except in the case of genocide and aggression, the court's jurisdiction is now more explicitly consensual and limited: It applies only with respect to states that have become parties to the statute and only with respect to those crimes over which that state has accepted the court's jurisdiction [article 22]. The criminal court is deemed to have jurisdiction once a party to the statute lodges a complaint against an individual (or individuals), and the state with custody of the suspect and the state on whose territory the crime occurred agree to accept the jurisdiction of the court [articles 21, 22, and 25]. Where an extradition request is pending under an extradition treaty, the consent of the requesting state is also required [article 21(2)].

Given the particular gravity of the crime of genocide, the court has inherent jurisdiction. All that is required, apparently, is that a party to the statute lodge a complaint alleging commission of acts of genocide in another state, whether or not that state is a party to the statute or has accepted the court's jurisdiction for any purpose [article 25(1)]. When it comes to crimes of aggression especially, the statute puts the Security Council in the driver's seat, recognizing the Council's primacy in matters of peace and security and desiring to establish an alternative to ad hoc tribunals. The court is given jurisdiction over *any* of the crimes identified in the statute if the Security Council, acting under Chapter VII of the U.N. Charter, has referred the matter to it [article 23(1)]. Indeed, it is up to the Security Council to determine that aggression has been committed before an individual can be charged as an aggressor [article 23(2)]. Further, no prosecution may be commenced "arising from a situation which is being dealt with by the Security Council as a threat to or breach of the peace or an act of aggression under Chapter VII of the Charter, unless the Security Council otherwise decides" [article 23(3)]. These limits on jurisdiction help to avoid "collateral challenges" to Security Council action and make the statute more palatable to permanent members—but at a price: Prosecutions for aggression will be subject to the vetoes of permanent members. The revised statute also attempts to clarify some of the rights defendants should enjoy [see, e.g., article 37, which provides only narrow exceptions to a prohibition on trials in absentia; and articles 48–49, which distinguish the scope of appeals by the prosecution from appeals by the defense].

Reaction to the newly revised statute in the ILC, the Sixth Committee of the General Assembly, and the ad hoc committee on the court has been generally positive [see *Issues/49*, pp. 261–62, for reaction to the first draft]. Even China, previously quite hostile to the idea of a court, is recorded as saying that the revised statute is "more balanced and realistic . . . and could serve as the basis for negotiation" [A/C.6/49/SR.18]. Others are far more enthusiastic, openly welcoming the idea of an independent, permanent (but not full-time) criminal court set on a secure constitutional base and with law defined in advance, finding this preferable to the ad hoc tribunals set up at Security Council whim, as with respect to the former Yugoslavia and Rwanda, and hoping this would deter the Council from further experimentation along such lines [see, e.g., James Crawford, "The ILC Adopts a Statute for an International Criminal Court," 89 *American Journal of International Law*, 4/95; and see, e.g., comments by the United Kingdom, press release GA/8871, and by Chile, A/C.6/49/SR.21]. Some others, such as the United States, remain cautiously optimistic about the prospects for an international criminal court but stress that prosecutions by national courts under national laws are usually to be preferred, given financial constraints, language difficulties, and familiarity with the substantive law, rules of evidence, and systems of punishments [see extensive U.S. comments on the revised statute, A/AC.244/1/Add.2]. Accordingly, the United States favors dramatically narrowing the proposed court's jurisdiction by, among other things: disfavoring international prosecutions where these would disrupt ongoing national criminal investigations; either excluding individual culpability for aggression or clearly defining what "aggression" is; clarifying when crimes are sufficiently "serious" to warrant international prosecution; restricting the prosecutor's discretion to initiate an investigation merely upon the filing of a complaint by a state; eliminating drug-related crimes from the court's jurisdiction; demanding the consent of additional states to jurisdiction (such as those of the nationality of the victim or those being targeted by the terrorist); and restricting prosecutions for crimes against humanity and war crimes to instances referred by the Security Council, with greater weight given to national prosecutions for these crimes [ibid.]. Having learned its lesson from issues left open with respect to the tribunals for the former Yugoslavia and Rwanda, the United States also wants to settle before the court is established the rules of evidence, court procedures, and financing [ibid.; for varying views on how the potentially expensive court ought to be funded, see GA/8876]. The United States, alike with others, has also expressed the need to ensure that the rights of the defendant will be protected under the statute [A/AC.244/1/Add.2; for varying views on this issue, see, e.g., GA/8873].

In meetings of the ad hoc committee and in the Sixth Committee, many governments echoed the U.S. call for greater precision with respect to the enumerated crimes and clarification of the court's relationship with prosecutions for international crimes by national courts [see, e.g., comments by Japan, A/C.6/49/SR.18], but considerable differences remain on how to clarify these issues, on the role of the Security Council, and on whether to include aggression and drug trafficking as cognizable crimes [see, e.g., press releases GA/8869–72]. Algeria, representing the views of many developing states, argued that giving the Council the authority to refer cases directly to the court gives that body powers that rightly belong to the judges and perhaps to the General Assembly [GA/8870 and see, e.g., comments by Tunisia and Greece, GA/8871; Gabon, A/C.6/49/SR.24; and Bahrain, A/C.6/49/SR.17]. Others, also distrustful of the Council, demand that the crime of aggression be defined more precisely [see, e.g., comments by Sudan, GA/8869 and A/C.6/49/SR.26, and Jamaica, A/C.6/49/SR.22]. Giving a political body like the Security Council the explicit authority to render what would amount to a quasi-judicial judgment in all cases of aggression continues to make many nonpermanent members uneasy; and some argue that, given the Council's historic reluctance to brand any state an aggressor, deferring to it in this way would dash all hopes of prosecuting aggressors [see, e.g., comments by Sri Lanka and Chile, A/C.6/49/SR.21, and the Netherlands, A/C.6/49/SR.18]. Other states continue to advocate a link between the proposed court and the Draft Code of Crimes against the Peace and Security of Mankind [see, e.g., comments by Morocco, A/C.6/49/SR.21; and see discussion of the Draft Code below]. Few issues with respect to the proposed jurisdiction of the court appear to be settled, and a number of states question even the proposal to give the court inherent jurisdiction in the case of genocide [see, e.g., comments by Jamaica, A/C.6/49/SR.22]. Although the very magnitude of some recent international crimes has injected a sense of urgency into the deliberations, the many issues yet to be resolved cast doubt on the immediate prospect of a functioning criminal court.

The ILC completed its work and submitted to the 49th Session of the General Assembly draft articles for a **framework convention on non-navigational uses of international watercourses.** The 33 articles of the proposed convention track those articles that were adopted on first reading in 1991 [see *Issues/47,* pp. 294–95]. These fall into six parts: introduction; general principles; planned measures; protection, preservation, and management; harmful conditions and emergency situations; and miscellaneous provisions. Intended to provide general principles and rules that would govern in the absence of specific agreement (and to serve as a guide to states in the negotiation of future agreements for specific watercourses), the proposed framework convention addresses both "international watercourses" (such as rivers or streams that form or cross a boundary, lakes through which a boundary passes, or tributaries of such watercourses) and the waters contained in such channels. It relates to all uses other than navigational ones and embraces "measures of conservation and management," including those relating to water quality, flood control, living resources, erosion, sedimentation, and saltwater intrusion [article 1; for text and commentary, see A/49/10, pp. 197–326]. The ILC compromised on whether to encompass confined groundwater that does not interact in some way with surface water: While such groundwater is not covered by the convention itself, the ILC adopted a resolution recommending that the same principles be applied to groundwater [A/49/10, p. 326].

Possibly the most fundamental provisions of the convention—a compromise between the interests of upper and lower riparian states—indicate that a watercourse state has both the right to utilize an international watercourse in an equitable and reasonable manner and the obligation not to deprive other riparian states of their right to equitable use [article 5]. The factors that states are entitled to take into account for purposes of "equitable and reasonable utilization" are enumerated [article 6]. Further, states are required to exercise "due diligence," so as to "utilize an international watercourse in such a way as not to cause a significant harm to other watercourse states" [article 7]. The commentary describes the due diligence standard as one assuring nonnegligent or intentional conduct but not constituting an absolute duty to ensure that no harmful results occur [A/49/10, p. 237]. A state that, despite due diligence, causes significant harm to another riparian state must nonetheless consult with the harmed state on the extent of use and on methods to mitigate the harm [article 7(2)].

Other important provisions of the draft framework convention on international watercourses identify states that are entitled to participate in consultations and negotiations relating to agreements on international watercourses [article 4]; provide for the regular exchange of data among riparian states [article 9]; ensure timely notification prior to the taking of "planned measures" that may have significant adverse effects [article 12]; obligate riparian states to "protect and preserve" the ecosystems of international watercourses [article 20]; and provide for impartial fact-finding and, subject to the agreement of all parties, for arbitration or judicial settlement to ensure the peaceful settlement of relevant disputes [article 33].

During discussion in the Sixth Committee, most governments praised the "well-balanced" proposed articles on watercourses, but some criticized the vagueness of key factors [see, e.g., Ethiopia, A/C.6/49/SR.28, and Finland, A/C.6/49/SR.22] while others differed about whether the competing interests of upstream and downstream states had been balanced adequately [compare, e.g., comments by Egypt and Iran arguing for greater restrictions on the activities of upstream states to those by Venezuela suggesting that the "due diligence" standard was already too severe, A/C.6/49/SR.24]. On the recommendation of the Sixth Committee, the 49th Assembly decided to convene a working group, which will meet October 7–25, 1996, to push ahead on a convention based on the ILC's work and with the participation of the ILC's Special Rapporteur [A/Res/49/52]. Whether a convention actually emerges from this process, the ILC's draft articles are a significant milestone in the codification and development of relevant law and are likely to serve as a model in the resolution of relevant disputes and the negotiation of particular agreements [see Stephen C. McCaffrey, "The International Law Commission Adopts Draft Articles on International Watercourses," 89 *American Journal of International Law*, 4/95].

Turning to its long-standing effort on a **Draft Code of Crimes against the Peace and Security of Mankind** [see the Special Rapporteur's 12th report, A/CN.4/460], the ILC focused on the first 15 draft articles, including many redrafted by Special Rapporteur Doudou Thiam. Although these provisions, dealing with definitional and general issues (such as the obligation to try or extradite, nonapplicability of statutory limitations, the rights of defendants, and nonretroactivity), were referred to a Drafting Committee, ILC discussions revealed continuing basic disagreements [see A/49/10, pp. 161–94; see also *Issues/47*, pp. 290–93]. Indeed, governments continue to disagree even about the proposed title—some noting that the word "code" is inappropriate unless the document includes a complete listing of all international crimes, others noting that the term "peace and security" is an inappropriate description of some of the crimes contemplated for inclusion, such as genocide and crimes against humanity [A/49/10, pp. 162–63]. A number of the thorny issues raised in the first 15 general articles cannot be resolved until it becomes clear which crimes the code will cover and whether it will have any relation to the proposed International Criminal Court or to prosecutions of international crimes in national courts. Much depends on the reception given to the Special Rapporteur's next report, which is intended to winnow down the crimes included in the code to the least contentious. The ILC is still committed to completing its second reading of the Code of Crimes by 1996.

The ILC's discussion of **state responsibility** continues to focus on the question of the right to take countermeasures in response to another state's action [see Special Rapporteur's 6th report, A/CN.4/461; *Issues/48*, pp. 276–78; and *Issues/49*, pp. 262–64]. Despite considerable discussion of the types of preconditions that might apply prior to the taking of some types of countermeasures, the Commission failed to resolve the issue, and there was still sharp disagreement about whether states, *as states,* can ever be guilty of international crimes [for a full discussion of this topic, see A/49/10, pp. 327–66 (on proposed article 19); compare, e.g., the views of the United States (A/C.6/49/SR.25) and France (A/C.6/48/SR.27), both opposing the criminal liability of states, to the views of Israel (A/C.6/49/SR.26) and Algeria (A/C.6/49/SR.27), both supporting the ILC's current draft article 19, which would permit the finding that a state is criminally liable for certain occurrences]. These continuing disagreements led the ILC to defer submission of draft articles on countermeasures until the 50th Session of the General Assembly [see also Robert Rosenstock, "The Forty-Sixth Session of the International Law Commission," 89 *American Journal of International Law*, 4/95, pp. 393–94].

In connection with **liability for injurious consequences arising out of acts not prohibited by international law,** the ILC produced a complete set of articles on preventive measures with respect to activities that give rise to the risk of transboundary harm [see Special Rapporteur's 10th report, A/ CN.4/459; A/49/10, pp. 367–437; and *Issues/49*, p. 264]. These articles, adopted on a first reading, require that states give prior authorization to activities that run the risk of causing "significant transboundary harm through their physical consequences" [articles 1, 11, and 13], that states contemplating such activity undertake a risk assessment and reveal any risks to affected states [articles 12 and 15], that states take legislative or other actions to prevent or minimize the risk of transboundary harm [article 14], and that states simply avoid transferring risky activities from one area to another or from one risk to another [article 14bis]. The articles also call for the exchange of information between states and the public, subject to the protection of national security and industrial secrets [articles 16–17] and consultations on preventive measures [articles 18–19]. Factors involved in an "equitable balance of interests" are enumerated [article 20]. The ILC's next effort will be to define, with greater precision, the activities that would be within the scope of these proposed articles. The Commission hopes to complete by 1996 a first reading of draft articles on activities having a risk of causing transboundary harm.

Continuing disagreement about the definition of a "state" and "state enterprise," about the criteria for determining the "commercial" character of a transaction or contract, and about the scope of permissible judicial measures of constraint against a state's property were among the reasons the 49th Session of the General Assembly put off yet again the scheduling of an international conference to conclude a convention on **jurisdictional immunities of states and their property** [A/Res/49/61; and see comments at A/C.6/ 49/SR.32–33. For a report on the informal consultations between states, see A/C.6/49/L.2]. The proposed convention, adopted by the ILC in 1991 and the subject of working groups during the 47th and 48th General Assemblies and of consultations during the 49th, will be discussed again formally during the 52nd. At that session or the next, a date and time for the conference will be set [A/Res/49/ 61; for background, see *Issues/49*, pp. 265–66].

2. Peace and Security

As has been true since the end of the Cold War, the Security Council continues to meet in virtually continuous session and to issue an unprecedented number of legally binding Chapter VII decisions. Among these were the resolutions renewing the mandate of UNOSOM II in Somalia [S/Res/923, 5/31/94], authorizing a multilateral humanitarian operation in Rwanda (UNAMIR) [S/Res/929, 6/22/94], empowering a multilateral force to use force if necessary to restore Haitian President Jean-Bertrand Aristide to power [S/Res/940, 7/31/94], extending economic sanctions to areas of Bosnia and Herzegovina under Serbian control [S/Res/942, 9/23/94], terminating economic sanctions on Haiti after the restoration to power of President Aristide [S/Res/944, 9/29/94], demanding the withdrawal of Iraqi military units that appeared to threaten Kuwait anew [S/Res/949, 10/15/94], establishing a war crimes tribunal for Rwanda [S/Res/955, 11/8/94], permitting airstrikes in support of the U.N. Protection Force in Croatia [S/Res/958, 11/19/94], authorizing the U.N. Confidence Restoration Operation in Croatia (UNCRO) [S/Res/ 981, 3/31/95], permitting a limited exception to its economic sanctions on Iraq [S/Res/986, 4/14/95], condemning violations of the cease-fire and attacks on U.N. personnel in Bosnia [S/Res/987, 4/19/95], and altering sanctions imposed on states of the former Yugoslavia [see, e.g., S/Res/988, 4/21/95]. Forceful enforcement actions were also carried out through NATO aerial bombardments in support of the U.N. Protection Force and to defend U.N.-proclaimed "safe areas" under the standing authority of Security Council Resolution 836 (1993) [see generally Security Council "Round-Up" for 1994, SC/5973, 1/3/ 95].

Some of these Chapter VII decisions, as well as others taken by the Council under Chapter VI, demonstrate that multifunctional peace operations, intended to accomplish many tasks beyond those of traditional peacekeeping operations (and sometimes involving the use of force), are here to stay. The Council continues to expand the definition of "threat to" or "breaches of the international peace," since it is authorizing these operations out of concern for human rights or the rights of noncombatants *within* states and not necessarily because of breaches of the peace between states, usually in the form of an act of aggression. Thus, *intrastate* banditry, violence, and attacks on humanitarian relief workers convinced the Council to determine, under Article 39 of the Charter, that the situation in Somalia "continues to threaten peace and security," leading it to renew the mandate of UNOSOM II through March 1995 [S/Res/923, 5/31/94; see also S/Res/929, 6/22/94, which finds that the "magnitude of the humanitarian crisis in Rwanda constitutes a threat to peace and security in the region"]. Meanwhile, the Council's extension of the mandate of its Assistance Mission for Rwanda II (UNAMIR II) made clear that this operation is not solely intended to mediate between the parties and obtain a cease-fire but is also expected to "secure" and "protect" displaced persons, refugees, and others at risk; secure humanitarian areas; provide security for the distribution of humanitarian relief supplies; and take action in self-defense if necessary [S/Res/925, 6/8/94]. Shortly thereafter, alarmed by systematic and widespread killings of particular civilian population groups within Rwanda, the Council crossed the threshold of Chapter VII to authorize a multilateral operation for humanitarian purposes to assist UNAMIR and humanitarian workers in Rwanda, and to contribute to the security and protection of threatened populations within that country [S/Res/929, 6/22/94]. These and other decisions continue to show a Council willing to give effect to the varying peacekeeping and other tasks spelled out in the Secretary-General's "An

Agenda for Peace." At the same time, the Council continues to give broad scope to its Chapter VI and VII powers, not least through operations that might be seen as "peacekeeping with teeth," wherein peacekeepers are thrust into situations in which there is as yet no peace to keep and considerable likelihood that peace would have to be imposed by U.N. force [see also *Issues/48*, pp. 281–88, and the various reports of the Secretary-General discussed in the Effectiveness of the Organization section below]. The effectiveness of these peace operations is another matter—and an ongoing subject of debate [see *Issues/49*, pp. 266–67, and see, e.g., the Secretary-General's call for a "fundamental review" of the U.N.'s operation in Bosnia, *New York Times*, 5/13/95].

The Council and its various **sanctions committees,** which during 1994 and 1995 dealt with Chapter VII-authorized sanctions against Libya, Iraq, states of the former Yugoslavia, Somalia, and Haiti, continue to devote considerable effort to the legal scope, implementation, and termination of **economic sanctions.** Due to political or humanitarian pressures to lift sanctions already in place (or to a reexamination demanded by prior Council decisions), the Council periodically evaluates the legal and political justification for existing sanctions regimes and investigates possible violations [see, e.g., Presidential Statement S/PRST/1994/76, one of several renewing sanctions on Libya (for the origins of the Libya sanctions, see *Issues/47*, pp. 301–4); see also S/Res/985, 4/13/95, seeking information from states concerning alleged violations of the Liberia weapons embargo, or S/Res/970, 1/12/95, or S/Res/988, 4/21/95, both dealing with alleged violations of border closings between the states of the former Yugoslavia].

Complaints about the inhumane effect of sanctions were probably responsible for the decision by the Security Council to give Iraq an opportunity to sell oil on world markets, provided part of the proceeds were used to compensate victims of the Gulf War [S/Res/986, 4/14/95; see also *New York Times*, 4/15/95, and discussion of Compensation Commission below]. Moreover, the Council's various sanctions committees continue to issue, on virtually a daily basis, legally binding determinations on whether particular shipments will be permitted into sanctioned states [see discussion of sanctions committees, *Issues/49*, p. 268]. During 1994 the Committee for Sanctions for the former Yugoslavia alone had to deal with more than 45,000 communications—prominently, requests for exceptions to sanctions [see, e.g., Report of the Secretary-General, "Building Peace and Development," 1994, p. 14]. Experience appears to have taught the Security Council that, for sanctions to begin to have the desired effect, it must spell out how these sanctions are to be given effect and who they affect [see, e.g., S/Res/942, extending economic sanctions to parts of Bosnia under Serbian control and detailing the types of commercial entity and "economic activity" targeted]. Such specificity by the Council, which in the case of Resolution 942 [9/23/94] includes instructions to national authorities on implementing economic sanctions, is intended to ensure uniformity in implementation and encourage compliance.

The Council's **Compensation Commission,** established in May 1991 to administer a system to provide compensation for claims for which the

Council found Iraq liable in its Resolution 687 of April 3, 1991 [see *Issues/ 49*, pp. 268–69], is processing 2.6 million claims valued at more than $160 billion, including about 3,200 claims (valued at $1.7 billion) submitted by the United States [see Ronald J. Bettauer, "The United Nations Compensation Commission— Developments Since October 1992," 89 *American Journal of International Law*, 4/95]. The Governing Council of that body, composed of members of the Security Council, as well as panels of Commissioners appointed periodically to review particular groups of claims, continues to issue decisions likely to be of interest to those who follow arbitral practice and issues of state responsibility.

Iraq's continued refusal to export oil certainly makes the long-term prospects for payment of Commission awards very dim indeed [see discussion of S/Res/986 above], and it is now clear that there will not be sufficient funds to pay all the awards. Accordingly, the Governing Council has compromised on the awarding of interest, deciding [Decision 16] to pay interest to claimants only after all have received payment of principal [see S/AC.26/1992/ 16], and the Governing Council has given some claims priority over others [see S/AC.26/1994, 12/17/94]. Decision 18 of the Governing Council attempts to ensure that payments rendered to governments actually reach individual claimants [see S/AC.26/1994, 12/18/94, imposing limits on the amounts governments may take from the awards as a processing fee, time limits on distributions, and reporting obligations], while Decision 19 determines that the members of the allied coalition are not eligible to recover the cost of the forces they supplied during the Gulf War [S/ AC.26/1994, 12/19/94].

Panels of Commissioners have thus far approved over $2.7 million to compensate 670 category "B" (death and serious injury) claims from 15 countries; and over $185 million to compensate 53,845 category "A" (departure from Iraq or Kuwait) claims from 60 countries and one international organization. Funds to pay the "B" claimants were transmitted to governments in June 1994 [S/AC.26/1994/1 and S/AC.26/1994/2 summarize the legal and evidentiary issues for both "B" and "A" claims]. The Compensation Commission now faces the daunting task of adopting further pragmatic approaches to facilitate the handling of the millions of remaining claims in these and other categories—"C" (individuals claiming up to $100,000, including Egyptian workers), "D" (individual claims in excess of $100,000), "E" (corporate claims, including Kuwaiti claims for costs related to extinguishing oil-well fires set by Iraq during the war), and "F" (government claims). The Compensation Commission, a subsidiary, quasi-judicial organ that the Council created under Chapter VII to deploy mass tort techniques to resolve millions of claims, remains unique in the annals of international dispute settlement institutions but, if successful, might be emulated [see David J. Bederman, "The United Nations Compensation Commission and the Tradition of International Claims Settlement," 27 *New York University Journal of International Law and Politics* 1 (1994)].

From a legal point of view, the Council's most innovative action in

1994 was probably **Resolution 940** [7/31/94] **authorizing force to restore the elected government of President Aristide.** Although the actual deployment of force proved to be unnecessary in that instance, international lawyers are likely to debate the precedent set under Chapter VII for a long time. What exactly constituted the "breach of the international peace" that prompted Council action in this instance? Resolution 940 offers several possible rationales, including the violation of agreements by Haitian military rulers, the deterioration of human rights within Haiti, the increased flow of refugees, and the U.N.'s stake in Aristide's government, since it had supervised his election. Some scholars have even suggested that 940 represents the Council's affirmation of an "emerging right to democratic governance." Depending on which rationale is chosen, the Council may have opened the door to authorizing the use of force considerably—far beyond the Gulf War precedent, in which force was authorized against a state that had invaded the territory of another, making for a clear breach of international peace. Discomfort with the Haitian precedent (and what it says about sovereignty, when an activist Council can delegitimize an existing government of which it disapproves), helps to explain the abstaining votes of Brazil and China on this resolution—one of the few instances during 1994–95 in which a Council resolution was passed by other than a unanimous vote [see also *New York Times* editorial of 8/1/94 inveighing against the "U.N. license" to invade Haiti]. For these reasons, some may prefer to regard the Haiti case as having, in the words of Resolution 940, a "unique character"—that is, as having no precedential value.

Whether this proves to be the case or not, 940 has other interesting legal features. For example, it supplied more details about what it was authorizing the multilateral force to do in Haiti than it had when authorizing force against Iraq "to restore international peace and security in the area" [S/Res/678, 11/29/90]. In the Haiti case, the operative text states that the Council,

> Acting under Chapter VII of the Charter of the United Nations, authorizes Member States to form a multilateral force under unified command and control and, in this framework, to use all necessary means to facilitate the departure from Haiti of the military leadership, consistent with the Governor's Island Agreement, the prompt return of the legitimately elected President and the restoration of the legitimate authorities of the Government of Haiti, and to establish and maintain a secure and stable environment that will permit implementation of the Governor's Island Agreement, on the understanding that the cost of implementing this temporary operation will be borne by the participating Member States.

While the allied forces authorized to use force against Iraq were requested only to keep the Council informed of their actions, the Council, circa 1994, demanded "unified command and control" even when, as in the

Iraq case, it was "contracting out" the authority to use force to member states acting on its behalf. The Council's attempt to assert greater control in this case may suggest a Council more sensitive to criticism and more likely to impose restraints on itself and those acting on its behalf [for a summary of these criticisms of the Council, now extending over a number of years, see, e.g., *Issues/49*, pp. 266–68, *Issues/48*, pp. 287–89, *Issues/47*, pp. 298–304, and *Issues/46*, pp. 246–49; and see generally, Keith Harper, "Does the United Nations Security Council Have the Competence to Act as Court and Legislature?" 27 *New York University Journal of International Law and Politics* 103 (1994). For a range of views by U.S. scholars on the legal implications of the Haitian action, see "Agora: The 1994 U.S. Action in Haiti," 89 *American Journal of International Law*, 1/95; and for the later Assembly resolution commending the restoration of Aristide and the consequent "strengthening of democracy," see A/Res/49/27].

The **ad hoc international war crimes tribunal for the former Yugoslavia,** created by the Council in 1993 [see *Issues/48*, pp. 284–85, and *Issues/49*, pp. 269–70], is now in full operation, with 11 judges and a prosecutorial staff of 20 investigators and lawyers. Dusan Tadić, a Bosnian Serb arrested in Munich in 1994, was formally charged with murder, torture, and the rape of Muslims in Bosnia and now faces trial for war crimes—the first to be conducted by an international tribunal since World War II. Tadić, a former cafe owner turned paramilitary commander, is charged with committing some of his crimes in 1992 at Omarska, a mine complex converted by the Serbs into a concentration camp, and other crimes during an attack on the town of Kozarac. The trial of Tadić, expected to start in June 1995, stems from a fortuitous arrest by the German authorities rather than from any contention that he might bear preeminent responsibility for war crimes in the region [*New York Times*, 4/27/95]. More significant for the future of the tribunal was the unexpected request by the tribunal's chief prosecutor, Richard J. Goldstone, that the Bosnian government defer its judicial investigation of Radovan Karadžić, the leader of the Bosnian Serbs, and General Ratko Mladić, their military commander—a request that amounts to a statement that these two high Serbian officials are suspected war criminals and will soon be formally indicted by the tribunal [*New York Times*, 4/24/95]. (The formal request for deferral is intended to avoid the possibility that the two men could be tried twice for the same crimes.) Although there is little immediate prospect that either Karadžić or Mladić will be transferred to The Hague for trial, the announcement suggests that the prosecutor believes his office has evidence to prove the existence of a campaign, carefully prepared at the highest political levels, to carry out a Serbian program of killing and eviction. The announcement is also expected to complicate the U.N.'s role in peace negotiations, since the Organization's negotiators will be dealing with two leaders the United Nations itself has named as possible war criminals. The expected indictment on charges of genocide, murder, rape, mistreatment of civilians, and torture could also make it difficult for either Karadžić or Mladić to travel outside

Serb-held Bosnia or Serbia—to attend Geneva peace talks, for example—since all states might be ordered to detain them for transfer to The Hague. By May 1995, the tribunal had indicted 22 Serbs for various crimes, including genocide, but only Tadić is in custody and the tribunal has decided that it will not conduct trials in absentia. Indictments of some Bosnian Croat leaders were also expected [for more on the tribunal, see, e.g., *World Chronicle,* 11/15/94; UNA-USA's *The InterDependent* (Spring 1995); and A/49/342—the first annual report submitted by the President of the tribunal, Antonio Cassesse—which includes a summary of the tribunal's procedural rules and the establishment of the registry and prosecutorial offices].

The Council's creation of a similar ad hoc **war crimes tribunal for Rwanda** raises anew the question of where the Security Council derives its authority for taking this action and whether this will have a salutary effect on the development of international law. As with the former Yugoslavia, the Council specifically found that the violations of humanitarian law, including acts of genocide, occurring in Rwanda constituted a "threat to the international peace and security" and that the prosecution of responsible persons would help restore international peace [S/Res/955, 11/8/94]. Acting under Chapter VII and upon the request of Rwanda, the Council approved a statute for the new International Criminal Tribunal for Rwanda, authorizing that tribunal to deal with "genocide and other serious violations of humanitarian law committed . . . between 1 January 1994 and 31 December 1994" [ibid.]. The Council's use of Chapter VII authority to establish this tribunal is both easier and more difficult to justify than in the case of the former Yugoslavia. On the one hand, the Council's power to create the Rwandan tribunal is easier to see: Rwanda requested the tribunal, and no one can claim that the Council is encroaching on "domestic jurisdiction." On the other hand, the alleged crimes were committed within the territory of Rwanda, had less "international" impact than those alleged to have been committed by Serbian forces within Bosnian territory, and are more difficult to characterize as breaches of the "international" peace.

The ad hoc tribunals for Rwanda and the former Yugoslavia are similar in structure and procedures, and the statute of the Rwanda tribunal anticipates that some of the same personnel will be involved in both tribunals. The prosecutor for the Yugoslav tribunal will also supervise the prosecutorial office for the Rwandan tribunal [S/Res/955, Annex (statute), article 15; and see also articles 11 and 12, which provide that while the Rwandan tribunal will have its own set of trial chamber judges (two trial chambers of three judges each, no two of whom may be nationals of the same state), it will share appeals judges with the Yugoslav tribunal].

There are far fewer similarities between the *types* of crimes over which each will have jurisdiction. Both tribunals will be able to prosecute persons for genocide and crimes against humanity (in fact, these crimes are defined in virtually identical terms in the respective statutes of the tribunals), but the Rwandan tribunal does not have authority to prosecute for grave breaches of the Geneva Conventions of 1949 (such as the unlaw-ful deportation of civilians) or for violations of the law of war. On the other hand, the Rwandan tribunal (unlike its Yugoslav counterpart), *does* have authority to prosecute violations of article 3 common to the Geneva Conventions and Additional Protocol I—that is, it can bring charges for murder, torture, mutilation, or any form of corporal punishment, collec-tive punishments, the taking of hostages, acts of terrorism, outrages upon personal dignity, pillage, non-judicially imposed sentences or executions, or threats to commit any of these acts [S/Res/955, Annex (statute), article 4].

Again, while the Yugoslav and Rwandan tribunals share some prob-lems (such as whether the Assembly will provide long-term financial sup-port), each faces particular challenges. In the Yugoslav case, there is the prospect of issuing indictments but having no actual defendants to sit in the dock. In the Rwandan case, there is the opposite problem—that of having so many potential defendants in custody that there is no prospect of quick indictments or trials and the very real possibility that defendants will be abused or even killed before the trial can take place. Indeed, given reports of mass atrocities in prison camps and other places where many of those likely to be prosecuted by the Rwandan tribunal are being held, the biggest challenge will be compliance with the tribunal's own article 20, which recognizes the international rights of accused persons, includ-ing the presumption of innocence, the right to be tried "without undue delay," and the right to counsel of choice [compare S/Res/978, 2/27/95 urging states to prevent abuses within refugee camps of Rwandan refugees]. The Rwandan tribunal, like the Yugoslav one, can impose a term of imprisonment but not the death pen-alty [article 23].

Through later resolutions, the Security Council extended the man-date of its peacekeeping force in Rwanda (UNAMIR) to include the pro-tection of personnel for the war crimes tribunal [A/Res/965, 11/30/94] and pro-vided that, subject to approval by Tanzania, the Rwandan tribunal would have its seat in the city of Arusha [S/Res/977, 2/22/95]. In January 1995 the former President of the Supreme Court of Madagascar, Honoré Rakoto-manana, was named chief prosecutor for the Rwandan tribunal, to work under the supervision of Goldstone [*New York Times*, 1/15/95].

The ad hoc committee established by the 48th Session of the General Assembly to elaborate an **international convention on the safety of U.N. and associated personnel** responded quickly to its mandate, and a proposed convention was approved during the 49th Session [A/Res/49/59; for the report of the ad hoc committee, see A/49/22]. The Secretary-General had recom-mended the elaboration of a new instrument, given attacks on U.N. peace-keepers in Bosnia and Somalia and threats to their safety elsewhere, and Ukraine and New Zealand were quick to put draft conventions on the table [A/48/349; see also *Issues/49*, pp. 272–73]. Since 1948 more than a thousand U.N. peacekeepers have been killed in the line of duty, more than a third of them since the beginning of 1993. An even larger number of civilian personnel have been attacked or forcefully impeded from undertaking their duties. These attacks, especially on peacekeepers in Bosnia and Somalia, have been the subject of innumerable, but ineffectual, condemnations by the Council, which has affirmed that such attacks and interference with the freedom of movement of U.N. personnel are clear violations of binding Council resolutions and, therefore, of the U.N. Charter [see, e.g., Council President's Statements S/PRST/1994/1, 11, 19, 46, 50, 57, and 69, and S/Res/987, 4/19/95; see also reports of the Serbian forces' taking, and treament, of U.N. peacekeepers, *New York Times*, 5/28–30/95].

The new convention on the safety of U.N. personnel, open for signature until December 31, 1995, will enter into force 30 days after the 22nd party had deposited its instruments of ratification at the United Nations. This convention is a significant achievement: It covers a gap in existing international criminal law while remaining faithful to existing legal precedents; establishes the conditions for the harmonization and unification of various national approaches; is the first multilateral instrument to define the concept of U.N. operations; and is likely to serve as a model for regional organizations that undertake peacekeeping operations.

The convention addresses two very different sets of issues. Least controversial are articles 3–8 dealing with the **status of peacekeepers in relation to host governments.** These articles obligate military and police components of U.N. operations to wear distinctive forms of identification and to respect the laws of the host country; require host states and the United Nations to conclude status of forces agreements that determine, for example, the scope of privileges and immunities of U.N. forces in those states; require host states to ensure unimpeded transit for U.N. forces; require that the United Nations secure host states' agreement to protect U.N. personnel; and impose a duty to release captured U.N. personnel.

More controversial are articles 9–21, which, taking aim at attacks on U.N. personnel, define new international crimes and impose on treaty parties the obligation to either prosecute or extradite alleged offenders. As with other antiterrorist treaty regimes for the internationally recognized crimes of aircraft hijacking and hostage-taking, parties to the convention must make sure that certain offenses are punishable under domestic law in certain circumstances (as when the alleged offender is one of their nationals or the crime is committed on their territory) and pledge to exchange information to facilitate apprehension and prosecution. The **crimes against U.N. personnel** will now become extraditable offenses under existing extradition treaties.

Among the crimes the new treaty covers are murder, kidnapping, and other forms of attack on personnel or their liberty; violence directed at the premises or means of transportation of U.N. personnel; and threats, attempts, or complicity in such attacks [article 9]. Other clauses in the treaty protect, among other things, the state's right to withdraw nationals from U.N. operations, to seek appropriate compensation for injuries to person- nel, to consent or deny entry to U.N. personnel, and to act in self-defense [articles 20–21]. Treaty parties may submit disputes about interpretation of the convention to arbitration or, failing that, to the International Court of Justice [article 22].

The single most controversial issue proved to be defining the **scope of persons to be protected by the convention,** since there were varying views on whether the new treaty should (1) be restricted to traditional peacekeeping alone, (2) extend to other humanitarian operations under U.N. auspices but carried out by others, or (3) cover Chapter VII enforce- ment actions. The compromise adopted—to include the first two but not the third [see article 1]—did not satisfy all members and may lead some states to enter reservations to the convention when they do ultimately accede to it. The definition of a covered "U.N. operation" now extends to any action undertaken in accord with the Charter and "conducted under United Nations authority and control," whether (a) "for the purpose of maintaining or restoring international peace and security" or (b) follow- ing a declaration by the Security Council or the Assembly that there "ex- ists an exceptional risk to the safety of the personnel participating in the operation" [article 1(c)]. It explicitly does not apply to enforcement actions under Chapter VII of the Charter "in which any of the personnel are engaged as combatants against organized armed forces and to which the law of international armed conflict applies" [article 2(2)].

The exclusion from the convention of U.N. enforcement actions, such as those in Korea and Iraq/Kuwait, is consistent with the long-estab- lished view, essential to the law of war and adopted by Allied war crimes tribunals after World War II, that ordinary soldiers not involved in policy- making are entitled to be treated as prisoners of war upon capture and should not be criminally liable for fighting on the wrong side in an illegal war. The convention reflects the view that to impose criminal liability on all armed forces opposing a U.N. Chapter VII operation would be both unjust and counterproductive, since U.N. forces would probably face even more desperate resistance to ending the conflict. At the same time, the convention, as drafted, puts a premium on an explicit Security Coun- cil determination that a particular action is "under Chapter VII" (and thus *not* covered by the convention) or that a particular humanitarian operation poses "exceptional risks" (and thus covered). And it also relies heavily on the premise that word of these determinations will reach those actually engaged in fighting against the U.N. forces, whether in trenches in Bosnia or in the jungles of Somalia. Representatives of Japan criticized the convention on this issue, suggesting that greater precision was needed as to the categories of operation and personnel covered, given the grave consequences for both U.N. peacekeepers *and* combatants. They also argued that those involved in U.N. humanitarian operations should have a better guarantee of protection, since there is no assurance that the Council or Assembly will make the necessary risk assessment in time and make the explicit finding needed to extend the convention's protections [A/C.6/49/SR.30]. The representatives of China, Cuba, and Iran argued, for their part, that the convention's coverage actually extended beyond ordinary peacekeeping and that they would have sought explicit language to the effect that covered U.N. operations were only those undertaken with "the consent and cooperation of the host state" and "under the command and control of the U.N." [A/C.6/49/SR.30, 32, and 35]. Most delegates to the Sixth Committee, however, endorsed the views of the United States, which argued that, given the pressing need to protect U.N. personnel, it was unreasonable to wait until a "perfect" convention could be elaborated [A/C.6/49/SR.30].

The strong support for the convention, particularly by troop-contributing members, feeds the expectation that it will obtain the required number of ratifications in fairly short order. Nonetheless, it is possible, and even likely, that once the convention enters into force, the parties will have to call a meeting to review problems with implementing it; this is anticipated in article 23 [for the Assembly's endorsement of the convention, see A/Res/49/238]. The sad truth is, however, that a new law to criminalize what all already know to be illegal is unlikely to deter actions occasioned by a mismatch between U.N. peacekeeping and other U.N. action, as when U.N. peacekeepers in Bosnia are mandated to show restraint while NATO planes, also authorized by the Council, apply direct force. In such instances, attacks on U.N. peacekeepers may be a foregone conclusion.

The 49th Assembly, as is now tradition, urged states to become parties to other agreements on the **protection, security, and safety of diplomatic and consular missions and representatives** as well as to take all measures to prevent violations of these agreements—a resolution that has lost none of its tragic relevance, given reports by the Secretary-General on the prevalence of such attacks [A/Res/49/49; and see A/49/295 and additions].

The General Assembly hall was the venue for the year's most significant event relating to nuclear arms control—the special review conference required by the **Treaty on the Nonproliferation of Nuclear Weapons,** which concluded on May 11, 1995 [see *New York Times*, 5/12/95]. The more than 170 states present, acting by acclamation to avoid a contentious formal vote, decided to extend in perpetuity that 25-year-old treaty—a remnant of the Cold War that strives to limit nuclear weapons to the United States, Britain, France, China, and Russia, and to pledge other countries to refrain from acquiring such weapons. The decision—a victory especially for the five nuclear powers—was the culmination of four weeks of bitter debate with the nuclear weapon have-nots, who argued that the treaty perpetuated a monopoly on nuclear technology and made that technology inaccessible to the developing states that wished to use it for peaceful purposes. Some argued that the treaty stands in the way of complete nuclear disarmament or the outright banning of the threat or use of such weapons. The fact of such controversy was apparent at the 49th General Assembly, which in December had invited states to present their views on whether the treaty should be extended in perpetuity (as the five nuclear powers wanted) or simply for a fixed term [A/Res/49/75F; vote: 103–40–25].

Responsible for the collapse of opposition to an indefinite extension of the treaty at the review conference itself was the intensive lobbying by the United States and the negotiation of side agreements calling for greater progress toward disarmament and a stronger system for monitoring compliance. Although some states critical of the extension indicated that they regarded the indefinite extension of the treaty as legitimizing nuclear weapons for eternity, a side statement affirms "the determined pursuit by nuclear-weapon states of systematic and progressive efforts to reduce nuclear weapons globally, with the ultimate goal of eliminating those weapons" [ibid.]. The treaty now has 178 parties—a sizable group—but absent from the list are a few countries that are believed to have nuclear weapons or the capacity to develop them on short notice, including Israel, India, and Pakistan [for a related Council resolution, see S/Res/984, 4/11/95].

The split of views concerning nuclear weapons and legal schemes to control them was most apparent in the vote on the 49th Assembly's detailed attempt to **reduce "step-by-step" the nuclear threat** [A/Res/49/75E; vote: 111–24–33, with most of the developing world in favor and the nuclear powers either against or abstaining]. Calling, as usual, for the Conference on Disarmament to serve as the negotiating forum, the Assembly detailed the actions states might take unilaterally, bilaterally, and multilaterally to counter the acquisition and processing of fissionable material, the manufacture and testing of nuclear warheads and their delivery vehicles, and the assembly and deployment of nuclear weapon systems. Among the specific actions suggested were prohibiting test explosions, cutting off production, enacting legally binding measures to deter the use or threat of use, withdrawing deployments and disassembling systems, storing and dismantling nuclear warheads, "standing down" nuclear weapon systems from high-alert status, and converting delivery vehicles and nuclear materials to other uses. The Assembly also called for preparation, under international auspices, of an inventory of nuclear arsenals, special fissile materials, nuclear warheads and delivery vehicles, and all facilities "devoted to the processing, manufacture, assembly and deployment of those items" [ibid.].

The difference of views between nuclear weapon "haves" and "have-nots" was also evident in the 49th Session's other attempts to strengthen **existing arms control regimes.** As during the 48th Session [see *Issues/49*, p. 277], these efforts proved controversial, especially with the United States, as in years past: voted against the Assembly's call to amend the Treaty Banning Nuclear Weapon Tests in the Atmosphere, in Outer Space and Under Water in such way as to convert that agreement into a comprehensive test-ban treaty (accompanied by a call for a moratorium on all nuclear test explosions pending agreement on a comprehensive ban) [A/Res/49/69; vote: 116–4–49]; voted against the Assembly's call for a review by the Disarmament Commission, of the Declaration of the 1990s as the Third Disarmament Decade [A/Res/49/75B; vote: 139–3–26]; and abstained on the Assembly's general call for "efforts for nuclear disarmament with the ultimate objective of the elimination of nuclear weapons in the framework of general and complete disarmament" [A/Res/49/75H; vote: 163–0–8] and its more specific call for an early agreement to reassure non-nuclear weapon states against the use or threat of use of nuclear weapons [A/Res/49/73; vote: 168–0–3]. The United States was also the sole abstaining vote on the Assembly's call for a consolidation and reinforcement of the legal regime relating to outer space in order to prevent an arms race there [A/Res/49/74].

Some non-nuclear weapon and developing states continue to look with disfavor on other arms control efforts, including the Assembly's call for compliance with the information demands posed by the Register of Conventional Arms (including the supply of data on the export and import of arms) [A/Res/49/75C; vote: 150–0–19] and for regional disarmament [A/Res/49/75O; vote: 164–0–7].

No such controversy attended the Assembly's resolutions calling for a **prohibition on the dumping of radioactive wastes** and effective implementation of the International Atomic Energy Agency's Code of Practice on the International Transboundary Movement of Radioactive Waste [A/Res/49/75A]; endorsing recent **arms control agreements between the United States and Russia** [A/Res/49/75L] and the **regime of military denuclearization in Latin America and the Caribbean (the Treaty of Tlatelolco)** [A/Res/49/83]; or directing the Disarmament Commission to study measures to curb the **illicit transfer and use of conventional arms** [A/Res/49/75M]. For the second year in a row the Assembly endorsed the opening of multilateral negotiations on a **comprehensive and internationally verifiable test-ban treaty** and that issue remains on the agenda for the 50th Session [A/Res/49/70; A/Res/48/70].

The Assembly also endorsed, by consensus, proposals that could result in the near future in amendments or additional protocols to two major arms control treaty regimes. It agreed to hold a review conference in Geneva in the fall of 1995 to discuss ways to improve the **Convention on Prohibitions or Restrictions on the Use of Certain Conventional Weapons Which May Be Deemed to Be Excessively Injurious or to Have Indiscriminate Effects,** and related protocols—such as by adding weapon categories not now covered by the Convention [A/Res/49/79]. It also endorsed the convening of an hoc group of parties to the **Convention on** the Prohibition of the Development, Production and Stockpiling of Bacteriological (Biological) and Toxin Weapons and on Their Destruction for the purpose of proposing verification measures [A/Res/49/86].

As has been the tendency in recent years, the Assembly issued its own appraisal of other peace and security issues, even those with which the Security Council was currently seized [compare *Issues/49*, pp. 270–78]. As at the 47th and 48th Sessions, the Assembly took a rhetorically hard line against **Serbia and Montenegro** and in defense of **Bosnia and Herzegovina,** urging once again that the Security Council "give all due consideration and exempt the Governments of . . . Bosnia and Herzegovina from the embargo on deliveries of weapons and military equipment originally imposed by the Security Council in resolution 713 (1991)" [A/Res/49/10; vote: 97–0–61]. Citing the International Court of Justice's provisional measures order of September 1993 that Serbia take all measures to prevent genocide [see *Issues/49*, pp. 290–91], the Assembly reaffirmed the territorial integrity of Bosnia and Herzegovina; commended all states for vigilant enforcement of sanctions against Serbia; condemned the Serbian-controlled occupation of parts of that region, Serbian refusal to accept the proposed territorial settlement, and the practice of "ethnic cleansing"; and encouraged the speedy resumption of work by the Yugoslav war crimes tribunal and its "full funding as well as voluntary contributions" [A/Res/49/10].

The question of financing this tribunal remains a contentious issue at the Assembly. In April 1995 it could not agree on a permanent mode of financing but did allocate over $7 million to allow the tribunal to continue its activities through July 14, 1995 [A/Res/49/242; see also Decision 49/471].

As during the 48th Session [see *Issues/49*, pp. 271–72], the Assembly addressed, with considerable specificity, **human rights violations within the former Yugoslavia,** "welcoming" and "commend [ing]" the report and recommendations of the Human Rights Commission's Special Rapporteur "on the situation of human rights in the territories of the successor states of the former Yugoslavia" and demanding that Serbia cooperate with the Rapporteur and other ongoing human rights efforts, including those by the Conference on Security and Cooperation in Europe (after February 1995, the Organization for Security and Cooperation in Europe, or OSCE) [A/Res/49/196; vote: 150–0–14]. The 49th Session cited, in particular, the numerous laws violated by the widespread rape and abuse of women and children in the former Yugoslavia, condemning these as a deliberate and impermissible weapon of war, urging states to take "joint and separate action, in cooperation with the United Nations" to end the abuses, condemning the denial of access by Bosnian Serb forces to U.N. human rights experts, and again calling on states to cooperate with the Yugoslav war crimes tribunal (by, among other means, supplying experts on the prosecution of crimes of sexual violence) [A/Res/49/205].

For the third year in a row, the Assembly called for an end to the economic, commercial, and financial embargo imposed by the United States against Cuba, contending that such unilateral economic sanctions interrupt the free flow of trade and have adverse extraterritorial effects on the sovereignty and legitimate interests of other states [A/Res/49/9; vote: 101-2-48]. This issue remains on the agenda for the 50th Session, which will have in hand a report on the subject by the Secretary-General.

As in years past, the Assembly devoted considerable attention to the "Question of Palestine," adopting various resolutions on the subject, each over the dissent of Israel and the United States. One of the most controversial, drawing 40 abstentions in addition to the two dissents, reaffirms the U.N.'s "permanent responsibility" with respect to Palestine "until the question is resolved in all its aspects in a satisfactory manner in accordance with international legitimacy," praises the work of the Committee on the Exercise of the Inalienable Rights of the Palestinian People, and endorses that Committee's recommendations [A/Res/49/62A]. A second, equally controversial, requests that the Secretary-General continue devoting resources to support the work of the Division for Palestinian Rights within the Secretariat [A/Res/49/62B; vote: 105-2-40]. The Assembly continues to suggest that a peaceful settlement in the region requires that Israel withdraw "from the Palestinian territory occupied since 1967" [A/Res/49/62D; vote: 136-2-7], and to affirm the rights of the Palestinian people to self-determination [A/Res/49/149; vote: 147-2-19].

Self-determination questions emerged in other contexts as well. As it has done periodically, the 49th Assembly condemned the use of mercenaries as a means to violate human rights and to impede the exercise of the right to self-determination, calling attention to the collusion between mercenaries and drug traffickers and urging states to ratify the International Convention against the Recruitment, Use, Financing and Training of Mercenaries [A/Res/49/150; vote: 118-19-33]. The vote on that resolution continued to reflect the diversity of views on the subject and on the convention [see *Issues/45*, pp. 202-3]. Considerably less problematic was the Assembly's reaffirmation of self-determination as a universal right of all peoples—a "fundamental condition for the effective guarantee and observance of human rights and for the preservation and promotion of such rights" [A/Res/49/147]. As has been an annual occurrence since 1973, the Assembly reaffirmed the sovereignty of the Islamic Federal Republic of the Comoros over the island of Mayotte, urging France to act on the results of the referendum on self-determination conducted in 1974 [A/49/18; vote: 87-2-38; see also A/Res/49/151 (vote: 113-5-51), which endorses the integration of Mayotte into the Comoros in the course of a broader resolution that condemns the violation of the human rights of people still under "colonial domination and alien subjugation"]. France continues to reject the Assembly's pleas with respect to Mayotte.

The 49th Session also endorsed the various institutional arrangements for securing peace in the Central American region that emerged from a number of regional summits (including the ones held in Guatemala, Costa Rica, Nicaragua, and Honduras in 1994). These arrangements deal, variously, with the verification of human rights and elections, regional security, and sustainable development. The Framework Agreement for the Resumption of the Negotiating Process between the Government of Guatemala and the Unidad Revolucionaria Nacional Guatemalteca was among the agreements the Assembly "noted with satisfaction" [A/Res/49/137].

3. Effectiveness of the Organization

The Secretary-General's third annual **Report on the Work of the Organization** [*Building Peace and Development 1994*] offered a sweeping tour d'horizon, with shots of many of the U.N.'s recent legal achievements. And it picks up the Secretary-General's overarching theme of the previous report—namely, that the U.N.'s attempts to protect the peace are necessarily related to its efforts to promote development, undertake humanitarian action, protect human rights and democracy, and pursue preventive diplomacy [compare *Issues/49*, pp. 278–80; *Issues/48*, pp. 293–94].

In 1994 the Secretary-General provided many concrete examples of the way in which the Organization's view of "security" has expanded beyond "questions of land and weapons" [*Building Peace*, p. 2] and, along the way, supplied mini-histories of many of the Organization's legal efforts. Included in the story of the U.N.'s often overlooked achievements in the legal area was an overview of the work of the Secretariat's Office of Legal Affairs, headed by Hans Corell. The Secretary-General described that Office's liaison with the U.N. Commission on International Trade Law and its successful promulgation of draft or model legislation (see Economic Relations section below), mentioned the informal consultations organized by Legal Affairs to settle outstanding issues related to the deep-seabed mining provisions of the Law of the Sea Convention prior to its entry into force on November 14, 1994 [see *Issues/49*, p. 298], and summarized that Office's other achievements, including the drafting of legal arrangements related to peacekeeping missions [*Building Peace*, pp. 26–29]. The Secretary-General also provided an overview of the work of the new U.N. High Commissioner for Human Rights [see *Issues/49*, p. 296, and "Social and Humanitarian Issues—Human Rights" in the present volume], the Centre for Human Rights of the Secretariat (including its work to strengthen the national administration of justice through the training of judges, prosecutors, lawyers, and police, prison, and military officials), and the U.N.'s efforts to secure universal ratification of human rights conventions [*Building Peace*, p. 145].

In the course of enumerating the Organization's ongoing efforts at peacekeeping, peacemaking, and preventive diplomacy, the report offers short histories and updates of the work of the U.N. Compensation Commission [see Peace and Security section above], the Commission of Experts to investigate allegations of genocide and other violations of humanitarian law as a precursor to establishing a war crimes tribunal for Rwanda, and the numerous U.N. efforts to prevent the proliferation of nuclear, chemical, and bacteriological weapons. It also notes the vast **increase in requests for U.N. electoral assistance** of various forms (52 states made such requests from January 1992 through June 1994) [ibid., pp. 198–204, 235, 262–65, and 273–74].

Also of legal significance is the increasingly important role that the Secretary-General (and the Secretariat generally) play in advising the Security Council to undertake legally binding action under Chapter VII and in recommending the nature or scope of particular Council actions [see, e.g., the description of the Secretary-General's efforts to identify oil-industry funds that might be reached as part of the fund to compensate victims in the context of the Compensation Commission, pp. 200–201]. Additional information about this role can be adduced from *Building Peace*'s description of how the Secretary-General's recommendations to the Council resulted in changes to the mandate of UNAMIR in Rwanda [pp. 225–35] and the description of his part in redefining the scope of action for UNOSOM II in Somalia [p. 243]. The report also makes note of the fact that the Security Council's work has been subject to increasing scrutiny— including demands for increased transparency in Council decision-making and greater sensitivity to financial constraints—and to increased attention by the General Assembly [see also Council Presidential Statement S/PRST/1994/81, which acknowledges the demand for more open meetings by the Council and an increased flow of information to the wider membership].

This annual report is as ambitious in scope as the Secretary-General's 1992 "An Agenda for Peace" (his special report on U.N. peace operations, intended as a benchmark in that field), but the 1994 document focuses on achieving peace through development. It ends with a call for a "new realism—an awareness that we had embarked upon a long path towards progress which would be marked by both successes and failures" [*Building Peace*, p. 279].

The Secretary-General addressed the question of **command and control of U.N. peacekeeping operations** more comprehensively in response to the 48th Assembly's request for a report on this subject [A/Res/48/42]. His report [A/49/681] distinguishes three levels of command: overall political direction (to be given by the Security Council); executive direction and control (provided by the Secretary-General); and operational command in the field (residing in the chief of mission, usually the Special Representative of the Secretary-General or the Force Commander or Chief Military Observer). As described here, "operational command" is less than "full command," and is limited by the specific Security Council mandate and the agreed period of time and geographical scope for deployment. At all times, the power to discipline or promote individual peacekeepers remains with the troops' national authority.

Any additional restrictions, the Secretary-General goes on to say, "would overly limit the necessary flexibility and freedom of manoeuvre which a head of mission must have in order to ensure operational effectiveness" [ibid., p. 3]. Further, to lessen the difficulties of leading a multinational operation and reduce possible casualties, command must be unified, coming only from U.N. Headquarters; an effective U.N. operation functions as "one integrated unit reflecting the will of the international community as a whole" [ibid.]. To ensure maximum cohesion among the three levels of command, the report recommends enhanced consultations among the entities involved—the U.N. Secretariat, the Security Council, and troop-contributing states—to include periodic meetings that will facilitate the exchange of information and views prior to the Council taking decisions to extend, terminate, or change the mandate of particular peace-keeping missions [see, to the same effect, the Council's own conclusions as expressed in a Presidential Statement of November 1994, S/PRST/1994/62]. The report also recommends some means of increasing the Secretariat's ability to direct and manage these operations, including its capacity for contingency planning and logistics [ibid., p. 5; see also the Secretary-General's report on restructuring the Secretariat, including changes to the Department of Peacekeeping Operations, A/49/336]. Finally, the report highlights, but does not purport to solve, the special command and control problems that arise when the U.N. "contracts out" enforcement action, delegating authority to particular members willing to take action on the Organization's behalf (as during the Gulf War, with respect to initial action in Somalia, and in Rwanda and Haiti). The report notes that members so authorized can "claim international legitimacy and approval for a range of actions which may in fact not have been envisaged by the Security Council," and it stresses the need to monitor such actions closely, particularly since the United Nations might find itself held accountable for these actions [ibid., p. 6]. Joint operations—with NATO and the Western European Union (WEU)—are cited as possible models for cooperative arrangements to ensure smooth command and control [ibid., p. 7].

Some of the Secretary-General's recommendations may collide with several bills pending in the U.S. Congress that are specifically intended to restrict U.S. participation in or funding of U.N. peacekeeping when there is no assurance that U.S. troops will remain under the operational control of a U.S. (not U.N.) commander [see, e.g., the International Peacekeeping Policy Act of 1995 (S. 420), the National Security Revitalization Act (H.R. 7), and the Peace Powers Act (S. 5), which are discussed in UNA-USA's *Washington Weekly Report*, 11/94–5/95].

The entire subject of post-"Agenda for Peace" peace operations remains under scrutiny. The Secretary-General returned to the issue in his **Supplement to An Agenda for Peace**, which reviews, in light of later developments, the Organization's various instruments for peace and security, including preventive diplomacy and peacemaking, traditional peacekeeping, post-conflict peace-building, disarmament, sanctions, and enforcement action [A/50/60–S/1995/1; for reactions, see, e.g., press releases SC/5982–84, 1/18–19/95]. Although the Secretary-General's paper focuses on policy issues, many of his recommendations (some of which echo previous ones [see, e.g., *Issues/47*, pp. 309–11, and *Issues/48*, pp. 280–81]) have legal implications. With respect to what the Secretary-General calls "multifunctional" peacekeeping operations, the report endorses unity of command, greater consultation and information-sharing with troop-contributing states and between the Secretariat and the Security Council, establishment of a "rapid reaction force," and experimenting with methods of financing (such as a suggestion to include financing for certain contingencies in regular budget assessments) [A/50/60, pp. 8–11].

The Secretary-General addressed once again the failure of members to abide by their legal duty to pay their assessed peacekeeping costs as well as their failure to provide troops and equipment for missions already authorized. He spoke of the debilitating impact this has on U.N. finances, not to mention the "continuing damage to the credibility of the Security Council and of the Organization as a whole when the Council adopts decisions that cannot be carried out because the necessary troops are not forthcoming," and indicated the need to make sure such cooperation will be available before new operations are authorized [ibid., p. 23].

With respect to sanctions, the Secretary-General expressed concern about their impact on vulnerable groups within the target country as well as on nontargeted, third states. To avoid problems, he recommended, among other things, greater involvement by humanitarian agencies, greater precision in sanctions, establishing objective criteria for determining when sanction objectives have been fulfilled, and providing assistance to third states that suffer collateral damage, as anticipated under Article 50 of the Chapter [ibid., pp. 16–18]. With respect to enforcement actions, the Secretary-General highlighted the difficulties of "contracting out" these actions to groups of states or other organizations and the need for close coordination and scrutiny of such actions [ibid., pp. 18–19].

The Security Council had its own response to the new post-Cold War challenges to peace operations, issued in the form of a May 3, 1994, Presidential Statement [S/PRST/1994/22]. Responding to the criticism that the Council had failed to elucidate criteria for new peacekeeping operations, the statement purports to identify some of the **factors that the Council "would henceforth take into account prior to authorizing peacekeeping"**:

- whether a situation exists the continuation of which is likely to endanger or constitute a threat to international peace and security;

- whether regional or subregional organizations and arrangements exist and are ready and able to assist in resolving the situation;
- whether a cease-fire exists and whether the parties have committed themselves to a peace process intended to reach a political settlement;
- whether a clear political goal exists and whether it can be reflected in the mandate;
- whether a precise mandate for a U.N. operation can be formulated;
- whether the safety and security of U.N. personnel can be reasonably assured. [ibid.]

The Statement endorsed more frequent consultations with non-Council members and the Secretary-General's initiatives for standby arrangements, and it recognized a need for greater stress on training for U.N. personnel involved in peacekeeping, U.N. "operational control" of peace operations, and financial estimates prior to the approval of mandates or extensions of existing ones [ibid.].

While these factors—essentially a recipe for "operational triage," or selectivity, in the deployment of the U.N.'s capacity for peacekeeping—were not presented as legally required under the Charter (which, after all, does not mention "peacekeeping" as such), they could, if applied consistently, become as much a part of institutional law as the original requisites for traditional peacekeeping (i.e., consent of the territorial sovereign and nonuse of offensive force). The factors identified by the Council, which track many of the Secretary-General's own recommendations, are also essentially consistent with the factors identified by the United States as part of its Presidential Directive on future participation and approval of U.N. peacekeeping operations [see "The Clinton Administration's Policy on Reforming Multilateral Peace Operations," 33 *International Legal Materials,* 5/94; but see H.R. 7, the National Security Revitalization Act pending before the U.S. Congress, which would, among other things, prohibit the U.S. from paying more than 25 percent of total U.N. peacekeeping assessments—down from the current 31 percent—and would also require extensive consultations between the U.S. executive and legislative branches prior to U.S. approval of or participation in a U.N. peace operation].

As during the 48th General Assembly, the 49th Session examined the report of the **Committee on Peacekeeping Operations** and adopted a comprehensive resolution that essentially endorsed the emerging consensus concerning the **whole question of peacekeeping operations in all their aspects** [A/Res/49/37]. This resolution affirms most of the recommendations of the Secretary-General and the Security Council discussed above, but the Assembly went on to assert that peacekeeping is not within the sole province of the Security Council, since the

> Charter . . . also provides for General Assembly functions and powers in this regard and that, in addition to its responsibility for financing peace-keeping operations, the Assembly could, *inter alia,* recommend,

in accordance with relevant articles of Chapter VI of the Charter, principles and guidelines for the conduct of peace-keeping operations, for their effective management and, consistent with the Charter, for encouraging support of their mandates. [ibid.]

The **Special Committee on the Charter of the U.N. and on the Strengthening of the Role of the Organization,** which met March 7–25, 1994, completed a **Declaration on the Enhancement of Cooperation between the U.N. and Regional Arrangements or Agencies in the Maintenance of International Peace and Security** and saw it adopted at the 49th General Assembly [A/Res/49/57]. The Declaration, which grew out of a paper submitted by Russia in 1992 [see *Issues/49*, p. 281], stresses the need for complementarity between U.N. and regional efforts in keeping the peace, exalts flexibility in coordinating such efforts, emphasizes the need for universal adherence to the Charter, and, while affirming the Security Council's primacy, encourages resort to regional forums before referring a dispute to the Council. The Declaration can be seen as an attempt to bring Chapter VIII of the Charter into the modern age, consistent with some of the recommendations made by the Secretary-General in his "An Agenda for Peace."

The Declaration, alike with Chapter VIII, indicates that enforcement actions may be authorized only by the Council, but it also recognizes the recent contributions that regional bodies have made to U.N. peace operations, whether through exchanging information, participating in consultations, or providing personnel [A/Res/49/57, Annex]. Significantly, in light of the recent problems the United Nations has encountered in the whole area of peace enforcement, the Declaration encourages regional entities to establish and train "groups of military and civilian observers, fact-finding missions and contingents of peace-keeping forces, for use as appropriate . . ." [ibid.]. In the Sixth Committee, this attempt to strengthen the role of "regional arrangements" was largely welcomed, seen as a necessary attempt to spread the burden of keeping the peace while keeping within the Charter structure for collective security [see, e.g., comments by Tanzania and the United States, A/C.6/49/SR.12, but see concern expressed by Pakistan, among others, that the Council might find itself delegating responsibilities to regional organizations with direct interests in particular conflicts, A/C.6/49/SR.10].

Much more controversial was the Special Committee on the Charter's consideration of a working paper by a number of developing and former East-bloc states concerning the **implementation of Article 50 of the Charter as it relates to assistance to third states affected by the application of Chapter VII sanctions** [discussed in A/49/33, pp. 11–19]. The paper proposed the establishment of a trust fund, consisting of assessed and voluntary contributions by U.N. members, to aid third states adversely affected by U.N. sanctions, which could approach the Security Council for redress, as anticipated by Article 50 of the Charter. Among the suggested uses for this aid were financing technical cooperation programs, providing direct cash or assistance in kind, and helping to promote investment in the countries affected [A/AC.182/L79]. As in past debates on the subject in the Special Committee and in the Sixth Committee, the division ran along North-South lines, with the former urging restraint and many developing countries stressing the need for urgent action, given the proliferation of U.N. sanctions programs [A/49/33, pp. 14–18; compare the views of, for example, Malaysia and the United States in A/C.6/49/SR.12; and see *Issues/49*, pp. 280–81].

Some argued that such a trust fund is sanctioned by the Charter, since Article 50 could not have spoken of consultations without the possibility of providing relief to affected states. Others argued that the whole idea is impractical anyway, since the trust fund would never have the resources to deal with claims of such magnitude. Still others asserted that there is nothing in the Charter about compensating states for consequent economic damage, and that the solution was not to set up new mechanisms but to go through existing ones—as, for example, international financial institutions and bilateral assistance programs. And there were a number of delegations, Chile's among them, that stressed the need for preventive action—such as consultations between the Security Council and states likely to be affected in order to devise sanctions unlikely to do severe damage to nontargeted states (and, as a pleasant side effect, apt to increase compliance with the Council's edicts) [A/C.6/49/SR.10 and 12]. In the end, the only thing on which all could agree was the need to consider the question further. The 49th Assembly invited the Secretary-General to submit to the Special Committee on the Charter for consideration in 1995 a further report on the question, including "possible practical ways and means" of dealing with the economic problems of third states [A/Res/49/58].

Similarly controversial was Cuba's revised working paper on **"Strengthening the Role of the Organization and Enhancement of Its Efficiency,"** which raised familiar complaints, voiced by many nonpermanent members, about the power and practices of the post-Cold War Security Council [see A/C.6/49/SR. 8–11 and *Issues/49*, p. 280]. Cuba is seeking the establishment of a working group within the Special Committee to examine the "current and future composition of the Security Council, in the light of the principle of equitable geographical distribution," and the effects of "special privileges" of the permanent members as well as the "viability of eliminating or modifying them." The working group would also explore definitive rules of procedure for the Council and changes that would enhance the transparency of the Council's reports and informal consultations [A/49/33, pp. 25–26].

As in the past, some states endorsed Cuba's "useful proposals" while others argued that the paper "was contrary to the scheme of the Charter," was outside the Special Committee's mandate, and was a waste of time [ibid., pp. 24–26; for comments favorable to Cuba's approach, see Libya's and Uganda's comments in A/C.6/49/SR.12].

The Special Committee on the Charter continues to work on Guatemala's proposal for **U.N. Model Rules for the Conciliation of Disputes between States** [A/49/33, pp. 27–43 (includes text of 29 draft rules); see also *Issues/49*, p. 281], on a new proposal by Sierra Leone for a **dispute settlement service** [A/49/33, pp. 44–46], and on a Russian paper suggesting **new issues for consideration in the Special Committee** [ibid., p. 26]. In its resolution approving the Special Committee's agenda, the 49th Assembly asked the Committee to consider the matter of deleting the **"enemy state" clauses of the Charter** (Article 107 and Article 53 [1] and [2]) and to recommend to the 50th Session the most appropriate legal action to be taken on this question [A/Res/49/58, adopted over the sole dissent of the Republic of Korea; see A/C.6/49/SR.40].

The **Committee on Relations with the Host Country**'s annual report to the Assembly raised long-familiar issues. Heading the list of complaints by the United States, as host, was the continuing and exacerbated problem of debt-ridden missions to the United Nations—a subject that a working group continues to examine [A/49/26, pp. 10–11; for the Assembly's approval of the Host Country Report, see A/Res/49/56; see also *Issues/49*, pp. 282–83]. Washington reported that, as of November 1994, missions to the United Nations and mission personnel owed more than $6 million to financial institutions (41 percent) and landlords (37 percent)—up from $4 million the previous year [A/C.6/49/SR.39]. This behavior, said the United States, was giving the entire diplomatic community a bad name: One prominent bank had decided against making any further loans to missions or diplomats, and some landlords were refusing to lease property to diplomats. The U.S. report also noted that it was working with other U.N. host countries, namely Switzerland and Austria, to find acceptable solutions [ibid., and A/29/26, p. 11].

The Cuban Mission complained again to the Host Country Committee about the "systematic failure" of the United States to protect the Mission, as is its duty under applicable law. Cuba cited "terrorism" by "well-known groups," which took the form of disruptive weekly demonstrations, harassment of personnel, bomb threats, vandalism, and attempted kidnappings [ibid., pp. 5–7]. To this, the United States reiterated its commitment to prosecute those who violate mission premises or threaten the security of mission personnel, called attention to the successful prosecution of some of those who had attacked the Cuban Mission, but went on to note America's "long and proud tradition of guaranteeing the freedoms of speech and assembly," suggesting that periodic demonstrations, even around mission premises, were "examples of those freedoms" [ibid., p. 7]. The United States also announced that it was removing the travel restrictions that had been imposed on U.N. staff members of Romanian nationality during the Cold War years.

At the recommendation of a working group of the Sixth Committee, the 49th General Assembly will grant **observer status in the Assembly** only to states and intergovernmental organizations "whose activities cover matters of interest to the Assembly" [Decision 49/26], not political bodies or interest groups. The rules for granting observer status in the Assembly are not addressed by the Charter or the Assembly's rules of procedure, and to date they have been determined anew by each session of the Assembly. As was suggested by Germany in the Sixth Committee, the decision reflects the view that the Charter remains an organization of states and that observer status is granted on an exceptional basis to serve the purposes of the U.N. system [A/C.6/49/SR.10]. The few cases where observer status had been given to nonstate or nongovernmental groups (the International Committee of the Red Cross was one) were deemed "too exceptional to provide a basis for the formulation of general criteria" [see A/C.6/49/SR.40]. Granting observer status more freely, it was suggested, would "erode the dignity of the Assembly and dilute its effectiveness" [see, e.g., comments by Kenya, A/C.6/49/SR.10]. Article 71 of the Charter, which provides that nongovernmental organizations may seek consultative status with the Economic and Social Council, continues in effect.

The 49th Assembly's decision is apt to be criticized by those who believe that the United Nations, to its detriment, reflects mainly the perspective of government elites and not at all the views of interest groups within states [see, e.g., comments in the U.N. Congress on Public International Law, press release L/2708, 3/16/95]. By separate decision [49/423], the Assembly voted to consider at a future session the **question of observer status for certain national liberation movements.**

4. Economic Relations

The most significant achievement of the 27th session of the **U.N. Commission on International Trade Law (UNCITRAL)**, held in May 1994, was its adoption of a **UNCITRAL Model Law on Procurement of Goods, Construction and Services.** This is a companion to its 1993 **Model Law on Procurement of Goods and Construction** [see *Issues/49*, pp. 284–85] and is also intended to assist states in restructuring or improving their rules governing transactions with government entities. It is directed at improving inadequate, outdated, and inefficient procurement practices that can impede economic development and the expansion of international trade. Both Model Laws have been particularly welcomed by developing countries and former East-bloc states, whose privatization efforts require attention to public-procurement policies and other market-oriented reforms.

UNCITRAL's working group on the new international economic

order, which had been entrusted with the task of drafting the latest model law, opted not to prepare a set of rules dealing only with services but a consolidated text that some states might readily adopt; others would be free to limit themselves to using the 1993 Model Law for goods and construction. The main difference between the procurement of goods or construction and the procurement of services is that the major criterion for selection in the latter case is not price but the professional competence and ability of the service provider. The new rules permit the procuring entity to give these factors greater prominence [see UNCITRAL Report, A/49/17, pp. 5–22; for text of Model Law, see A/CN.9/389].

The five chapters of the Model Law address general issues (such as scope of application), methods of procurement and conditions for use, tendering proceedings, procurement methods other than tendering, and review procedures. Public-procurement policies have increased in importance due to the need for greater efficiency in the management of increasingly scarce public funds—a fact reflected in the recent extension of the GATT Agreement on Government Procurement to cover services and in a recent Directive of the European Union on contracts for services [see A/C.6/49/SR.3]. The UNCITRAL Law is consistent with these other efforts.

As with the 1993 Model Law, the Commission adopted a **Guide to Enactment of the Model Law** that is intended to assist executive branches of government and parliaments to adapt their domestic legislation to the new Model Law [see A/CN.9/392–94; A/49/17, pp. 22–24]. In the Sixth Committee there was praise for the new law, and special praise for its attempt to secure better management of resources through competitive pricing, transparency, responsibility, accountability, and fairness to both the procuring state and the contractor [see, e.g., comments by Nigeria, A/C.6/49/SR.5]. The 49th Session approved the new law and recommended that states consider it when enacting or revising their procurement laws [A/Res/49/54].

UNCITRAL also discussed draft **Guidelines for Preparatory Conferences in Arbitral Proceedings,** an attempt to enhance the predictability of arbitrations and save costs and time [A/49/17, pp. 25–37]. The Guidelines provide advice to practitioners on how to plan for such conferences, designed to take place early in arbitral proceedings and rendered necessary by the broad discretion and flexibility that characterize such proceedings. Many believe that, without such conferences, arbitrations can lead to misunderstandings, delays, and increased costs. Although the Guidelines are a relatively recent effort for the Commission and grow out of proposals made at UNCITRAL's May 1992 Congress on International Trade Law [see *Issues/49*, p. 286], UNCITRAL has made substantial progress toward a text that now includes "general considerations," information on "convening and conducting preparatory conferences," and an "annotated check-list of possible topics for preparatory conferences" [A/49/17, pp. 26–28].

There are still some differences about the topics to be addressed in the Guidelines, given the existence of established rules of arbitral procedure, such as those in UNCITRAL's Model Law on International Commercial Arbitration. In the Sixth Committee, most states expressed strong support for the effort, but the French representatives were skeptical, arguing that preparatory conferences are "superfluous in the case of simple proceedings, could add unnecessary rigidity in complex cases, and significantly increased the cost of the proceedings." France also suggested that such conferences favored the better-organized parties and could deprive the arbitrators of the option to pronounce on questions of procedure, contravening the UNCITRAL Arbitration Rules [A/C.6/49/SR.4]. The Commission expects, in any case, to finalize the Guidelines in 1995.

UNCITRAL and its working group on international contract practices continue their work on a draft **Convention on Independent Guarantees and Stand-by Letters of Credit** with which the working group has been grappling since 1989 [A/49/17, p. 38; A/CN.9/391; and see *Issues/49*, pp. 285–86]. The process was expected to be completed in May 1995 and the draft convention submitted to the 50th Session of the General Assembly.

UNCITRAL does not expect to be able to complete work on **legal rules on electronic data interchange** for that session, however, given the requirement that these rules take into account rapidly changing technological developments [A/49/17, pp. 39–40; A/CN.9/390]. The Commission also discussed ways to enhance the utility of its systematization of **Case-Law on UNCITRAL Texts (CLOUT),** which now contains abstracts of 52 court decisions and arbitral awards relating to the U.N. Convention on Contracts for the International Sale of Goods and the UNCITRAL Model Law on International Commercial Arbitration [A/49/17, pp. 41–42; A/C.6/49/SR.3; and see *Issues/49*, p. 286].

There was some concern in the Commission and in the Sixth Committee that the attempt to harmonize the liability regime governing the transport of goods by sea had so far been less than successful as a result of two rival regimes governing the transport of goods by sea: the **Hamburg Rules** and the International Convention for the Unification of Certain Rules Relating to Bills of Lading (**Hague Rules**). States noted that the mixing of legal regimes increases legal costs, makes it difficult for the carrier to assess its liability exposure, complicates settlement negotiations, hinders the use of uniform transport documentation, distorts competition among carriers, and results in an unequal treatment of the carrier's customers [A/C.6/49/SR.3]. UNCITRAL recommended against any revisions in the Hamburg Rules to deal with these problems and urged, instead, that the Hamburg Rules themselves be adopted more widely [ibid.].

As to its future program, UNCITRAL is examining the possibility of working on legal aspects of **receivables financing** (that is, claims for payments of sums of money that arise from international commercial transactions, such as assignments by way of sale or as a security); **cross-**

border insolvency (problems arising from the lack of harmonized rules for the handling of international bankruptcies); and **build-operate-transfer (BOT) projects** (private consortiums authorized by governments, which operate until they recoup their construction costs and then are transferred to the government) [A/49/17, pp. 43–47; A/CN.9/397–99; for the 49th Session's approval of UNCITRAL's report and agenda, see A/Res/49/55; for the report on annual status of UNCITRAL conventions, see A/CN.9/401; for a bibliography of recent writings on UNCITRAL, see A/CN.9/402].

As is customary, the General Assembly considered the **external debt problem of developing countries** in several resolutions, emphasizing, among other things, the need for structural adjustments to attract foreign investment and the need to implement fully the Uruguay Round (GATT) agreements [see A/Res/49/93 and A/Res/49/94]. It also renewed its call for cooperation between the United Nations (and specifically the U.N. Conference on Trade and Development) and the new **World Trade Organization** [A/Res/49/97; and see A/Res/49/99].

More controversial was a resolution on the implementation of the **right to development,** which touted the importance of "unconditional international cooperation" for development, urged the increase flow of resources for this purpose, and challenged the idea that certain rights have priority over the right to development by affirming:

> that a primary aim of international cooperation in the field of human rights is a life of freedom, dignity and peace for all peoples and for every human being, that all human rights and fundamental freedoms are indivisible and interrelated and that the promotion and protection of one category of rights should never exempt or excuse States from promoting and protecting the others. [A/Res/49/187; adopted by a vote of 110–35–24 (the "North" dissenting)]

5. Space Law

Over the sole dissent of the United States, the 49th Session approved an increase in the membership of the **Committee on the Peaceful Uses of Outer Space,** from 53 to 61 [A/Res/49/33; the United States was of the view that this did not reflect the agreement reached at the Committee's previous session and that bringing the issue to a vote was an undesirable departure from the Committee's commitment to consensus (see press release OS/1674, 2/9/95)]. The breach of consensus-based decision-making on this occasion might have further consequences, since the United States cited this instance—and budgetary constraints—in opposing a proposal, favored by many developing states and contained in Resolution 48/39, for a third **U.N. Conference on the Exploration and Peaceful Uses of Outer Space (UNISPACE III)** [press release OS/1678, 2/10/95]. Other states, such as the United Kingdom, Japan, and Argentina, indicated that such a conference required further study of agenda, objectives, and costs, and the issue remains under study [ibid.].

The Assembly endorsed the Outer Space Committee's annual report, including the long-standing **agenda of its Legal Subcommittee,** which addresses three issues: (1) whether there is a need to review or revise the principles adopted by the General Assembly in 1992 governing the use of nuclear power sources in outer space in light of subsequent technological developments; (2) how to arrive at a commonly agreed definition and de-limitation of outer space and how to ensure the rational and equitable use of the geostationary orbit without prejudicing the role of the International Telecommunications Union (ITU); and (3) whether there is a need for legal principles to ensure that all states share the benefits of space exploration and research [A/Res/49/34; see *Issues/49*, pp. 287–89]. The Assembly approved the first item on the Legal Subcommittee's agenda but, in a somewhat contradictory move, also endorsed the Committee's recommendation that the Legal Subcommittee suspend for now its consideration of principles relevant to the use of nuclear power sources, pending results within the Scientific and Technical Subcommittee, which is examining the same question [ibid.].

There was little discernible progress (and frequent reiteration of long-established positions) on the items on the Legal Subcommittee's agenda [see summary in the Outer Space Committee's annual report, A/49/20, pp. 18–22], which were taken up again during the Legal Subcommittee's 34th session (Vienna, March 27–April 13, 1995). As the delegate from Spain observed late in the session, national positions on such questions as the definition of outer space and the utilization of the geostationary orbit had taken on the character of a "theological debate" with static, dogmatic repetition of perennial arguments in place of cooperation [press release OS/1689, 3/28/95].

Many states, the United States among them, continued to resist the move to reexamine the **Principles Relevant to the Use of Nuclear Power Sources in Outer Space** recently adopted by the Assembly [see *Issues/48*, p. 303; *Issues/49*, p. 287], arguing that prolonging the debate on those principles would not be a good use of the Committee's scarce time and resources [press release OS/1690, 3/29/95; see also comments by China, Germany, and Ecuador to the same effect]. With respect to the **delimitation of outer space,** the delegate from the Netherlands was perhaps the most outspoken in stating the traditional position of the North: that the Committee has sought for 36 years to make an unnecessary demarcation because "we lawyers like to regulate things" but that the world has been able to function without a legal line between air space and outer space. The Committee ought to deal with real problems instead, he said, and noted a need for laws covering air vehicles that pass in and out of outer space boundaries [ibid.]. The Russian delegate had a different take on the study of air vehicles (called "aerospace objects" by some). This, he said, could lead to conclusions as to the legal boundaries of sovereignty, and he went on to propose a concept of the "right to innocent flight" whereby states would be permitted free access to place such objects in orbit and return them to earth [press release OS/1691, 3/29/95]. A questionnaire to seek the views of the Committee's membership with respect to aerospace objects, including the definition of such objects, was approved at the end of the Legal Committee's 1995 session [press release OS/1697, 4/11/95].

There were similar (and familiar) sharp exchanges with respect to the need to establish principles on the **use of the geostationary orbit,** with Japan, for instance, arguing that there is no need for such principles, given the ITU's legal principles for fair use, and China, among others, expressing astonishment at that suggestion and reiterating the position of many developing states that the ITU's technical regime falls short of the "comprehensive scheme" needed to ensure equitable access to the orbit [compare press release OS/1690, 3/29/95, to press release OS/1691, 3/29/95; see also comments by Colombia, which contended that reference to the ITU was an unproductive "ping-pong" approach, since broader equity issues were not discussed within the ITU on the grounds that these were within the ambit of the Outer Space Committee (ibid.)].

Many developing states favored as a starting point a working paper prepared by Colombia in 1993, which proposed criteria for the application of preferential rights to ensure developing countries equitable access to the orbit, in place of the ITU's regulations [see *Issues/49*, p. 288]. There was also considerable support by developing states for examining, as a legal issue, the question of space debris in connection with the geostationary orbit [see, e.g., comments by Mexico, press release OS/1691, 3/29/95].

With respect to the issues of **sharing benefits of space activities,** the Legal Subcommittee examined rival working papers on the subject, clearly dividing along North-South lines: a draft nonbinding declaration, sponsored by Germany and France, that stresses the freedom of states to determine all aspects of their cooperation and specifies that such cooperation should be guided by the need to allocate resources efficiently; and a set of draft binding principles, sponsored by Brazil and ten other developing states (inspired by the 1967 Treaty on Principles Governing the Activities of States in the Exploration and Use of Outer Space, including the Moon and Other Celestial Bodies), which addresses the development of indigenous space capabilities of all states, including the exchange of material and equipment, and transfer of technology [press releases OS/1693–94, 4/4/95; and see *Issues/49*, pp. 288–89]. Many developing states stressed the need for new law to protect the rights of states that have few or no space capabilities at present. Others, such as the United States, saw no need for law on international cooperation beyond that already contained in the 1967 Outer Space Treaty [press release OS/1696, 4/10/95].

6. The International Court of Justice

The opening on the Court occasioned by the death of Judge Nikolai K. Tarassov (Russia) was filled by Judge Vladlen S. Vereshchetin (Russia), who was elected to the post by the General Assembly and the Security Council on January 26, 1995. The other two vacancies on the Court, occasioned by the death of Judge Roberto Ago (Italy) and the resignation of Judge Sir Robert Yewdall Jennings (United Kingdom), were filled through elections slated for June 21 and July 12, 1995, respectively. The Court's docket—with a dozen contentious cases and two advisory opinions (both on the legality of nuclear weapons)—is unusually full. Nonetheless, in the period May 1994 to May 1995, the Court issued only two judgments.

The Court's two judgments came in the jurisdictional phase of the **Case Concerning Maritime Delimitation and Territorial Questions Between Qatar and Bahrain.** Qatar had filed an application instituting proceedings against Bahrain in July 1991 relating to sovereignty over the Hawar Islands, sovereign rights over the shoals of Dibal and Qit'at Jaradah, and the delimitation of the maritime areas of the two states [see *Issues/ 47*, p. 330]. Qatar had asserted that the Court had jurisdiction to decide the case under article 36(1) of its statute, based on two alleged agreements between the parties: an exchange of letters between the King of Saudi Arabia and the Amir of Qatar dated December 19 and 21, 1987, and between the King of Saudi Arabia and the Amir of Bahrain dated December 19 and 26, 1987; and a document entitled "Minutes" signed at Doha on December 25, 1990, by Bahrain, Qatar, and Saudi Arabia. From the outset, Bahrain contested the Court's jurisdiction, and the Court finally found in favor of Qatar through two orders, one on July 1, 1994, and the other on February 15, 1995.

In its **Order of July 1, 1994,** the Court determined, Judge Shigeru Oda (Japan) dissenting, that the exchanges of letters and the Minutes of December 25, 1990, were both valid international agreements and could serve as a basis for the jurisdiction of the Court. The Court observed that under the Vienna Convention on the Law of Treaties, international agreements may take any form and bear any title, and that the Court must examine the actual terms and the particular circumstances to determine whether the parties have entered into binding obligations as well as the nature of those obligations. The Court found unconvincing Bahrain's evidence that its foreign minister never intended to commit his country to a legally binding agreement and that he considered the Minutes a mere political understanding; the Court was equally untroubled by Qatar's six-month delay in registering the Minutes with the U.N. Secretariat, as is required by Article 102 of the Charter [Order, 7/1/94, par. 27–29]. The Court was more circumspect, however, on the question of just what the parties had decided to submit to the Court for a decision through their exchange of letters or the "Bahraini formula" determining the scope of jurisdiction contained in the Minutes. In its July order, the Court stated that the Bahraini formula "permitted the presentation of distinct claims by each of the Parties" but "nonetheless presupposed that the whole of the dispute would be submitted to the Court" [ibid., par. 33]. The Court decided to afford the parties the opportunity to ensure that the entire dispute would be submitted to the Court and gave them until November 30, 1994, to approach the Court "jointly or separately" to this end.

Although joined by 15 of the 16 judges who heard this phase of the proceedings, the July 1 order was not without its critics. As Judge Stephen M. Schwebel (United States) noted in his separate opinion, the Court's judgment was at the very least unusual, since it ducked the very issue that the parties had asked it to determine: whether it had jurisdiction to consider Qatar's claims. The Court had decided instead, he said, and contrary to the parties' expectations, that it would give them another chance to litigate the jurisdictional issue. The Court had done nothing but delay a resolution of the issue, since its attempt to get the parties to agree to submit the case jointly had failed.

On November 30, 1994, Qatar again submitted, unilaterally, the whole of the dispute to the Court, including the following subjects it considered to be within the Court's jurisdiction: the Hawar Islands, including sovereignty over the island of Janan; Fasht al Dibal and Qit'at Jaradah; the archipelagic baselines; sovereignty over Zubarah; the areas for fishing for pearls and other types of fishing; and any other matters connected with maritime boundaries. Bahrain, for its part, continued to contest the jurisdiction of the Court on any of these issues, arguing that it understood the Court's July 1 order to mean that the Court's jurisdiction was contingent on *both* parties' agreement to submit the dispute to the Court.

In its **Judgment of February 15, 1995,** the Court, by a vote of 10 to 5, gave a definitive answer. It affirmed that the Bahraini formula had indeed constituted the parties' consent to jurisdiction and had determined the subject matter of the dispute, thereby affirming Qatar's jurisdictional claims and finding them admissible. The Court noted that in the letters of December 19, 1987, Qatar and Bahrain had agreed that "All disputed matters shall be referred to the International Court of Justice . . . for a final ruling binding upon both parties, who shall have to execute its terms," but also agreed to form a Tripartite Committee "for the purpose of approaching" the Court and "satisfying the necessary requirement to have the dispute submitted to the Court" [Order, 2/15/95, par. 26]. The Court disagreed with Bahrain's contention that this meant that final submission to the Court was subject to conclusion of a Special Agreement between the parties setting forth the specific questions both parties would agree to submit to the Court, finding no evidence either in the exchange of letters or in the parties' subsequent conduct for this interpretation [ibid., par. 26–29]. It also interpreted the Minutes, particularly the statement that "the two parties [*al-tarafan* in Arabic] may submit the matter to the International Court of Justice" to mean that the parties had agreed that one of them, unilaterally, could apply to the Court [ibid., par. 34–42].

As the vote suggests, the judgment of the Court was controversial and perhaps reminiscent of the Court's stretch to find jurisdiction in the Nicaragua Case [Case Concerning Military and Paramilitary Activities In and Against Nicaragua (Nicaragua v. United States), 1984 ICJ Rep. 392]. (For one view, suggesting that the Court majority entirely misread or ignored the negotiating history of the Minutes, see Judge Schwebel's dissenting opinion to the 2/15/95 Order.) The parties are now expected to proceed to pleadings dealing with the merits of their dispute, with a final judgment on the merits likely to be years away.

In March 1995, Spain instituted proceedings against Canada with respect to a dispute relating to the Canadian Fisheries Protection Act and measures taken on the basis of that law [press communiqué, 3/29/95]. In this **Fisheries Jurisdiction Case (Spain v. Canada),** Spain alleges that Canada is violating various principles and norms of the Law of the Sea, including the fundamental principle of the freedom of the high seas, in derogation of the sovereign rights of Spain. More specifically, it alleges that Canadian law imposes on all persons on board foreign ships a broad prohibition against fishing on part of the high seas, outside of Canada's exclusive economic zone, and that Canada permits the use of force to enforce this prohibition. In Spain's view, the Court has jurisdiction under article 36(2) of the Statute of the Court, despite Canada's attempt to exclude such disputes from the jurisdiction of the Court, and Madrid seeks (among other things) a finding that Canadian law cannot be applied against Spain, that reparations for damages must be paid, and a declaration that the boarding of a Spanish ship, the *Estai,* was illegal [ibid.].

In an April 1995 letter, Canada contested the jurisdiction of the Court, and the Court decided (Order of May 2, 1995) that memorials by the parties must initially address the matter of jurisdiction. It determined that the Memorial by Spain would be due on September 29, 1995, and the Counter-Memorial by Canada on February 29, 1996 [press communiqué, 5/2/95].

Over the dissents of the United States, Russia, and most of the wealthier states of the North, the **General Assembly** voted to ask the ICJ a deceptively simple question under the Court's advisory jurisdiction: "**Is the threat or use of nuclear weapons in any circumstance permitted under international law?**" [A/Res/49/75K; vote: 78–43–38]. This is an attempt to implicate the Court in a fractious subject that came up at the 49th Session [see Peace and Security above]. The resolution presumes that the question involves an interpretation of the Charter's prohibition on the threat or use of force—and that it is, in any case, a "legal question" that the Assembly is entitled to pose under Article 96(1) of the Charter. The Assembly itself, notes the resolution, has often declared that the use of nuclear weapons would be a "violation of the Charter and a crime against humanity" [ibid., citing its prior resolutions 1653 (XVI), 33/71B, 34/83G, 35/152D, 36/92I, 45/59B, and 46/37D].

By asking the question on its own authority, the Assembly is apparently trying to ensure that the Court will address an issue that the **World Health Organization** had already put on the Court's advisory question agenda: ". . . would the use of nuclear weapons by a state in war or other armed conflict be a breach of its obligations under international law, including the WHO Constitution?" Thirty-five states, including the United States, have filed written statements in response to WHO's request for an advisory opinion [press communiqué, 9/23/94], and further written comments on that request are due on June 20, 1995. Indeed, since the Assembly's question is posed so generally, it will become more difficult for the Court to avoid the issue: It can no longer say, as it might with respect to WHO's question, that the legality of the use of nuclear weapons lies beyond the jurisdiction of the entity asking the question.

Answering the question may put the Court at odds with most, if not all, the members of the Security Council, four of which voted against Resolution 49/75K (China was not present for the vote). Any opinion would be purely advisory and nonbinding, however. Written statements on the General Assembly's question were due on June 20, 1995, with a second round of statements expected by September 20, 1995 [Order, 2/1/95].

Public hearings in the case of **East Timor (Portugal v. Australia)** [see *Issues/46*, p. 269] were held from January 30 to February 16, 1995, and a judgment is expected soon. The public hearings in one of the cases filed by Iran against the United States pending before the Court, **Aerial Incident of 3 July 1988** [see *Issues/46*, p. 267], scheduled for September 12, 1994, were postponed at the joint request of the parties. Other contentious cases are at various stages of pleading: Oil Platforms **(Iran v. United States)** [see *Issues/48*, p. 308], Questions of the Interpretation and Application of the 1971 Montreal Convention Arising from the Aerial Incident at Lockerbie **(Libya v. United Kingdom, and Libya v. United States)** [see *Issues/47*, pp. 325–27], Application of the Convention on the Prevention and Punishment of the Crime of Genocide **(Bosnia and Herzegovina v. Serbia and Montenegro)** [see *Issues/48*, pp. 304–5, and *Issues/49*, pp. 290–91], Gabcikovo-Nagymaros Project **(Hungary v. Slovakia)** [see *Issues/49*, p. 293], and Question of Sovereignty over the Peninsula of Bakassi **(Cameroon v. Nigeria)** [see *Issues/49*, p. 293; for a summary of the nature of the claims in these and all other cases and advisory opinions pending before the Court, see the Report of the ICJ, A/49/4].

Acting at the recommendation of the Sixth Committee, the 49th Assembly deferred until the 50th Session the question of terminating the procedure under **article 11 of the Statute of the Administrative Tribu-**

nal of the United Nations whereby the judgments of that body, which adjudicates staff grievances, can be indirectly appealed to the ICJ by the Committee on Applications for Review of Administrative Tribunal Judgments [Decision 49/425; and see *Issues/49*, pp. 294–95]. That review procedure continues to draw criticism, eliciting such descriptions as (in the words of the U.N.'s Deputy Legal Counsel) "deficient, unsatisfactory, ineffective, complex and contradictory" [AC.6/49/SR.38], and is slated for abolition. The question is what to leave in its place—whether ombudsman panels, or a different type of appeal (perhaps by member states) to the ICJ's advisory jurisdiction, or nothing at all [see A/49/258; and see the Secretary-General's report, A/C.6/49/2]. The matter of deleting article 11 of the statute appears on the agenda of the 50th Session. The delegates will have had the time to consider how any changes to this system will comport with reforms considered by the Fifth Committee in respect to the administration of justice vis-à-vis U.N. employees [Decision 49/425].

The ICJ reported that, as of July 1994, 58 states had made declarations accepting the so-called **"compulsory" jurisdiction of the Court** under article 36(2) of the Court's statute [A/49/4, p. 3].

7. Other Legal Developments

The United Nations marked the midpoint of the **U.N. Decade of International Law (1990–99)** by convening in New York in March 1995 a **Congress on Public International Law** [see *Issues/49*, pp. 299–300]. The Congress, intended to promote the rule of law in international relations, drew nearly a thousand scholars and practitioners from 146 states for discussions of five topics, one for each day of the Congress: (1) theoretical and practical aspects of the promotion and implementation of principles of international law; (2) means of peaceful settlement of disputes; (3) new developments in the codification and progressive development of international law; (4) new approaches to research, education and training in international law; and (5) new challenges for the 21st century [U.N. press releases L/2699, L/2702–7, L/2709, and L/2712].

Addressing the Congress, the President of the ICJ, Mohammed Bedjaoui (Algeria), urged greater use of the Court's advisory question jurisdiction by extending to states and additional organizations the ability to ask such questions [U.N. press release L/2704; see also his comments at the Sixth Committee, A/C.6/49/SR.16].

The 49th General Assembly adopted a program of activities for the third term of the U.N. Decade (1995–96), including continued efforts to encourage states to ratify and implement existing multilateral treaties, to strengthen means and methods of peaceful dispute settlement, and to identify areas ripe for codification or progressive development [A/Res/49/50 and Annex]. The Assembly also took this opportunity to stress the importance of international humanitarian law, invited states to disseminate the International Red Cross revised Guidelines for Military Manuals and Instructions on the Protection of the Environment in Times of Armed Conflict, and asked the Red Cross to continue to report on this issue [A/Res/49/50; and see reports from the Secretary-General on the Decade, A/49/323 (with additions and annex with the Red Cross Guidelines), and from the working group on the Decade, A/C.6/49/L.10].

Within the Sixth Committee, the subject of the U.N. Decade provided an opportunity for taking stock of achievements since the Decade began and for trumpeting individual efforts to promote international law [see, e.g., the Secretary-General of the Permanent Court of Arbitration's summary of efforts to improve the functioning of that body, A/C.6/49/SR.34]. Some delegates took the occasion to suggest topics worthy of increased attention by the legal community, such as the use of economic sanctions by the Security Council [see, e.g., comments by Bulgaria and Ukraine, A/C.6/49/SR.36] and particular environmental concerns [see, e.g., comments by Kazakhstan, A/C.6/49/SR.37]. Russia advocated the convening of a third international peace conference to strengthen international dispute settlement, fill gaps in international humanitarian law, and create an "international criminal justice system to try those responsible for crimes against humanity and offenses against peace and international law" [A/C.6/49/SR.34]. Libya's representatives, who noted their own country's unsuccessful attempt to secure ICJ consideration of the Security Council's use of sanctions for "political reasons" in the Lockerbie Case [see *Issues/47*, pp. 325–27], argued that the

> goals of the Decade would be unattainable if States continued to use international law when it suited them and to ignore it when it conflicted with their aims and interests. The law of the powerful still held sway. The United Nations should therefore be more active in urging all States, both big and small, to respect international law, in particular Chapter VI . . . concerning the peaceful settlement of disputes. [ibid.]

Representatives to the Sixth Committee continue to divide over the need to convene an international conference to elaborate a new convention on **international terrorism,** and a decision was not reached on the subject. Such divisions appeared to be put aside when it came to condemning "terrorism" and adopting the 49th Assembly's **Declaration on Measures to Eliminate International Terrorism** [A/Res/49/60, Annex]. The Declaration summons the support of the Charter, prior U.N. resolutions on Friendly Relations and defining Aggression, human rights instruments, and the large number of antiterrorism multilateral conventions to condemn "all acts, methods and practices of terrorism, as criminal and unjustifiable, wherever and by whoever committed" and to proclaim that all states must refrain from such acts and take effective and resolute measures to eliminate terrorism, including the apprehension, prosecution or extradition of all perpetrators [ibid.].

Discussions in the Sixth Committee revealed that despite over-whelming agreement on a resolution that mounts an attack *against* terrorism, consensus remains elusive on *defining* it (indeed, "terrorism" is proving as difficult to define as "aggression"). Some states continue to proclaim, as does Sudan, that it is "equally important to draw a distinction between terrorism as such and the legitimate right of peoples subject to the yoke of imperialism, racism, or foreign domination to fight against such oppression, exercise their right to self-determination and self-defense, live in freedom and independence, and determine their own choices . . ." [A/C.6/49/SR.14–15; and see *Issues/49*, pp. 298–99].

Alarmed by continuing reports that the law of war is being violated throughout the world in virtually every case of armed conflict, the Sixth Committee considered ways to better implement such humanitarian law [see, e.g., A/C.6/49/SR.6], and the 49th Session adopted a resolution urging all states to become parties to the Geneva Conventions of 1949 and its additional Protocols and to participate in the international fact-finding machinery under article 90 of Protocol I [A/Res/49/48]. The Assembly decided to revisit this issue at the 51st Session.

The 49th Assembly issued its traditional slew of resolutions addressing the **human rights situation** in particular countries [see A/Res/49/196–207] and urging states to adhere to particular human rights conventions [see, e.g., A/Res/49/175]. It also addressed the need for better implementation of human rights law and, as in the case of the Rights of the Child Convention (in force since September 1990) [see A/Res/49/211], went beyond urging universal ratification to suggest that states parties withdraw reservations to that convention and submit timely reports to the Committee on the Rights of the Child, with specific recommendations for remedying that Committee's heavy workload [see also A/Res/49/153 (on implementing the Standard Rules on the Equalization of Opportunities for Persons with Disabilities), A/Res/49/167 (on implementing the strategic plan of action for the improvement of the status of women within the U.N. Secretariat), A/Res/49/212 (on compliance measures to ameliorate the plight of street children), A/Res/49/210 (on measures to prevent the sale of children, child prostitution, and child pornography), A/Res/49/209 (on measures to protect children in armed conflicts), Decision 49/448 (directing that parties to the Convention on the Elimination of All Forms of Discrimination consider an amendment to the treaty to permit longer meetings of the Committee charged with implementation), and, more generally, A/Res/49/178 (on implementation of human rights treaties, especially reporting obligations), A/Res/49/194–95 (on strengthening the U.N.'s Centre for Human Rights), and A/Res/49/208 (urging compliance with the Vienna Declaration and Programme of Action to improve implementation of human rights instruments)].

More controversial was a resolution delineating certain **rights for migrants** (the main sponsor, Cuba, undoubtedly had U.S. policies toward the island in mind) that called on all states "to allow . . . the free flow of financial remittances by foreign nationals residing in their territory to their relatives in the country of origin" and "to discourage and reverse legislation that adversely affects the family reunification of documented migrants and the transfer of financial remittances" [A/Res/49/182; vote: 88–5–70]. The same resolution requested that this issue—cast as one involving respect for "the universally recognized freedom of travel" of all foreign nationals residing in a state's territory—be considered at the next (51st) session of the U.N. Commission on Human Rights. In the Third Committee discussion, Argentina explained that it was abstaining because the resolution "reflected political concerns which went beyond the question of migrants." Chile and Mexico noted that, even though they had voted in favor, the resolution should have indicated that the right to travel included the right to leave any country, including one's own [A/C.3/49/SR.63].

When it comes to what a number of scholars have called the "emerging right" to democratic governance, the Assembly continues to exhibit a mild schizophrenia. At the 49th Assembly, as in the past, most of the South voted in favor of a resolution encouraging **respect for the principles of national sovereignty and noninterference in the internal affairs of states in their electoral processes** and affirming that there is "no universal need for the United Nations to provide electoral assistance to Member States, except in special circumstances such as cases of decolonization, in the context of regional or international peace processes or at the request of specific sovereign States, by virtue of resolutions adopted by the Security Council or the General Assembly in each case . . ." [A/Res/49/180; vote: 97–57–14; see also *Issues/49*, pp. 295–96, and *Issues/48*, p. 309]. (Chile abstained on the grounds that this language might be construed as limiting the sovereign right of states to request electoral assistance in circumstances other than those specified in the resolution, while Germany, representing the views of many states of the North, noted that the resolution "detracted from efforts made by many States to enhance the principle of periodic and genuine elections" and that the European Union "objected to the selective use of the Charter to deny peoples their rights to free and democratic elections" [A/C.3/49/SR.63].) On the other hand—and by an even larger margin [vote: 155–1–12]—the Assembly passed a resolution on **strengthening the role of the United Nations in enhancing the effectiveness of periodic and genuine elections and the promotion of democratization** ("provided only at the specific request of the Member State concerned") [A/Res/49/190]. (Notwithstanding this proviso, Iran cast a negative vote. China, Cuba, North Korea, Iraq, Libya, Myanmar, Sudan, Syria, Uganda, Tanzania, Vietnam, and Zimbabwe abstained.)

With respect to **international crime control,** the 49th Assembly authorized preparations for the Ninth U.N. Congress on the Prevention of Crime and the Treatment of Offenders (Cairo, April 29–May 10, 1995) [A/Res/49/157]. The 50th Session will have a report of the recommendations of that Congress [for a preview, see "Other Social Issues: Crime" in the present volume; for a summary of the issues explored by the Eighth Congress, see *Issues/46*, pp. 249–52; for recommendations made by the 49th Session with respect to strengthening U.N. criminal justice and crime prevention programs, see A/Res/49/156, 158, and 159]. In connection with efforts to strengthen the U.N. International Drug Control Programme and in the course of encouraging states to implement the many existing drug control conventions, the 49th Session reaffirmed, as it has in the past, that the **"fight against drug abuse and illicit trafficking should not in any way justify violation of the principles enshrined in the Charter** . . . and international law, particularly respect for the sovereignty and territorial integrity of States and non-use of force or the threat of force in international relations"** [A/Res/49/168; for a report by the Secretary-General on the work of the Commission on Crime Prevention and Criminal Justice, see A/49/593; see also *Issues/47*, p. 306].

With respect to the **Law of the Sea,** the 49th Session called on states to ensure, consistent with the Law of the Sea Convention, that no foreign fishing vessels fish in zones under the national jurisdiction of other states unless so authorized. That resolution reaffirms the treaty-protected rights and duties of coastal states to ensure proper conservation and management measures with respect to living resources in zones under their national jurisdiction [A/Res/49/116]. The 51st Assembly will have on its agenda a comprehensive report on the impact of the **entry into force of the Law of the Sea Convention** [see A/Res/49/28, which, among other things, requests the Secretariat's assistance in establishing that convention's own international tribunal].

The Assembly also welcomed the entry into force of the **Convention on Biological Diversity** and the convening in 1994 of the first meeting of its conference of parties, and it put on the agenda for the 50th Session a review of the results of that meeting and of progress toward implementing the convention. The 50th Session will also examine the progress made in implementing the U.N. **Framework Convention on Climate Change,** which entered into force in March 1994 [A/Res/49/120].

VII
Finance and Administration
By Toula Coklas

The discussions and decisions of a number of items on the agenda of the Fifth Committee at the 49th Session of the General Assembly were postponed to the resumed 49th Session in early 1995, and it was anticipated that their consideration would continue even further into the year.

Aside from recurring items of the Fifth Committee's agenda, at the 50th Session the General Assembly will most certainly be concerned with the overall question of peacekeeping activities, documentation, and conference services, as well as its review of the administrative and financial functioning of the Organization.

1. U.N. Finances

Financial Reports and Audited Financial Statements and Reports of the Board of Auditors

In Resolution 47/211, paragraph 18, the General Assembly invited the Board of Auditors, in its concise summary of principal findings, conclusions, and recommendations, to report in a consolidated fashion on the major deficiencies in program and financial management and in cases of inappropriate or fraudulent use of resources, together with measures taken by the United Nations in that regard.

The findings, conclusions, and recommendations of the Board for the following organizations are summarized in the Secretary-General's report A/49/214 (the detailed findings for each of the organizations are found in the relevant volumes of document A/49/5): the United Nations, peacekeeping operations, International Trade Center (UNCTAD/GATT [ITC]), U.N. University (UNU), U.N. Development Programme (UNDP), U.N. Children's Fund (UNICEF), U.N. Relief and Works Agency in the Near East (UNRWA), U.N. Institute for Training and Research (UNITAR), voluntary funds administered by the U.N. High Commissioner for Refugees (UNHCR), U.N. Environment Programme

(UNEP), U.N. Population Fund (UNFPA), U.N. Habitat and Human Settlements Foundation, and U.N. International Drug Control Programme (UNDCP). The Board also examined the accounts of the U.N. Joint Staff Pension Fund, and the audit reports thereon are included in the report of the U.N. Staff Pension Board. In each of its individual reports the Board included a section on the implementation of its past recommendations. At the start of the deliberations in the Fifth Committee [A/C.5/49/SR.10] the Deputy Controller and Auditor General of the United Kingdom, in presenting the reports of the Board of Auditors on behalf of the Chairman of the Board of Auditors, made the following observations:

For the first time, the Board had presented a separate report on the financial statements of the peacekeeping operations in 1992–93. In preparing the report the Board had been very conscious of the importance of that work and of the request in General Assembly Resolution 47/212. With regard to those financial statements, it disagreed with the evaluation placed on assessed contributions because, in its view, there was scant likelihood of collecting those contributions.

As far as financial issues were concerned, the Board had qualified its audit opinion of the financial statements of four organizations. In three cases, namely UNDP, UNFPA, and UNDCP, the Board had limited the scope of its opinion, as it had in 1990–91, since it had been unable to obtain sufficient evidence in the form of audit certificates from governments and nongovernmental organizations that funds advanced to them for technical cooperation projects had been used for those purposes. Nevertheless, the problem had been much reduced compared to the previous biennium, and the organizations had taken steps to improve the situation still further.

As to management issues, the Board was well aware of its role in helping to reduce waste within the United Nations and to enhance program performance. In the 1992–93 biennium, the Board had carried out horizontal studies—in other words, it had examined the same topic in each of the organizations it audited—in two important areas: the procurement of goods and services and the implementation of the Integrated Management Information System (IMIS). In the procurement area, the Board felt that there were a number of areas in which significant improvement was required if the United Nations and its organizations were to secure better value for the money. The Board made three recommendations: first, the United Nations must actively manage procurement and plan it more effectively, developing measures to enable it to monitor trends and identify potential problems; second, the Organization must test the market much more thoroughly than had been its previous practice, and a greater use of open tenders for major procurement and better use of advertising and of supplier rosters is recommended; and third, the United Nations must act as an "intelligent" customer. It must have sufficient in-house expertise to work with the market in the way the market expected, both for letting and for monitoring contracts.

The Integrated Management Information System had remained a project with little detailed planning for implementation, either in New York or at offices elsewhere, such as Geneva and Vienna. In addition, the resources required had been considerably underestimated. The rapid response of the United Nations to the shortcomings identified, as set out in the sixth progress report on the project [A/C.5/48/12/Add.1], was encouraging.

With respect to program management, the Board had commented on various shortcomings in a number of detailed cases, such as those concerning conference services, UNHCR, UNICEF, UNEP, and the U.N. Habitat and Human Settlements Foundation. The Board generalized the reasons for those shortcomings, which it said stemmed essentially from a lack of clear objectives and from the absence of performance measures and effective monitoring.

The Board, once again, had found it necessary to comment extensively on the failure of several organizations, especially in the peacekeeping area, to maintain adequate inventories of nonexpendable property. Those inventories formed the basis for the safeguarding and management of the organizations' assets. The United Nations would be ill-equipped to make the best use of its assets if it did not know what assets it had or where those assets were.

The Board also paid special attention to the management of technical cooperation projects carried out by the United Nations, UNDP, UNFPA, ITC, and others. A number of general themes had again emerged, in particular a failure to establish quantifiable objectives, a tendency to administer projects mechanically, persistent overruns on timetables and budget, and a failure to disseminate the lessons of previous experience. The Board's key recommendation in that regard was that such projects must be managed more proactively and within a structure which clearly established the lines of responsibility and accountability.

Finally, during the 1992–93 biennium, the impact of the changes in the implementation of development projects, in particular the switch to national execution, had had a major effect on some organizations. For example, the United Nations and ITC had experienced a sharp decline in program support cost income, as a result of which it had been necessary to review their staffing levels and to implement painful reforms.

With regard to cases of fraud or presumptive fraud, the Board was provided with information on some 74 cases involving a total of $1,911,223 that became known to nine organizations during 1992–93. Of this amount, approximately $1,076,160 had been recovered; these cases involved staff members and non-staff members, and disciplinary action in the form of summary dismissal was taken against some of the staff members, and other cases are still under investigation.

The Board of Auditors welcomed the proposals put forward by the Secretary-General to change the management culture of the Organization, with emphasis on responsibility, authority, accountability, and transparency [A/C.5/49/1], which could do much to help attain the Organization's objectives and to solve the more specific problems identified in the Board's report. The Board also welcomed the creation of the Office of Internal Oversight Services, and the consequent strengthening of the internal audit capacity of the United Nations. It had always worked closely with the Internal Audit Division and subsequently with the Office for Inspections and Investigations with a view to coordinating their activities, and it hoped that the same kind of collaboration would be developed with the new Office.

At the request of the Assembly in its Resolution 48/216, the Board had submitted, in document A/49/368, its views on the implications of extending the term of office of the members of the Board to four or six years. The Board favored the adoption of the six-year term of appointment, meaning that each member would serve for three biennial financial periods, thus giving that person sufficient time to become familiar with the Organization and to make an effective contribution.

In recent debates, a number of member states had expressed concern about the capacity of Board members to provide sufficient numbers of professionally qualified staff to carry out the full range of required audit activities, and it had been questioned on that point by the Advisory Committee on Administrative and Budgetary Questions (ACABQ). The Board was pleased to note that it had no difficulty in providing the requisite number of professional staff, by drawing on its respective national audit institutions or by obtaining the services of outside experts.

Over the previous years, the Board had received an increasing number of requests from the General Assembly for special audits of particular topics. In most cases, those requests could be addressed within the Board's program by adjusting the focus of particular audits to cover the necessary ground. In certain cases, however, especially where requests were made at short notice or required particular expertise, the Board might have to seek additional funding to meet those requirements.

The Chairman of the ACABQ, commenting on the reports of the Board of Auditors, stated that in studying the Board's reports it had kept in mind the concern which had been expressed in the Fifth Committee regarding the adequacy of audit coverage and related resources. The Board had taken account of the General Assembly's wish to have broader audit coverage for peacekeeping operations, and for the first time the Board had prepared a separate report on peacekeeping operations [A/49/5, vol. II, section II]. In the future, the Board might have to consider issuing separate reports on the larger peacekeeping operations. As to the question of additional reports the General Assembly might request, the Advisory Committee, in paragraph 8 of its report [A/49/547], noted that the Board was able to cope with additional audits the Assembly might request. However, if the audit had to be completed within a short period, more resources might be needed. Before deciding on additional audits, the Board needed to prepare a statement of financial implications. On the question of extending the term of office of the members of the Board of Auditors to four or six years, the Advisory Committee, after considerable discussion, had concluded that the final decision rested with the General Assembly; if the term of office was changed, the Assembly would have to adopt appropriate transitional measures. The Advisory Committee regarded as an encouraging development the inclusion by the Board in its reports of a section on the implementation of its past recommendations. The Chairman stressed the importance of the Advisory Committee's observations in paragraph 8 of its report with respect to the Advisory Committee's intention of meeting with the Board of Auditors and to explore with it, and with representatives of the Secretary-General, the most acceptable means of putting into practice the procedures outlined in paragraph 36 of its report.

During the discussions in the Fifth Committee, the representative of Sweden, speaking on behalf of the Nordic countries, stated that while the Nordic delegations generally endorsed the recommendations of the Board of Auditors and the related comments of the ACABQ, they were concerned about some of the findings and conclusions regarding financial matters and, in particular, deficiencies in budgetary control. With few exceptions, the Board had found rather serious shortcomings in program and project management in all the organizations and funds under review. As major contributors, the Nordic countries were particularly concerned to note the Board's observations with regard to UNDP, UNICEF, and UNFPA. Monitoring in UNDP had become highly mechanical. Although examples of good monitoring existed in UNFPA, progress reports often did not clearly establish what had been done, whether it was relevant to achieving stated objectives, or what remained to be done. In UNICEF, monitoring needed to be improved in order to promote program delivery of supplementary-funded projects.

The representative of India stated that some of the Board's observations on accounts and financial reporting were both relevant and important in a systemic sense. For example, the fact that only two of the 17 peacekeeping missions had presented evidence of a cash count as of December 31, 1993 to confirm the accuracy of cash-in-hand balances seemed to suggest that even rudimentary accounting procedures were absent in the field. Also, the absence of proper inventories of nonexpendable properties at duty stations away from Headquarters was symptomatic of certain systemic deficiencies. His delegation shared the Board's view that the Integrated Management Information System, on which there had already been considerable expenditure without significant results, should now be taken up on a priority basis for completion. The project team should be appropriately strengthened and detailed targets established for all key responsibility centers for the project so that IMIS could fulfill its purpose early in 1995. With regard to the hiring of consultants, given the recent expansion of the Organization's activities, greater use should be made of the considerable in-house capabilities available in the Organization, and the use of external consultants, especially for peacekeeping purposes, should be kept to an absolute minimum.

The representative of Germany, speaking on behalf of the European Union and Austria, agreed completely with the Board's view that, where procurement was concerned, the use of a relatively narrow range of suppliers and the limited extent of bidding made it unlikely that the Organization was receiving the best value for its money. Financial rule 110.18, establishing international competitive bidding on high-volume contracts, must be strictly adhered to. The representative of the Russian Federation stated that the Board of Auditors in its report [A/49/214] mentioned that it had received information concerning 74 cases of fraud or presumptive fraud involving a total of almost $2 million in nine organizations during 1992–93. The Ad Hoc Intergovernmental Working Group of Experts established pursuant to General Assembly Resolution 48/218 A had indicated in its report [A/49/418] that the Secretariat gave an extremely narrow interpretation of the term "fraud." The Secretariat, in considering the new mechanisms of internal control, should address that problem and find an adequate definition of the terms "fraud" and "presumptive fraud."

The representative of Brazil commented that the shortcomings identified in connection with peacekeeping operations in the area of procurement were part of a larger problem that stemmed mostly from the fact that the Organization lacked a management culture designed to ensure impartiality, transparency, and open competition.

The representative of the United States observed that the reports of the Board of Auditors revealed that the deficiencies in financial controls, procurement, and control of nonexpendable property which the Board had criticized repeatedly in previous bienniums had still not been rectified, despite promises of action by the Secretariat. The Integrated Management Information System, which had been put forward as a cure for many of the problems, had not been adequately implemented. His delegation noted that the Board had drawn attention to continuing problems in the area of budgetary control and had described the excess of expenditures over allotments in the 1992–93 biennium as unprecedented. The fact that IMIS was still not in place did not absolve the Secretariat of responsibility for the proper administration of resources. It was expected that with the advent of the new system of accountability and responsibility, the necessary internal controls would be put into place without delay. Regarding the term of office of the Board's members, his delegation favored an extension of the term from three to four years, with a limit of two consecutive terms, to permit synchronization with the budget cycle and to allow a greater number of member states to participate in the important external oversight function. Much remained to be done to bring the United Nations into compliance with the findings of the Board of Auditors, and his delegation urged the new senior management of the Department of Administration and Management to place that task at the top of its agenda; that was a precondition for restoring the faith of the membership in the Secretariat.

The representative of the Islamic Republic of Iran referred to the report of the Board concerning voluntary funds administered by the U.N. High Commissioner for Refugees [A/49/5/Add.5]. His country suffered from a considerable shortfall between the increasing needs of its large refugee population and the available international assistance. The total spending of UNHCR was less than its total income; moreover, the UNHCR report for 1993–94, as well as its proposed program budget for 1995, showed a sharp decrease with respect to his country. His delegation called on UNHCR to revise and increase the budget allocation.

The representative of Ukraine welcomed the creation of the Office of Internal Oversight Services. The concentration of all auditing, inspection, control, evaluation, and monitoring functions within a single structural unit would not only result in a more rational use of resources but would also enhance the effectiveness of internal oversight within the Secretariat and consequently increase the confidence of member states in the Organization. The internal oversight machinery of the Board of Auditors and the Joint Inspection Unit should also be strengthened and the Board should have greater independence in its activities. The irregularities with respect to procurement were a matter of particular concern. The Secretariat should focus on the Board's recommendations, which called for a review of the policy with regard to the acquisition of equipment and supplies, for clarification of the concepts of urgency and exceptions to the rules in connection with the acquisition of equipment for peacekeeping operations, and for increased use of competitive bidding and the list of suppliers.

The representative of Canada, speaking on behalf of Australia and New Zealand, stated that the adoption of common accounting standards for the U.N. system represented an important step forward. Notwithstanding the fact that the Panel of External Auditors and ACABQ have estimated that it would, in fact, take a number of years for them to be fully applied throughout the system, three of the standards should be applied as early as possible. First, provision should be made for possible delays in the collection of contributions; second, the value of any accumulated surplus of deficit should be disclosed in such a manner as to indicate the amounts actually available for distribution; and third, liabilities for end-of-service benefits should be provided for in the accounts. Only pledged contributions received or relating to the fiscal period under audit should be included in the reports and those relating to future periods should appear in the notes to statements. The application of accounting standards throughout the system was essential for fair and equitable comparisons between organizations. Given that spending on peacekeeping operations accounted for some 32 percent of the total expenditures of the system, proper controls must be applied. With regard to the term of office of Board members, he supported the proposal that the term be extended to six years, since under the current system auditors might leave just when the knowledge they had acquired could be used to the best effect.

On December 23, 1994, at its 95th plenary meeting, the General Assembly adopted Resolution 49/216 on financial reports and audited financial statements, and reports of the Board of Auditors, without a vote. In section A of the resolution, the General Assembly, having considered for the period ended December 31, 1993 the financial reports and audited financial statement of the United Nations and its organizations, inter alia, accepted the financial reports and audit opinions and reports of the Board of Auditors and the concise summary of principal findings, conclusions, and recommendations for remedial action of the Board of Auditors; noted with concern that the Board issued qualified audit opinions on the financial statements of U.N. peacekeeping operations, UNDP, UNFPA, and UNDCP; approved the recommendations and conclusions of the Board and the comments thereon in the report of the ACABQ; and requested the Board of Auditors to consider, in the light of the report of the Office of Internal Oversight Services on the security access system, whether it is necessary for the Board to undertake a further review of the project, including its development and the method of procurement and managerial accountability, both at the inception and execution of the project. The General Assembly also requested the Secretary-General to continue to monitor closely the costs and benefits to the Organization of the lump-arrangements, including an analysis of the level of cash incentive provided to staff by the current 75 percent procedures, and to make any necessary adjustments to ensure that the arrangements do not offer scope for abuse. Noting also that in some cases inventory control was deficient, the General Assembly endorsed the view of the Board that these issues should be reviewed as a matter of high priority, and requested the Secretary-General and the relevant executive heads of the U.N. organizations and programs to address these issues accordingly.

In section B the General Assembly welcomed the submission of a separate document covering all peacekeeping operations, and invited the Board to develop this format further, in particular for the larger peacekeeping operations; expressed concern that the Board was unable to confirm cash-in-hand balances for the majority of peacekeeping operations and requested the Secretary-General to ensure that, for each peacekeeping operation, the cash counts are reconciled on a regular basis with the accounting records; expressed concern at the findings of the Board regarding nonexpendable property and requested the Secretary-General to ensure strict compliance with the provisions of financial rules 110.25 and 110.26 in that regard; and, finally, requested the Secretary-General to consult with the Board of Auditors on appropriate measures to avoid the recurrence of the qualification of the audit opinion of the financial statements of the U.N. peacekeeping operations.

Section C of the resolution dealt with the question of procurement. In its operative part the General Assembly took note with concern of the findings of the Board on the aspects of procurement that require remedial action; requested the Secretary-General to take immediate action to implement the recommendations of the Board, taking into account the views expressed by member states during the discussions in the General Assembly, and to keep the Board fully informed of the ongoing measures taken; and requested the Board to report thereon to the Assembly at its 50th Session. It also requested the Secretary-General to report to the General Assembly through the ACABQ, no later than April 30, 1995, with respect to proposals for the improvement of certain procurement activities of the Secretariat.

Section D of the resolution was concerned with the Organization's accounting standards. The General Assembly requested the Secretary-General and the executive heads of the U.N. organizations and programs to pursue their effort to ensure full compliance with the common accounting standards in submitting the financial statements for the biennium 1994–95, inter alia, disclosure of valuation of property, contributions in kind, and cash held in nonconvertible currencies and calculation and disclosure of delays in the collection of assessed contributions, with a view to improving disclosure in the financial statements.

In section E of the resolution, the General Assembly welcomed decision 94/30 of October 10, 1994 of the Executive Board of the UNDP/UNFPA and decision 1994/R. 3/6 of October 5, 1994 of the Executive Board of UNICEF, on the harmonization of the presentation of budgets and accounts, and requested the executive heads of the UNDP, UNFPA, and UNICEF to report, through the ACABQ, to their respective governing bodies on the implementation of those decisions, and to the Economic and Social Council at its substantive session of 1995.

Scales of Assessments

The approval of the scale of assessments for the regular budget for the years 1995–97 was one of the major items considered by the Fifth Committee at the 49th Session.

A lengthy discussion in the Committee at the 48th Session resulted in a consensus resolution, the preamble of which reaffirmed that the capacity to pay of member states is the fundamental criterion for determining the scale of assessments [Res/48/223 B]. In operative paragraph 1 of the consensus resolution, the General Assembly requested the Committee on Contributions to recommend to the Assembly at its 49th Session a scale of assessments for the period 1995–97 on the basis of the average of two separate machine scales, and laid down specific instructions to the Committee as to the following criteria to be used in the construction of the scale.

1. The scale was to be based on the average of two separate scales, one of which would have a seven-year statistical base and the other an eight-year base.

2. Uniform exchange rates should be used for converting local statistical data into U.S. dollars.

3. The adjustment for external indebtedness should remain the same as that used for the 1992–94 scale.

4. The low per capita income allowance applied in calculating the assessments of countries with a per capita income below the average world per capita income for the statistical period would be retained and a "gradient" of 85 percent applied.

5. There should be no change in the floor rate of 0.01 percent and the ceiling rate of 25 percent.

6. The scheme of limits, the purpose of which is to prevent excessive fluctuations in assessment rates between one scale and the next, would be phased out in two equal steps over the scale periods 1995–97 and 1998–2000.

The Assembly further decided that in phasing out the scheme of limits, the allocation of additional points resulting from the phasing out to developing countries benefiting from its application should be limited to 15 percent of the effect of the phase-out.

In the operative paragraphs of Resolution 48/223 C, the General Assembly requested the Committee on Contributions to undertake a thorough and comprehensive review of all aspects of the scale methodology with a view to making it stable, simpler, and more transparent while continuing to base it on reliable, verifiable, and comparable data, and to report to the Assembly at its 50th Session. It also reaffirmed the principle of capacity to pay as the fundamental criterion for determining the scale of assessments, and agreed, in principle, to establish an ad hoc body to study the implementation of this principle in determining the scale of assessments.

At its 54th session, the Committee on Contributions discussed at length the issues involved in the construction of a scale of assessments for the period 1995–97. In its report to the General Assembly at its 49th Session [49/11], the Committee submitted to the Assembly a draft resolution with a proposed new scale for the contributions of member states to the regular budget for the years 1995, 1996, and 1997 [49/11, par. 60,1, as well as annexes II.A, II.B, III.A, and III.B].

In paragraphs 7 and 8 of its report, the Committee stated that the capacity to pay is the fundamental criterion for determining the scale of assessments and described briefly the following components of the methodology and criteria used to approximate the capacity to pay:

1. The national income data provided by all states for the statistical period.

2. Debt relief reduces the annual national income of eligible countries with high levels of external debt.

3. The low per capita income allowance formula reduces the national income already adjusted for debt relief on the basis of its two parameters, namely the upper per capita income limit of the average world per capita income for the statistical base period and the relief gradient of 85 percent.

4. The rates of assessment of member states may not be lower than 0.01 percent (floor rate) or exceed 25 percent (ceiling rate).

5. The assessment rates of least-developed countries may not exceed 0.01 percent.

6. The scheme of limits avoids excessive variations of individual rates of assessment between successive scales.

In introducing the report of the Committee to the Fifth Committee [A/C.5/49/SR.3], the Chairman of the Committee on Contributions stated that the proposed new scale was prepared pursuant to the mandate as set out by rule 160 of the rules of procedure of the General Assembly and in conformity with General Assembly Resolution 48/223 B. It reflected a 50 percent phase-out of the effects of the scheme of limits on a country-by-country basis, spread out over the three years of the scale.

Annexes II.A and III.A of the report show the step-by-step adjustments to the national income averages for the two statistical base periods 1986–92 and 1985–92 and the resultant machine scales. Annexes II.B and III.B show the number of points which are redistributed among member states by each of the steps. Columns 8 through 10 of annexes II.A and III.A added up to less than 100 percent because some points remained unallocated on account of the 15 percent limitation on allocation of additional points resulting from the 50 percent phase-out of the effects of the scheme of limits to developing countries benefiting from its application, in accordance with General Assembly Resolution 48/223 B, paragraph 2.

In order to obtain a scale adding up to 100 percent and prepared on the basis of the average of two machine scales, the corresponding points on the two scales for each country were averaged and the unallocated points distributed, on a pro rata basis, among countries which were not subject to the ceiling, were not least-developed countries, and were not developing countries benefiting from the 15 percent provision.

The national income data had been provided to the U.N. Statistical Office by member states and non-member states. In the case of certain countries for which national income data were not available, per capita income averages for neighboring countries had been used. Similarly, estimates of real growth rates computed by the Economic Commission for Europe had been used in the case of the five countries formerly part of Yugoslavia.

The exchange rates which the Committee had applied were those specified in General Assembly Resolution 46/221 B, paragraph 3(b). Some complexities and ambiguities inherent in the use of multiple sources and types of exchange rates had been noted, as were some inherent in the increasing effect of money speculation on market exchange rates, and the Committee would address those issues at its next session in the context of its review of the methodology with a view to establishing well-defined criteria for converting national income data to U.S. dollars.

With regard to the 50 percent phase-out of the scheme of limits, the Committee had explored both a global phase-out through broadening of the scheme's parameters and a country-by-country phase-out through reducing 50 percent of the scheme's effect on each country. The latter approach had been preferred because it avoided distortions in the rates for individual countries and made for greater transparency.

The main difficulty in making a choice between the one-step phase-out and the three-step phase-out of 50 percent of the effect of the scheme of limits was to balance the interests of those member states whose rates of contribution would decrease under the proposed scheme and those whose rates would increase. In the opinion of the Committee, a three-step phase-out would not necessitate a review of the scale during the scale period and was, moreover, in accordance with rule 160 of the rules of procedure of the General Assembly, which permits the revision of the scale if "substantial changes in relative capacity to pay" occurred since the scale was approved.

The Committee also recommended new rates of assessment for non-member states [49/11/par. 60,2(c)]; since the proposed rates fell within the parameters of the scheme of limits, they would remain unchanged in the years 1995, 1996, and 1997.

During the discussion in the Fifth Committee [A/C.5/49/SR.3–SR.7] on the proposed scale of assessments for the period 1995–97, certain member states, including Ukraine and Belarus, stated that their assessment rates had been basically distorted because of the General Assembly's decision 47/456, and did not reflect their special circumstances and their capacity to pay. Latvia, speaking on behalf of Estonia and Lithuania, stated that although there had been some improvement in the scale by the 50 percent phase-out of the scheme of limits, the rates recommended for the Baltic countries were between 2 and 3.5 times higher than their capacity to pay. Romania observed that the consensus reached on the proposed scale in the Committee on Contributions reflected the technical divisiveness of the issue. The proposed scale had to be established in the context of the profound political and economic transformation that had taken place in the countries of Central and Eastern Europe and the former Soviet Union, which had determined an entirely new approach to the calculation of their rates of assessment. Romania's position continued to be that the economic difficulties of certain countries could be resolved instead through political decisions of the General Assembly. Poland felt that the proposed scale seemed to reflect the capacity to pay better than earlier scales, and met, at least in part, the concerns of a number of developing countries and of Central and Eastern European countries with economies in transition. Libya and Iraq called attention to their difficult economic situation due to sanctions imposed on them; and the Syrian Arab Republic complained that consideration had not been given to its particular economic situation due to the fact that part of its fertile agricultural land was under occupation.

Most of the member states taking part in the discussion in the Fifth Committee were satisfied with the manner in which the Committee on Contributions had conformed with its mandate in Resolution 48/223 B and expressed various views on the components that made up the proposed scale.

1. *The methodology used.* In paragraph 2 of Resolution 48/223 C, the General Assembly requested that an ad hoc body be established to study the implementation of the principle of capacity to pay in determining the scales.

India observed that the current methodology used was a result of the experience of member states over the past half-century and had stood the test of time. There were areas that could be improved and his delegation was ready to cooperate with others in reviewing the methodology so that it more effectively reflected the principle of capacity to pay; the scale, however, represented a "delicate political balance" and it was important to adopt a consensus approach in refining the methodology. Kuwait agreed that the present methodology was a result of a great deal of study and that it would be preferable to introduce any necessary changes gradually rather than devising an entirely new methodology. Pakistan pointed out that the Committee on Contributions was already mandated to advise the General Assembly on the apportionment of the expenses of the Organization according to capacity to pay and that the proposed new body was likely to duplicate the work of the Committee and cause a further drain on the resources of the United Nations. Poland and Egypt expressed the belief that the ad hoc body would make a valuable contribution to the issue of capacity to pay if the work it was assigned complemented rather than duplicated the work of the Committee on Contributions. A large number of member states emphatically supported the establishment of the ad hoc body. Norway, speaking on behalf of the five Nordic countries, expressed the hope that this would be the last time the General Assembly would be called upon to adopt a scale based on the present methodology; it was important for the methodology to enjoy the confidence, or at least the acceptance, of all member states. The numerous criteria which currently determined the capacity to pay and the distortions that had evolved over the years had led the Nordic countries to support a "clean slate" approach (the scale should be based solely on national income and should not be regarded as an instrument for income distribution), which, however, would include a relief mechanism for countries with below-average per capita incomes. Egypt, Bangladesh, and Iran were opposed to the "clean slate" approach; they felt that a gradual approach to reform was preferable. Most of the other member states supporting the establishment of the ad hoc body emphasized that its mandate should be carefully defined and that its membership should reflect an equitable geographical distribution. India, Jordan, and Iran stated that the members of the ad hoc body should be appointed by the president of the General Assembly in consultation with member states.

2. *Exchange rates.* The Committee on Contributions, in paragraph 50 of its report [A/49/11], noted the significant effect of different exchange rates on the scale of assessments and expressed the opinion that the provisions of paragraph 3(b) of General Assembly Resolution 46/221 B had several technical problems which should be addressed in the context of the review of methodology. The Committee asked the Secretariat to prepare a comprehensive critical study on the subject for the Committee's consideration at its next session. A number of member states in the Fifth Committee, recognizing the complexity of the issue, were encouraged by the intention of the Committee on Contributions to address the issue with a view to establishing a well-defined criterion for converting national income data to U.S. dollars. It was generally agreed that the use of market

exchange rates (MERs) should be maintained in preference to price-adjusted rates of exchange (PARs).

3. *Phasing-out of the scheme of limits.* In paragraph 1(f) of Resolution 48/223 B, the General Assembly requested the Committee on Contributions when developing the scale for the period 1995–97 to take into account a scheme of limits "whose effects would be phased-out 50 percent with a view to its complete phasing-out in the scale for 1998–2000."

Accordingly, the Committee, after much deliberation and compromise, decided on a 50 percent three-step phase-out, on a country-by-country basis, in its formulation of the proposed scale for 1995–97. A number of member states during the discussion in the Fifth Committee agreed that the 50 percent phase-out during the three-year period 1995–97 was an important step toward the elimination of the "distorting" effects of the current methodology and was fully in accord with rule 160 of the rules of procedure of the Assembly. Although the decision to spread the 50 percent phase-out over the three-year period did not meet the expectations of all member states, it represented a reasonable compromise which would avoid excessive changes in the rates over the 1995–97 period. Certain member states, mainly some of those admitted to membership in the United Nations following the dissolution of Czechoslovakia, the USSR, and Yugoslavia (the so-called "22 States"), maintained that a one-step phasing-out of 50 percent of the effects of the scheme of limits was more within the spirit of Resolution 48/223 B. The Russian Federation disagreed with the assumption made in paragraph 20 of the Committee's report [49/11] that developing countries would be better served by a six-step phase-out of the scheme of limits; the multiple-step phase-out was highly beneficial to but a few developed countries. The Nordic countries observed that the distorting effects of the phasing-out of the scheme of limits would be felt until the year 2000. On the grounds of fair burden-sharing and the financial soundness of the United Nations, they favored the immediate abolition of the scheme of limits and supported a one-step phasing-out rather than a three-step phasing-out over the years 1995–97.

4. *Statistical base period.* In its Resolution 48/223 B the General Assembly requested the Committee on Contributions to develop the scale of assessments for 1995–97 on the basis of the average of two separate machine scales using statistical base periods of seven and eight years, rather than the ten-year base used in the previous scale. During the discussion in the Fifth Committee, the People's Republic of China agreed to the modification in the statistical base period but felt a greater stability would be achieved through the maintenance of a longer base period. Belarus observed that it was difficult to understand why some member states wished to maintain the longer base period when even the seven-year and eight-year base periods did not make it possible to evaluate objectively the real capacity of member states to pay. The Czech Republic believed

that the reduction of the base period from ten to seven and eight years, together with the 50 percent phase-out of the scheme of limits, was a step toward compliance with the principle of the capacity to pay. Poland felt that a further reduction in the statistical base period would make it possible to apply fairer rates to those member states which had formerly been part of larger entities. Iran observed that with the structural adjustments taking place in the national economies of many member states, a base period of three years would be preferable.

5. *The debt adjustment.* The General Assembly decided in its Resolution 48/223 B that the debt adjustment approach used in the preparation of the scale of assessments for the period 1992–94 should continue to be used in the 1995–97 scale. The national income of countries identified for debt relief, i.e., those with per capita incomes below $6,000, is reduced by an amount based on a theoretical debt-service ratio. On the assumption that total external debt outstanding is repaid on the average in approximately eight years, 12.5 percent of this debt is deducted from the national income of eligible countries.

6. *Low per capita income allowance.* In its Resolution 48/223 B, the General Assembly requested the Committee on Contributions to use a low per capita income allowance formula with a per capita income limit of the average world per capita income for the statistical base period and a gradient of 85 percent. In that respect, the Committee used the national income figure resulting from the debt relief adjustment and further adjusted for low per capita income. The national income of countries whose per capita national income is below the per capita limit of $3,055 for the period 1985–92 or $3,198 for the period 1986–92 is reduced by the percentage resulting from calculating 85 percent of the percentage difference between the country's per capita income and $3,055 and $3,198, respectively. For example, for a country with an average per capita income of $1,000 for the period 1985–92, the average total national income, adjusted for debt relief, is reduced by 57.2 percent ($3,055 − $1,000 = $2,055; $2,055 = 67.3 percent of $3,055; 85 percent of 67.3 = 57.2 percent). The total amount of relief granted increases the proportion of national income adjusted for debt relief of the countries not affected by the formula in proportion to their respective share (pro rata) of their collective national incomes. The national income figures thus adjusted constitute the assessable income. In the Fifth Committee the view was expressed by some member states that the low per capita income allowance formula, which had for many years played an important part in the search for greater equity, raised some complex problems. Australia, speaking on behalf of Canada and New Zealand, observed that the element which most distorted the scale of assessments was the low per capita income allowance formula, with the result that the assessment of some member states had fallen to a "derisory" level.

7. *The floor rate of 0.01 percent and ceiling rate of 25 percent.* There was to be no change in the floor rate of 0.01 percent, applied to the assessment of the least-developed countries, and the ceiling rate of 25 percent, applied to the assessment of the United States.

The scale of assessments for the period 1995–97, as recommended by the Committee on Contributions, was adopted by the General Assembly (Resolution 49/19 B) without a vote at its 95th meeting on December 20, 1994. It reads as follows:

The General Assembly

1. *Resolves that* the scale of assessments for the contributions of Member States to the regular budget of the United Nations for the years 1995, 1996, and 1997 shall be as follows:

Member State	1995	1996	1997
		(percentage)	
Afghanistan	0.01	0.01	0.01
Albania	0.01	0.01	0.01
Algeria	0.16	0.16	0.16
Andorra	0.01	0.01	0.01
Angola	0.01	0.01	0.01
Antigua and Barbuda	0.01	0.01	0.01
Argentina	0.48	0.48	0.48
Armenia	0.08	0.07	0.05
Australia	1.46	1.48	1.48
Austria	0.85	0.85	0.87
Azerbaijan	0.16	0.14	0.11
Bahamas	0.02	0.02	0.02
Bahrain	0.02	0.02	0.02
Bangladesh	0.01	0.01	0.01
Barbados	0.01	0.01	0.01
Belarus	0.37	0.33	0.28
Belgium	0.99	1.00	1.01
Belize	0.01	0.01	0.01
Benin	0.01	0.01	0.01
Bhutan	0.01	0.01	0.01
Bolivia	0.01	0.01	0.01
Bosnia and Herzegovina	0.02	0.02	0.01
Botswana	0.01	0.01	0.01
Brazil	1.62	1.62	1.62
Brunei Darussalam	0.02	0.02	0.02
Bulgaria	0.10	0.09	0.08
Burkina Faso	0.01	0.01	0.01
Burundi	0.01	0.01	0.01
Cambodia	0.01	0.01	0.01
Cameroon	0.01	0.01	0.01
Canada	3.07	3.08	3.11

Member State	1995	1996	1997
		(percentage)	
Cape Verde	0.01	0.01	0.01
Central African Republic	0.01	0.01	0.01
Chad	0.01	0.01	0.01
Chile	0.08	0.08	0.08
China	0.72	0.72	0.74
Colombia	0.11	0.10	0.10
Comoros	0.01	0.01	0.01
Congo	0.01	0.01	0.01
Costa Rica	0.01	0.01	0.01
Côte d'Ivoire	0.01	0.01	0.01
Croatia	0.10	0.09	0.09
Cuba	0.07	0.06	0.05
Cyprus	0.03	0.03	0.03
Czech Republic	0.32	0.29	0.25
Democratic People's Republic of Korea	0.04	0.05	0.05
Denmark	0.70	0.71	0.72
Djibouti	0.01	0.01	0.01
Dominica	0.01	0.01	0.01
Dominican Republic	0.01	0.01	0.01
Ecuador	0.02	0.02	0.02
Egypt	0.07	0.07	0.08
El Salvador	0.01	0.01	0.01
Equatorial Guinea	0.01	0.01	0.01
Eritrea	0.01	0.01	0.01
Estonia	0.05	0.05	0.04
Ethiopia	0.01	0.01	0.01
Fiji	0.01	0.01	0.01
Finland	0.61	0.61	0.62
France	6.32	6.37	6.42
Gabon	0.01	0.01	0.01
Gambia	0.01	0.01	0.01
Georgia	0.16	0.14	0.11
Germany	8.94	8.99	9.06
Ghana	0.01	0.01	0.01
Greece	0.37	0.38	0.38
Grenada	0.01	0.01	0.01
Guatemala	0.02	0.02	0.02
Guinea	0.01	0.01	0.01
Guinea-Bissau	0.01	0.01	0.01
Guyana	0.01	0.01	0.01
Haiti	0.01	0.01	0.01
Honduras	0.01	0.01	0.01
Hungary	0.15	0.14	0.14
Iceland	0.03	0.03	0.03
India	0.31	0.31	0.31
Indonesia	0.14	0.14	0.14
Iran (Islamic Republic of)	0.60	0.52	0.45
Iraq	0.14	0.14	0.14
Ireland	0.20	0.21	0.21

Member State	1995	1996	1997
		(percentage)	
Israel	0.26	0.26	0.27
Italy	4.79	5.02	5.25
Jamaica	0.01	0.01	0.01
Japan	13.95	14.79	15.65
Jordan	0.01	0.01	0.01
Kazakhstan	0.26	0.23	0.19
Kenya	0.01	0.01	0.01
Kuwait	0.20	0.19	0.19
Kyrgyzstan	0.04	0.04	0.03
Lao People's Democratic Republic	0.01	0.01	0.01
Latvia	0.10	0.09	0.08
Lebanon	0.01	0.01	0.01
Lesotho	0.01	0.01	0.01
Liberia	0.01	0.01	0.01
Libyan Arab Jamahiriya	0.21	0.21	0.20
Liechtenstein	0.01	0.01	0.01
Lithuania	0.11	0.10	0.08
Luxembourg	0.07	0.07	0.07
Madagascar	0.01	0.01	0.01
Malawi	0.01	0.01	0.01
Malaysia	0.14	0.14	0.14
Maldives	0.01	0.01	0.01
Mali	0.01	0.01	0.01
Malta	0.01	0.01	0.01
Marshall Islands	0.01	0.01	0.01
Mauritania	0.01	0.01	0.01
Mauritius	0.01	0.01	0.01
Mexico	0.78	0.78	0.79
Micronesia (Federated States of)	0.01	0.01	0.01
Monaco	0.01	0.01	0.01
Mongolia	0.01	0.01	0.01
Morocco	0.03	0.03	0.03
Mozambique	0.01	0.01	0.01
Myanmar	0.01	0.01	0.01
Namibia	0.01	0.01	0.01
Nepal	0.01	0.01	0.01
Netherlands	1.58	1.58	1.59
New Zealand	0.24	0.24	0.24
Nicaragua	0.01	0.01	0.01
Niger	0.01	0.01	0.01
Nigeria	0.16	0.13	0.11
Norway	0.55	0.56	0.56
Oman	0.04	0.04	0.04
Pakistan	0.06	0.06	0.06
Panama	0.01	0.01	0.01
Papua New Guinea	0.01	0.01	0.01
Paraguay	0.01	0.01	0.01
Peru	0.06	0.06	0.06
Philippines	0.06	0.06	0.06
Poland	0.38	0.36	0.33

Member State	1995	1996	1997
		(percentage)	
Portugal	0.24	0.26	0.28
Qatar	0.04	0.04	0.04
Republic of Korea	0.80	0.81	0.82
Republic of Moldova	0.11	0.10	0.08
Romania	0.15	0.15	0.15
Russian Federation	5.68	4.98	4.27
Rwanda	0.01	0.01	0.01
Saint Kitts and Nevis	0.01	0.01	0.01
Saint Lucia	0.01	0.01	0.01
Saint Vincent and the Grenadines	0.01	0.01	0.01
Samoa	0.01	0.01	0.01
San Marino	0.01	0.01	0.01
Sao Tome and Principe	0.01	0.01	0.01
Saudi Arabia	0.80	0.75	0.71
Senegal	0.01	0.01	0.01
Seychelles	0.01	0.01	0.01
Sierra Leone	0.01	0.01	0.01
Singapore	0.14	0.14	0.14
Slovakia	0.10	0.09	0.08
Slovenia	0.07	0.07	0.07
Solomon Islands	0.01	0.01	0.01
Somalia	0.01	0.01	0.01
South Africa	0.34	0.33	0.32
Spain	2.24	2.31	2.38
Sri Lanka	0.01	0.01	0.01
Sudan	0.01	0.01	0.01
Suriname	0.01	0.01	0.01
Swaziland	0.01	0.01	0.01
Sweden	1.22	1.22	1.23
Syrian Arab Republic	0.05	0.05	0.05
Tajikistan	0.03	0.02	0.02
Thailand	0.13	0.13	0.13
The former Yugoslav Republic of Macedonia	0.01	0.01	0.01
Togo	0.01	0.01	0.01
Trinidad and Tobago	0.04	0.04	0.03
Tunisia	0.03	0.03	0.03
Turkey	0.34	0.36	0.38
Turkmenistan	0.04	0.04	0.03
Uganda	0.01	0.01	0.01
Ukraine	1.48	1.29	1.09
United Arab Emirates	0.19	0.19	0.19
United Kingdom of Great Britain and Northern Ireland	5.27	5.30	5.32
United Republic of Tanzania	0.01	0.01	0.01
United States of America	25.00	25.00	25.00
Uruguay	0.04	0.04	0.04
Uzbekistan	0.19	0.16	0.13
Vanuatu	0.01	0.01	0.01
Venezuela	0.40	0.36	0.33

Member State	1995	1996	1997
		(percentage)	
Viet Nam	0.01	0.01	0.01
Yemen	0.01	0.01	0.01
Yugoslavia	0.11	0.11	0.10
Zaire	0.01	0.01	0.01
Zambia	0.01	0.01	0.01
Zimbabwe	0.01	0.01	0.01
Grand total	100.00	100.00	100.00

2. *Resolves also* that:

(a) In accordance with rule 160 of the rules of procedure of the General Assembly, the scale of assessments given in paragraph 1 above shall be reviewed by the Committee on Contributions in 1997, when a report shall be submitted to the Assembly for consideration at its fifty-second session;

(b) Notwithstanding the terms of regulation 5.5 of the Financial Regulations of the United Nations, the Secretary-General shall be empowered to accept, at his discretion and after consultation with the Chairman of the Committee on Contributions, a portion of the contributions of Member States for the calendar years 1995, 1996 and 1997 in currencies other than United States dollars;

(c) In accordance with regulation 5.9 of the Financial Regulations of the United Nations, States which are not members of the United Nations but which participate in certain of its activities shall be called upon to contribute towards the 1995, 1996 and 1997 expenses of the Organization on the basis of the following rates:

Non-member States	Percentage
Holy See	0.01
Nauru	0.01
Switzerland	1.21
Tonga	0.01

These rates represent the basis for the calculation of the flat annual fees to be charged to non-member States in accordance with General Assembly resolution 44/197 B of 21 December 1989.

2. The Expenses of the Organization

Program Budget for the 1994–95 Biennium

Pursuant to discussions in the Fifth Committee on revised estimates for the 1994–95 biennium [A/C.5/49SR 20, 21, 32, 34–36, 38, 40, 42, 44, 47, 48] the General Assembly in part A of its Resolution 49/220, on revised budget appropriations for the 1994–95 biennium, resolved that the amount of

$2,580,200,200 (U.S. dollars) appropriated by it in its Resolution 48/231 A of December 23, 1993, shall be increased by $28,074,200 as summarized in Table VII-1. In part B of the resolution, the General Assembly resolved that, for the 1994–95 biennium, the estimates of income of $477,401,700 shall be decreased by $45,321,200 as indicated in Table VII-2.

In part C of the resolution the General Assembly decided that:

1. Budget appropriations in a total amount of $1,335,407,400—consisting of $1,290,100,100, being half of the appropriations initially approved for the 1994–95 biennium by the General Assembly in its Resolution 48/231 A of December 23, 1993, plus $28,074,200, being the increase in the appropriations approved during the 49th Session by Resolution A above, plus $17,233,100, being the increase in the appropriation for the biennium 1990–91 approved by the Assembly in its Resolution 49/218—shall be financed in accordance with regulations 5.1 and 5.2 of the Financial Regulations of the United Nations as follows:

    (a) $75,295,460, consisting of:
- (i) An amount of $33,018,750, being the net half of the estimated income, other than staff assessment income, approved for the 1994–95 biennium by the General Assembly in its Resolution 48/231 B, December 23, 1993;
- (ii) $2,826,300, being the increase in estimated income other than staff assessment income approved in Resolution B above;
- (iii) $37,468,110, being the balance of the surplus account as at December 31, 1993;
- (iv) $1,982,300, being the increase in income other than staff assessment income for the 1990–91 biennium approved by the Assembly in its Resolution 49/218;

    (b) $1,260,111,940, being the assessment on member states in accordance with its Resolution 49/19 B of December 23, 1994 on the scale of assessments for the years 1995, 1996, and 1997.

2. There shall be set off against the assessment on member states, in accordance with the provisions of General Assembly Resolution 973 (X), December 15, 1955, their respective share in the Tax Equalization Fund in the total amount of $167,334,119, consisting of:

    (a) $205,682,100, being half of the estimated staff assessment income approved by the Assembly in its Resolution 48/231 B;

    (b) Less $48,147,500, being the estimated decrease in income from staff assessment approved by the Assembly in Resolution B above;

    (c) Plus $2,501,819, being the increase in income from staff assessment compared to the revised estimates for the 1992–93 biennium approved by the Assembly in its Resolution 48/219, December 23, 1993;

    (d) Plus $7,297,700, being the increase in income from staff assessment for the 1990–91 biennium approved by the Assembly in its Resolution 49/218.

Table VII-1

Section		Amount approved by the General Assembly in Resolution 48/231 A	Increase or (decrease)	Revised appropriation
		(United States dollars)		
	PART I. *Overall policy-making, direction and coordination*			
1.	Overall policy-making, direction and coordination	37 049 800	168 700	37 218 500
	TOTAL, PART I	37 049 800	168 700	37 218 500
	PART II. *Political affairs*			
3.	Political affairs	67 923 600	(1 807 400)	66 116 200
4.	Peace-keeping operations and special missions	101 573 200	30 648 700	132 221 900
	TOTAL, PART II	169 496 800	28 841 300	198 338 100
	PART III. *International justice and law*			
5.	International Court of Justice	18 329 400	986 600	19 316 000
7.	Legal activities	32 490 000	(1 057 500)	31 432 500
	TOTAL, PART III	50 819 400	(70 900)	50 748 500
	PART IV. *International cooperation for development*			
8.	Department for Policy Coordination and Sustainable Development	50 355 600	1 201 000	51 556 600
9.	Department for Economic and Social Information and Policy Analysis	46 815 700	(589 800)	46 225 900
10.	Department for Development Support and Management Services	29 385 800	(3 424 400)	25 961 400
11A.	United Nations Conference on Trade and Development	108 296 400	5 283 400	113 579 800
11B.	International Trade Centre UNCTAD/GATT	19 982 200	960 100	20 942 300
12A.	United Nations Environment Programme	11 384 500	2 893 400	14 277 900
12B.	United Nations Centre for Human Settlements (Habitat)	11 854 300	3 322 200	15 176 500
13.	Crime control	4 638 200	201 500	4 839 700
14.	International drug control	13 998 700	695 200	14 693 900
	TOTAL, PART IV	296 711 400	10 542 600	307 254 000

Table VII-1 (continued)

Section		Amount approved by the General Assembly in Resolution 48/231 A	Increase or (decrease)	Revised appropriation
		(United States dollars)		
	PART V. *Regional cooperation for development*			
15.	Economic Commission for Africa	78 020 100	(6 362 500)	71 657 600
16.	Economic and Social Commission for Asia and the Pacific ...	59 846 200	1 432 200	61 278 400
17.	Economic Commission for Europe	44 684 500	2 694 800	47 379 300
18.	Economic Commission for Latin America and the Caribbean	79 992 600	(1 013 200)	78 979 400
19.	Economic and Social Commission for Western Asia	38 226 600	(3 013 500)	35 213 100
20.	Regular programme of technical cooperation	42 910 000	1 904 700	44 814 700
	TOTAL, PART V	343 680 000	(4 357 500)	339 322 500
	PART VI. *Human rights and humanitarian affairs*			
21.	Human rights	36 063 300	7 644 900	43 708 200
22A.	Office of the United Nations High Commissioner for Refugees	45 329 400	3 243 300	48 572 700
22B.	United Nations Relief and Works Agency for Palestine Refugees in the Near East	21 007 900	342 400	21 350 300
23.	Department of Humanitarian Affairs	18 541 200	493 500	19 034 700
	TOTAL, PART VI	120 941 800	11 724 100	132 665 900
	PART VII. *Public information*			
24.	Public information	133 145 300	(1 702 700)	131 442 600
	TOTAL, PART VII	133 145 300	(1 702 700)	131 442 600
	PART VIII. *Common support services*			
25.	Administration and management	876 856 000	19 964 800	896 820 800
	TOTAL, PART VIII	876 856 000	19 964 800	896 820 800

Table VII-1 (continued)

Section		Amount approved by the General Assembly in Resolution 48/231 A	Increase or (decrease)	Revised appropriation
		(United States dollars)		
	PART IX. *Jointly financed activities and special expenses*			
26.	Jointly financed administrative activities	26 192 800	1 028 400	27 221 200
27.	Special expenses	31 780 400	1 014 700	32 795 100
	TOTAL, PART IX	57 973 200	2 043 100	60 016 300
	PART X. *Staff assessment*			
28.	Staff assessment	404 949 000	(47 150 900)	357 798 100
	TOTAL, PART X	404 949 000	(47 150 900)	357 798 100
	PART XI. *Capital expenditures*			
29.	Technological innovations	18 841 500	6 556 800	25 398 300
30.	Construction, alteration, improvement and major maintenance	58 306 900	140 200	58 447 100
	TOTAL, PART XI	77 148 400	6 697 000	83 845 400
	PART XII. *Internal oversight services*			
31.	Office of Internal Oversight Services	11 429 100	598 600	12 027 700
	TOTAL, PART XII	11 429 100	598 600	12 027 700
	PART XIII. *International Seabed Authority*			
32.	International Seabed Authority	—	776 000	776 000
	TOTAL, PART XIII	—	776 000	776 000
	GRAND TOTAL	2 580 200 200	28 074 200	2 608 274 400

95th plenary meeting
23 December 1994

Table VII-2

		Amount approved by the General Assembly in Resolution 48/231 B	Increase or (decrease)	Revised estimates
Income section			*(United States dollars)*	
1.	Income from staff assessment	411 364 200	(48 147 500)	363 216 700
	TOTAL, INCOME SECTION 1	411 364 200	(48 147 500)	363 216 700
2.	General income	59 258 800	1 671 000	60 929 800
3.	Services to the public	6 778 700	1 115 300	7 934 000
	TOTAL, INCOME SECTIONS 2 AND 3	66 037 500	2 826 300	68 863 800
	GRAND TOTAL	477 401 700	(45 321 200)	432 080 500

95th plenary meeting
23 December 1994

In its Resolution 49/219, on questions relating to the program budget for the 1994–95 biennium, the General Assembly took the following decisions. In Part I, *Financing for the Expansion of the United Nations Observer Mission in South Africa,* it approved an appropriation of $19,266,000 under section 4 (Peacekeeping operations and special mission) of the program budget for the 1994–95 biennium and an appropriation of $1,464,200 under section 28 (Staff assessment), to be offset by income in the same amount under income section 1 (Income from staff assessment). It requested the Secretary-General to submit to the General Assembly a full final performance report relating to the final expenditure of the U.N. Observer Mission in South Africa and to the activities budgeted and implemented. It also requested the Secretary-General to include in the next report detailed financial statements of the Observer Mission and an inventory of assets, including information concerning their final disposition, and to assess the experiences and budget performance of the Mission with a view to formulating recommendations for similar future operations.

In Part II of the resolution, *Agreement Relating to the Implementation of Part XI of the United Nations Convention on the Law of the Sea of December 10, 1982,* the General Assembly, inter alia, approved an additional appropriation of $776,000 under section 32 (International Seabed Authority) of the program budget for the 1994–95 biennium, offset by a reduction in the same amount under section 7 (Legal activities), and decided that, should additional resource requirements arise, the General Assembly would consider whether to authorize the Secretary-General to enter into related commitments, as appropriate.

In Part III, *Human Rights,* the General Assembly, inter alia, decided to appropriate, on an exceptional basis, an amount of $4,473,000 under section 21 (Human rights) of the program budget for the 1994–95 biennium on the understanding that the posts requested by the Secretary-General in his report [A/C.5/49/53] for the Office of the U.N. High Commissioner for Human Rights, the Centre for Human Rights, and the U.N. human rights presence in Cambodia are approved on a temporary basis and that all these posts shall be subject to a detailed review by the ACABQ and by the General Assembly at the earliest opportunity at its resumed 49th Session. It also decided to appropriate an amount of $1,022,900 under section 28 (Staff assessment), to be offset by an increase in the same amount under income section 1 (Income from staff assessment); and requested the Secretary-General to provide justification for the establishment of the posts on a permanent basis and an explanation with regard to the observations and recommendations contained in the report of ACABQ [A/49/Add.6 and Corr.1] to the General Assembly for consideration during its resumed 49th Session.

In Part IV, *Revised Estimates Under Sections 3A, 3B, 3C, 4, 8, 15, 24, and 28 and Income Section 1,* the Assembly approved the continuation of six temporary posts for the servicing of the Security Council sanctions committees, with the related costs to be met from resources currently appropriated under section 3 (Political affairs) of the program budget for the 1994–95 biennium; decided to accept the redeployment of $576,600 from section 3 to section 8 (Department for Policy Coordination and Sustainable Development) for activities related to the international convention to combat desertification, as proposed by the Secretary-General [A/C.5/49/44], subject to review and adjustment by ACABQ and the General Assembly; and also decided to consider the remaining proposals of the Secretary-General at the resumed 49th Session on the basis of the report of ACABQ referred to in its report [A/49/7/Add.4].

In Part V, *Africa: Critical Economic Situation, Recovery and Development,* the General Assembly, inter alia, decided to accept the redeployment of $428,500 from section 3 to section 8 of the program budget for the 1994–95 biennium; requested the Secretary-General to review his proposals for additional resources in the light of the comments of member states in the Fifth Committee at the 49th Session and of the ACABQ, and to submit it through the Committee for Program and Coordination and the ACABQ to the General Assembly in the context of the proposed program budget for the 1996–97 biennium; and also requested the Secretary-General to prepare a draft budget section containing his proposals, for implementation during the 1996–97 biennium, for activities mandated under program 45 of the medium-term plan for the period 1992–97, entitled "Africa: critical economic situation, recovery and development," taking into account the views expressed by member states in the Fifth Committee at the 49th Session and those of ACABQ, and to submit it through the Committee for Program and Coordination and the ACABQ to the General Assembly at its 50th Session.

In Part VI, *First Performance Report,* the General Assembly approved a net decrease of $21,036,900 in the appropriations approved in the program budget for the 1994–95 biennium, and a net decrease of $49,085,100 in the estimates of income for the 1994–95 biennium, to be apportioned among expenditure and income sections as indicated in the report of the Secretary-General [A/C.5/49/43].

In Part VII, *Contingency Fund,* the General Assembly noted that a balance of $1,362,800 remained in the contingency fund.

Program Budget for the 1990–91 Biennium

Additional appropriations for the 1990–91 biennium as reflected in the Secretary-General's report [A/C.5/47/77 and Add.1 and Corr.1] and commented upon by ACABQ in its report [A/47/915] were discussed in the Fifth Committee at its 32nd and 36th meetings during the 49th Session. During the short discussion, the outstanding issue was the question of "supernumerary" staff, i.e., staff members who had remained in employment with the Organization despite the fact that there were no posts for them in the staff table. It was noted that this was a serious issue and posed the issue of budgetary prerogatives of the General Assembly and the importance of not presenting member states with a *fait accompli.* Consultations were held within the Committee in the interest of reaching a consensus, as a result of which a draft resolution was adopted for recommendation to the General Assembly.

The General Assembly, on the recommendation of the Fifth Committee, adopted Resolution 49/218, final appropriation for the 1990–91 biennium, without a vote. In its resolution, the General Assembly decided to appropriate for the 1990–91 biennium an additional $17,233,000 and to increase the estimates of income for the biennium by $7,297,700 under income section 1 and $1,982,300 under income sections 2 and 3. It also decided that the net increase in appropriations for the 1990–91 biennium, as approved above, shall be set off against the budgetary surplus available to member states for the 1992–93 biennium.

Program Planning

At its 48th Session, in its Resolution 48/218 B, the General Assembly decided to give the issue of program planning in-depth consideration at its 49th Session, and requested the Secretary-General to submit at that time a prototype of a new format for the medium-term plan. The proposed program budget outline for the 1996–97 biennium and the proposed new format for the medium-term plan were considered jointly at the 49th Session. The principal reports before the Fifth Committee were the report of the Secretary-General on the proposed program budget outline for the 1996–97 biennium [A/49/310], the report of the Secretary-General on the prototype of a new format of the medium-term plan [A/49/301] and the report of the Committee for Program and Coordination (CPC) on its 34th session [A/49/16, Parts I and II].

The medium-term plan provides the framework for the program budget. The usefulness of the plan as currently conceived had been increasingly called into question by member states. The CPC, at its 32nd session, recommended that a prototype of a possible new format be formulated; the Assembly endorsed the decision and requested the Secretary-General to submit such a prototype at its 48th Session through the CPC and the Administrative Committee on Administrative and Budgetary Questions (ACABQ). At the 48th Session the Secretary-General submitted proposals designed to obtain agreement on the principles by which the current planning system would be revised before developing a prototype. The General Assembly decided to request the Secretary-General to submit at its 49th Session a prototype of a new format of the plan that would take account of the views expressed at the 48th Session [A/Res/48/218 I.B].

The prototype submitted by the Secretary-General comprised a perspective and program framework for a four-year period beginning in 1998. The perspective would be a concise forward-looking policy document which would contain an analysis of persistent problems and challenges and emergency trends to be addressed within the next four to six years, and the role of the Organization in that undertaking. The program framework would list only major programs and subprograms and would provide guidelines against which the preparation and implementation of the budget would be assessed. The narrative of each program would consist of a brief one-page chapter detailing its objectives and mandates. The framework would be reviewed regularly every two years in the off-budget year in an effective manner to reflect new mandates. The plan would thus state clearly the Organization's strategic imperatives and would be amended only when a change in strategic direction was required. Should the General Assembly approve the proposed new format, the medium-term plan for the period 1998–2001 would be submitted to the Assembly at its 51st Session through the CPC and the ACABQ.

In its report, the CPC welcomed the proposed new format for the plan on the understanding that Annexes I and II to the report [A/49/310] were for illustrative purposes only; that relevant legislative mandates should be indicated in the narrative of the program; and that the narrative of the subprograms should reflect all the mandated activities. It recommended that the perspective strictly observe the balance between persistent problems and emerging trends, and stressed the need for all proposed revisions to be submitted to the relevant Main Committees of the Assembly prior to consideration by the Fifth Committee.

With regard to the latter recommendation of CPC, the representative of Mexico was concerned that in revising the medium-term plan, consideration had not been given to the legislative mandates supporting the proposed revisions and that the intergovernmental bodies concerned had not been consulted. The representatives of Cameroon, Uganda, Cuba, and other countries were disturbed by the fact that some Main Committees had not taken decisions on the proposed revisions, and suggested that the chairmen of the Main Committees be informed of their responsibilities for planning and programming. The representative of the Russian Federation welcomed the proposed new format, and was pleased that the emphasis would be placed on objectives and the means of attaining them rather than on detailed descriptions of activities and outputs as in the past. The representative of the United States welcomed the new and concise format of the medium-term plan, which should be a dynamic policy document reflecting evolving priorities. Establishing the perspective for a four-year rather than a six-year period would help to ensure that it was more in tune with current thinking. The program framework would take its cue from the overall perspective, and by reviewing that framework every two years, member states would be able to ensure that it reflected current priorities, which, in turn, would be reflected in the following biennial budget request. The representative of Canada, speaking on behalf of Australia and New Zealand, stated that the prototype did not represent adequate progress; program and subprogram objectives should be more precisely defined, as should the priorities, otherwise the measurement of output would continue to consist merely of a listing of activities, which would not permit their effectiveness to be measured. The representative of Norway, speaking on behalf of the Nordic countries, commented that as a framework for biennial budgets the proposed new format represented an improvement over the current medium-term plan. However, further improvement was possible regarding the description of expected results and planned outputs. The prototype did not fully meet the criterion that the framework identify the objectives and expected results of the subprograms to be achieved at the end of four years. The relationship between the medium-term plan and biennial budgets needed further clarification. The representative of Germany, speaking on behalf of Austria and the European Union, noted that the results with regard to the proposed new format were not completely satisfactory because the Secretariat had been unable to provide the necessary documents within a reasonable timeframe, which had greatly complicated the task of CPC.

Informal consultations in the Fifth Committee to reach a consensus resolution on this matter were unsuccessful. The Committee decided to defer its consideration to the resumed 49th Session. As of this writing, no decision has been reached on the prototype of a new format for the medium-term plan.

Pursuant to its consideration of the outline for the proposed program budget for the 1996–97 biennium [A/49/310], CPC recommended that the General Asssembly consider the preliminary estimates of resources submitted by the Secretary-General as a basis for its decisions, taking into account: (1) that the estimate should be adequate to permit the implementation of all mandated activities; (2) that the preliminary estimate was of a general indicative nature and the breakdown by major programs was illustrative; (3) that although the preliminary estimates did not contain provision for inflation or for anticipated effects resulting from currency fluctuations in 1996–97, consideration should be given to paragraph 7 of General Assembly Resolution 47/213; (4) that the preliminary estimate proposed by the Secretary-General had been prepared on a minimum-requirements basis and included provisions for which there was no legislative mandate yet and the financing for new mandates to be legislated by the General Assembly would be dealt with in conformity with paragraph 9 of Annex I to General Assembly Resolution 41/213; (5) that the intention of the Secretary-General was to conduct a review to achieve further efficiency gains; and (6) that the projected implications of General Assembly decisions contained in the outline would be reviewed and adjusted on the basis of actual decisions taken by the General Assembly. CPC also endorsed the size of the Contingency Fund, expressed as the percentage proposed by the Secretary-General, and recommended that the working of the Fund be kept under review.

The representative of the Russian Federation, welcoming the proposed outline, stated that for the first time the Secretariat had provided for specific measures for redistributing resources to activities of increasing importance. The representative of the United States welcomed the overall budget ceiling of $2,574,000,000. It was the first time the Secretary-General had presented a budget outline which proposed to do more with less. The representative of Canada, speaking on behalf of Australia and New Zealand, attached great importance to the principle of zero real growth. The Secretary-General had done well to strive to implement the principle in his preliminary estimates of resources to be allocated for the 1996–97 biennium. However, that approach should be applied on the basis not of appropriations for the 1992–93 biennium but of actual expenditure, which was now known to amount to nearly $36,000,000 less. Those savings should be factored into the 1994–95 performance reports, as well as into the 1996–97 program budget outline. The representative of Uganda, noting the anticipated negative growth rate of 3.2 percent of the preliminary estimates as compared to the projected revised estimates for 1994–95, urged the Secretariat, in making proposals on the draft program budget for 1996–97, to ensure that development programs, more particularly those relating to Africa and the least-developed countries, were not adversely affected by the projected reduction in resources. The representative of Mexico stated that it was unfortunate that certain functional activities were being accorded the same weight as substantive activities. While the Mexican delegation considered internal oversight services to be important, it was concerned that strengthening the budget for those services, as had been proposed, might make it difficult to ensure the necessary financing of the growing number of substantive activities.

The General Assembly adopted Resolution 49/217 on the proposed program budget outline for the 1996–97 biennium without a vote. In its resolution, the General Assembly, inter alia, invited the Secretary-General to prepare his proposed program budget for the 1996–97 biennium on the basis of the total preliminary estimate provided by the ACABQ [A/49/796] of $2,574,000,000 at the initial 1994–95 rates, recosted to $2,548,400,000 at revised 1996–97 rates and taking into account also actual expenditure data available for 1994; decided that the contingency fund shall be set at the level of 75 percent of the preliminary estimate at 1996–97 rates, namely, at $20,600,000; and requested the Secretary-General to submit, in the context of his proposed program budget for the 1996–97 biennium, information on the nature of expenses charged to the contingency fund thus far, as requested by the ACABQ in paragraph 10 of its report.

3. Review of the Efficiency of the Administrative and Financial Functioning of the United Nations

The restructuring of the U.N. Secretariat received considerable attention during the 47th and 48th Sessions of the General Assembly. At the 49th Session, pursuant to Resolution 48/218, various aspects of the issue of reconstruction of the Secretariat were addressed in the wider context of the agenda item on the review of the efficiency of the administrative and financial functioning of the United Nations.

In Resolution 48/218, the General Assembly took a number of decisions. Section IA dealt with the implementation of mandates and prerogatives relating to the timely and substantive dialogue and consultations between member states and the Secretary-General. Section IB was concerned with proposed revisions to the medium-term plan in the context of program planning. Section IC requested the Secretary-General to submit to the Assembly's 49th Session, through the Committee for Program and Coordination (CPC) and the Advisory Committee on Administrative and Budgetary Questions (ACABQ), an analytical report on all aspects of the restructuring of the Secretariat and its programs, including those relating to the U.N. Conference on Trade and Development (UNC-TAD) and transnational corporations. Section ID dealt with the number and distribution of high-level posts. Section IE requested the Secretary-General to include the following elements in the system of accountability and responsibility:

1. The establishment of clear responsibility for program delivery, including performance indicators as a measure of quality control.
2. A mechanization ensuring that program managers are accountable for the effective management of the personnel and financial resources allocated to them.
3. Performance evaluation for all officials, including senior officials, with objectives and performance indicators.
4. Effective training of staff in financial management and responsibilities.

The Secretary-General was to submit to the Assembly at its 49th Session through the CPC and the ACABQ a report on the establishment of the system.

Section II of the resolution dealt with the need to establish an enhanced oversight function to ensure the effective implementation of U.N. activities in the most cost-effective manner possible.

At its resumed 48th Session, the General Assembly, in paragraph 5 of Resolution 48/218 B, decided to establish an **Office of Internal Oversight Services** under the authority of the Secretary-General, the head of which would be at the rank of Under-Secretary-General (USG). The USG so appointed was to exercise operational independence under the authority of the Secretary-General and was to be an expert in the fields of accounting, auditing, financial analysis and investigations, management, and law or public administration. The new USG was to be appointed by the Secretary-General following consultations with member states and approved by the Assembly with due regard to geographic rotation. In so doing, the Secretary-General was to be guided by paragraph 3(1) of Assembly Resolution 46/232 in which it decided, as a general rule, that no national of a member state should succeed a national of that same state in a senior post, and that there should be no monopoly in senior posts by nationals of any state or group of states. The USG would serve for one fixed term of five years without possibility of renewal and could be removed by the Secretary-General only for cause and with the approval of the Assembly.

The purpose of the Office of Internal Oversight Services was to assist the Secretary-General in fulfilling his internal oversight responsibilities in respect of the resources of staff of the Organization through the exercise of the functions of monitoring, internal audit, inspection and evaluation, investigations, implementation of recommendations and reporting procedures, and support and advice to management. In this latter function the Office could advise program managers on the effective discharge of their responsibilities, provide assistance to managers in implementing recommendations, and ascertain that program managers were given methodological support and encourage self-evaluation. Any relevant reports were to be submitted to the Secretary-General, who would submit them to the General Assembly together with any comments the Secretary-General might consider appropriate. The Board of Auditors and the Joint Inspection Unit were also to be provided with the reports, as well as any comments of the Secretary-General, and would provide the Assembly with their comments as appropriate.

In paragraph 6 of Resolution 48/801/Add.2, the Secretary-General was requested to ensure that the Office of Oversight Services had procedures in place that provided for "direct confidential access of staff members to the Office and for protection against repercussions, for the purpose of suggesting improvements for programme delivery and reporting perceived cases of misconduct." Furthermore, in paragraph 7 of the resolution the Secretary-General was requested to ensure that procedures were also in place to preserve individual rights and the anonymity of staff members, and observe due process where all parties are concerned; that falsely accused staff members are fully cleared; and that disciplinary and/or jurisdictional proceedings are initiated where the Secretary-General considers them justified. In paragraph 8 the Assembly decided that the Office of Internal Oversight Services would be financed from appropriations approved under section 31 (Office of Inspections and Investigations) of the program budget for the period 1994–95. In paragraph 11 the Secretary-General is requested to submit to the 49th Session of the Assembly a detailed report containing recommendations on the implementation of the resolution as it pertains to internal oversight functions of the U.N. operational funds and programs, including methods by which the Office could assist such funds and programs in enhancing their internal oversight mechanisms. Finally the Assembly decided to include in the provisional agenda of its 50th Session an item entitled "Report of the Secretary-General on the activities of the Office of Internal Oversight Services"; it also decided to evaluate and review the functions and reporting procedures of the Office at its 53rd Session.

At the start of its deliberations on the review of the efficiency of the administrative and financial functioning of the United Nations at the 49th Session of the General Assembly, the Fifth Committee had before it the report of the Secretary-General on the establishment of a transparent and effective system of accountability and responsibility [A/49/1]; the report of the Secretary-General on the reconstruction of the U.N. Secretariat [A/49/336]; and other relevant reports.

In his report on accountability and responsibility [A/49/1], the Secretary-General stated that an integrated system should be based on the following premises: responsibility must be clearly defined; managers and staff must have the resources and authority to carry out their respective responsibilities effectively; and accountability must be established at all levels. This process-oriented approach is supported by strengthening accountability mechanisms and including a bona fide reward system to motivate staff at all levels, as well as sanctioning legitimate and viable administrative measures for nonperformances.

On the question of responsibility and authority in Section III of the Secretary-General's report, under part A, clear definitions of responsibility for achieving strategic imperatives were enumerated.

1. *Mandates and directives.* For a system of accountability and responsibility to be effective, the responsibilities of senior officials, directors, and staff at all levels must be clearly defined. There were two essential management tools available to the Secretary-General and his senior managers in this connection: one was the medium-term plan, which is the principal directive for the work of the Organization, and the other is the program budget, which provides an inventory of the outputs, services, and activities to be delivered during the biennium in relation to the resources appropriated by the General Assembly for that purpose. These two instruments have been recognized both by member states and by the Secretariat as requiring major improvement. As mandated by the Assembly in its Resolutions 47/214 and 48/218, a prototype for the medium-term plan was prepared [A/49/301] that provides more clearly defined and result-oriented objectives. As to the program budget, the budget instructions provided to guide program managers in the preparation of their submissions for the proposed program budget for the 1996–97 biennium were designed to achieve improvements in that document.

2. *Definition of the statutory and organizational framework of the Organization.* The legislative norms to which staff members at all levels are to be accountable must be "clear, unambiguous, coherent, comprehensive, duly promulgated, and available to both supervisors and the supervised. This is accomplished only if the established hierarchy of the internal laws of the Organization is recognized and respected. In this regard a review of the Financial Regulations and Rules is being undertaken for submission to the Assembly at its 50th Session. The revised text is to reflect developments in terms of how to deal, inter alia, with emergency situations and how to improve delegation of authority. The procurement process, and related management issues at Headquarters, for field missions and in the field were being reviewed by an independent high-level

group of procurement experts drawn from member states. A review was being made of the Staff Regulations and Rules with a view to creating a more coherent, simplified, and easily updated body of rules and procedures. A new format for the Organizational Manual would be developed by the end of 1994. The standards of conduct for staff members in international organizations are the subject of a report prepared in 1954 by the International Civil Service Advisory Board (ICSAB) and is commonly referred to as the "Code of Conduct." The report contains ethical guidelines for the conduct of international civil servants. An examination and updating of the report was being considered in the light of experience gained in its application over the past 40 years and in anticipation of new challenges the Organization will face in the future. The Personnel Manual, the Financial Manual, and the field administration handbook will be issued in a format that permits easier reference, retrieval, and updating.

3. *Provision of information and policy guidance.* While precise and comprehensive written instruments assigning responsibility are essential for providing a sound basis for a system of accountability and responsibility, policy guidance, information, and instructions should nevertheless be provided through ongoing communication between the Secretary-General and the heads of departments, offices, and main organizational units, between those senior managers and their directors and managerial staff, between directors and their managers, and with all staff. In this connection, a number of initiatives were taken by the Secretary-General during the past year. (1) The Secretary-General's Task Force on Operations was established, in response to the need for greater coordination and sharing of information and experiences between the departments responsible for action in the political, peacekeeping and humanitarian areas. (2) The Secretary-General decided to resume the practice of periodic meetings of senior managers in the economic and social field. (3) An advisory panel on Management and Finance was established consisting of all senior managers at Headquarters, the purpose of which is to discuss, inter alia, the modalities for implementing General Assembly resolutions and the development of a new initiative for improving efficiency of the administrative and financial functioning of the Organization, the medium-term plan, and the program budget. With the assistance of the Training Service of the Office of Human Resources and Management, workshops were organized throughout 1994 at the level of individual departments, offices, and main organizational units with the purpose of clarifying for each their mission, objectives, allocation of responsibility, priorities, constraints, and challenges. In addition, training is to be provided to all managers and staff involved in setting work objectives and translating them into concrete assignments and actions to meet the objectives and setting indicators to assess performance. Effective January 1, 1995, the entire staff was to be subject to a new work program-based performance appraisal system (PAS)

that emphasizes performance management, the issuance of guidelines, and the discussion of assignments and responsibilities by managers and supervisors and their staff.

The need for managers and staff to have the necessary authority and fully understand that authority, with regard to all available resources and relevant policies, directives, and regulations, for the effective discharge of their responsibilities is covered in Section III B of the report, and was comprised of the following elements.

1. *Information and available resources.* It was necessary that managers have access to all relevant information required for them to exercise their authority effectively. Through the facilities offered by the Integrated Management Information System (IMIS), once in place, directors and senior management staff, as well as heads of departments, offices, and main organizational units, will have at their disposal up-to-date and complete information on the resources available to them and how the resources allocated to their programs are being deployed.

2. *Delegation of authority.* In light of the reorganization of the Department of Administration and Management, the issue arises of the extent to which that Department's authority for managing the Secretariat's human and financial resources should be delegated to departments, offices, and main organizational units, both at Headquarters and in the field. It had become apparent that, to make day-to-day operations as effective as possible, a greater decentralization was required. It was cautioned, however, that it was important to achieve a proper balance between administrative decentralization and central control to ensure that decentralization would not result in the loss or weakening of coherent overall policies consistently applied. The USG for Administration and Management was establishing a working group to review the issue of delegation of authority at Headquarters and, based on preliminary findings and conclusions, the working group would study the situation away from Headquarters. As early as possible in 1995, and subject to decisions of the Assembly at the 49th Session, the appropriate rules and administrative instructions concerning delegation of authority for peacekeeping operations will be issued by the Secretary-General. In areas other than peacekeeping and field operations, starting in early 1995, a review of the Financial Regulations and Rules under article X, internal control, will be carried out on the basis of the findings of the working group on the review of the delegation of authority, with a view to submitting revisions to the regulations for consideration by the Assembly at its 50th Session.

3. *Empowerment of managers.* Individual managers must be empowered to make decisions not only on the use of approved and available resources, but also on the implementation of the programs and activities

at their level. They must be clear about their authority to make decisions and carry out their assigned responsibilities; and the expected level of performance must be specified, including the constraints under which the subordinates operate, the level of initiative required, and in many cases, the type of action required. Starting in 1994, departments and offices at Headquarters began preparing statements to define the authority of each manager as well as to elaborate the responsibilities assigned to them and the accountability measures for monitoring and controlling the implementation of their programs and activities. A similar exercise will begin in 1995 with respect to offices away from Headquarters.

4. *Training of program managers and supervisors.* To allow program managers and supervisors to utilize the full resources available to them, particularly through their staff, the Training Service of the Office of Human Resources and Management established a comprehensive training program emphasizing leadership, planning, managing financial and human resources, and the linkages between their responsibilities and the accountability framework.

5. *Training of staff.* The Training Service has developed a training program to update the professional and technical knowledge and skills of staff, with a view to providing the staff with the tools necessary to respond to the new challenges and perform diversified tasks efficiently and effectively as required by the changing work programs of the Organization. Similar training programs were being developed for support personnel for peacekeeping and other field operations.

Section IV of the report [A/C.49/1] is concerned with the question of **accountability mechanisms.**

1. *Reporting by the Secretary-General to intergovernmental and expert bodies.* Accountability starts with the obligation of the Secretary-General to report to policy organs on the implementation of the programs they have mandated. This is currently done by the program performance report, the medium-term plan, and the program budget performance report. The purpose of the program performance report is to apprise member states of the degree to which the outputs and services cited in the program budget are implemented, and to provide explanations for the changes that occur during the biennium. In its current form the report remains a largely mechanical summation of outputs and services that differ widely in their nature and significance, and is a heavily centralized exercise based on the review and tabulation of large volumes of data submitted quarterly by the respective program managers. It is proposed to make program reporting and monitoring less descriptive and quantitative and more of an assessment of the problems and results of implementation which could be achieved through the utilization of the findings

generated by the self-evaluation system. Guidelines are being developed to assist program managers in the implementation of activities and in assessing performance.

Because the in-depth evaluation studies take an average of three years to prepare and focus on relating programs to objectives set in the medium-term plan, they are usually very general and their usefulness as an input for subsequent planning and programming has been increasingly questioned. A more management-oriented and problem-solving approach to evaluation is being considered rather than one centered solely on objectives. The Secretary-General has proposed a drastic shortening of the evaluation cycles, from a norm of three years for a study to one year, and a substantially heavier schedule of in-depth evaluations to match the more intense cycle [A/49/99].

The program budget performance report that the Secretary-General submits to the Assembly through ACABQ at the end of the biennium should allow member states to verify that the expenditures of the Organization remain within the appropriations approved, and are incurred only for the purposes approved by the General Assembly. The presentation of the budget performance report has been revised to show projected expenditures by main objects of expenditure, on a basis allowing for easy comparison with the corresponding appropriations in the program budget. The analytical content of the report is being strengthened so as to present member states with a clear indication of the various factors that had an impact on resource utilization.

2. *Accountability of program managers for the implementation of management plans.* The successful implementation of the medium-term plan and of the programs of the Organization as defined in the program budget depends in the first instance on effective management planning by heads of the departments, offices, and main organizational units. The Secretary-General initiated in 1992 a practice whereby all program managers are required to prepare and submit to him management plans every six months. This practice has helped to clarify and sharpen the focus of the contribution of each organizational entity to the attainment of the substantive policy objectives set out in the medium-term plan and program budget. As to the monitoring of budget performance, new procedures were instituted within the central administration. In addition to the current annual review, detailed monitoring of expenditures against allotments is now carried out on a monthly basis with a view to providing greater understanding of the needs and performance of all units of the Organization.

3. *Staff accountability for the delivery of outputs and services.* Staff accountability as well as performance management will be greatly strengthened and facilitated by the application Secretariat-wide of the new PAS (work program-based performance appraisal system). During

1994, the PAS was to be tested in selected units of the Secretariat, the results evaluated, and appropriate modifications made to the system. The new system would begin in January 1995. The PAS set out the importance of having a structured, but balanced, awards system designed to encompass all levels of management, as well as staff, including the most senior program managers. Elements of such a reward/sanction system are already in the Staff Regulations and Rules, some of which are proposed in the PAS, and others are under discussion in such interagency forums as the Consultative Committee on Administrative Questions (CCAQ) and the International Civil Service Commission (ICSC). Until now, the elements in question have been imprecise, not necessarily transparent to staff, and scattered over a number of issuances and differing systems and processes. It is anticipated that by the end of 1994 a review will take place of the guidelines designed to ensure that administrative actions affecting the status or career of staff members will be more directly linked to performance. In addition, the USG for Administration and Management has established a task force to review the whole process by which career appointments are granted.

4. *Administration of justice.* The main observation of the task force created by the USG for Administration and Management pursuant to General Assembly Resolution 47/226 was that there is a need for an overhaul in the administration of justice in such a way as to reduce delays and streamline the numerous applicable policies, regulations, rules, and administrative issuances. A number of new measures were proposed by the task force for priority implementation in 1995. These include a complete reform of the administrative review system. Moreover, measures were proposed to encourage settlement through informal channels, such as through the office of an ombudsman. Finally, the existing system whereby the Secretary-General receives advice from the Joint Disciplinary Committee in disciplinary cases and from the Joint Appeals Board in cases of appeal against administrative decisions is to be completely revamped in order to create a more transparent and credible system.

5. *Development of the organizational oversight machinery.* A significant initiative toward strengthening accountability within the Secretariat was the establishment of the Office of Inspections and Investigations, an independent oversight mechanism, reporting directly to the Secretary-General, as a first step toward the establishment of a broader audit, evaluation, and investigation authority. The Office was established by the Secretary-General's bulletin ST/SGB/262 of August 24, 1993, and a detailed description of its functions is contained in bulletin ST/GB/268 of November 23, 1993, as well as a note by the Secretary-General to the General Assembly [A/48/640].

The Office of Internal Oversight Services was established by General Assembly Resolution 48/218 B and was to assume the functions prescribed for the Office of Inspections and Investigations as indicated in the Secretary-General's note [ibid.]. The establishment functions and modalities of the Office are described above in the introduction to this agenda item.

The report of the Secretary-General on the *Restructuring of the Secretariat* [A/49/336] provided an analysis and assessment of the impact on programs of the restructuring measures introduced by the Secretary-General during the past biennium. The analysis in the report focused in particular on the impact of the restructuring measures adopted at Headquarters and of the redeployment of activities and resources undertaken both to and away from Headquarters, which were acted on by the General Assembly in its Resolution 47/212 A. It did not review in detail later measures introduced in the various U.N. programs and entities and the regional commissions, which were the subject of separate reports to the concerned intergovernmental bodies.

In Section II, part A, Implementation of Restructuring, the Secretary-General's restructuring initiatives had distinct aims for three different sectors of the Secretariat: (1) in the political and humanitarian sector, the aim was to consolidate, streamline, and enhance capacity; (2) in the economic and social sector, the aim was to build linkages and rationalize and simplify the work of the Organization; and (3) in the administrative and management area, it was to integrate, minimize levels of management, and clarify policy and operational responsibility.

In the political and humanitarian area, the work of the Secretariat, which was dispersed in a large number of offices and units, was now consolidated in three departments: the Department of Political Affairs, Department of Peacekeeping Operations, and Department of Humanitarian Affairs. In the economic and social sectors, special emphasis was placed on a better integration of the economic and social dimensions of development, and on the elimination of duplication and the promotion of an integrated approach in the interrelated fields of trade, finance, investment, and technology. New Headquarters structures in the economic and social sectors were established around three clusters of functions: policy coordination and sustainable development; economic and social information and policy analysis; and development support. Significant relocations of activities both to and away from Headquarters were effected, including the integration into the new Department for Policy Coordination and Sustainable Development of the functions of the Social Development Division and of the Division for the Advancement of Women located at Vienna, as well as the functions of the World Food Council (WFC) secretariat at Rome, and the transfer to the United Nations Conference on Trade and Development (UNCTAD) of responsibilities for transnational corporations and science and technology. In the administrative and management area, the objective was to achieve through reorganization a more integrated, streamlined structure, with clear lines of responsibility. The basic elements of the new structure were now in place. The Organization's capacity for internal oversight services was also enhanced through the consolidation of all audit, inspection, and evaluation functions, and would be further strengthened through the establishment of a new Office of Internal Oversight Services, as mandated in General Assembly Resolution 48/218 B.

In part B of Section II of the report, a general assessment was made of the restructuring measures taken with regard to the three general areas. It was pointed out, however, that because of the rapidly changing context and the relatively short time that had passed since the process was initiated, an assessment of the impact at the present stage was bound to be somewhat tentative and limited in scope.

1. *In the political and humanitarian sectors,* the new structures of the Department of Political Affairs, the Department of Peacekeeping Operations, and the Department of Humanitarian Affairs now in place had enabled the Organization to respond more effectively to the unprecedented demands in the areas of preventive diplomacy, peacemaking, and peacekeeping, and has made it better equipped to address the challenge of providing a coherent response to complex humanitarian emergencies, the magnitude of which has escalated continuously in recent years. Thus, although the Organization's structures in the peacekeeping, political, and humanitarian areas have been streamlined and reinforced, a wide gap remains between the unprecedented needs arising from recent humanitarian emergencies and the Organization's capacity to respond. Although the Organization has done what it can to fill that gap, it is, however, ultimately for the member states to determine what the capacity should be.

2. *In the economic and social sectors,* a significant policy contribution introduced through the restructuring process has been to identify and clarify those economic and social functions which are best performed by the central secretariat. The resulting establishment of three new Headquarters departments, namely the Departments for Policy Coordination and Sustainable Development, for Economic and Social Information and Policy Analysis, and for Development Support and Management Services, is in turn contributing to a more focused and effective exercise of central secretariat functions. It is also providing the basis for an improved distribution of responsibilities within the Organization as a whole. Alongside improvements in the division of labor, the promotion of greater synergies between functions and activities was a main aim of the Secretary-General's restructuring initiative in this sector. It is, however, difficult to measure progress in that area, certainly in quantitative but also in qualitative terms. Measures are being taken to establish or reinforce internal coordination mechanisms. In addition to continuing consultations among the

heads of the three economic and social departments at Headquarters, periodic meetings of the executive secretaries of the regional commissions are held under the chairmanship of the Secretary-General, with the participation of the heads of the U.N. programs and entities. The measures of consolidation and streamlining introduced have made it possible to avoid potentially significant additional costs by enabling the Secretary-General to provide, by and large, within available resources, for major new mandated activities, including the secretariat capacity for the follow-up to the U.N. Conference on Environment and Development and the preparation for major forthcoming conferences.

3. *In the administration and management area,* the basic elements of a new streamlined structure in the Department of Administration and Management are now in place. The process of modernizing management practices still needs priority attention, with particular emphasis on the delegation of authority in both financial and personnel administration. The introduction of new management approaches will require a complete overhaul of existing rules and regulations. Training programs for staff need to be revamped. Initial steps have already been taken to improve the quality of training for senior managers and to expand training at all levels. The Secretary-General also remains committed to the establishment of an integrated system of skills training for all categories of staff, including staff to be deployed to peacekeeping and humanitarian missions.

The **impact of restructuring** is covered in Section III of the report [A/49/336].

A. *Political and peacekeeping and humanitarian functions.* In the past three years there has been an explosion in the number and size of U.N. peacekeeping operations. In 1991 there were some 11,000 military and 1,400 civilian personnel deployed on peacekeeping missions; the corresponding figures for 1994 were an estimated 100,000 and 6,500 respectively. Those operations have undergone major qualitative changes. The mandates of peacekeeping missions now may cover such responsibilities as disarmament and demobilization of combatants, coordination and even an active role in the delivery of humanitarian assistance, human rights monitoring, electoral verification, and direct support to governmental functions (e.g., civilian police). The main changes introduced in the structure and functioning of the Secretariat entities involved follow.

1. *The Department of Political Affairs.* The Department was established in 1992 to enhance the Organization's capacity to provide good offices and to conduct preventive diplomacy and peacemaking activities. It incorporated five former departments and offices dealing with political affairs and the servicing of a number of U.N. principal organs and subsidiary bodies. The Department was initially headed by two USGs, each

with geographically defined responsibilities and functions. With a further view to streamlining and consolidation, the two parts of the Department were merged a year later under the direction of a single USG, supported by two Assistant Secretaries-General (ASGs). The cooperation with regional organizations is entrusted to six regional divisions (two for Africa, two for Asia, one for the Americas, one for Europe). Each division is headed by a director who reports to one of the two ASGs. The Department also provides secretarial services to the General Assembly, the Security Council, the Trusteeship Council, and a number of related intergovernmental organizations. This function has been entrusted to two divisions, one for the General Assembly and Trusteeship Council and related bodies, and the other for the Security Council and its subsidiary organs, each headed by a director reporting to one of the two ASGs. As the result of restructuring, it has been made possible for the Center for Disarmament Affairs, previously headed at the USG level and supported by several directors, to carry out its established functions without adverse impact and to assume new responsibilities.

2. *The Department of Peacekeeping Operations.* The Department was established in response to the major expansion of the peacekeeping activities of the Organization, incorporating the former Office for Political Affairs as part of its first phase of restructuring. The staff resources of the Department have been strengthened and its internal structure reorganized. The transfer of the Electoral Assistance Division from the Department of Political Affairs to the Peacekeeping Operations Department has consolidated operational responsibilities in the latter. Two offices, headed by an ASG, have been created: an Office of Operations and an Office of Planning and Support. New units were established within the two Offices as well as in the Office of the USG. In 1993 came the Situation Center, which operates around the clock and is staffed mainly by military officers on loan to the Secretariat from member states at no cost to the United Nations. In late 1993, the nucleus of the Policy and Analysis Unit was established. The integration into the Department of the division handling administrative aspects and field operations in the Department of Administration and Management (the Field Operations Division, renamed the Field Administrative and Logistics Division) is contributing to more coherent planning and management of field operations. A Mission Planning Service was created, the staff of which participate in technical missions sent in advance of an operation's establishment, and they are involved in the initial phase of setting up in the field the missions they have planned. In order to provide the Department with the expertise required to provide effective Headquarters management of those activities, a Civilian Police Unit was established in 1993 (as of July 1994, a total of 1,915 civilian police officers were engaged in peacekeeping operations). In order to put the Department's capabilities on firm and durable foundations, there is a

need for further strengthening of the Department at Headquarters and for a marked streamlining in procedures for acquiring and deploying resources. The role of member states will remain crucial in this respect.

3. *Department of Humanitarian Affairs.* In accordance with General Assembly Resolution 46/182, the Secretary-General appointed an Emergency Relief Coordinator with overall responsibility for the coordination of emerging relief activities undertaken by the U.N. system. The Department of Humanitarian Affairs was established in 1992 through the consolidation of existing offices dealing with disaster relief and complex emergencies. The new Department absorbed the functions performed by the U.N. Disaster Relief Office, the Unit for Special Emergency Programs, and various other relevant units. Centralized mechanisms, established by the Department to strengthen the standby capacity of the Organization for emergency responses, include the U.N. Disaster Assessment and Coordination Standby Teams and the International Emergency Readiness and Response Information System. The Department works closely with the Department of Peacekeeping Operations and humanitarian organizations to address issues arising as the result of the widespread presence of land mines in countries requiring U.N. assistance. Recently the internal structure of the Department has been further reviewed in light of experience, and its capabilities for responding to complex emergencies were consolidated into a single, unified desk structure under a Complex Emergency Branch in New York. A capacity for addressing itself to those areas will also be maintained in Geneva. A number of other initiatives were taken in 1994 to strengthen field coordination capacities, develop a resource mobilization strategy, and enhance horizontal cooperation between humanitarian, political, and peacekeeping components of the U.N. system, which should reinforce substantially the system's ability to respond in a timely and properly coordinated manner. Although it is difficult to quantify savings generated by the restructuring, there is no doubt that the coordinating efforts put into place have resulted in economies.

4. *Human rights.* The World Conference on Human Rights, through the Vienna Declaration and Programme of Action [report of the World Conference on Human Rights, Vienna, June 14–25, 1993—A/Conf.157/24, Part I, chap. III] has provided the United Nations with clearly stated objectives and a framework for action in the field of human rights. One of the principal results of the World Conference has been the establishment by the General Assembly, in its Resolution 48/141, of the post of High Commissioner for Human Rights, with principal responsibility for U.N. human rights activities. A significant strengthening of advisory services and technical assistance programs is taking place, particularly in areas of building national human rights infrastructures, conducting free and fair elections, the administration of justice, and training law enforcement officials. The specific mandate of the High Commissioner, together with the provisions of the Vienna Dec-

laration, implies a significant reorientation and expansion of the U.N. human rights program in general, and of the activities of the Centre for Human Rights, under the supervision of the High Commissioner, in particular.

B. *Economic and social sectors.* In line with the approaches outlined in his note of December 3, 1992 [A/47/753], the Secretary-General initiated in 1993 a number of measures for the further restructuring of the economic and social sectors of the Secretariat, which were reflected in the revised estimates submitted to the Assembly at its resumed 47th Session [A/C.5/47/88], and acted on by the Assembly in its Resolution 47/212 B. That restructuring involved the establishment of three new departments at Headquarters, namely the Department for Policy Coordination and Sustainable Development, the Department for Economic and Social Information and Policy Analysis, and the Department for Development Support and Management Services. It also involved the redistribution among U.N. entities at Headquarters, Geneva, and Vienna of activities and resources in such areas as transnational corporations, science and technology, social development, and food security. The key objective was that the activities of the Organization in the economic and social fields should function as a single integrated program. The frequent structured meetings and consultations among the USGs in charge of the three new Departments, and the administration of the U.N. Development Programme (UNDP), have proved to be an effective tool in coordinating policy matters as well as carrying out specific tasks, such as the preparation of key policy documents. A task force was established in 1993 by the Secretary-General with a view to identifying substantive areas of activity that lent themselves to decentralization from Headquarters to regional commissions. With a view to improving the effectiveness of the development system at the country level, the Administrator of UNDP has been requested to assume overall responsibility for the strengthening of the resident coordinator system.

1. *Department for Policy Coordination and Sustainable Development.* The basic rationale for the establishment of the Department was set out in the report of the Secretary-General on institutional arrangements to follow up the U.N. Conference on Environment and Development [A/47/598] and his subsequent note [A/47/753] which referred to the desirability of a single streamlined structure that would provide a common framework for the provision of overall support to the Economic and Social Council on the one hand, and the Secretariat follow-up to the Conference on the other. Those interrelated functions focus on the analysis and synthesis of inputs and the provision of support for central coordinating, policy review, and policy-making functions. By placing them under common direction, a synergy is created, which contributes to both efficiency and overall policy coherence. The central focus of the new Department

is in providing support for the central coordinating and policy-making function, vested in the Economic and Social Council and its subsidiary bodies, including the new Commission on Sustainable Development, and in the Second and Third Committees of the General Assembly. Some of the features of the consolidation of the Department are (1) to establish a totally new work program and an entirely new division in sustainable development, including the servicing of the three new bodies— intergovernmental, interagency, and advisory—established to follow up on the U.N. Conference on Environment and Development; (2) the location in the Department of virtually all units transferred to New York from other duty stations (including the Division for the Advancement of Women and the Division for Social Policy and Development transferred from Vienna and the World Food Conference (WFC) secretariat from Rome), and the resulting weighty logistical, administrative, and programmatic considerations and responsibilities that devolved to the executive direction of the Department; (3) the assignment to the Department of the responsibility for the preparation of the World Summit for Social Development (March 1995, Copenhagen) and the fourth World Conference on Women (September 1995, Beijing).

The process of consolidation of the Department has only recently been completed. It was a rather complex exercise in view of the need to conceptualize and institutionalize the extremely varied mandates of the Department in a manner conducive to optimal effectiveness while avoiding excessive structural complexity and lengthy procedure governing the redeployment (including from locations outside New York), placement, and recruitment of staff, as well as the allocation of office space.

2. Department for Economic and Social Information and Policy Analysis. The principal responsibility entrusted to this Department in the context of the restructuring process was to enhance the role of the United Nations in the elaboration of economic and social data and in the analysis of development policies, trends, and interactions. In addition, the restructuring allowed for the mutual reinforcement of substantive and operations activities relating to population and statistics by assigning to the Department responsibilities for carrying out technical cooperation activities in those two areas. The overall impact of restructuring on the programs entrusted to the Department has been positive both in relation to its ability to identify new and emerging issues within its area of responsibility, responding to the information and policy analysis needs of member states, and in respect of the delivery of effective technical cooperation.

3. Department for Development Support and Management Services. The Department was established with a view to sharpening the focus of U.N. technical assistance to meet priority needs of developing countries and countries in transition in the broad field of governance and management, particularly institution-building and human resource development.

Through the incorporation of the Office of Project Services of UNDP as a semiautonomous entity, it was intended that the Department would provide operational and administrative services to developing countries with a view to strengthening their operational capabilities in the context of national execution. This has been a difficult and complex task for the Department, involving redeployment of staff and programs, adoption of the profile of its personnel to the new mandate, and establishment of working modalities that would reflect the new multidisciplinary approach that is to characterize its activities. The resulting dimunition of staff resources available, corresponding to 29 percent of the Department's technical and professional staffing and 32 percent of its total staff, was reflected in a low rate (47 percent) of delivery of program budget outputs for 1992–93. The delivery of technical cooperation projects, which constitutes the major portion of its activities, dropped less significantly (to 70 percent of the authorized project budgets in 1993, as compared to 81 percent in 1991). Despite these intervening difficulties, it was able to consolidate its new structure, which is now organized into two major substantive divisions: one dealing with management of the economy, social development, and natural resources and energy planning and management; the other with governance, public management, financial management, and capacity-building.

4. *U.N. Conference on Trade and Development.* The main objective of the deployment to UNCTAD of the programs on transnational corporations and science and technology was to reflect more effectively the growing interplay of trade, investment, and technology services and their financial underpinnings. Since the 1993 meetings of the Commission of Science and Technology took place before the effective transfer of the two programs to UNCTAD, the programmatic impact of the transfers for the 1992–93 biennium was quite limited. Following the approval by the Assembly in its Resolution 48/228 of the program budget for the 1994–95 biennium, the UNCTAD secretariat was realigned, taking full account of the relevant intergovernmental decisions of the resolution. A central feature of the realignment was the establishment of two new divisions, namely the Division on Science and Technology and the Division of Transnational Corporations and Investment. The heads of the two departments are at the director level, and their work is coordinated by the Deputy to the Secretary-General of UNCTAD. In addition, a common investment-technology advisory service has been established to tap the potential for synergies between the activities of the two divisions. An UNCTAD-wide reference service has also been set up within the Division of Transnational Corporations and Investment on the basis of the separate reference units of the transferred programs and the preexisting UNCTAD reference unit.

The evolution of UNCTAD programs, as well as the developments in the relevant intergovernmental bodies, justifies a generally positive initial assessment of the restructuring measures affecting UNCTAD. This preliminary conclusion relates to the substantive objectives the Secretary-General had identified for the transfer of the two programs and to some of the more general managerial objectives that have guided the overall restructuring exercise.

5. *Decentralization of the regional commissions.* The General Assembly noted in Resolution 47/212 B that the further reconstructing of the Secretariat in the economic and social sectors would, inter alia, entail the decentralization of the activities of the regional commissions, and stressed that such decentralization should be in accordance with the criteria agreed by the General Assembly and the Economic and Social Council on the basis of clearly identified relevant advantages. As indicated by the Secretary-General in his report on the revised estimates to the program budget for 1992–93 [A/C.5/47/88], and in the introduction to the proposed program budget for 1994–95, an interdepartmental task force reviewed possible decentralization measures to strengthen the regional commissions. Based on its recommendations, a redistribution of budgetary resources for advisory services was proposed for the 1994–95 program budget. Another area identified for decentralization related to the program on energy and natural resources, including water and minerals. Other activities mentioned by the task force, although not requiring significant reallocation of resources, would benefit from a more effective division of labor among global departments and programs and regional commissions. The Secretary-General intends to keep the question of improving the division of labor within the Organization in these and other areas under active consideration.

6. *Strengthening the U.N. presence at Nairobi.* Nairobi hosts the headquarters of the U.N. Environment Programme (UNEP) and Habitat, as well as other national and regional U.N. offices. For two decades the growth of Nairobi into a fourth hub of global activities, along with New York, Geneva, and Vienna, has been purposeful but not always fully coordinated, resulting in the development of parallel management and administrative structures which have at times detracted from the original intent of the Assembly in placing UNEP and Habitat programs in the same location. The separate administrative structures that emerged did not encourage collaboration and did not allow for full advantage to be taken of potential synergies and efficiencies. Several studies over the years have concluded that the creation of a central administration would eliminate duplication of services and redundancies in posts, ensure better use of resources, and improve the administrative support provided to other Secretariat functions requiring services at Nairobi. At the program level, enhanced collaboration between the two entities is producing better results in several areas. Close collaboration between UNEP and Habitat, and a

shared managerial framework, including common administrative support services, may be achieved in a way that strengthens both organizations without in any way jeopardizing the mandates and programmatic identity of either. Administrative reforms under consideration should contribute to a more efficient use of scarce resources and more coherent management, and also provide the foundation for a stronger headquarters center in Kenya and added visibility to the U.N. presence in Africa.

7. *United Nations at Vienna.* Within a short period of time, the U.N. entities at Vienna have gone through a number of major readjustments. Divisions of the Center for Social Development and Humanitarian Affairs were redeployed to the Department for Policy Coordination and Sustainable Development in New York; the Office of Outer Space Affairs, which was part of the Department for Political Affairs, was relocated to Vienna in 1993; and Responsibility for legal matters related to the Committee on the Peaceful Uses of Outer Space, previously shared between the Office of Legal Affairs and the Office of Outer Space Affairs, was transferred to the latter pursuant to Assembly Resolution 45/248 A. A Division of Administrative and Common Services was established in 1991 and entrusted, inter alia, with the responsibility for negotiating a rationalization of the joint common services shared by the United Nations, the U.N. Industrial Development Organization (UNIDO), and the International Atomic Energy Agency (IAEA), and in 1992 the United Nations and IAEA agreed that the Conference Services of the U.N. Office in Vienna would provide interpreting services to IAEA. An important decision, predating the reconstruction process, was the consolidation of three pre-existing drug control units with the U.N. Drug Control Programme. The relocation of the Office of Outer Space Affairs to Vienna has substantially improved cooperation between it and various national and international space agencies located in Europe, and has also opened the possibility of cooperation between the Office and the U.N. Drug Control Programme in integrating the use of space technology into drug control activities.

The restructuring of administrative arrangements at Vienna has not yet been completed, and there is limited experience in judging the program implications of the organizational adjustments. The consolidation process, including efforts to reinforce synergies among the various programs, was continuing in 1994.

C. *Administration and management, common services, and other activities.*

1. *Department of Administration and Management.* The reorganization of the Department was pursuant to a decision of the General Assembly [48/491] and was designed to achieve three strategic objectives: (a) a Department with clear lines of policy and operational responsibilities and accountability; (b) an integrated Department with constant interactions

between the constituent parts in order to permit budgetary, personnel, and other interrelated managerial considerations to be taken into account collectively in decision-making; and (c) a lean, streamlined Department with minimum levels of management consistent with the scope and depth of activity. In line with the first objective, the responsibilities of the USG and the three ASGs have been clearly defined. To achieve the strategic objective of an integrated Department, it has been decided to establish, at the highest possible level, a consolidated front office, comprising the USG and the three ASGs with supporting staff, in order to promote common planning, easy and frequent cross-functional communication, and a collective sense of accountability and responsibility. The achievement of this objective, namely a streamlined department, is reflected in the fact that there were 15 senior posts (D-2 and above) in the budget for the 1994–95 biennium compared with 19 for the 1992–93 biennium.

As the new structure of the Department has only recently been formalized, it is obviously not yet possible to assess its effectiveness.

2. *Office of Inspections and Investigations.* The Secretary-General established the Office in 1993 [ST/SGB/262] to provide comprehensive audit, inspection, and investigation services to the Organization. It was created as an integral part of the Secretariat but functioned independently in the conduct of its duties and responsibilities, and had the authority to initiate any audit, inspection, or investigation without any hindrance or need for prior clearance. Its activities were coordinated with the Board of Auditors of the United Nations and with the Joint Inspection Unit (JIU) with respect to the implementation of their recommendations and in order to minimize duplication of effort. The Office was created from a merger of the Internal Audit Division, the Central Evaluation Unit, the Central Monitoring Unit, and the Management Advisory Services. Pursuant to its establishment, the Management Advisory Services merged with the Internal Audit Division to form the Audit Control and Management Control Division, the Investigation Unit was formed, and the inspection function was added to the Central Monitoring Unit.

In July 1994, the General Assembly, in Resolution 48/218 B, created a new Office of Internal Oversight Services, replacing the Office of Inspections and Investigations, resulting in the introduction of a significant upgrading of capability and a more independent structure. The merger—of the offices responsible for internal audit, monitoring and evaluation, management assessment, and investigations—enables greater interaction among those functions and a more efficient use of resources. The increase in delegation of authority to regional commissions, coupled with the increase in the number and complexity of peacekeeping missions, requires a substantial increase in the audits of those overseas activities. Greater emphasis needs to be given to compliance audits to ensure that regulations and rules are complied with. The Office will establish appropriate policies and procedures for investigating reports of alleged misconduct, malfeasance, deliberate mismanagement, and abuses of violations of the U.N. regulations. Where necessary, it will address certain reports to program managers and will expect them to indicate corrective action taken or planned. The Department of Administration and Management has focused additional resources on the periodic follow-up to recommendations and findings of both the Office and the Board of Auditors in order to assure the Secretary-General and the Assembly of appropriate implementation of corrective action.

3. *The Department of Public Information.* Several reconstructuring measures have taken place in the Department with a view to consolidating and streamlining its activities. The transfer of publishing services from the Office of Conference Services to the Department has contributed to streamlining the delivery of print products and to gearing cost-effective production to the needs of specific audiences. The transfer of the Dag Hammarskjöld Library to the Department has proven beneficial in light of the Department's various audiences that are increasingly interested in the information services available by the Library. There has been a successful integration of 16 U.N. Information Centers with UNDP offices, resulting in a unified image of the United Nations in the field through enhanced information activities in all areas, including those relating to development, and a more effective interagency cooperation and the sharing of common services. The electronic access to information materials provided by the Department to various U.N. bodies has strengthened the outreach potential of the Organization. The function of providing secretariat services to the Committee on Information, the Joint U.N. Information Committee, and the Publications Board, as well as the representations of the Department at Interagency Meetings on Language Arrangements, Documentation, and Publications, has been centralized in the Office of the ASG. Finally, efforts have been made to reduce expenditures at some high-cost duty stations, which have led to successful negotiations for the release of the Organization from the contract at the current premises of the U.N. Information Center in London and the transfer of the center to a much less expensive, yet equally effective location.

Other reports before the Fifth Committee during its discussion on this agenda item were the two reports of the Joint Inspection Unit (JIU). One stressed the importance of strengthening and improving the effectiveness of the external oversight mechanisms [A/49/34]. The other was concerned with the review and assessment of efforts to restructure the regional dimensions of U.N. economic and social activities. The report of the Ad Hoc Intergovernmental Working Group of Experts [A/49/418], established pursuant to General Assembly Resolution 48/218 A on the jurisdictional and procedural mechanisms for the proper management of resources and funds of the Organization, after an in-depth study on the magnitude of alleged cases of fraud, concluded that the procurement for peacekeeping activities constituted a major area with the risk of possible fraud, given the high level of expenditures involved. The report of the Committee for Program and Coordination (CPC) in the second part of its 34th session [49/16 (Part II)], in its observations on the report of the Secretary-General on the establishment of a transparent and effective system of accountability and responsibility, proposed a new format of the medium-term plan, which would consist of a perspective and a program framework for a four-year period beginning in 1998. It also took note of the Secretary-General's recommendations in A/49/336 on the procedures and norms for the creation, suppression, reclassification, conversion, and redeployment of posts, and recommended further study by the relevant Main Committees of the Assembly at its 49th Session. The views of the Board of Auditors on the improvement of oversight functions were transmitted by the Secretary-General in his note A/49/471, in which the Board, inter alia, outlined measures it had taken to improve the quality of external audit work, and considered that its budget should be put on at least the same basis as that of the new Office of Internal Oversight Services, thus serving to reinforce its independence. The Secretary-General reported [A/49/301] on a prototype of a new format of the medium-term plan.

During the deliberations in the Fifth Committee, most delegations expressed appreciation of the efforts of the Secretary-General and the Secretariat to achieve a new system of accountability and responsibility. Some delegations, among them Ukraine's, observed that the time had come for a phase of consolidation without further major structural changes. The representative of China stated that consolidation of the restructuring measures, with no further major changes in the near future, would reassure the Secretariat staff and improve its morale as well as enable member states to make a comprehensive evaluation of what had been achieved. The representative of Cuba regretted that the report of the Secretary-General on restructuring [A/49/336] lacked the analytic approach required in the relevant Assembly resolutions, which would make member states aware of how the restructuring affected the implementation of various programs. The establishment of the Office of Internal Oversight Services was enthusiastically welcomed. It was generally agreed that the Office should be granted increased human and financial resources. The representative of Canada, speaking on behalf of Australia and New Zealand, observed that in national economies it had frequently been found that savings identified by such internal oversight could more than offset any additional resource implications. Her delegation as well as others agreed that the Board of Auditors' budget should be put on the same basis as that of the oversight office and be identified in a separate section of the program budget. The sharper focus being given by both internal and external bodies was welcome, and the wider coverage given to management issues and systems in the reports of the Board of Auditors was particularly commendable.

It was generally agreed that the new format for the medium-term plan recommended by the Secretary-General in his report [A/49/301] would make a considerable contribution to improved efficiency. The representative of Poland observed that the medium-term plan should be the Organization's basic strategic document, for four years rather than six.

The need for significant improvement in the contracting and procurement area was emphasized. The Secretary-General's proposal for an independent review of procurement processes was welcomed, particularly in view of the increasing costs of peacekeeping missions. The representative of Egypt stressed the need for international bidding and more openness in contract evaluation. India observed that the procedures for inviting and evaluating bids must be nondiscriminatory, the decisions of the Committee on Contracts should be transparent, and the roster of suppliers to the United Nations should be published periodically.

A number of delegations praised the efforts of the Secretariat to develop a performance appraisal system of rewards and sanctions. The representative of the Russian Federation remarked that the current performance system had resulted in indifferences and stifled initiative and creativity. On the question of much needed increased training of staff, the representative of Norway, speaking on behalf of the Nordic countries, and the representative of Singapore stated that training requirements should be adopted as part of the organizational development process, and the Secretariat should propose a plan for further training of all personnel, particularly in the management and financial area. The representative of Zambia underscored the importance of providing training to program managers.

The representative of Japan welcomed the efforts made by the Secretariat to change the Organization's "management culture." The representative of the United States remarked that the measures proposed for accountability and responsibility fit into the overall framework for management reform. The representative of Finland observed that the current management system should not be underestimated, and firm and persistent commitment on the part of the member states was essential for the successful implementation of the system of accountability. The representative of Canada stated that in the process of restructuring, the member states had sought a responsive Secretariat in which senior officials saw their role as one of serving member states and, at the same time, had expressed the desire to empower managers, giving them freedom to act and innovate within a framework of basic rules. Member states must, therefore, stop micromanaging the Organization and resist the urge to request endless reports and budget estimates.

Some delegations felt that the reforms made in the economic and social sectors fell short of stated objectives. The representatives of Tunisia and Kenya observed that the operating rules for UNEP and Habitat in Nairobi required further clarification. The representative of Uganda was concerned that development programs, including UNCTAD, UNEP, Habitat, and the Department for Development Support and Management Services, had the lowest rate of program implementation. While he recognized that a number of factors had contributed to the decline, it was logical to conclude that the restructuring had a negative impact on some programs, especially those concerned with development. Specific recommendations would be made to the General Assembly to ensure increased human and financial resources for programs and activities relating to the recovery of Africa and the least-developed countries, and the Secretariat should have the high level of enthusiasm and motivation on this issue that it had in the restructuring of the political, humanitarian, and human rights sectors. The representative of Benin echoed the concerns of Uganda and stressed that attention must be paid to the structures that needed to be set up in order to ensure the implementation of the strategies adopted by the Assembly for the U.N.'s New Agenda for the Development of Africa in the 1990s.

At the resumed 49th Session, the Secretary-General reported to the General Assembly on procedures in place for implementation of article III, section 29, of the Convention on the Privileges and Immunities of the United Nations, adopted by the General Assembly on February 13, 1946 [A/C.5/49/65]. In addition, the Secretary-General provided the General Assembly with a note transmitting a report of the Office of Internal Oversight Services on "investigation of allegations of irregularities and mismanagement" made by Frank Ruddy, former Deputy Chairman, Identification Commission, U.N. Mission for the Referendum in Western Sahara.

Administrative and Budgetary Aspects of Peacekeeping Operations

The reports of the Secretary-General on effective planning, budgeting, and administration of peacekeeping operations [48/945 and Corr. 1 and A/49/557] were introduced to the Fifth Committee by the Controller. He called attention to the fact that the number and size of peacekeeping operations had dramatically increased in recent years, and their cost had increased eightfold since 1990. The scope of mission mandates had also expanded, and there was a need for improvement in the quality of back-stopping, not only in terms of the work to be done by the Secretariat but also in terms of the commitment of member states to pay their assessments in full and on time. As of November 15, 1994, outstanding contributions amounted to $1.6 billion and the Peacekeeping Reserve Fund had been depleted. Assessment of member states was lagging as a result of the lengthy budget review and approval procedures, and late payments resulted in severe cash flow difficulties. Monthly expenditures for peacekeeping operations totaled some $300 million, and late payments by member states had prevented the Organization from reimbursing troop contributors.

The Secretary-General outlined three categories of issues which needed to be addressed: finance, personnel, and equipment; within those categories, eight priority areas were suggested for the Committee's consideration. The first priority area was **financial authority.** An increase in the Advisory Committee for Administrative and Budgetary Questions (ACABQ) commitment authority from $10 million to $50 million was proposed in order to avoid delays in implementing mandates given by member states. It was further proposed that, beyond that limit, the General Assembly should approve commitment authority for expenditures for at least three months of operation on the basis of preliminary estimates. It was also proposed that the General Assembly should authorize assessment on member states of one-third of the preliminary estimates of an operation, or the level of commitment authority—whichever was lower—prior to review and approval of the full budget. With regard to the second priority area, **the peacekeeping budget cycle**, it was pointed out that current procedures involving differing mandate periods had resulted in a large number of budgetary reports which overburdened ACABQ as well as member states, and that delays in the process, combined with late payment of assessments, were causing severe operational difficulties. The Secretary-General therefore proposed an annual budget cycle. As for the third priority area, **budget formulation and presentation**, the Secretary-General proposed that the presentation and cost estimates of budgets be standardized and the budget format simplified. The fourth priority area related to the need for an increase in the level of the **Peacekeeping Reserve Fund**. The Fund currently stood at $64.2 million, as against an authorization level of $150 million. The Secretary-General proposed that the Fund's level be increased to $800 million. With regard to the fifth priority area, **international contractual personnel**, the use of such personnel, especially in peacekeeping operations, represented an innovative approach toward alleviation of the acute shortage in civilian personnel in existing and future field operations. As for the sixth priority area, **death and disability benefits** for contingents, the Secretary-General sought the Committee's guidance on two options: one, to apply the policy currently used for military observers whereby reimbursement was limited to twice the annual salary excluding allowances, or $50,000, whichever was greater; or two, to maintain the current arrangements, whereby the troop-contributing state was reimbursed for compensation paid. The seventh priority area, **mission start-up kits,** would allow new missions to become operational in a timely manner prior to the approval of peacekeeping budgets. In connection with the eighth priority area, **contingent-owned equipment,** it was proposed that procedures be simplified through the preparation of standard depreciation tables, including standardized lists of equipment; that such tables indicate reimbursement rates depending on whether the United Nations or a member state was responsible for the maintenance of the equipment; and that tables should be provided to the General Assembly and included in the notes to troop-contributing countries.

In introducing the report of the ACABQ [A/49/664], its Chairman stated that a change in several administrative and budgetary aspects of peacekeeping operations was long overdue, and that the reports of the Secretary-General and the ACABQ offered a unique opportunity to consider that change. The ACABQ endorsed the measures taken by the Secretariat and those which were under way to improve mission planning. The Secretariat should be given broad guidelines and should have the opportunity to plan in accordance with the requirements of each mission as mandated by the Security Council. The planning exercise should enable the Secretariat to determine as accurately as possible the sum total of inputs and the related cost required to achieve mission mandates as decided by the Security Council. As for financing, the Peacekeeping Reserve Fund had been established to solve the problem of ready cash, but it had not lived up to expectations because of the long-standing problem of late payment of assessments. The ACABQ did not endorse the Secretary-General's proposal to increase the Fund. With reference to the Secretary-General's proposal to increase from $10 million to $50 million the commitment authority granted to ACABQ, the ACABQ felt that it could result in very large sums of money being committed under its authority and that, even though developments in the Security Council had not required ACABQ to authorize the commitment of large sums, it was nevertheless doubtful that member states would wish to increase so dramatically the authority currently granted to ACABQ. As to the Secretary-General's proposal for an assessment of one-third of the total estimates presented in the preliminary estimates provided to the Security Council in order to meet the "start-up" costs, it appeared to ACABQ that, given the varying needs of different missions, an across-the-board assessment of one-third of the total projected cost of each mission would be arbitrary and that, on the basis of recent experience, it would be unrealistic to expect the Assembly to accept either the preliminary estimate or the one-third assessment without discussion or debate. On the subject of the peacekeeping budget cycle, ACABQ agreed with the Secretary-General's proposal that the cycle should not be linked to the respective mandate period as approved by the Security-Council; missions with operational requirements not subject to fluctuations during the year should have annual budgets approved by the General Assembly. The ACABQ recommended that the budget cycle of all peacekeeping missions start on July 1 and end on June 30, and that 1995 be a transition year. The new budget and financial cycle should take effect July 1, 1996. With regard to the budget format and performance reports, it was pointed out that the usefulness of a budget document lies in its ability to facilitate review and decision-making. Many peacekeeping budgets did the opposite, largely as a result of demands by member states for massive amounts of data and statistics. The Secretariat's preparation of a standard cost manual should make future budget documents more user-friendly. Performance reports should be based on final data and not on projections. The introduction of the new budget and financial cycle should permit the preparation of true performance reports and allow in-depth review by ACABQ and the General Assembly. ACABQ endorsed the steps taken to strengthen the internal audit function in peacekeeping operations and, in particular, called for clearer guidelines with respect to roving finance officers and for the provision of management advisory services from within existing resources. With regard to the use of international contractual personnel, the way in which the pilot project had been implemented in the case of the U.N. Protection Force (UNPROFOR) and the status of international contractual personnel had raised a number of questions that needed to be addressed urgently before the procedure was extended to other missions. ACABQ recommended that an independent investigation and evaluation be undertaken and that future recruitment of such personnel for UNPROFOR or the extension of the practice to other missions be suspended pending the outcome of that exercise. ACABQ made no specific recommendation on the question of death and disability benefits, a matter which required a political decision by the General Assembly. It recommended, however, that the Secretary-General review the question of staff entitlements, including mission subsistence allowances. The concept of start-up team rosters needed further refinement, and practical ways should be found to ensure the full implementation of the standby arrangements for military personnel approved by the General Assembly as well as to ascertain from member states the circumstances in which they would provide troops and equipment requested by the United Nations. ACABQ believed that greater efforts should be made to obtain seconded personnel from member states. Problems relating to the valuation of and reimbursement for contingent-owned equipment had been a matter of serious concern to ACABQ for many years. It supported the Secretariat project aimed at setting comprehensive standards for each category of equipment; pending completion of the project, interim measures would be implemented. Finally, on the question of liquidation, ACABQ concurred with the Secretary-General's proposals, and an attempt should be made to reach agreement with governments for compensation for the residual value of surplus mission assets.

In the Fifth Committee there was general support for the recommendation of ACABQ that the level of the Peacekeeping Reserve Fund not be increased. It was felt that an increase would not be necessary if member states met their obligations in paying their assessment. An increase in the Fund would not significantly alleviate the cash flow problem and might merely increase the burden on those member states which meet their obligations. As to the question of death and disability benefits, it was generally agreed that they should be based on the principle of equal compensation regardless of nationality, with the adoption of a formula that would preclude any differences in actual payments to beneficiaries.

The representative of New Zealand, speaking on behalf of Australia and Canada, supported the proposal of the Secretary-General to assess up to one-third of the estimated cost of operations in order to cover start-up and expansion costs. They also supported the proposal to increase the commitment authority which ACABQ was authorized to grant, provided that caution was exercised and that an effort was made to achieve cost-effectiveness. Nigeria had difficulty in accepting an increase in the commitment authority, and had reservations concerning the assessment of member states at one-third, or any other fraction, of the preliminary estimates, as this appeared to encroach upon the authority of the General Assembly. Iran agreed that the present level of the commitment authority might not be commensurate with the cash needs for the start-up costs of a new or expanded mission, but it could not support so sharp an increase as the one proposed.

Australia, Canada, and New Zealand supported the proposals of the Secretary-General and ACABQ to annualize estimates on a July/June basis. They did not, however, agree with ACABQ that 1995 should be a transitional year, but rather believed that the new cycle should be introduced from July 1, 1995, at least in respect of those operations for which budgets had not yet been considered. They fully concurred with the Secretary-General's proposal for a new, more user-friendly budget format based on standardized cost modules and ratios containing a uniform set of annexes, and agreed with ACABQ that performance reports should be based on actual expenditure. The representative of the United States supported efforts to improve performance reporting; timely reliable data on how funds were actually spent were of enormous help for future spending decisions. A computerized system linking operations in the field and Headquarters was required to collect and transmit such data. A number of delegations, including Argentina, Austria, the European Union, the Russian Federation, Norway, and Thailand, supported the Secretary-

General's proposal on annual budgets. Besides reducing the work of preparing documentation, it would also enable member states to schedule payment of their contribution effectively and this would, in turn, reduce the cash flow problem.

The representative of the Russian Federation fully shared the Secretary-General's view that the current procedures for reimbursement of contingent-owned equipment were cumbersone, time-consuming, and expensive, and supported the proposals to change the procedures and set comprehensive standards for each category of equipment. Military experts might usefully be invited to participate in the process, and other alternatives—such as a system of rental fees for different categories of equipment, including delivery to and from the designated area, maintenance, spare parts, and insurance—should not be excluded. The representative of Norway commented that it was a "vexatious" issue which should be given priority. The Nordic countries endorsed the Secretary-General's proposal for a standardized project. As a troop-contributing country, Thailand stated that it was well aware of the shortcomings of current procedures for reimbursement for contingent-owned equipment, and agreed with the Secretary-General that the process should be simplified by developing standard tables of depreciation rates.

The representative of the United States believed that the concept of using international contractual personnel had merit in that it offered the potential advantages of more rapid deployment of support staff and lower cost; an evaluation should be undertaken by the Office of Internal Oversight Services, and efforts should then be made to correct the problems that had been identified. The representative of Nigeria stated that since no two operations were identical, international contractual personnel who had served in one operation should not automatically be considered for other operations. Given the limited geographical representation in that category of personnel, his delegation called for a prompt investigation by the Office of Internal Oversight Services into current recruitment. Regarding the deployment of international contractual personnel in UN-PROFOR, the European Union and Austria could not endorse the ACABQ's recommendation that further recruitment of such personnel be suspended; a suspension could have adverse effects on the operation, and make it more difficult to ensure that a maximum of troops perform core peacekeeping tasks. Egypt, on the other hand, endorsed the ACABQ's recommendation and was generally concerned over the irregular recruitment procedure and contractual arrangements for such personnel; their use could lead to the creation of parallel systems of recruitment outside established U.N. rules and regulations, and would not be subject to geographical representation or the principle of equal pay for equal work. The representative or Kenya shared the concerns of ACABQ with regard to international contractual personnel, and felt that the "back-door" entry to the U.N. system must also be addressed. There was need for transparency in connection with such recruitment, which must respect the principle of equitable geographical distribution.

The representative of India welcomed the proposals for strengthening internal audit functions and agreed that the use of resident auditors should be decided on a case-by-case basis. The Philippines shared the concern of ACABQ regarding the use of resident auditors and believed that the Board of Auditors should continue its coverage of peacekeeping operations and report separately on large operations like UNPROFOR. A number of delegations felt that the interpretation placed by ACABQ on the inclusion of humanitarian assistance in peacekeeping budgets was too narrow, and stressed the need to maintain the separate identity of each. The representative of Kenya welcomed the Secretary-General's acknowledgment of the crucial role played by neighboring countries in providing essential logistical support and his recommendation that the General Assembly give consideration to "good neighbor" agreements with countries neighboring a mission area. The United States and the Russian Federation drew attention to the lack of detailed information on the methodology for the determination of mission subsistence allowance rates. The Secretary-General should carry out a complete review of the subsistence allowance system, which should be comprehensive and transparent and take due account of the authority of the Secretary-General to assign staff to any U.N activity or office in the world.

The report of the Secreatry-General on the support account for peacekeeping operations [A/49/717 and Corr.1] indicated the criteria for deciding which support activities should be funded from the regular budget and which from the support account, the extent to which the regular budget was already providing support, and the threshold for establishing core posts to be funded from the regular budget. It was the Secretary-General's wish to increase the Secretariat's capacity to provide back-stopping for the increased level of peacekeeping activities. The total number of posts required in the support account for back-stopping functions had been estimated at 630. However, the current funding of the support account under the peacekeeping budget represented 8.5 percent of the civilian component costs of peacekeeping operations. It was estimated that the 1995 level of the account would be the same as in 1994; it was therefore proposed that 431 posts, including the conversion of 65 posts currently under general temporary assistance and an additional 24 posts, be funded from the support account in 1995. In its related report [A/49/778], the ACABQ stated that the General Assembly had already authorized the financing of 342 posts from the support account, while ACABQ had previously recommended the establishment of 60 additional posts, which, with the addition of 5 posts by ACABQ and the Fifth Committee as general temporary assistance, made a total of 407 posts. The ACABQ recommended that the General Assembly should, for the period January 1 to June 30, 1995, authorize funding of $14,105,900 from the support account in respect of those posts.

Pursuant to the report of the Fifth Committee [A/49/803/Add.1] the General Assembly adopted a 14-part Resolution 49/233 on the administrative and budgetary aspects of the financing of the U.N. peacekeeping operations. In part I, **budget cycles,** the General Assembly decided that the financial period for each peacekeeping operation shall be from July 1 to June 30, and requested the Secretary-General to submit the necessary draft amendments to Financial Regulations for approval by the Assembly at its resumed 49th Session; decided that for peacekeeping operations with budgetary requirements not subject to fluctuation there would be consideration and approval of a budget once a year and that for other peacekeeping operations, budget estimates would be considered and approved by the Assembly twice a year, i.e., for the periods July 1 to December 31 and January 1 to June 30; urged the Secretary-General to submit, in the context of the consideration of peacekeeping budget estimates, the related performances report for each operation for the previous financial period, together with such supplementary, up-to-date financial performance data for the current period as are available; decided that the assessments on member states of appropriations approved by the General Assembly for peacekeeping operations are subject to the approval of mandates by the Security Council; and requested the Secretary-General to submit twice a year to the General Assembly a table summarizing the proposed budgetary requirements of each operation for the period July 1 to June 30, including a breakdown of expenditures by major line item and the aggregate total resource requirement.

Part II, **contingent-owned equipment,** authorized the Secretary-General to proceed with the project outlined in the annex to the resolution, which is aimed at setting comprehensive standards for each category of equipment, as well as establishing rates of reimbursement, on the understanding that member states, in particular troop-contributing countries, will be invited by the Secretary-General to participate in the process, and that proposals for establishing new rates of reimbursement will be submitted to the General Assembly for approval.

Part III, **death and disability benefits,** decided that underlying any system of compensation for death and disability should be the need for equal treatment of member states, compensation to the beneficiary that is not lower than reimbursement by the United Nations, simplification of administrative arrangements to the extent possible, and speedy settlement of claims; requested the Secretary-General to submit concrete proposals, based on these principles, on possible revisions to the current compensation arrangements, including detailed information on the administrative and financial implications; and also requested the Secretary-General to submit these proposals to the Assembly through the ACABQ by May 31, 1995.

Part IV, **financial authority,** decided that, if a decision of the Security Council relating to the start-up phase or expansion phase of peacekeeping operations results in the need for expenditure, the Secretary-General is authorized, with the prior concurrence of ACABQ and subject to Financial Regulations, to enter into commitments not to exceed US$50 million per decision of the Security Council. The cumulative total of outstanding commitment authority, in respect of the start-up expansion phase of operations, was not to exceed $150 million at any one time; however, appropriation by the Assembly of any outstanding commitments shall automatically restore the balance of the limit of $150 million to the extent of the amount appropriated. Part IV also decided that, if a decision of the Security Council results in the need for the Secretary-General to enter into commitments for the start-up or expansion phase of operations in an account exceeding $50 million, per decision of the Security Council, or exceeding the total of $150 million, the matter shall be brought to the General Assembly, as soon as possible, for a decision on commitment authority and assessment; decided further that the question of assessment of an appropriate amount of the costs relating to the start-up and expansion phases of peacekeeping operations shall be considered by the Assembly at its 50th Session in the light of experience gained from the implementation of the resolution; and resolved that the Secretary-General of the resolution; and resolved that the Secretary-General and the ACABQ shall report to the Assembly on any exercise of the commitment authority given under the provisions of the resolution, together with the circumstances relating thereto, in the context of the next report submitted to the Assembly on the financing of the relevant peacekeeping operation.

Part V, **host country agreements,** requested the Secretary-General to include in his reports to the Assembly on the financing of each operation or mission information related to the status of the negotiation of the host country agreement and its implementation insofar as it relates to the administration of the peacekeeping operation.

Part VI, **international contractual personnel,** decided that pending the outcome of the investigation and evaluation and the decision by the Assembly on the use of international contractual personnel in UNPROFOR, the pilot project for the use of international contractual personnel shall not be extended beyond UNPROFOR.

Part VII, **liquidation,** requested the Secretary-General to report to the General Assembly no later than March 31, 1995, on the feasibility of procedures for valuation and transfer of costs for assets to be redeployed from a peacekeeping operation during its liquidation phase to other peacekeeping operations or other U.N. bodies, and for reimbursement to the special account for the liquidating operation as expeditiously as possible.

Part VIII, **mission subsistence allowance,** requested the Secretary-General to review the entitlements of staff assigned to field missions, including the purpose of and basis for the establishment of a mission subsistence allowance, and to submit a report thereon to the Assembly at its 50th Session.

Part IX, **review of the Office of Internal Oversight Services,** requested the Secretary-General to direct the Office of Internal Oversight Services to undertake an inspection of the units within the Secretariat responsible for logistical, operational, and administrative arrangements in peacekeeping and other field operations, with a view to identifying problems and recommending measures to enhance the efficient utilization of resources, and to report thereon to the Assembly at its resumed 49th Session.

Part X, **oversight,** requested the Secretary-General to examine alternative methods for enhancing the audit functions in peacekeeping operations that will not have resident auditors, and their relative costs, and to make proposals to the Assembly by the 50th Session; and endorsed the recommendations of ACABQ with respect to the concepts of a roving finance officer and a management review officer, and requested the Secretary-General to clarify further those concepts, as well as the accountability of program managers, in a report to the Assembly by its 50th Session.

Part XI, **Peacekeeping Reserve Fund,** decided to maintain the Peacekeeping Reserve Fund at its present level at the present stage.

Part XII, **rotation of troops,** requested the Secretary-General, given the operational implications of the question of the tours of duty of contingents, to submit the report referred to in paragraph 77 of the report of ACABQ to the Special Committee on Peacekeeping Operations.

Part XIII, **standardization of the budget process and format,** welcomed the development of the Standard Cost Manual and requested the Secretary-General to provide it with a mock-up budget for a single peacekeeping operation, based on the manual, taking into account the comments of ACABQ and the views expressed by member states; and requested the ACABQ to review the proposed manual and the mock-up budget by August 31, 1995, with a view to submitting its views on them to the Assembly at its 50th Session.

Part XIV, **start-up kits,** endorsed the request of ACABQ for a detailed report—including further information regarding the financial and personnel arrangements, cost parameters, legislative justification, issues of ownership and inventory control of stocked equipment, accounting procedures, and alternatives for mission start-up kits, as well as on the use of the Brindisi logistics base for storage and maintenance—to be submitted to the Assembly before the end of the 49th Session.

The General Assembly also decided [49/470], with reference to the re-location of Belarus and Ukraine to the group of member states set out in paragraph 3(c) of General Assembly Resolution 43/232, to consider, as an exceptional measure, any arrears of Belarus and Ukraine as at January 1, 1995, and for 1995 in the financing of peacekeeping operations, as being due to conditions beyond their control and, accordingly, that the question of the applicability of Article 19 of the Charter of the United Nations relating to the loss of voting rights in the Assembly in this respect would not arise. It called upon Belarus and Ukraine to prepare during the re-sumed 49th Session proposals for the treatment of their arrears concern-ing the financing of peacekeeping operations.

Budgets of Peacekeeping Operations

During the regular 49th Session and the resumed 49th Session of the General Assembly, commitments were provided (see Table VII-3) for the following operations: the U.N. Disengagement Observer Force (UNDOF); the U.N. Angola Verification Mission (UNAVEM); the U.N. Observer Mission in El Salvador (ONUSAL); the U.N. Protection Force (UN-PROFOR—in the former Yugoslavia); the U.N. Operation in Somalia (UNOSOM); the U.N. Peacekeeping Force in Cyprus (UNFICYP); the U.N. Assistance Mission for Rwanda (UNAMIR); the U.N. Interim Force in Lebanon (UNIFIL); the U.N. Iraq-Kuwait Observation Mission (UNIKOM); the U.N. Observer Mission in Georgia (UNOMIG); the U.N. Mission in Haiti (UNMIH); the U.N. Observer Mission in Liberia (UNOMIL); the U.N. Operation in Mozambique (UNOMOZ); the U.N.

Table VII-3
Peacekeeping: Commitment Authority

Operation	$ (gross)	Period
UNDOF	2,677,583 per month	6/1–11/30/95
ONUSAL	5,643,700 total	9/16–11/30/94
UNAVEM	3,500,000 per month	2/9–5/8/95
UNPROFOR	134,731,500 per month	4/1–6/30/95
UNOSOM	253,704,400 total	10/1/94–2/28/95
UNFICYP	11,316,600*	1/1–6/30/95
UNAMIR	140,000,000 total	12/10/94–6/9/95
UNIFIL	67,407,000 total	2/1–7/31/95
UNIKOM	4,000,000*	4/1–6/30/95
UNOMIG	1,720,000 per month	1/13–7/12/95
UNMIH	151,545,100 total	2/1–7/31/95
UNOMIL	1,593,800 per month	1/13–7/12/95
UNOMOZ	40,000,000 total	11/16/94–3/31/95
UNMOT	3,251,200 per month	12/16/94–4/26/95
MINURSO	5,400,000 total	1/95

* Net of voluntary contributions.

Mission of Observers in Tajikistan (UNMOT); and the U.N. Mission for the Referendum in Western Sahara (MINURSO).

4. Staffing and Administration

Human Resources Management

At the start of the deliberations on this item in the Fifth Committee [A/C.5/49/SR.15], the USG for Administrative and Budgetary Questions said that the Organization was facing serious problems in terms of the morale, capability, and dedication of its staff, and that in order to address those problems it was necessary to rekindle in every staff member a sense of pride in serving the United Nations. To that end, management must be improved and staff development encouraged. That would involve a change in the management culture and in the system of justice, from adversarial to supportive. On a positive note, the current strategy to reform human resources management and the system of administration of justice had the support of the staff and a good beginning had been made. The reports before the Committee represented the first step in remedying management shortcomings and in developing the Organization's main asset—its staff.

The ASG for Human Resources Management introduced the report of the Secretary-General on the composition of the Secretariat [A/49/527], which indicated a decrease in the number of both unrepresented and over-represented countries, with a corresponding increase in the number of member states within range. The report on the improvement of the status of women in the Secretariat [A/49/587] reflected the progress toward the achievement of gender balance and outlined initiatives required to achieve the goals set by the Secretary-General. The report on staff training [A/49/445] provided a retrospective of the activities of the Office of Human Resources Management (OHRM) during the reporting period. The report on the reform of the internal system of justice [A/C.5/49/13] set out a series of steps to address the current inadequacies of the system.

The ASG stated that the strategy for human resources management identified a series of interrelated initiatives for improving management in the Secretariat. The key elements were human resources planning, career management, development of a responsive management culture, good staff-management relations, performance appraisal, enhanced attrition, and delegation of authority to program managers. The strategy also included greater use of a buyout/early retirement option to enable management to better satisfy needs for greater staff turnover, skill reengineering, enhanced manager leadership, and morale building.

The ASG for Conference and Support Services and U.N. Security

Coordination stated that the report in respect of the privileges and immunities of officials of the United Nations and the Specialized Agencies and related organizations [A/C.5/49/6 and Add.1 and Corr.1] was submitted by the Secretary-General on behalf of and with the approval of the Administrative Committee on Coordination (ACC). It covered the period from July 1, 1993 to June 30, 1994, but all cases involving the death of a staff member up to October 3, 1994 had been included. There was serious concern about the safety and security of staff members because in some countries their work for the United Nations meant that they were the targets of attack. The issue was one of paramount importance since the United Nations was conducting an increasing number of complicated operations, often in a hostile environment. If staff members were willing to risk their lives to achieve the goals of the Organization, they must be fully protected. Annex III to the report contained detailed information about the arrest and detention of officials, and annex II contained a consolidated list of staff members who were under arrest or detention or were missing as at June 30, 1994. Respect for the privileges and immunities of U.N. officials was one of the paramount conditions for the effective exercise of the responsibilities entrusted to U.N. organizations by member states.

A representative of the Joint Inspection Unit (JIU) said the report of JIU on the advancement of the status of women in the Secretariat [A/49/176] reviewed action taken to eliminate bias against women and establish and maintain gender equity in the Secretariat, and focused on the opportunity to improve the status and advancement of women under the new policies of greater transparency and accountability and strategic management of human resources. The report also summarized the disappointing history of the efforts to enhance the role of women and examined the failure to overcome the obstacles thereto in the light of the new policy initiatives. The extensive tables and statistics contained in the report painted a gloomy picture. The Steering Committee for the Improvement of the Status of Women in the Secretariat had concluded in 1991 that the Secretariat had fallen far short of its obligations to gender equity. That conclusion remained true in 1994. Three of the JIU recommendations for improving the status of women in the Secretariat dealt with dynamic human resources management. First, the Secretary-General was urged to continue the comprehensive report on personnel matters appearing in document A/C.5/49/5 as a biennial human resources report. The second recommendation called for strengthening the OHRM, and the third called on the Secretary-General to ensure that future reporting on human resources reflects greater accountability and follow-up. The fourth recommendation recognized that those measures were not sufficient to secure improvement of the status of women and called for replacement of the ineffective action programs with a new result-oriented program. The recommended program included 10 steps, which were set out on pages iv and v of the report.

Introducing the report of the Joint Inspection Unit entitled "Towards a new system of performance appraisal in the United Nations Secretariat: requirements for successful implementation" [A/49/219], a representative of JIU said that the new system was intrinsically connected with the review of the efficiency of the administrative and financial functioning of the United Nations, and more specifically with the establishment of the system of accountability and responsibility called for in General Assembly Resolution 48/218. One of the elements to be included in the new system was a performance evaluation for all staff, including senior officials. The report summarized three important sources of knowledge for the new system: the work of the International Civil Service Commission (ICSC), with emphasis on principles and guidelines for performance appraisals; the work of the Consultative Committee on Administrative Questions (CCAQ), especially that relating to performance appraisal of managers; and the organizations in which strengthened performance appraisal systems had recently been implemented, such as those for UNDP, UNICEF, and UNFPA, and the World Meteorological Organization (WMO). Under the proposed new system, performance objectives would be established in advance and supervisor/staff communication would be improved through regular discussions of performance and feedback. The new system stressed the importance of involving staff in the development of performance agreements and assessment of their own performance, making them accountable for results using measurable and objective performance standards. In order for the new system to succeed, the Secretary-General and the General Assembly should exercise their respective oversight functions through careful monitoring of its development and implementation. A number of requirements, broken down into three recommendations, also needed to be met. The first dealt with fundamental prerequisites, namely the introduction of a performance appraisal system within a supportive management and organizational culture and environment. The second set of recommendations addressed key technical elements. Among other requirements in this area, the Secretary-General should ensure objective, transparent, and fair ratings and make the new performance appraisal reports the key input for rewards and sanctions to be vigorously implemented. The last set of recommendations stemmed from constraints that might adversely affect the successful implementation of the new system. The Secretary-General and the General Assembly should revise and expand staff training plans for the new system in order to ensure that all Secretariat staff, including managers, were prepared for the new system rather than continue the current rush to complete training by the end of 1994 without adequate resources. The necessary resources could be obtained by delaying staff salary increments.

In future, the granting of such increments should be based exclusively on performance-based considerations.

In a statement before the Fifth Committee [A/C.5/49/SR.19], the president of the Staff Union stated that he wholeheartedly supported the proposals put forward in the report of the Secretary-General [A/C.5/49/5], particularly those pertaining to training and its application to career development and to accountability for all staff members. One of the most important changes would be the introduction in 1995 of a new performance appraisal system. The Staff Union was also in favor of a reform of the internal system of justice that would make for an open, fair system that would speed up procedures, but warned against hasty implementation, without consultation, of the steps that would be taken. It also suggested that the Fifth Committee contemplate the possibility of merging the Administrative Tribunal in New York with the Administrative Tribunal of the International Labour Organisation, which would result in savings to the U.N. Organization and in a unified jurisprudence. It was hoped that the General Assembly would approve the necessary funds for the training of managers responsible for the new personnel and accountability systems. Senior officials must be held to standards of accountability as strict as those for the rest of the staff, which had not been the case in the past. In that context, the Staff Union recommended that the 1954 Code of Conduct be revised, as proposed by the Secretary-General in his report of the establishment of a transparent and effective system of accountability and responsibility [A/C.5/49/1], but with staff participation. The situation of staff in the General Service and related categories was a veritable "time bomb." Their salaries had been frozen since 1989 and the career development plan approved in 1986 had still not been implemented, with the result that hundreds of staff members were blocked at the top of their level with no possibility of promotion. The Staff Union wholeheartedly supported the proposal of OHRM that it initiate a triennial review of the career situation of staff members who had not been promoted under the current system, as well as the request for an increase, from 30 to 40 percent, in the proportion of P-2 posts available for the promotion of staff in the General Service and related categories. Moreover, the overall need to maintain two different categories of staff members should be reviewed and consideration be given to the establishment of a single category of international civil servants. As to the security and safety of staff on missions, in the past two years, 86 civilian staff members had been murdered and yet no one had been brought to justice. Referring to the draft convention on the safety of U.N. and associated personnel then before the Sixth Committee, the Staff Union leader reiterated the request he had made to the ACC that the draft convention cover all personnel, civilian and military, working directly or indirectly for the United

Nations, not only with peacekeeping but also with humanitarian missions and electoral assistance and other operations.

Many delegations welcomed the Secretary-General's strategy to modernize and reenergize human resources management in the global Secretariat of the United Nations [A/C.5/49/5]. In his report the Secretary-General set out a series of human resource management elements that he deemed essential for the United Nations: a new management culture; enhanced management of human resources in particular; strictly competitive recruitment; full gender balance; meaningful performance appraisal; additional decentralization; optimal conditions of service; greater delegation of authority; advanced transparency; an attitude of service in human resources management; greater staff mobility; more training; simplification of policies and procedures; security and safety of staff; improved communications; and greater manager/staff accountability. The Secretary-General stated, however, that while the Organization had continued to witness a substantial expansion of its role and of its mandates, commensurate changes and modernization in human resources management had not occurred. As a result, the management of its human resources was fragmented, bureaucratic, and incapable of dealing expeditiously with the ever-changing demands at hand. In addition, an increased workload had found the OHRM able to react only to the more administrative aspects of human resources management functions which are so essential in a changing environment.

The representative of China expressed the hope that the process set in motion by the Secretariat with a view to modernizing the human resources management system would produce concrete results and go beyond reports, resolutions, and program budgets. The representative of Germany, speaking on behalf of the members of the European Union, stated that it was important to recall that recruitment was governed by the principles of the Charter, particularly Article 101, paragraph 3, and Article 8. The members of the European Union would do their best to offer qualified candidates to the Secretary-General, but they believed that recruitment should be speeded up. National competitive examinations were a good means of recruitment but, there again, the posts should be filled within a reasonable period. Furthermore, the European Union did not support the Staff Union's recommendation of a change in the quota of P-2 posts reserved for General Service staff who had been successful in the internal competitive examination for promotion to the Professional category. In addition, the same standards should be applied to that examination as to national examinations, particularly in respect of the level of university education required of applicants. Australia, speaking on behalf of Canada and New Zealand with regard to the suggestion that there should be a triennial review for staff who had not benefited from the promotion process, felt that there was no reason to single out such employees for special treatment or to assume that they should be promoted periodically. A related issue was that qualification requirements identified in vacancy notices were seriously out of step with the market reality. The representative of Poland observed that the efforts of member states to provide the Organization with suitable candidates should be closely related to the work of OHRM in identifying the Organization's needs.

The status of women in the United Nations system was widely commented upon in the Committee. The representative of Cuba was alarmed by the low figures given in the report on the advancement of the status of women in the Secretariat [A/49/527]. The number of women in the Organization had increased only by 10 percent in a decade; if the same rate of increase was maintained, it would be difficult to achieve the target of 35 percent by 1995. The representative of the Philippines stated that the slow progress in improving the status of women in the Secretariat was regrettable, and that the present level of 14 percent of women at the D-1 and higher levels was even more so. The majority of women still worked in the General Service and related categories, and their concerns were equally deserving of the Committee's attention. Women could be helped to advance to the Professional category if a larger number of posts were set aside for qualified women in the internal examination system. The Secretary-General should give serious attention to the 10-step program recommended by JIU [A/49/176], especially in view of the forthcoming Fourth World Conference on Women. The representative of New Zealand, speaking on behalf of Australia and Canada, expressed disappointment at the slow progress in improving the status of women in the Secretariat and stated that effort should be made to reach the 35 percent target by 1995. Moreover, the lack of any change in the proportion of women in senior policy-making positions was disturbing; according to the most optimistic projections, the 1995 target of 35 percent would not be reached until 1997. The three delegations supported the 10-step program recommended by JIU [A/49/176] with a view to ensuring equitable work policies and practices throughout the Secretariat, and called for the incorporation of an equal opportunity employment program in the recruitment and selection procedures of OHRM, and for efforts by member states to propose more qualified women candidates, encouraging women to apply for vacant posts and publicizing employment opportunities. The representative of Germany, speaking on behalf of the members of the European Union, stated that although progress had been made in the recruitment of women to the P-2 and P-3 levels, the percentage of women was particularly low in duty stations away from Headquarters and in senior posts. Steps should be taken to remedy such examples of imbalance, through training programs which give women better preparation for managerial positions and through the creation of a more supportive working environment for women.

On the question of training, the representative of Thailand believed that the Organization's efficacy was directly related to the quality of its staff and advocated an increase in funding for training. The United Nations spent less than 1 percent of its staff costs on occupational and management training. The representative of Poland observed that while training had been the focus of attention for some time, the report on staff training [A/49/406] suggested that the system had just begun to work. Expenditures on training in priority areas should be regarded as an investment rather than a cost. The representative of the Russian Federation, although recognizing the important role of training, had, nevertheless, assumed that only highly trained professionals were recruited by the Organization. The only purpose of training should be to upgrade the qualifications of staff or to familiarize them with the Organization's most recent areas of activity; the United Nations should not be converted into a personnel training center. The representative of Ukraine observed that it was possible to recruit personnel who already had high-level qualifications. In that connection, the introduction of a new management culture and the policy of recruiting only on a competitive basis was welcome; no priority should be given to internal candidates.

The delegations of Germany (including the European Union), Austria, and Australia (including Canada and New Zealand) expressed their preference for an enhanced attrition/early retirement arrangement. It was felt that greater use should be made of agreed separation and the early retirement option in order to free the Organization of staff who performed poorly or whose skills were no longer needed. The representative of South Africa supported in principle the system of early retirement, since it would ensure flexibility in the filling of senior posts and redress the gender imbalance in the Secretariat. The representative of Sweden welcomed the emphasis on staff mobility, which could revitalize both the Organization and individual staff members and lead to a greater sense of unity of purpose. The United Nations had an obligation to consider the family situation of its employees and to assist dual careers and the employment of spouses.

Commenting on the correlation between permanent and fixed-term contracts, the representative of the Russian Federation could not support the clearly discernible tilt in favor of permanent contracts, felt that the share of fixed-term contracts should at the very least be no smaller than approximately 40 percent, and thought that it would be even better to establish a parity between the two types of contract. The representative of China pointed out that while permanent contracts provided for a stable work force familiar with its task, fixed-term contracts could attract equally qualified people who would give the Organization the flexibility to adjust to the ever-changing demands.

The representative of Germany stated that the European Union particularly welcomed the setting up of the new performance appraisal system, which was a central component of the new system of accountability and responsibility and would help to change the basic nature of supervisory-staff relationships, while permitting a real evaluation of professional performance. The representative of Thailand pointed out that the proposed performance appraisal system could be successful only if it ensured objectivity, transparency, and fairness in its implementation, and if staff participated in it.

A number of delegations were concerned with the safety of U.N. personnel and welcomed the adoption by the Sixth Committee of the draft convention on the safety of U.N. and associated personnel, and urged all states to give early consideration to becoming parties to the convention. The representative of the Russian Federation was particularly concerned that international civil servants continues to be victims of violence. Despite repeated appeals by the General Assembly, not all states strictly fulfill their obligations to provide security and protection for officials of the United Nations and related organizations. Germany, speaking on behalf of the European Union, stated that the question of respect for the privileges and immunities of U.N. officials was of such importance that it should not be biennialized. The privileges and immunities of U.N. officials were dealt with in the Charter and the 1946 Convention on Privileges and Immunities of the United Nations. The German delegate appealed to governments concerned to cease their violations; the situation of the staff of peacekeeping and humanitarian missions gave particular cause for concern, and in time of crisis, locally recruited staff should benefit from the same protection as international officials.

The principal concerns of delegations with regard to the composition of the Secretariat were the interrelated questions of the geographical distribution of staff and the underrepresentation of some member countries in the Secretariat. The representative of India stated that having studied the report of the Working Group of the Fifth Committee, set up under General Assembly Resolution 47/226 to consider the formula for the determination of equitable geographical representation of member states in the Secretariat, his delegation considered it necessary to give greater weighting to the population factor in determining desirable ranges. Contrary to the recommendation of Resolution 41/206 C, the percentage of posts allocated in proportion to a member state's population had been reduced from 7.2 percent to 5 percent in 1987, and it was time to rectify that anomaly. He also noted that only 17 percent of Secretariat posts were subject to geographical distribution. That proportion fell to 7.5 percent in relation to the total number of posts in the U.N. system. The representative of China commented that during the period June 1992 to June 1994 the number of staff members holding posts subject to geographical distribution had decreased by 58, whereas during the same period there had been an increase of 241 staff members in the Secretariat in the Professional category and above. The representative of Algeria stated that the three factors used in calculating ranges with reference to geographical distribution—membership, budget contribution, and population—were too restrictive. The representative of Indonesia commented that, notwithstanding the system of desirable ranges, 26 member states, including Indonesia, were still underrepresented. While supporting the maintenance of the desirable ranges, the representative of Japan noted that the number of staff members of Japanese nationality, which had increased slightly from 86 to 91 in the previous year, was still far below the desirable range. His government had done its utmost to propose qualified candidates; it was up to the Secretariat to take appropriate measures. The representative of Ukraine observed that the continuing situation in which many member states, including Ukraine, were significantly underrepresented in the Secretariat was regrettable. His delegation was not calling for a moratorium on the consideration of candidates from significantly overrepresented countries, but it should be noted that the number of personnel recruited from Ukraine amounted to only 60 percent of the mid-point of its range.

Pursuant to the recommendations of the Fifth Committee in its report to the General Assembly [A/49/802] on Human Resources Management, the General Assembly adopted Resolution 49/222 without a vote. The resolution consists of six parts. Part I deals with **human resources management planning.** The operative part of the resolution, inter alia, endorses the strategy for the management of human resources; approves the establishment of a planning unit within the OHRM; approves the proposals of the Secretary-General for the implementation of the performance appraisal system; requests the Secretary-General to implement the performance appraisal system at the USG level; notes that the strategy for the management of the human resources of the Organization requires the active implementation as a management tool, over a period of several years beginning in 1995, of an enhanced attrition program; and requests the Secretary-General to report on the initial phase of implementation of the program in the context of the agenda item on the proposed program budget for the 1996–97 biennium. Part I also requests the Secretary-General to integrate, for budgetary presentation and management purposes, Professional posts P-1 and P-2, and P-3 and P-4 (and directs that these recommendations be implemented on an experimental basis in his proposed program budget for the 1996–97 biennium); requests the Secretary-General to continue to hold national competitive examinations at the P-3 level, with due regard to the promotion prospects at the P-2 level and a maximum of efficiency and economy; urges the Secretary-General to take all necessary measures to ensure that successful candidates at the P-2 and P-3 levels are offered positions within one year after their selection, subject to the availability of approved posts; and requests the Secretary-General to give due priority to training and implementation of the strategy in drafting the proposed program budget for the 1996–97 biennium.

Part II, **composition of the Secretariat**, reaffirms that no post should be considered the exclusive preserve of any member state; recognizes that the system of desirable ranges is the principal guideline for the recruitment of staff for geographical representation of member states; urges the Secretary-General, whenever making appointments at all levels to posts subject to geographical distribution, to continue his efforts to ensure that in particular the unrepresented and underrepresented member states are adequately represented in the Secretariat; and requests the Secretary-General in this regard to exercise flexibility in the application of desirable ranges in individual recruitment cases, keeping in mind all parts of the present resolution. In Part II the Assembly also requests the Secretary-General to sustain the present ratio between career and fixed-term appointments, and to submit to the 51st Session of the General Assembly specific proposals on what proportion of appointments should be made on a fixed-term basis; requests the Secretary-General to increase his efforts at improving the composition of the Secretariat by ensuring a wide and equitable geographical distribution of staff in all departments; and decides to continue its consideration of this issue at the resumed 49th Session, in the light of the report to be submitted by the Joint Inspection Unit.

Part III, **status of women in the Secretariat**, expresses concern that the goals set in Resolution 45/239 C may not be met; urges the Secretary-General to implement fully the strategic plan for action for the improvement of the status of women in the Secretariat 1995–2000; requests the Secretary-General to include full implementation of the strategic plan of action as a specific performance indicator in the performance appraisal of all managers; and appeals to all member states to support the efforts of the United Nations, the Specialized Agencies, and related organizations to increase the participation of women in posts in the Professional category and above. Part III also notes the intention of the Secretary-General to include the activities of the Focal Point for Women in his proposed program budget for the 1996–97 biennium; requests the Secretary-General to enable, from within existing resources, the Focal Point for Women effectively to monitor and to facilitate progress in the implementation of the strategic plan of action; and urges member states to make voluntary contributions.

Part IV, **administration of justice in the Secretariat**, welcomes the intention of the Secretary-General to consult fully with the staff representatives in the development of a new system of internal justice and requests the Secretary-General to submit a detailed proposal covering, inter alia, the specific institutional, legal, and procedural changes required in this regard.

Part V, **reporting**, requests the Secretary-General, in the light of the information on staff representation provided to the Fifth Committee during the 49th Session, to issue a corrigendum to its report on the costs of staff representation activities [A/C.5/49/14] and to report separately to the General Assembly, at the earliest possible opportunity, on the modalities and costs of staff representation since 1992. Part IV and also requests the Secretary-General to report comprehensively to the General Assembly at its 51st Session on the implementation of all issues covered in the present resolution.

Part VI, **amendment to the staff regulations**, approves the amendment to staff regulation II.I, substituting for the existing text "The Secretary-General shall establish administrative machinery with staff participation to advise him in case of an appeal by staff members against an administrative decision alleging the non-observance of their terms of appointment, including all pertinent regulations and rules."

At the resumed 49th Session, the representative of the Joint Inspection Unit introduced to the Fifth Committee [A/C.5/49/SR.45] Part I of the report of JIU entitled "Inspection of the application of United Nations recruitment, placement and promotion policies" [A/49/845]. In Resolution 47/226, the General Assembly had urged the Secretary-General to review and improve, where necessary, all personnel policies and procedures with a view to making them simple and more transparent and relevant. Since only limited progress had been made in that regard, JIU, in its first recommendation, emphasized the need to comply with Resolution 47/226 as a matter of priority and to bring together the improved policies and procedures in a human resources management manual to be used as a main reference source by all program managers and other officials concerned. JIU had identified a number of deficiencies and anomalies in recruitment, such as the reappointment of a considerable number of former staff members who were over the retirement age and the fact that some posts, including posts at the managerial level, had remained vacant for a long time. The main objective of the job-specific criteria which JIU had in mind was to enable OHRM to perform the fundamental task of recruitment, in other words, to assess the ability of candidates to fulfill the functions of the post. Noting that the roster of internal candidates was of extremely limited usefulness, JIU hoped that when the Integrated Management Information System became fully operational, OHRM would be able to create rosters which would use the same descriptors as were used in vacancy announcements and job design. JIU also recommended that the authority and professional skills of OHRM be strengthened; that its functions as the central human resources authority for policy formulation, planning, control, and monitoring of human resources be clearly spelled out in the Organizational Manual; and that OHRM management capacities be strengthened and its human resources upgraded both through the hiring of officials with specific and solid professional education and experience in human resources management and through specified human resources training of the staff already on board. JIU was in favor of the decentralization of human resources management, but only after the necessary conditions had been met, in other words, only after the formulation of human resources management policies and the establishment of appropriate mechanisms for reporting, accountability, and follow-up, both for human resources separately and as a part of overall program performance. Other JIU recommendations related to employment beyond the retirement age, the need for a certain geographical balance among both staff sent on missions and those employed as their replacements, modernization of recruitment methods, and the format of candidate rosters.

After some discussion of the JIU report, the Fifth Committee decided to recommend to the General Assembly that it take note of the report of the JIU entitled "Inspection of the application of United Nations recruitment and promotion policies" [A/49/845] as well as the Secretary-General's comments on that report, and approve the recommendations of the JIU contained therein.

The Common System

As at the 48th Session, the reports of the International Civil Service Commission (ICSC) and the U.N. Joint Staff Pension Board were considered jointly at the 49th Session.

Pursuant to its consideration of the report of ICSC [A/49/30], the General Assembly adopted without vote Resolution 49/223 in which it, inter alia, decided (1) to approve with effect from March 1, 1995, a revised scale of gross and net salaries for staff in the Professional and higher categories (appearing in Annex I to the resolution); (2) to approve with effect from January 1, 1995, an increase of 10.26 percent in the levels of the children's and the secondary dependent's allowances; and (3) with reference to the education grant, to approve increases in the maximum reimbursement levels in seven currency areas as well as other adjustments to the management of the reimbursement of expenses under the education grant. It was also agreed that a comprehensive review of the applications of the methodology used as a basis for determining the conditions of service of the General Service and related categories should be undertaken upon completion of the current round of surveys at Headquarters duty stations.

The General Assembly, in its Resolution 49/224 on the U.N. pension system, and pursuant to its consideration of the report of the U.N. Joint Staff Pension Board [A/49/9], decided, inter alia, (1) to approve with effect from July 1, 1995, an increase in the maximum number of years of creditable contributory service, so that the years of contributory service in excess of 35 and performed as from July 1, 1995, shall be creditable at an accumulation rate of 1 percent per year, subject to a maximum total accumulation rate of 70 percent, and amends accordingly, with effect from July 1, 1955, article 28 of the Regulations of the Fund; (2) to approve with effect from April 2, 1995, amendments to article 54 of the Regulations of the U.N. Joint Staff Pension Fund (set out in annex I to the resolution) to include the latest scale of pensionable remuneration for staff in the Professional and higher categories, to define the pensionable remuneration of ungraded officials and of participants in the U.N. Field Service category and to include references to, and place limitations on, the extent to which merit and/or longevity step increments are deemed to be pensionable; (3) to approve, with effect from July 2, 1995, the application to staff in the General Service and related categories of the longer-term modification of the pension adjustment system that entered into effect on April 1, 1992, the consequential revisions in the schedule of cost-of-living differential factors and the schedule for special adjustments of small pensions under section E of the pension adjustment system, and the consequential changes in the pension adjustment system (set out in annex II of the resolution); and (4) to approve additional expenses of $390,200 (net) for the 1994–95 biennium, chargeable directly to the U.N. Joint Staff Pension Fund, for the administration of the Fund.

Review of Conference Services

In its Resolution 47/202 B, the General Assembly had decided to undertake a comprehensive review of the need for and usefulness and timely issuance of verbatim and summary records on the basis of a report submitted by the Secretary-General through the Committee on Conferences. In reviewing that report [A/49/276] the Committee on Conferences had found verbatim and summary records to be particularly costly in financial and human terms and had noted that their timely issuance was often prevented by constraints in resources, resulting in the undermining of their usefulness. The Committee stressed the importance of summary records and recommended that their timely issuance be improved. It further recommended that the General Assembly again request the chairmen of the relevant organs and subsidiary bodies to propose the adoption of time limits for speakers, as it had done in Resolution 48/222 A. While the Committee agreed on the need for verbatim and summary records for bodies of a political or legal nature, it believed that there was a need to review procedures and streamline the provision of meeting records. In its report [A/49/32] it recommended which bodies should continue to receive verbatim records, which should receive summary records in lieu of verbatim records, which should be provided with summary records and might be invited or requested to review their need, and which should no longer receive meeting records. The Committee also recommended that the General Assembly invite the bodies established by the Charter of the United Nations to review their entitlement to meeting records and it appealed to the treaty bodies authorized to establish their own practice to review their need.

The Chairman of the Committee on Conferences observed that judging from the draft revised calendar of conferences and meetings for 1955, the upcoming year would be particularly busy. An effort has been made to devise a program that met the needs of the Organization while avoiding as far as possible any overlapping of meetings relating to the same sector of activity in the same location. The Committee had considered the question of unified conference services at Vienna, which become a reality on January 1, 1995, and urged the General Assembly to complete its consideration of the matter by the end of 1994. With respect to meetings of subsidiary bodies away from their established headquarters, the Committee on Conferences recommended that the waiver granted the Legal Subcommittee of the Committee on the Peaceful Uses of Outer Space and the functional commissions of the Economic and Social Council itself be reformulated in the light of General Assembly Resolution 45/264, Annex, paragraph 5(c). The Committee further recommended that the General Assembly, in considering exceptions under Resolution 40/243, take into account the financial implications of the waiver, its effect on the work of the organ in question, and the volume of work at the headquarters of the organ involved and at Headquarters.

The ASG for Conference and Support Services and U.N. Security Coordinator stated that the calendar of conferences for 1995 was particularly full; in addition to a considerable number of regular meetings, four special conferences had been scheduled. Moreover, the Fifth Committee planned to continue meeting through the first half of 1995 and might also meet in the second half of the year. Since 1989, the demand for conference services had continued to increase. The problem of meeting that demand with the available staff resources and physical facilities was compounded by seasonal fluctuations. Much of the increased demand resulted from intensified activity by the Security Council: the Council held 424 meetings in 1993, compared with 149 in 1989. More meetings also brought more requests for documentation. The total translation workload relating to political and Security Council activities had increased from 22,000 pages in 1989 to 87,000 in 1993. It might be appropriate to have conference servicing resources specifically allocated to the Security Council and its subsidiary bodies and budgeted accordingly, since the overnight processing of Security Council documentation currently displaced other work. The large number of meetings now held by the Fifth Committee and ACABQ might justify a similar arrangement. Intensified peacekeeping activity accounted for much of the increased workload of ACABQ and of both servicing and substantive departments. On the question of control and limitation of documentation, notwithstanding the many resolutions on the matter, the reality was that there was virtually no control or limitation. The volume had overwhelmed the processing capacity of the Office of Conference and Support Services. For the most part, the increased demand made on the documentation-processing services had been met through the introduction of new technology and, more importantly, through increases in productivity. Between 1990 and 1994 the average daily output per translator at Headquarters had risen by almost 40 percent. Such increases in productivity should have allowed for improvements in quality and timeliness, but instead they had been consistently overtaken by growth in demand. It was clear also from the report on compliance with the six-week rule for the issuance of pre-session documentation [A/49/531] that the crisis was also due to delays in the submission of documents for processing. The Committee on Conferences had recognized the need to streamline the provision of written meeting records. Written records were costly, the nominal cost of one verbatim record in six languages being $13,800, and of one summary record $12,400. However, no intergovernmental organ would actually say that it no longer required meeting records. Consequently, any decision to rationalize the provision of records needed to be taken at a high level.

During the discussion in the Fifth Committee, the representative of Finland, speaking on behalf of the Nordic countries, stated that despite efforts to streamline the work of the General Assembly, new items were constantly being included in its agenda and the Secretariat had been unable to meet the increased demand. He therefore appealed to member states to consider the high costs involved and to exercise restraint in requesting new reports from the Secretary-General. At the same time, however, departments in the Secretariat responsible for preparing reports should improve the quality and timeliness of documentation, which should be more action-and-result-oriented. With regard to the problems concerning the preparation of the verbatim and summary records of various bodies, the representative of Cuba commented that while it was necessary to reduce the cost of those records, the proposal to discontinue verbatim records for the sessions of the Conference on Disarmament, the First Committee, and the Committee on the Peaceful Uses of Outer Space, all of which were negotiating forums, was not acceptable. The Nordic countries also agreed that the Conference on Disarmament was a negotiating body rather than a deliberating body and, as such, should be allowed to retain its verbatim records if it considered them necessary. They welcomed the initiatives taken by the governing bodies of UNICEF and UNDP/UNFPA to dispense with summary records, as well as the measures taken by the Economic and Social Council to limit documentation. In addition to reducing their in-session documentation, UNDP/

UNFPA and UNICEF had decided, with respect to pre-session documentation, that Secretariat reports should normally not exceed three pages and should include sections identifying the report's objective, the means of implementation, and the decision which the governing body was requested to make. The representative of Germany, speaking on behalf of the European Union and Austria, stated that it was regrettable that, despite the introduction of new technology, improved productivity, and the reduction of costs in the area of conference servicing, the situation with respect to the timeliness and quality of documentation remained critical. The member states and the Secretariat, within their respective fields of competence, had a common responsibility to take corrective action. The member states expected the Secretariat to produce the documentation required in compliance with the page limits and time limits mandated by the General Assembly. The European Union and Austria supported the recommendation that the chairmen of bodies that have consistently underutilized conference-servicing resources be requested to review their need for meeting records and that these chairmen propose to member states that time limits on statements should be adopted at the beginning of each session. The representative of Benin was concerned with the proposal to reduce the staff in the Translation Services. It was well known that the delays experienced by non-English-speaking delegations in obtaining working documents were due to the insufficient number of translators. The representative of Cuba noted that certain regional groups had not been able to meet for lack of interpretation services, and expressed regret at the failure to restore 19 posts to the Office of Conference and Support Services. The representatives of Benin and Egypt stressed that training for conference-serving staff was a priority, not only in order to reduce dependence on temporary assistance, but also to ensure that the language and terminology used by interpreters in meetings and by translators in the Organization's documents were consistent with those currently used by member states.

Pursuant to the report of the Fifth Committee to the General Assembly [A/49/805], the General Assembly adopted Resolution 49/221, Pattern of Conferences, without a vote. In part A, it decided that the waiver to the Headquarters rule contained in General Assembly Resolution 40/243 shall be discontinued in the case of the Legal Subcommittee of the Committee on the Peaceful Uses of Outer Space, reformulated in the case of the Economic and Social Council, and discontinued in the case of the functional commissions of the Economic and Social Council.

In part B, it invited the bodies established by the Charter to review their entitlements to meeting records, and appealed to the treaty bodies that are authorized to establish their own practice to begin reviewing their need for such records; and decided that meeting records shall be provided as set forth in the annex to the resolution. Part B also requested the U.N.

Administrative Tribunal, the Committee on the Peaceful Uses of Outer Space, the First Committee, the Special Committee on the Situation with regard to the Implementation of the Declaration on the Granting of Independence to Colonial Countries and Peoples, the subsidiary organs of the General Assembly that meet on the occasion of international days of solidarity proclaimed by the Assembly, and the executive committee of the Program of the U.N. High Commissioner for Refugees to submit to the General Assembly at its 50th Session, through the Committee on Conferences, justifications for the continuation of the current entitlement to meeting records. The Assembly went on to reiterate its request that the chairmen of the relevant organs and subsidiary bodies of the Assembly, the Economic and Social Council, its subsidiary bodies, and other U.N. bodies propose to member states, at the beginning of each session, the adoption of time limits for speakers; and decided to adopt specific measures (as outlined) for limiting documentation. Part B then took note of the content of Annex II to the report of the Committee on Conferences [A/49/32 and Corr. 1] and requested the Secretariat to follow up on it and to report thereon to the Committee at its substantive session of 1995.

In part C, the Assembly requested the Secretary-General, within the context of the program budget for the 1996–97 biennium, to take into account the possible negative effects, if any, of the elimination of 19 posts in the Office of Conference and Support Services; requested the Secretary-General to take into account, in particular, the requirements for conference services arising from the increased workload of the Security Council and, consequently, of the Fifth Committee and the ACABQ; requested the Secretary-General in the context of the proposed program budget for the 1996–97 biennium to include more transparent performance indicators, better cost information on meetings and documentation, and a detailed analysis of real demand for conference services; and requested the Secretary-General to submit to the Assembly recommendations on language training to be included in the program budget proposals for the 1996–97 biennium, for the purpose of keeping interpreters and translators current with the latest developments in the six official languages.

In part D, Resolution 49/221 requested the Secretary-General, as a matter of priority, to improve the arrangements and meeting facilities in the Indonesian and Chinese lounges with a view to enabling more bilateral meetings and contacts among member states to take place; requested the Secretary-General to make available other venues for such meetings; called upon the Secretariat to examine the possibility of instituting an equitable and efficient system for the use of these facilities and venues; requested the Secretariat to implement these improvements in time for the 50th anniversary of the United Nations; and decided that such improvements shall be made within existing resources.

Index

An Invitation...

 TIRED OF MERE TALK about post-Cold War cooperation while global problems such as international drug trafficking, human rights abuses, ageing and health issues, and atmospheric pollution cry out for attention? Wish you could do something positive to help translate all that talk into global action?

There is something you can do! Join with thousands of your fellow citizens who have already discovered the vital work of the United Nations system—and who have lent their support by joining the United Nations Association of the USA!

UNA-USA is a nonprofit, nonpartisan organization working in Washington, D.C., at U.N. Headquarters in New York, and in hundreds of communities across the country to build public understanding of — and support for — greater international cooperation. That cooperation can only be achieved through the United Nations.

Hear and be heard

Founded a half-century ago by Eleanor Roosevelt and other concerned Americans, UNA-USA today boasts a national membership of more than 20,000 people — people who, like you, want to know about the global issues that affect their lives. And who want to know what's being done to address them.

As a UNA-USA member, you will receive the Association's acclaimed journal, *The InterDependent*, with expert analysis that takes you beyond daily newspaper headlines and into the halls where global policy is made. In fact, as a UNA-USA member you can actually help develop such policy! Each year you will be invited to take part in the Association's unique Global Policy Project — a program designed to find answers to specific international problems, and which reaches the highest levels of decision-makers, both at U.N. Headquarters and in our nation's capital.

Be a part of it all

In addition to the benefits that come with being a national member (listed below), you are also invited to participate in your local UNA-USA Chapter to whatever degree you wish. Many of our members enjoy the opportunity to come together with like-minded citizens in their immediate community to discuss current events, participate in various projects and programs, to plan the observance of U.N. Day (October 24), or to attend a lecture or conference — often featuring senior U.N. officials and representatives of foreign governments. It's like having a small piece of the United Nations right in your town! But remember, participation is strictly voluntary.

Sign on and receive . . .

■ A subscription to the highly acclaimed UNA-USA journal, *The InterDependent*.

■ A new membership kit, full of insider information on global issues and the many parts of the U.N. system that address them.

■ Discounts on all UNA-USA materials.

■ An opportunity to become active in your local UNA-USA Chapter (if you wish).

■ The knowledge that you are a part of the decision-making process that affects you, your family, and your world.
